HOMERIC SOUNDINGS

Homeric Soundings

The Shaping of
The Iliad

OLIVER TAPLIN

CLARENDON PRESS · OXFORD

OXFORD

UNIVERSITY PRESS

Great Clarendon Street, Oxford OX2 6DP

Oxford University Press is a department of the University of Oxford.
It furthers the University's objective of excellence in research, scholarship,
and education by publishing worldwide in

Oxford New York

Athens Auckland Bangkok Bogotá Buenos Aires Cape Town
Chennai Dar es Salaam Delhi Florence Hong Kong Istanbul Karachi
Kolkata Kuala Lumpur Madrid Melbourne Mexico City Mumbai Nairobi
Paris São Paulo Shanghai Singapore Taipei Tokyo Toronto Warsaw
and associated companies in Berlin Ibadan

Oxford is a registered trade mark of Oxford University Press
in the UK and in certain other countries

Published in the United States
by Oxford University Press Inc., New York

ISBN 0-19-815014-8

Printed in Great Britain
on acid-free paper by
Bookcraft (Bath) Short Run Books
Midsomer Norton

For Colin
καὶ εἰν Ἀΐδαο δόμοιϲι

PREFACE

It is a measure of how long this book has been in the making that I discussed it at the start with Colin Macleod, before his death in December 1981. His widow Barbara kindly gave me his texts of Homer, but, while I have drawn here and there on their minuscule and cryptic marginalia, I have learned much more from his Commentary on the last book; and, most important, I have been constantly strengthened by the example of his scholarship and his perception. Although he made unbearable demands on himself, he remains an enlivening inspiration for all who knew—and shall yet come to know—his searching mind.

Ten years ago I intended to write some sort of general intoduction to Homer's poetic artistry. Since then, however, several excellent introductions have appeared, and this has enabled me to pursue the more detailed and specialist observations which I have been developing year by year in my lectures at Oxford. There are at root two subjects. One is ethics in the broad sense—issues of justifiable controversy such as the politics of the Achaian alliance, the guilt or innocence of the Trojans, the glory and waste of slaughter in battle. The other is Homer's poetic form and narrative techniques, all the way from touches of phrasing to the shaping of whole scenes and the interaction between scenes, often separated by thousands of lines. What I have come to appreciate is that these two approaches to the *Iliad*—through 'form' and through 'content'—are not only related but are inextricably worked together. That is why this book takes the form of a sequence of larger arguments which grow out of observing details in the formation of particular passages.

There might seem to be an inhibition, even a prohibition, against finding all this complex and large-scale correlation in the *Iliad* of all poems. Homer was, after all, archaic, pre-classical; and even if he could laboriously write (which for myself I think highly unlikely) he surely created his poems to be heard. Does this not make all this intricacy, the fruit of many rereadings, inapposite? The more I have dwelt on this problem, the more I have come to believe the contrary: the kind of artistry which I have uncovered, especially the long-distance interconnections, would be more rather than less accessible when perceived aurally. Extended sessions of performance can induce a kind of spellbound attentiveness, such as cannot be sustained in the more disjointed process of reading. Furthermore, if the form and timing of the long sessions are arranged by the performer, then this opens up further opportunities for shapings that would be far more apparent when heard in real time than they are when ironed out in the uniform format of printed pages.

While this book purports to be advanced rather than elementary, it may, I hope, be of interest to those experienced in literatures and cultures other than Greek. So all quotations have been given in translation also. For the *Iliad* I have gratefully used the close and thoughtful prose version of Martin Hammond. I have also taken over his principles for the spelling of Greek proper names, thus avoiding my own decisions in that inevitably thorny thicket! There are some Greek words which encapsulate concepts, particularly of ethics or politics, too complex or alien to be replaced by an equivalent English word. In at least some such cases I have used the transliterated Greek, and given some explanation in the Glossary. The abbreviated references to books and articles are spelt out in the Bibliography; and other abbreviations for journals, reference-books, etc. will, I hope, be easily decipherable for specialists.

I have two institutional debts which I am glad to acknowledge. Since I became a Tutorial Fellow in 1973, Magdalen College has invariably been ready, indeed generous, in the granting of sabbatical leave and of other kinds of assistance which do something to lighten a very heavy burden of teaching and related responsibilities. Secondly, the British Academy elected me to a Research Readership for two years from autumn 1989. Much of the first year has been spent on completely rewriting this book; and I cannot imagine how else I would have ever finished it.

It is a delight, finally, to signal some personal thanks. Two colleagues and friends, Richard Rutherford and Edith Hall, read the whole manuscript through and made many valuable suggestions, great and small. I have inevitably to select among the many who have helped me in various ways, and I trust that no one will be offended by omission. Much thanks, then, to Hilary O'Shea (of OUP), Tony Harrison, Oswyn Murray, Andrea Wilson

Nightingale, Robin Osborne, Fabienne Pagnier and Rachel Woodrow (for word-processing), Nicholas Richardson, Beaty Rubens, Gregory Sifakis, Laura Slatkin, Christiane Sourvinou-Inwood, Stephanie West, and Malcolm Willcock.

OLIVER TAPLIN

Magdalen College
31 March 1991

The translations of the *Iliad* in this volume are from *The Iliad: A New Prose Translation* by Martin Hammond, published by Penguin Books in the Penguin Classics series.

CONTENTS

I

Exploratory Charts

1.1 *Book as pilot*

The last line of Derek Walcott's potent poem *Omeros*[1] is:

> when he left the beach, the sea was still going on.

Walcott's epic has, I find, a deeper affinity with Homer—in scope and humanity as well as in its many reverberations—than anything in English poetry since Tennyson—deeper and perhaps greater even than David Jones's *In Parenthesis*. One crucial affinity is the ever-presence of the sea, its traversability and its danger. Walcott's Aegean is the Caribbean that surrounds St Lucia and the other islands, crossed by slaves from Africa, colonizers from Britain, tourists from America, as well as by exiles and homecomers:

> and *O* was the conch-shell's invocation, *mer* was
> both mother and sea in our Antillean patois,
> *Os*, a grey bone, and the white surf as it crashes
> and spreads its sibilant collar on a lace shore.

Of all the metaphors that have been applied to Homer over the centuries—the sun, a great edifice, a deep-browed king, a copious nursery—the most widespread has been the sea.[2] Poet and poem become fused in this image.

To hear or read the *Iliad* is to embark on a voyage, whether

---

[1] Derek Walcott, *Omeros* (New York and London, 1990). I first read this in October 1990, as I was completing this book. Since then I have written an essay on the relation of Walcott's poem to Homer, published in *Arion*, 3rd ser., 2 (May 1991).

[2] For some illustrations from ancient times and down to Byron, see F. Williams' commentary on Callimachus' *Hymn to Apollo* (Oxford, 1978), 87–9, 98–9; R. Jenkyns, *The Victorians and Ancient Greece* (Oxford, 1980), 96–7 gives further illustrations from, among others, Swinburne and Andrew Lang. I think also of Odysseus Elytis, who in *To Axion Esti* speaks of his own work as 'my poor house on the sandy shores of Homer'.

undertaken for pleasure, exercise, experience, or whatever mixture of motives. I see it as my role to chart, to map the coast, trace currents, document weather patterns, take soundings. This book aspires to be a pilot and to enhance the epic journeying of others. Each section, or sounding, takes a substantial passage as a starting-point, and it works outward from that quotation in an attempt to place it within the shaping of the poem as a whole. As soundings are taken to build up a chart, a map which shows at a glance the topographical shape which is not immediately obvious to the eye of a traveller, so my 'soundings' add up, I hope, to a kind of chart for those who embark upon the *Iliad*. What I call 'shaping' can extend all the way from basic construction, theme, and ethics to the smallest details of wording and narrative technique. So in some ways this is a kind of Introduction,[3] Commentary, and Interpretation, except that there is much that it does not introduce, it is shamelessly selective, and it forms a kind of sequential collation of arguments and observations rather than an integrated perspective or total reading.

Three very different activities or experiences are in play here: (1) hearing poetry, like Homer's own public; (2) reading poetry, as we read the *Iliad*; (3) making use of works of criticism and interpretation, as you are of this book. My linking of them is an attempt to exploit the third activity in order to enrich the second by means of sharpening awareness of the first. There is a vital difference of reception between (1) and (2). Listening to poetry, performed live, is a co-operative undertaking, involving at least two people: reading is normally a solitary business, self-contained, self-absorbed. The text seems to be a mere passive given for the reader to handle at will, choosing when, how, where, and in what order to activate it. It may try to influence its treatment and reception by means of indicators like page numbering and typography; but the apparently omnipotent reader feels free to reject all such guidance. (This can sometimes foster delusions of grandeur, such as that the reader *creates* all the meaning.) In reality, of course, a thousand unexamined assumptions and habits remain

---

[3] The 1980s have produced a rush of books in English which are, in various ways, 'introductions' to the *Iliad*, including Camps, Griffin's *HLD* and *Homer*, Schein, Mueller, Silk, and Edwards. On the whole these are very good, and there is no point in adding to their number. These *Soundings* are, then, for those who have already set off, rather than for those about to embark.

active. And a thousand mundane pressures external to the text—
telephone, children, chores, sleepiness—interrupt and shape the
act of reading. The collaboration of listening to a performance usually sets
aside a special time and place, partly to enhance the experience,
but also to avoid the kind of interferences that beset reading. Also
to limit its freedom—or formlessness. The audience agrees to
receive the work within forms imposed by the performers, including the sequential order of the work and its divisions. The performers also control, to a large extent, pace, tone, extent and
degree of impersonation, musical accompaniment, and so forth.

This does *not* mean, however, that audiences are the passive
subjects of a dictatorial regime.[4] The artists need to capture the
attention and goodwill of their public in the first place, and then
they need to retain it. Virtually all creative artists (I assert) seek
the attention of those whose time and opinion and praise they
value; and most like their public to be larger than smaller, and
responsive rather than impassive. A plant needs nourishment to
live: 'il pubblico è il concime alla radice di ogni vegetazione
artistica' ('the public is the manure round the roots of every artistic
burgeoning').[5] Poet and audience meet in a kind of symbiosis.

Then again, this does *not* mean that the artist has merely to
follow after, or pander to, the tastes and demands of the public.
The interactions and benefits work in both directions. In fact,
most of the best creative artists challenge, revise, and form afresh
those tastes and demands. This was no doubt true of Homer. Yet,
however unorthodox or challenging he was, Homer must still have
made his poetry to *meet* the values, concerns, anxieties, and satis-
factions of his audiences. And, more tangibly, he must have made
use of (in modern terminology) the media, venues, publicity, and
technology available to him in his historical time and place—
which comes down to practicalities like where and when he performed and to how large a gathering. I do not intend by any
means to restrict my attention to those audiences who originally
heard Homer 'in the flesh'. At the same time, out of his myriad

---

[4] Nor, I should add, in view of some misunderstanding of my past work on the
stagecraft of tragedy, does the performance impose a single or simple meaning.

[5] The poet Cesare Pavese, cited by Gentili, 126. From a different relationship
Derek Walcott sees Homer and Greek literature as feeding his poetry: 'All that
Greek manure under the green bananas . . .' (*Omeros*, 271).

audiences across time and place, they do hold a special place, since the *Iliad* was made *for* them in a much more formative sense than it was made for any others, including you and me. My thesis is that there are shapings that emerge from a poem when it is heard that are not so clear to a reader. This is another sense of 'soundings'.

1.2   *Opening conclusions*

In external historical terms we know next to nothing about Homer or about his own audience—though there is room to speculate, as I shall in § 1.5. The poems themselves, the *Iliad* and *Odyssey*, are by far the chief evidence for their own reception. If the way can be found to tap them, they may suggest something about the tastes, values, preoccupations, attentiveness, and mentality of the public they were created for. I should make it clear, however, that this method of working outwards from within the poetry cannot say anything about what responses the consciousness of any member of any audience actually, as a matter of fact, formulated during a performance. Quite apart from being necessarily irrecoverable, the experience of an audience-member is far too complex and rapid and layered to make any distinction between conscious and unconscious response appropriate. My concern is with what went *into* the audience's perception. So when I use verbs like 'hear', 'notice', and 'appreciate' I am talking about levels of prominence in the poem rather than levels of consciousness in any audience-member. Hearing a poem and reading an interpretation of it are, as I said, two very different kinds of mental activity.

Since this book is fragmented into over thirty soundings, it will be as well to set out some of its persistent and underlying theses here at the start. Some of them will be familiar, even orthodox, others are novel. Since it is my purpose to establish these theses by the accumulation of internal evidence from the poem, it is methodologically somewhat dubious to pull them out and collect them at the beginning. The truth is (of course) that this only reflects the element of inevitable circularity in my own research. Which came first: the observation of a pattern which prompted a working hypothesis, or the working hypothesis which, when applied, brought the pattern to light? This poses a false dichotomy, since the two procedures work in a kind of cumulative interplay. As my aspiration is to enrich the appreciation of Homer for others, I am not distressed by the ineradicable traces of circularity in my method. I am putting my conclusions before the observations that give them substance, then, not because that reflects my own process, but because it will be clearer for the reader. I shall group these theses and working hypotheses into a cluster of ethical or evaluative claims (1–4), and a cluster of aesthetic or technical claims (5–7). This division between what used to be called 'content' and 'form' is, I believe, misleading, and I hope that this book as a whole will show their inseparability.

1. I start with a point that may seem self-evident; but, if so, it has seldom been formulated. The symbiotic collaboration of poet and audience decides what to include in the poem (and what not) and how to treat it; it decides, in other words, whom and what to celebrate or make notorious through poetry. The characters in Homeric epic are all striving for attention: their ultimate goal is immortal fame, *kleos*. But this is achieved not by them, but by the future generations who sing and hear about them. There is no court of appeal for the characters—Meriones cannot complain that he has been unfairly neglected or that Diomedes has been overrated. Such choices lie with the poet, taking due consideration of the expectations of his audience.

And the poet–audience symbiosis not only determines who are given time and attention, but what they are given it for. There is no other external, impersonal power (not even 'the plot' or 'tradition') which determines that Agamemnon's rejection of Chryses is the very first incident of the poem, or that he plays virtually no part after book 19; that Antilochos and Agenor win the first two kills of the poem; that the Hektor–Andromache scene is included; that the poem does not end with the death of Hektor, and that Achilleus' last great exploit is, instead, his meeting with Priam; that his last participation is his going to bed with Briseïs, and so on and so on. By including some things and not others, emphasizing some more than others, putting them in a particular sequence, the poet wields mighty power. That extends to the power to influence his audiences, to stimulate change or encourage stability in various ways and degrees in their aesthetics, their values, and their politics. At the same time that power is not unlimited, because of the need to catch a public and to retain it. He has to persuade them that his particular poetry and its choices are worth their time and attention and approval.

2. One of the characteristics for which Homer's audience evidently valued him was his abstinence from moralizing: he does not derive lessons from, or pass judgements on, his own story. In Schiller's terms he is naïve, not sentimental. There are very few epics—or even novels—where the narrator's explicit evaluation is heard so little. But this is not by any means to say that the *Iliad* is without ethical colouring or amoral or (as it has often been put) 'objective'. The poem is full of *implicit* evaluation or 'focalization'.[6] Much of this book is spent on trying to tease that out.

It may be the absence of explicit judgements that has misled many scholars into regarding the assessments of the characters themselves as somehow definitive, as though they obliged the audience to share them. Just as the characters cannot determine their own prominence, they cannot impose their evaluations. They are always caught up in their narrative and rhetorical context and can never be definitive. The context makes it clear that there are partialities in, for example, Nestor's assessment of the quarrel in book 1, or in Agamemnon's apology in book 19. The narrator allows the audience the independence to evaluate for themselves, including evaluation of the characters' own values. In other words Homer is constantly challenging his audience to do the really interesting work, to reach their own assessments. The issues are complex and largely insoluble; and there is no final opinion, no court of appeal to settle differences. One reason for the *Iliad*'s greatness is that there can never be the last word on the issues it raises.

3. So I am reacting against talk of 'the world of heroes', 'Homeric values', 'the heroic code'—the widespread supposition that the ethics of the *Iliad* are clear, established, and unanimously accepted by characters and audience alike.[7] This is untenable if only because the participant characters spend so much time and energy on *dis*agreeing about ethics and values. Issues of approval, respect, justification, sanction, and their contraries, are open for dispute,

---

[6] The term favoured by de Jong.
[7] This is epitomized by Finley: see the extreme quote on p. 50.

both by the characters within the poem, and by the audience outside. It is, indeed, vital to the quality of the poem that such matters are *not* closed.

Most such issues are, broadly speaking, 'anthropological', that is to say they involve human relationships and social expectations. The *Iliad* is also, I would maintain, a highly *political* poem. It is concerned with the problems of individuals living together in groups; and some fundamental issues of 'political philosophy' are opened up. Are there circumstances (for instance) in which an agreed obligation may be regarded as annulled? Can material goods pay off a great offence, or is some personal 'price' called for? Does the glory of victory outweigh the suffering of defeat? Which is better: to face reproach from people you have let down, or to die for them even if it exposes them to defeat? The *Iliad* is largely made up of shifting sequences of questions like these, some set in momentous circumstances, some relatively slight. The questions are seldom clear-cut, and seldom, if ever, answered. Clearly Homer's audience wanted to have such issues given an airing; and they found poetry a good way of doing this.

4. The essential issues of the *Iliad* are political but they shade into concerns which could be called private. For example, does the bond of Phoinix with Achilleus make it wrong for him to plead on behalf of Agamemnon? Does Hektor's relationship with Andromache affect his obligations to Troy? Does Lykaon have special claims for mercy from Achilleus? Individual though such questions are, they are not personal in the narrow sense. They have a social or political dimension, and they are broadly universalizable. These private questions are also set within the same ethical framework as the public issues, and expressed with the same words such as *aidōs*, *charis*, and *tīmē*.

So too with the gods, the essential issues are human but they shade into the religious. There is a consistent framework but its application, its interaction with the human world, is again beset with questions. Do human rights and wrongs matter to the gods? May humans blame the gods for their mistakes? How far does piety influence them? Do they kill us for their sport? If the gods have conflicting interests, how do they resolve them, and what happens if they clash? As with 'the heroic code', neither audience nor characters have a clear, unequivocal theology that makes all these issues agreed and tidy. Again the interest lies not in any solution, but in the airing of the issues within a shared framework.

So one of the aims of this book is to attempt to build up, by the accumulation of passages, at least some of the underlying network of personal, social, political notions and practices. It seems to me that a remarkably consistent—which is not to say neat or straightforward—'anthropology' and 'athanatology' begin to emerge.

5. The consistencies of Homer are far more impressive than the inconsistencies. *Even* Homer nods—but not much. His prosopography is a good instance. Whether it is largely a product of the tradition or largely the construct of the master-poet, or (most probably) a combination, there are a remarkable number of human characters (not to mention gods) who are recognizably individualized. They recur, that is, with consistent attributes and life-stories. I reckon that there are over thirty such characters, male and female, old and young, Achaian and Trojan, from the greatest heroes to relatively minor figures (such as, say, Lykaon or Meriones). They often have a consistent network of relationships, public and private, as well as their individuality. Furthermore, in many cases there is a control over the shaping of the role of the particular character within the poem as a whole. Special attention is paid to such things as first and last participation and the relative placing of the scenes where he or she is prominent. This means that the audience, or at least some significant members of it, were eager to follow the fortunes of a large number of individual characters; and that they appreciated their continuity and recognizable individualization.

6. This is all, of course, in keeping with the strongly unitarian tendency of most Homeric criticism in the last quarter of the twentieth century. More than a century and a half of zealous searching by analyst scholars has bequeathed little that is impressive. The high degree of *consistency* in the plot and narrative generally far outweighs the correspondingly sparse inconsistencies. Much analysis now looks trivial, or based on misunderstandings, especially of the explanations for repeated diction.

Much of this book is spent on tracing the coherence of foreshadowings, back-references, cross-references, interlocking sequences—the 'cobwebbing' of motifs and ideas. Until recently there was a kind of a priori prohibition on even searching for such phenomena. It was claimed that oral poets quite simply cannot do such things, that they are too busy concentrating on the immediate lines in hand. 'Delicate and subtle preparation *now* for what will follow in five hundred lines; veiled and indirect allusions *now* to what happened five hundred lines ago—such artifice lies beyond his power, even supposing that it lay within the bounds of his imagination.'[8] I believe that I have accumulated here an overwhelming quantity of observations to contradict that.

If an oral poet were by definition incapable of such things, then that would prove that Homer was not an oral poet. But I do not see why an outstanding oral poet, developing a great poem over many years, should not be capable of building up this kind of complexity and this degree of cross-reference. Indeed, oral composition might actually help rather than hinder the kind of cobwebbing that I have documented. Most obviously the technique of using recurrent scene-shapes (feast-scenes, debate-scenes, etc.—§ **2.**4) would help the poet to keep a grip on all the occurences of any such type-scene in the poem, and so to mould each in relation to the others. The division of the oral poem into large-scale parts would also encourage connections, especially between the beginnings and endings—see further pp. 19–22 for illustration.

Even on the smallest scale, oral technique might help rather than hinder distant connections. Individual names, objects, and places bring with them their recurrent epithets and phrases. So, while the repetition of common formulae is not in itself significant, the technique could help an experienced poet to build up cross-references. All this points to an audience with highly developed attentiveness both to detail and to larger shapings. The links between widely separated scenes would not be there if the audience did not appreciate them (not necessarily 'consciously'—see p. 4). And they would not be there unless the audience was ready and willing to hear the whole poem through.

7. I believe that I have in this book charted such an extent of interconnection (and it is only a selection) that the only reasonable

[8] D. L. Page, *The Homeric Odyssey* (Oxford, 1955), 142.

explanation is that the poem came into existence to be delivered as a whole. I maintain that it is still best appreciated if taken as a whole. The next step is crucial: the *Iliad* was and is shaped to be received by its audience in sequence, from the beginning to the end in that order. This is not invalidated simply because *we* have the power to *read* it in any order we choose.

That is why these soundings come (with rare exceptions) in the order that they come within the poem. It is of the essence that the narrative flows in a single direction, and that the scenes follow in an order given by the poet. Earlier scenes foreshadow later ones, the more so for an audience already familiar with the poem. It is far more important, however, that later scenes, with or without direct back-reference, accumulate significance in the wake of the earlier narrative. Some motifs come in a series of just two or three (for example Andromache's laments, death-speeches), others gather associations and significance by a kind of 'snowball' effect built up from many recurrences—a couple of examples would be the significance of the river Skamandros and the impending death of Achilleus. As well as motifs (which I would prefer ideally to call 'themes') there is the recurrence of scene-shapes and scene-sequences (where I shall avoid the usual, but inappropriate, term 'themes'). Two examples of paired scenes will give some preliminary idea of how important this technique can be to the entire poetic construction: the two evening battlefield assemblies of the Trojans in books 8 and 18, and the deaths of Patroklos and Hektor in 16 and 22. It should be obvious that these scene-pairs need to be taken in their proper sequence, and that the significance of either element is greatly diminished if it is taken without the other.

The recurrent scene-shapes are as characteristic a product of oral poetry as the stock epithets. And, like the epithets, they provide artistic opportunities for difference-within-similarity which would be difficult, if not impossible, for a writing poet. Since recurrent scenes are longer and more flexible and less frequent than recurrent phrases, they are more important for critical interpretation of the kind attempted here. While I occasionally point to the effect of a common formulaic phrase, it is more often the departure which draws attention to significant shaping.

I do not wish to make out that Homer's audiences were homogeneous—though they will have had much in common. They would have included the experienced and inexperienced, old and young, some attentive and with good memories, others less so. It is part of Homer's great achievement that his poems could and still can be appreciated at many different levels. What, I believe, does follow from the shaping of the poem for its public is the inbuilt hope and request that they should hear the whole from start to finish. While parts can no doubt be enjoyed in isolation, I aim to show how there are innumerable craftings which are greatly enriched if they are seen to be connected with other parts of the poem, often far distant.

1.3 *The* Iliad *in three movements*

The core thesis is, then, that each part of the *Iliad* is enriched by its placing within the whole, and by the way it interacts with other parts both near and distant. This is evidently incompatible with certain other views that have been held about the structuring of the poem. Obviously, for a start, I must reject any analyst claims that the poem is made up of separable elements put together by some sort of editor or by random agglomeration. My soundings, if valid, entail that whoever put the *Iliad* together, whether or not we can still separate out earlier constituents (as neo-analysis maintains), was the master-craftsman. The greatness of the *Iliad* is inseparable from its construction.

I have to concede one significant exception, the one which proves the rule: the 579 lines of the 'Doloneia', book 10.[9] I shall (§ **6.1**) add some arguments to those raised by others to show that it does not fit in the structure as a whole, and that it contains elements intrusively alien to the character of the rest of the *Iliad*. Above all, to be blunt, there are no other parts of the poem, so far as I can see, which would be impoverished by the removal of book 10. There would be impoverishment resulting from the removal of any other passage of more than (say) 50 lines—and I include the catalogue of ships and the battles of book 13 in that assertion!

---

[9] See Schadewaldt, *IS* 142 f.; Reinhardt, *ID* 248–50. The most important recent work (with full bibliog.) is G. Danek, *Studien zur Dolonie* (*WSt* Beiheft 12 (Vienna, 1988)), who concludes that book 10 is the work of another poet, who knew the *Iliad* as a fixed text.

Next, I totally disagree with the claim that the *Iliad* is paratactic.[10] This maintains that the oral tradition composed in many
small sections, each integral in itself; and that these could be
combined, added, subtracted, moved, and exchanged to produce
any number of valid paratactic poems. The *Iliad* is just one such
combination. This book cumulatively constitutes a case for the
opposite view (which Notopoulos was at pains to reject): the
Aristotelian view that the *Iliad* is organic, somewhat like a living
creature. To cut parts out is to maim, to move parts around is to
wound the whole, even fatally. Cross-references, narrative links,
and scene-sequences would all be damaged if sections were moved
or removed (except for the 'appendix' of book 10).

The whole tendency of these soundings seems also to be at odds
with a widely held view of the delivery of the *Iliad*: that it was
created to be performed in extracts of (say) one or two hours'
length. The prime argument in favour of this is the practice of
the bards Phemios and Demodokos in the *Odyssey*. It is also not
uncommon for oral performances in various places in the twentieth
century to be of this sort of length, and this is, in fact, the case
with the south-Slavic tales which have dominated comparative
studies with Homer. But far longer performances are common in
many other traditions—see further below in § 1.4.

Sections could be extracted from the *Iliad*, and on the whole
they would not become baffling or drastically incomplete. They
would, however, be significantly impoverished by lacking their
context (that is true even of book 10); and they would include a
lot of loose ends, incomplete correspondences, partial sequences,
and so forth (that is not true of book 10). It is quite possible that
Homer would himself have sung extracts on occasion, presumably
with some adaptation to limit damage. But the poem that we have
could not have come into existence in the first place in order to
be performed in extracts. These soundings all indicate that the
poem was shaped to be conveyed as a whole to its audience.

Yet within the whole there is structuring. For all its highly
developed narrative continuity, the *Iliad* surely is, in some way or
other, divided into parts. And it must necessarily have been performed punctuated with *some* breaks. By taking different criteria

---

[10] Particularly well argued, however mistakenly, by James Notopoulos in a
series of articles which developed considerably from the extreme manifesto of
1949.

for division, scholars have arrived at many different analyses.[11] On the smallest scale, using such considerations as change of scene, change of participant characters, etc., one may arrive at over one hundred sections of (normally) between 50 and 300 lines, but such frequent division cuts across many continuities. A bibliographer in Antiquity, possibly Aristarchos himself (see pp. 285–6), determined to divide the *Iliad*—and the *Odyssey*—into twenty-four parts. While the job has on the whole been well done, several of the divisions come at one place when several alternatives would have done just as well; and a few of them are downright badly placed, obscuring crucial continuities. These traditional book-divisions are inevitably deeply ingrained in the reception of Homer. Some scholars have been led to try to defend them as reflecting the fundamental structuring of the poem, and even of its original performance. They are demonstrably mistaken—I discuss this matter fully in the Appendix, in which I try to break down the authority that the book-divisions have accumulated by scrutinizing their placements one by one.

Most interpreters sense that at the most significant level of structuring the segments are on a larger scale. The majority have, however, juggled with blocks of the traditional books, even while acknowledging that the book-divisions have no special authority.[12] Thus, Kirk has recently defended, with reservations, a division into six blocks of four books; and Thornton has settled on the same segmentation, though for quite different reasons.[13] Once they have posited their blocks, scholars tend to find a distribution among them of a rather arbitrary selection of features: that each section contains, for example, an *aristeia* or an invocation of the Muses, a supplication, or an edict of Zeus, or whatever. But if the search is to be for an underlying framework, then it should be

[11] For a whole book on the subject, arriving finally at 33 'chapters', see Nicolai, *passim*, esp. 136ff., 154ff.

[12] Thus, for example, Bowra, in *CH* 43, divides into 1 (prologue)/2–8 (7 books)/9–15 (7)/16–22 (7)/23–4 (epilogue); Camps, 104 (omitting book 10) has blocks of two books and five books in the pattern 2/5/2/5/2/5/2; Schadewaldt, *Aufbau*, 39ff., goes for 1/2–7/8–9/11–17/18/19–22/23–4.

[13] Kirk, i. 44–5. On p. 45 he says the book division is 'probably itself, to some extent at least, a product of post-Homeric activity over the presentation and storage of the text'; yet on p. 115 a book division is treated as Homeric. Thornton (46ff.) never explains why she regards it as axiomatic that the sections should be equal in length.

some feature which is sustained throughout, not a scattering of occasional features. I propose that the shaping of *narrative-time* provides a good starting-point. The highly developed control of the time-scheme will be shown throughout (especially in Chapter 6). It may have been a traditional way of structuring narrative, to judge from Nestor's miniature epic of past exploits which he tells to Patroklos at 11. 670–761. He keeps close track of the time-scheme, with indicators at 682–6, 707, 716 ff., 723, 726, 730–2, and 735. The sequence of night, dawn, midday, night, and sunrise at 716–35 is especially relevant.

And it may, I suggest, be an indication of the importance of narrative-time for Homer that he makes much of it in the closing lines of the poem. Achilleus asks Priam how long a truce he needs for the burial of Hektor. He replies:

> "ἐννῆμαρ μέν κ' αὐτὸν ἐνὶ μεγάροις γοάοιμεν,
> τῆι δεκάτηι δέ κε θάπτοιμεν δαινῦτό τε λαός,
> ἐνδεκάτηι δέ κε τύμβον ἐπ' αὐτῶι ποιήσαιμεν,
> τῆι δὲ δυωδεκάτηι πολεμίξομεν, εἴ περ ἀνάγκη."

'We would lament him for nine days in our houses, then bury him on the tenth day and hold the funeral feast for the people. On the eleventh day we would build the grave-mound over him, and on the twelfth day let us fight again, if that must be.' (24. 664–7)

This temporal framework is then acted out:

> "ἦ γὰρ Ἀχιλλεὺς
> πέμπων μ' ὧδ' ἐπέτελλε μελαινάων ἀπὸ νηῶν,
> μὴ πρὶν πημανέειν, πρὶν δωδεκάτη μόληι ἠώς."

> . . . .

> ἐννῆμαρ μὲν τοί γε ἀγίνεον ἄσπετον ὕλην·
> ἀλλ' ὅτε δὴ δεκάτη ἐφάνη φαεσίμβροτος ἠώς,
> καὶ τότ' ἄρ' ἐξέφερον θρασὺν Ἕκτορα δάκρυ χέοντες,
> ἐν δὲ πυρῆι ὑπάτηι νεκρὸν θέσαν, ἐν δ' ἔβαλον πῦρ.
> Ἦμος δ' ἠριγένεια φάνη ῥοδοδάκτυλος Ἠώς,
> τῆμος ἄρ' ἀμφὶ πυρὴν κλυτοῦ Ἕκτορος ἔγρετο λαός.

'Achilleus promised me, when he sent me on my way back from the black ships, that they will do us no harm until the twelfth dawn comes.' . . . For nine days they brought in vast quantities of wood. But when the tenth dawn appeared bringing light for mortals, then they carried out brave Hektor with their tears falling, and placed his body at the top of the pyre, and put fire to it.

When early-born Dawn appeared with her rosy fingers, then the people collected around the pyre of famous Hektor. (24. 779–81, 784–9)

That day, the eleventh, ends with the feast that closes the poem on the verge of the twelfth day. I shall argue more fully on pp. 282–3 that this achieves a fine poetic effect. The point for now is Homer's artful control of narrative-time.

The observation that it was an excellence of technique special to Homer to select a short and crucial period of time rather than covering the Trojan war from start to finish goes back to Aristotle. And the attempts to add up the number of days contained goes back at least to Alexandria, probably Zenodotos.[14] What is not usually spelt out, however, is how small is the number of days (and nights) on which events are actually narrated, because about three-quarters of the days covered by the whole poem are lumped together in blocks in the opening and closing phases.

There are, in fact, fourteen days of actual narrated events, and just four of them are days of battle. Here is the narrative calendar:

Day 1   Chryses' visit and rejection (1. 12–52), followed by nine days of plague (53).

2   On the tenth day there is the great *agorē*, followed by the fetching of Brisēïs, the visit of Thetis, and the return home of Chrysēïs (1. 54–476).

3   Next day the ship returns from Chryse (477–87), and this leads into the transition which includes the days while the Olympians are visiting the Ethiopians.

4   After twelve days away the gods return to Olympus, as predicted by Thetis (425, 493), and she visits Zeus. This day (493–611), which ends with divine revelry, is the last before battle is joined.

5   The day which dawns at 2. 48, after Agamemnon's dream, goes on until after the sunset, which means after 7. 380 (see 7. 282, 293, 313 ff.). The actual battle is joined at 4. 446 ff. and ends at 7. 57. It is a day of heavy casualties on both sides.

6   On the next morning (see 7. 378, 381, 421–2), after the

---

[14] Aristotle, *Poet*, 1459ᵃ 30 ff. For Zenodotos see Pfeiffer, 116–17. For other analyses of the narrative-time see Myers (cited in n. 16); F. Pfister, *WJbA*. 3 (1948), 137–46; Hellwig, 40 ff.

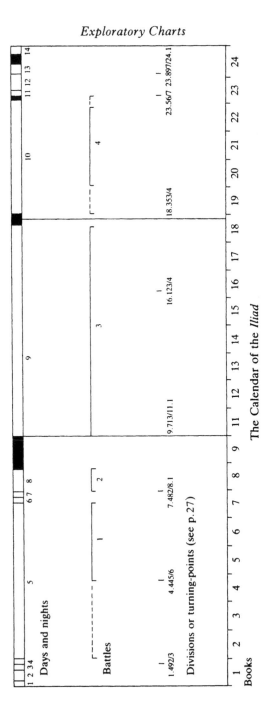

The Calendar of the *Iliad*

initial *agorē* of the Achaians, the dead of both sides are gathered and cremated.

Day 7 On the next day (433) the ashes are buried, and the Achaians hastily build their wall and ditch (465).

8 The second day of battle lasts from 8. 1 to 8. 484—it was known as the κόλος μάχη (curtailed battle). It gives Hektor and the Trojans the clear upper hand.

The *night* that follows runs from 8. 489 to the end (8. 565) and then through book 9. If book 10 belongs, then that too falls within the same night—in fact the apparently final closure at the end of book 9 is one of the objections to book 10—see p. 152.

9 The next day is Hektor's great day of triumph; it lasts from the sunrise at 11. 1 till the sunset at 18. 239-42, over 5,000 lines, and is by far the longest day in terms of performance-time.

The following *night* lasts from 18. 243 to the end of that book (18. 617). I shall argue on pp. 200-2, however, that the night is significantly divided between the human aftermath of the previous day in 243-353, and the scenes on Olympus at 354 ff., which are leading towards the next day.

10 This third successive day of battle is the fourth and last in the poem as a whole. It is, of course, dominated from start to finish by Achilleus, who is the only Achaian to kill. And Hektor's death is the last battle-death of the poem (the last altogether except for the twelve youths slaughtered at the pyre of Patroklos). The day dawns at 19. 1, and comes to a close with sleep in the evening of 23. 55-61.

11 On the next day, after his dream appearance, Patroklos is put on the pyre (see 23. 49, 109). All night the winds and flames roar (23. 217 ff.).

12 Next morning (266 ff.) the ashes are buried, and all day the funeral games are celebrated.[15]

13 After the games there is a lapse of days, apparently nine, during which Achilleus maltreats Hektor's corpse

---

[15] Macleod, 32 sees a 'correspondence' between these two days of funeral and the two at the end of book 7 (nos. 6 and 7 in my calendar).

before the gods intervene (24. 31, 413).[16] The day that Apollo speaks out comes to its evening at 24. 351 as Priam is crossing the Trojan plain. The great meeting between Priam and Achilleus takes place during the *night* after that day.

Day 14 Priam is awoken by Hermes before the dawn which rises at 24. 695. This day includes the laments for Hektor and closes with Priam's instructions for the eleven days of funeral (24. 777 ff.)—see above.

Once the handling of narrative-time is set out like this, one feature stands out as by far the most remarkable: the huge central day lasts all the way from book 11 to book 18—day 9 in the calendar. It is held together as a narrative unit by Zeus' promise of success to Hektor until the sun goes down (11. 187 ff. = 202 ff.)—see further pp. 155–6. The story of Patroklos is skilfully interwoven with Hektor's day right through to the closing moments before sunset when Achilleus' arousal saves his friend's body from the Trojans (though this does not of course save the borrowed armour).

I can see no major division across this narrative sequence. There is a narrative break between 12. 471 and 13. 1 (see further pp. 167–8), but it is not fundamental. It marks the beginning of the great retardation between 13. 1 and 15. 405, during which the battle makes very little progress in strategic terms. But this is indeed a retardation: it only makes sense as a block within the narrative sequence on either side of it. There is also a major turning-point at 16. 123/4, where the Hektor-plot and the Patroklos-plot are first synchronized—see § **6.5**. But, again, this is a turning-point as opposed to a closure and a narrative division, in much

---

[16] ἐκ τοῖο δυωδεκάτη in 24. 31 (see Macleod, ad loc.) must refer to the stretch of time since the death of Hektor, and so the tenth not twelfth day of divine quarrelling (107–8). So Kirk, i on 1. 493–4 is wrong to refer 24. 31 and 413 to two different lapses of narrative-time. At the same time I am inclined to agree with Kirk that not too much should be made of the 'symmetry' of the time-lapses in books 1 and 24, as was done by J. L. Myres in *JHS* 52 (1932), 264–96, with *JHS* 53 (1933), 115–17, and by Whitman, Ch. 11 (249 ff.). The analogy with Geometric pottery is doubly dubious. Apart from the difference between a sequence spread over many hours and an object which, however monumental, is static, the *Iliad* has, it seems to me, crucially broken out of the poetic equivalent of the repetitive patterning which characterizes Geometric art—see further pp. 34–5. Furthermore the building up of 'Chinese boxes' or ring-composition diagrams is only interesting when the labelling of the balancing pairs can be justified (cf. Tsagarakis, 3–5).

the same way as the joining of battle at 4. 445/6 is a turning-point within the day that lasts from book 2 to book 7 (day 5 in the calendar—see further p. 288).

From the appreciation of the massive structural unity of the central day follows the observation that the poem as a whole is constructed in three parts, or three movements, the first two about equal in length, the third appreciably shorter.[17] Part I concludes with Hektor's first day of victory and with the failure of the Achaians to resolve the quarrel between Achilleus and Agamemnon: this is all leading up to the central day. Part III tells of the aftermath of that day: Achilleus' vengeance for Patroklos and the burials of the two great and closely connected dead.

Before elaborating on this tripartite structure, I should confess that I cannot claim that the *Odyssey* is also structured in three parts. While this may count against my theory in some ways, it also supports my claim to be working from inside the poem and not imposing preconceived notions. On internal grounds it is clear, I believe, that the *Odyssey* is, at a fundamental level, divided into *two* parts. Until 13. 92 the poem has told of the adventures of many years and all over the 'real' and 'fantasy' world. From 13. 93 it is set on Ithaka, mostly in Odysseus' house, and it takes up only six days of narrative-time.[18]

To return to the tripartite structure of the *Iliad*, the roles of the two predominant characters of the poem are both, I suggest, articulated within it. Achilleus' participation in part I comes at the beginning and the end, i.e. the quarrel in book 1 and its reassertion in book 9. In part II he has very little direct role except

---

[17] In stichometric terms the three parts add up to:

Part I (omitting book 10)   5,691 lines
Part II   5,405 lines
Part III   4,018 lines

A three-part structure has been posited for the *Iliad* by various scholars in the past, including J. T. Sheppard, *The Pattern of the Iliad* (London, 1922) (but with little argument), and Wade-Gery, esp. 15–16, who has book 10 as the opening of part II, which would be disastrous. Kirk (i. 45–6) speaks of three 'movements' as 'the most natural division', but then elaborates a quite different six-part division. It is worth recalling that Aischylos composed a trilogy based on the *Iliad*: *Myrmidons, Nereids, Phrygians*.

[18] This most basic division of the *Odyssey* is widely recognized. The line count there is:

Part I   6,345 lines
Part II 5,883 lines

for his arousal and the shift in the object of his anger at the end
in book 18. Part III is, of course, dominated by him almost
throughout, on the battlefield, in the public setting of the funeral,
and finally in private grief and consolation. The articulation of
Hektor's role works in a completely different yet skilfully comple-
mentary way within the structure. He is introduced in the central
sections of part I, especially in public in book 3, in private in 6
(his last scene in Troy—see § 4.2), and in successful battle in
book 8. Part II he dominates as he breaks into the Achaian camp,
brings fire to the ships, kills Patroklos, and takes over his armour.
All this is made possible, of course, by the corresponding absence
of Achilleus until they are eventually brought into juxtaposition
by their responses at the very end of the day (18. 1–353). Part III
leads relentlessly to Hektor's death, and finally, after the exhaustion of Achilleus' vengeance, to his funeral.

It is worth setting beside these two heroes the structuring of
the roles of two relatively subsidiary, yet crucial, characters, neither of whom even speaks until part II. Patroklos in part I is a
silent attendant on Achilleus—see pp. 78–9. He first speaks at
11. 606, and, as traced in § 6.5, his part is woven through the
central day, until his hour of glory and his consequent death form
the 'third quarter', so to speak, of part II (rather as the death of
Hektor will be positioned in the trajectory of part III). In part III,
as in part I, Patroklos is silent, at least in the waking world of the
living—yet his presence is still very much felt, first as the
unavenged corpse, then as the unburied dream-ghost, and finally
as the dedicatee of the funeral games. On the other side, Poulydamas, the cautious counterpart to Hektor's confidence, is not
even named until 11. 57. He is then quite prominent throughout
part II, both as adviser to Hektor and as a warrior, culminating
in his contribution to the Trojan debate at 18. 243 ff.—see § 6.2.
The only reference to him in the whole of part III is when Hektor
recalls that advice:

> "ὤ μοι ἐγών, εἰ μέν κε πύλας καὶ τείχεα δύω,
> Πουλυδάμας μοι πρῶτος ἐλεγχείην ἀναθήσει,
> ὅς μ' ἐκέλευε Τρωσὶ ποτὶ πτόλιν ἡγήσασθαι
> νύχθ' ὕπο τήνδ' ὀλοήν, ὅτε τ' ὤρετο δῖος Ἀχιλλεύς."

'What am I to do? If I go back inside the gates and the wall, Poulydamas
will be the first to lay blame on me, because he urged me to lead the

Trojans back to the city during this last fatal night, when godlike Achilleus had roused himself.' (22. 99–102)

In further support of the substance of this basic tripartite structure I would point out that several of the most important corresponding scenes in the poem occur at the beginnings and endings of the sections. These will be fully discussed in the actual soundings, so I merely introduce them here. Thus, for instance, the quarrel of Achilleus and Agamemnon at the start of part I is called off in the corresponding *agorē* of the Achaians at the start of part III (book 19—see p. 205).[19] This also leads to the return of Briseïs, balancing her departure—see p. 81. Then there are correspondences between Achilleus' complaints at the beginning and at the end of part I (i.e. book 9—see § 2.3). There are yet others between Agamemnon's apologies in 9 at the end of part I, and in 19 at the start of part III. Indeed at 19. 141 and 195 he explicitly refers to his previous offer of ransom as χθιζός, 'yesterday' (more precise would be 'the night before last').[20]

The interventions of Thetis are placed very significantly in relation to this structure. At the beginning of part I she visits Achilleus, and takes to Olympos the request which greatly aggravates the strife. At the end of part II (18. 35 ff.) she again visits Achilleus in his grief and again goes to Olympos on his behalf, though this time it is to further his anger against the Trojans, not the Achaians (see § 7.3). Her mission is a kind of bridge over into the opening of part III. Finally, towards the end of part III (24. 74 ff.) her summons to Olympos leads into the concluding sequence and the resolution of Achilleus' anger—see further pp. 263–4.

As fundamental as any correspondence in the construction of the poem is that between the old father Chryses at the beginning of part I and the old father Priam at the end of part III—see pp. 77–8. There are also telling connections between Priam at the end of part III and the night-time visit of old Phoinix to offer reparation to Achilleus at the end of part I—see p. 80.

---

[19] Note the temporal signals pointing back from 19 to 1, such as ἤματι τῶι ὅτε...πρῶτον... (89, 136, 'on that day when'..., 'on that first day...').

[20] There are other back-references in narrative-time which refer across the parts. At 13. 745 in part II Poulydamas refers to the Trojan victories of book 8 (part I) as χθιζὸν χρεῖος (debt of yesterday). At 21. 5 (part III) the narrator places Achilleus on the battlefield by referring back to Hektor's rout of the Achaians in book 15 (part II) ἤματι τῶι προτέρωι (on the day before).

These binding correspondences or 'rings' between the apertures and closures of the three parts make obvious sense in terms of narrative technique. They help to hold the plot together and to give it a shape which, even on so grand a scale, can be grasped by the audience.

1.4   *Shape and performance*

Virtually every one of the fourteen days of action in the *Iliad* looks forward in some way to what is going to come the next day or in the imminent future. Narrative-time is used to keep the plot moving onward. At the end of each of the four battle-days (5, 8, 9, and 10 in the calendar on pp. 15–18) a similar device is used to close the day and anticipate the next: there are what might be called 'post-mortem' scenes which show the responses of both sides to the day's events. Thus at 7. 313–420 both hold despondent meetings which lead to diplomatic communications between them. Next at 8. 489 ff. the Trojans meet out on the battlefield and in high spirits agree to spend the night out there; meanwhile (9. 1 ff.) the Achaians decide to send the embassy to Achilleus. Next evening, at the end of part II, the Trojans again meet in the field and again decide to stay out in the plain (18. 243 ff.). On the Achaian side (18. 314 ff.) there is all-night lamentation for Patroklos— debate is inappropriate in the circumstances and is postponed until next morning, the early scenes of part III. Finally, after the next day of battle, debate is inappropriate for both sides: the Trojans on the wall grieve for Hektor, culminating with Andromache (22. 405); and the Achaians scatter while Achilleus and the Myrmidons lament for Patroklos (23. 114).

There are especially strong correspondences between the 'post-mortem' scenes in 8–9 and in 18, the evenings of two consecutive days, and the endings of part I and part II. Poulydamas expressly refers back from 18 to 8:

"ὄφρα μὲν οὖτος ἀνὴρ Ἀγαμέμνονι μῆνιε δίωι,
τόφρα δὲ ῥηΐτεροι πολεμίζειν ἦςαν Ἀχαιοί·
χαίρεςκον γὰρ ἔγωγε θοῆιc ἐπὶ νηυcὶν ἰαύων
ἐλπόμενος νῆας αἱρηςέμεν ἀμφιελίςςας.
νῦν δ' αἰνῶς δείδοικα ποδώκεα Πηλεΐωνα·"

'As long as this man kept up his anger against godlike Agamemnon, the
Achaians were easier to fight—and I too was glad to be camping close
by their fast fleet in the hope of capturing the balanced ships. But now
I am terribly afraid of the swift-footed son of Peleus.' (18. 257–61)

But the most notable recurrence is the cluster of forward-markers
in narrative-time at these two junctures of the poem. In fact very
nearly every reference to 'tomorrow', 'when the sun rises', etc.
occurs in anticipation of part II from the end of part I, or of
part III from the end of part II.[21]

Zeus himself first raises the motif, warning Hera before the sun
has even set:

> "ἠοῦς δὴ καὶ μᾶλλον ὑπερμενέα Κρονίωνα
> ὄψεαι, αἴ κ' ἐθέλῃιςθα, βοῶπις πότνια "Ηρη,
> ὀλλύντ' Ἀργείων πουλὺν ϲτρατὸν αἰχμητάων·"

'In the morning, ox-eyed queen Hera, if you have the mind for it, you
will see the son of Kronos in yet greater power, destroying the Argive
spearmen in great numbers.' (8. 470–2)

In his speech on the battlefield Hektor turns the anticipation of
the dawn into his rallying cry: see 8. 508, 525, 530, 535, 538, all
quoted on pp. 144–5. In his last line he is sure that νῦν ἡμέρη ἥδε
κακὸν φέρει Ἀργείοιϲιν (this coming day brings disaster to the
Argives) (541, cf. his rallying cry at 13. 828). The Trojans settle
down by their fires παννύχιοι (all night long) (554), and even the
horses ἑϲταότεϲ παρ' ὄχεϲφιν ἐΰθρονον 'Ηῶ μίμνον (stood beside their
chariots waiting for the throned dawn). So the narrative of the
Trojan side reaches a major closure, while at the same time being
infused with anticipation of what is to follow in the morning.

Much the same effect is then achieved during the course of
book 9 for the Achaian side—see further pp. 148–52. In particular
Odysseus' report that Hektor and the Trojans eagerly await the
dawn to attack prompts Achilleus to counter that this does not
worry him since first thing in the morning he will be embarked
and setting sail for home (9. 356ff.). Although he modifies his
threat in response to Phoinix and Aias, it is this strong version

---

[21] Apart from in Nestor's 'epic within an epic' in book 11—see p. 14 above—
the only forward temporal markers of this 'next day' kind are at 7. 331, where
Nestor is talking of collecting the casualties of the first day's battle, and at 24. 660,
when Achilleus tells Priam that he should not see Hektor till next day.

which is reported back to the other Achaian leaders by Odysseus.
Diomedes arouses them from despondency:

> "αὐτὰρ ἐπεί κε φανῆι καλὴ ῥοδοδάκτυλος Ἠώς,
> καρπαλίμως πρὸ νεῶν ἐχέμεν λαόν τε καὶ ἵππους
> ὀτρύνων, καὶ δ' αὐτὸς ἐνὶ πρώτοισι μάχεσθαι."
> Ὥς ἔφαθ', οἱ δ' ἄρα πάντες ἐπήινησαν βασιλῆες,
> μῦθον ἀγασσάμενοι Διομήδεος ἱπποδάμοιο.
> καὶ τότε δὴ σπείσαντες ἔβαν κλισίηνδε ἕκαστος,
> ἔνθα δὲ κοιμήσαντο καὶ ὕπνου δῶρον ἕλοντο.

'Then when rosy-fingered dawn appears in her beauty, you, Agamemnon, should quickly draw up your forces, men and chariots, in front of the ships and urge them on, then fight yourself among the leaders.'
So he spoke, and all the kings applauded his proposal, delighted at the speech of Diomedes the horse-tamer. And then after libations they went each to his own hut. There they lay down and took the benison of sleep.
(9. 707–13)

So, as with the Trojans, but in very different spirits, there is both heavy closure, and keen suspense. If book 10 is discounted,[22] then the next lines of the _Iliad_ after the previous quotation are:

> Ἠὼς δ' ἐκ λεχέων παρ' ἀγαυοῦ Τιθωνοῖο
> ὄρνυθ', ἵν' ἀθανάτοισι φόως φέροι ἠδὲ βροτοῖσι·
> Ζεὺς δ' Ἔριδα προΐαλλε θοὰς ἐπὶ νῆας Ἀχαιῶν
> . . . .

Dawn now rose from her bed beside lordly Tithonos, to bring light to deathless gods and mortal men. And Zeus sent Strife down to the fast ships of the Achaians . . . (11. 1–3)

The other cluster of forward-pointers to the next day comes at the evening of the great central day, exactly one circuit of the sun later in the narrative-time. The battle over the corpse of Patroklos is so urgent for the mortals that it takes, again, the perspective of a god to raise the motif of what will happen next day: Thetis tells Achilleus to wait until morning when she will bring him new armour (18. 134–7, see p. 60). Once the sun sets, the Trojans meet on the battlefield as they did on the previous evening in book 8. But while there only Hektor spoke, this time Poulydamas speaks first (18. 257–61 are quoted above—see further pp. 157–9). He takes up the 'tomorrow' motif from Hektor's book 8 speech, but

---

[22] There is an awareness of the narrative-time at 10. 251–3, though it does not anticipate the future.

adapts it to his cautious advice: they should spend the night inside the city and fight in the morning from the walls (18. 254–7, 266–7, 277–9—the lines are quoted on pp. 158–9). Hektor contradicts him phrase for phrase: they should stay out in the plain and fight in the morning by the ships (18. 297–9, 303 ff.). The Trojans all applaud Hektor, and δόρπον ἔπειθ' εἵλοντο κατὰ στρατόν (so then they took their supper throughout the army) (18. 314). The scene then shifts to the Achaian camp: αὐτὰρ Ἀχαιοὶ παννύχιοι Πάτροκλον ἀνεστενάχοντο γοῶντες (Meanwhile the Achaians mourned all night long in lamentation for Patroklos). The mourning is then narrated until

> παννύχιοι μὲν ἔπειτα πόδας ταχὺν ἀμφ' Ἀχιλῆα
> Μυρμιδόνες Πάτροκλον ἀνεστενάχοντο γοῶντες·
> Ζεὺς δ' Ἥρην προσέειπε κασιγνήτην ἄλοχόν τε·
> "ἔπρηξας καὶ ἔπειτα, βοῶπις πότνια Ἥρη,
> ἀνστήσας' Ἀχιλῆα πόδας ταχύν."

Then all night long the Myrmidons gathered round swift-footed Achilleus and mourned in lamentation for Patroklos. And Zeus spoke to Hera, his sister and wife: 'So you have achieved it in the end, ox-eyed queen Hera—you have stirred swift-footed Achilleus into action . . .' (18. 354–8)

These are, I shall maintain in pp. 201–2, the opening lines of part III. The awaited dawn and Thetis' return come at 19. 1 ff., after the scenes on Olympos and the description of Achilleus' armour.[23] This day will eventually come to a close at 23. 4 ff., when Achilleus brings the body of Hektor to Patroklos, as he vowed he would in the closing moments of part II:

> "νῦν δ' ἐπεὶ οὖν, Πάτροκλε, σεῦ ὕστερος εἶμ' ὑπὸ γαῖαν,
> οὔ σε πρὶν κτεριῶ, πρίν γ' Ἕκτορος ἐνθάδ' ἐνεῖκαι
> τεύχεα καὶ κεφαλήν, μεγαθύμου σοῖο φονῆος."

'But now, Patroklos, since I shall be going under the ground after you, I shall not give you burial until I have brought here the armour and the head of Hektor, the great man who murdered you.' (18. 333–5)

The combination of closure and anticipation does not need to be as heavily emphasized here in 18 as earlier in 8 and 9, because of that preparatory sequence. There is also more of a narrative bridge from part II to part III through the all-night lamentation

---

[23] Part II begins with the dawn of 11. 1, but 19. 1 cannot be the first line of part III—see pp. 291–2.

for Patroklos and the mission of Thetis to obtain new armour. I am confident, none the less, that these two junctures on either side of the central day are the two most important divisions in the whole structure of the *Iliad*.

Until now I have been arguing from internal indicators, basing my analysis on the shaping of the plot within the narrative-time. I shall now elaborate a related hypothesis about the original performance of the *Iliad*. I would maintain the tripartite structural analysis on its own grounds, whether or not these further speculations about performance are acceptable.

My theory is, simply, that the three-part structure matches and arises from Homer's own performance; and that the two clusters of forward-markers to 'tomorrow' in *narrative-time* also serve as forward-markers in *performance-time*. Hence the combination of closure and anticipation: 'that's all for now, but come back to hear what happens tomorrow'. Anyone who had heard the *Iliad* up to book 9 or up to book 18 would be very reluctant to stop with the closure at those junctures.

So the *Iliad* was created to be delivered in three huge sessions on three consecutive days. Any attempt to work out what this hypothesis might mean in practice must turn to comparative evidence on performance of oral poetry, especially heroic and epic poetry. This used to be dominated by the south-Slavic material studied by Parry and Lord, but it has now been documented world-wide.[24]

Performance-speeds vary enormously in various traditions. Rapid delivery is not, however, usually sustained over long poems,

---

[24] Hatto, *THEP* ii. 152 describes Serbo-Croat heroic song as 'a tradition largely not of *epics* but of *lays*'. For a long time C. M. Bowra (see *Heroic Poetry* and *AJA* 54 (1950), 184–92) stood alone as the Homerist who explored beyond the territory of Parry and Lord. Recently, however, many Homeric scholars have been venturing further afield: see, for example, Jensen, 47 ff.; Thornton, 9 ff.; Hainsworth, *THEP* ii. 11 ff.; Martin, *passim*, esp. 5–10, 232–9. Some specialist publications on the local traditions are: A. T. Hatto (ed.), *Traditions of Heroic and Epic Poetry*, i (London, 1980); J. B. Hainsworth (ed.), *Traditions of Heroic and Epic Poetry*, ii (London, 1989), esp. the contribution on 147–294 by A. T. Hatto, 'Towards an Anatomy of Heroic Epic Poetry'; N. K. Chadwick and V. Zhirmunsky, *Oral Epics of Central Asia* (Cambridge, 1969); S. H. Blackburn, P. J. Claus, J. B. Flueckinger, and S. S. Wadley (edd.), *Oral Epics in India* (Berkeley, Calif., 1989); D. P. Biebuyck, 'The African Heroic Epic', in F. Oinas (ed.), *Heroic Epic and Saga* (Bloomington, Ind., 1978); I. Okpewho, *The Epic in Africa: Towards a Poetics of the Oral Performance* (New York, 1979); J. Vansina, *Oral Tradition as History* (London and Nairobi, 1985), esp. Ch. 2 (33f.).

and reasonable comparisons with Homer seem to agree more or less with modern experiments in performing his poems.[25] There is something of a consensus that the whole of the *Iliad*, with some musical accompaniment but without any interruption, would take approximately 25 hours, perhaps somewhat less, rather more likely somewhat more. If 25 hours are divided proportionately between the three parts (omitting book 10) we arrive—with a specious semblance of exactitude—at

> I: 9 h. 25 m.
> II: 8 h. 56 m.
> III: 6 h. 39 m.

The two parts of the *Odyssey*, if sung at the same average pace, would come out at 10 h. 30 m. and 9 h. 44 m.

Intervals need to be added to these extremely approximate timings. Comparative evidence indicates intervals occurring every few hours (surprisingly rarely by some accounts) and lasting between 5 and 15 minutes. These might, then, add at most a further hour to each session. Whether or not it damages my theory, I can find no clear placements for intervals within the narrative construction of the *Iliad*. Without giving the arguments here (they are explained in the Appendix) I find the most significant structural subdivisions at the following places:

> I: 1. 492/3; 4. 445/6; 7. 482/8. 1
> II: 16. 123/4
> III: 23. 56/7; 23. 897/24. 1

These are so irregular—giving sections varying from 492 to 3,547 lines—that I am obliged to propose that intervals, apart from the two main ones, were not built into the artistic construction of the poem.[26] In that case it is likely that the brief breaks were variables

---

[25] See Notopoulos, 'Studies', 4–7; Thornton, 47–8; Jensen, 46–50. For variety of performance-speeds see Finnegan, 122–3. In some traditions each line is repeated by an assistant or apprentice. If this were true of Homer—and there is no evidence to suggest it—the *Iliad* would take too long for my theory to stand.

[26] In the *Odyssey*, on the other hand, it is quite easy to place some fairly regularly spaced intervals which significantly reflect the poetic construction. Within *Od.* part I (1. 1–13. 92) they come at the dividing-points between books 4 and 5, and books 8 and 9. Within part II (13. 93 to the end) they come at the division of books 16 and 17 and at 20. 90/1 (or 20. 344/21. 1). I have no explanation of why the *Odyssey* divides so much more readily into regular sections than the *Iliad*; but I strongly suspect that there *is* an explanation, and that it has to do with performance circumstances.

at the discretion of the poet, using his sensitivity to audience response.

In a book-bound world where attention-span is greatly influenced by electronic media, live performances on such a scale may well seem incredible, in terms both of the stamina of the performer and of the attention of the audience. And south-Slavic oral poetry seemed to confirm that a session of a couple of hours was the most that could be expected or endured under normal circumstances. There is now, however, a great deal of evidence from other parts of the world which shows that very long sessions of heroic poetry are possible, and are even perhaps the norm—see footnote 24 above. This makes it clear that the leading performers have highly practised and resilient vocal powers that can go on for hour after hour (actually the same is true of many professional opera-singers).[27] It is also evident that in technologically less-developed societies, especially those with low literacy, audiences are ready and able to remain attentive during extremely long performances.

These long sessions are not normally, however, available as everyday experiences; they tend to be part of special extended occasions such as festivals and marriages. Indeed we know that the Greeks of classical times spent many hours at festivals listening to and watching various kinds of music and poetry, usually organized in contests.[28] The most celebrated is, of course, the four days devoted annually to tragedy, comedy, and dithyramb at the City festival of Dionysos at Athens. But there were also contests between rhapsodes (professional performers of Homeric epic); and these were by no means completely displaced by other genres of heroic narrative such as tragedy, even though the competitors were more musical, spectacular, and innovative.[29] It seems that

---

[27] The mistaken assumption that no performer could go on with such vocal stamina led to unfortunate theories which, while advocating a three-session performance, supposed that the Homeric poems were originally delivered by teams of performers. See G. Murray, *The Rise of the Greek Epic*, 3rd edn. (Oxford, 1924), 187 ff.; T. B. L. Webster, *From Mycenae to Homer* (London, 1958), 267–72; Whitman, 81–3.

[28] The subject has recently been surveyed by Herington (*Poetry into Drama*) and the evidence usefully collected (in translation), esp. in app. 1 (161 ff.).

[29] Burkert ('Making') puts forward the speculative thesis that in the sixth century there was a kind of melting-pot of genres competing for the narration of heroic stories. He attributes to this era the emergence of rhapsodic performances of a set masterpiece rather than the creation by bards of new hexameter epic. I find this reconstruction of the literary history very interesting and attractive, though it has to suppose that Homer was somehow preserved in a fixed form during an age (about a century?) when his poems were not being performed.

rhapsodic performances were already well established at Sikyon in the early sixth century, when Kleisthenes, in conflict with Argos, 'stopped rhapsodes from competing because of the Homeric epics, since in them the Argives and Argos are celebrated all over the place'.[30] It was later than this, under Peisistratos, that the performance of Homer by rhapsodes was made into an important element in the Panathenaia at Athens. We know very little of how this was organized—much less than scholars like to think. While it is clear that each rhapsode had to take up the story at the point where the previous one left off,[31] we do not know, for example, whether the whole of the *Iliad* or the *Odyssey* was covered during one (four-day) festival, whether the performances lasted for more than one day (or night) of it, whether they went on simultaneously with the athletics or whether they were for their duration the central attraction. Whatever happened, it is evident that Homeric performances at Athens and elsewhere attracted the attention of audiences for many hours in succession, even in an age when many rival kinds of performance had developed, including some others which also conveyed heroic narrative.

It is a striking feature of the comparative evidence that in many parts of the world the long performances of heroic narrative take place not by day but at night, sometimes even for three or more successive nights.[32] It is normal for such a performance to start some time towards sunset and to go on into the small hours, or even till dawn. The occasions tend, naturally, to be those where work is not called for next morning, that is to say some festivity.

I would speculate, therefore, that the *Iliad* was created in the form in which we know it, to be performed during three successive

[30] Hdt. 5. 67. 1. These epics were not necessarily the *Iliad* and the *Odyssey*. E. Cingano, in *QUCC*, n.s. 20 (1985), 31 ff., argues for the Theban cycle.

[31] See [Plato] *Hipparchus*, 228b, and (amid much dubious material) Diog. L. 1. 57 (Solon). See, among others, Jansen, 145–6. Wade-Gery, 30 and n. 77, argues that this high degree of organization should really be attributed to Pericles. This may be right; but I see no good reason, on the other hand, to follow his belief (14 and n. 38) that the *Iliad* was performed at the Panathenaia over the course of three days. The wording of Xen. *Symp.* 3. 6 cannot be forced to support this. On the other hand the Xenophon passage is evidence that by that time 'busking' rhapsodes had become quite a regular phenomenon.

[32] For central Asia, see the citations of Zhirmunsky in Thornton, 29, 31; for Africa, see Biebuyck, op. cit. (n. 24 above), 24; for India, see Blackburn *et al.*, op. cit. (n. 24 above), 65, 78, 104, and the handy chart of 'Performance features of Indian oral epics' on 254–62. Even Lord (15) reports that in Yugoslavia there was singing during the nights of Ramadan 'fostering songs of some length'.

nights—rather than days—and the *Odyssey* during two successive nights. This breaks the exactness of my proposed 'synchronism' between narrative-time and performance-time. Part I and part II end in narrative-time in the evening and anticipate resumption at dawn, while in performance-time the morning and evening would be reversed. This makes the theory less neat, but I do not see it as a fatal objection. The closure still anticipates resumption next day.

So, once again, I am driven away from the model supplied by the bards of the *Odyssey*. They do sing in the evening, but only short songs, with no suggestion that they perform far into the night. While I take it as perfectly possible that Homer was ready and able to sing shorter poems, and even to supply adapted extracts of the *Iliad* and *Odyssey*, if there was sufficient incentive, I persist in the belief that the poems could not have come into existence to be purveyed in extracts. The underlying three-part and two-part structures lead to the hypothesis of very long sessions, even all-night sessions.

There is just one performance within Homer which mirrors the reconstruction I have built up—the performer is Odysseus. It has already been a long day before he begins at *Od.* 9. 39 ff. to tell the story of his adventures Ἰλιόθεν (starting from Troy). There have been athletics, poetry ('Ares and Aphrodite'), and dancing during the day, followed after sunset by bathing, gift-giving, supper, and then Demodokos' telling of the sack of Troy. So it is late at night in the narrative-time when Odysseus begins, and well into the small hours when he flags in the middle of telling what he saw in the underworld:

> "πάcαc δ' οὐκ ἂν ἐγὼ μυθήcομαι οὐδ' ὀνομήνω
> ὄccαc ἡρώων ἀλόχουc ἴδον ἠδὲ θύγατραc·
> πρὶν γάρ κεν καὶ νὺξ φθῖτ' ἄμβροτοc. ἀλλὰ καὶ ὥρη
> εὕδειν, ἢ ἐπὶ νῆα θοὴν ἐλθόντ' ἐc ἑταίρουc
> ἢ αὐτοῦ· πομπὴ δὲ θεοῖc ὑμῖν τε μελήcει."
>   Ὣc ἔφαθ', οἱ δ' ἄρα πάντεc ἀκὴν ἐγένοντο cιωπῆι,
>   κηληθμῶι δ' ἔcχοντο κατὰ μέγαρα cκιόεντα.

'But I cannot name and tell of every one of the great men's wives and daughters that I saw. The night would not be long enough. And it is time to sleep now, whether I go to my crew on board or sleep here. My send-off is for you and the gods to organize.' So he spoke. They all sat

there long in silence, still held under the spell through the shadowy hall.
(*Od*. 11. 328–34)

After some conversation Alkinoös urges him to press on:

> "coì δ' ἔπι μὲν μορφὴ ἐπέων, ἔνι δὲ φρένες ἐςθλαί,
> μῦθον δ' ὡς ὅτ' ἀοιδὸς ἐπισταμένως κατέλεξας,
> πάντων Ἀργείων σέο τ' αὐτοῦ κήδεα λυγρά.
> ἀλλ' ἄγε μοι τόδε εἰπὲ καὶ ἀτρεκέως κατάλεξον,   370
> εἴ τινας ἀντιθέων ἑτάρων ἴδες, οἵ τοι ἅμ' αὐτῶι
> Ἴλιον εἰς ἅμ' ἕποντο καὶ αὐτοῦ πότμον ἐπέσπον.
> νὺξ δ' ἥδε μάλα μακρὴ ἀθέσφατος· οὐδέ πω ὥρη
> εὕδειν ἐν μεγάρωι· cὺ δέ μοι λέγε θέσκελα ἔργα.
> καί κεν ἐς ἠῶ δῖαν ἀνασχοίμην, ὅτε μοι cὺ   375
> τλαίης ἐν μεγάρωι τὰ cὰ κήδεα μυθήcαcθαι."

'Your words are fine and your mind is good, and you have told your story
as skillfully as a poet, all the dire trouble you and all the Argives went
through. But tell me this and tell me true, did you see any of your heroic
comrades, who went to Troy along with you and met their death there?
The long night still stretches ahead, and it is not yet time to sleep in this
hall. Please tell us of your wonderful deeds. Indeed I could stay till dawn,
as long as you could bear to go on telling in this hall your sufferings.'
(*Od*. 11. 367–76)

If my theory is right, then there is still about one hour to go in
the *performance-time* of part I of the two-part *Odyssey*, and this
passage would have come at—very approximately—4 a.m. This
seems about the right time to reassure the audience and to revive
their attention for the final stretch, which will bring Odysseus'
story back to Scherie, and end by putting him—asleep—on the
boat for Ithaka.

1.5 *Genesis and transmission*

To give a frame to these exploratory charts I shall attempt my
own literary-historical version of the possible genesis and early
transmission of the *Iliad*.[33] I must emphasize, however, that there
is little in this book which depends for its validity on the final

[33] If I were to accompany this sketch with full bibliography, the footnotes would
displace the text. As well as the bibliography in standard books, there is fuller
documentation in Lesky, *RE*; Heubeck, *HF*; and J. P. Holoka, *CW* 66 (1973),
257–93; *CW* 73 (1979), 65–150; *CW* 83 (1990), 393–461; *CW* 84 (1991), forthcoming.

truth of any particular one of these inferences and speculations. My soundings work out from the poem: they try not to super-impose an occasion and audience arrived at by external means. There are, I suppose, two essential working hypotheses, already proposed, which are so fundamental that, if either were to be falsified, then much in this book would suffer considerable dam-age. They are (1) that the poem was created to be conveyed as a whole to its audience, and (2) that the poem transmitted to us is substantially that created by the master-poet.[34] Much of the recon-struction that follows serves to supply a historical setting within which those hypotheses are plausible.

Place

The poet of the *Iliad*, who might as well be called Homer, was very probably a man.[35] Ancient tradition and the predominant dialect of his poetic diction both point to northern Ionia as his geographical base, though there is so little allusion in the poem to that particular area as to be positively strange.[36] One might ask: whereabouts would audiences be gratified by the prominence of their land or by the admirable ·portrayal of their predecessors (rather than a mere passing mention)? Some answers would be: first of all, the Troad and Lesbos,[37] then Phthia, Argos, Sparta, Pylos, Crete, even Ithaka, even Lycia and Paionia. But not Ionia.

---

[34] I have already indicated (p. 11) that book 10 is the exception that proves the rule.

[35] I find Samuel Butler's case for an authoress of the *Odyssey* unconvincing— unfortunately. On the whole the women serve the gratification of Odysseus— though J. Winkler, *The Constraints of Desire* (New York, 1990), 129 ff., puts Penelope in a different light. If either Homeric poem were to be by a woman it would be the *Iliad*, with its keen awareness of the victims of war.

[36] There is not so much as a mention of Samos, Smyrna, Ephesos, or Chios (once in passing in the *Odyssey*). Miletos and Mykale figure in the Trojan catalogue at 2. 869 ff. as the home of the barbarophone Carians (see p. 113). The leading Ionian touch is the beautiful simile of the Kaÿstrios valley at 2. 459 ff.; for other small east-Aegean touches, see G. L. Huxley in *Maynooth Review*, 3 (1977), 73–84. I am far from convinced by Kirk's argument (i. 248, 262–3) that the omission of Ionia is calculated 'archaizing' because the poet and his audience would be aware that Greeks had arrived there since the time of the Trojan War. Mythopoeia very quickly supplants factual historical memory. In any case Greeks had been in Ionia for over 200 years by Homer's day, and in some places, especially Miletos, since Mycenaean times.

[37] There is interesting but highly speculative material in A. Aloni, *Tradizioni arcaiche della Troade e composizione dell'Iliade* (Milan, 1986).

A possible explanation might be that, although Ionia was Homer's home-base, it was not his main territory for performance. An interesting corollary of this 'neglect' of Ionia is that if the poem was initially or primarily transmitted through Chios (see p. 43) then it was not subject to much tampering, not even for that most obvious of motives, local pride and politics.[38]

Period

Very few would now dispute that Homer came within the chronological limits of 800 BC and 650 BC, though this is considerably later than used to be commonly supposed before the development of modern archaeology. There has even grown up a widespread consensus of *c*. 730 BC, but for no conclusive reason that I can see.

To put a huge issue simply and intuitively, I sense that Homer fits better with the Greek world after 700 rather than before. I am aware of no irresistible reason to put him before 700.[39] On the other hand, there are various 'novelties' from the mid-eighth century at the very earliest, which might well have stood out as obtrusive 'anachronisms' if introduced into heroic poetry before 700. One is the roofing of temples, which is boasted of prominently early in the *Iliad*, at 1. 39.[40] Two others are the great wealth of

[38] Some important places that are given at best marginal allusion in the *Iliad* are Sikyon (yet see Herodotus, quoted on p. 29), Corinth, Eretria, Chalkis, and above all, Athens. The sparsity of material to gratify Ionia and Athens (with the exception of Salamis, which was not properly Athenian until later) seems to be evidence against making too much of the alleged Athenian centrality in the transmission of Homer—see p. 44 below. The notorious disputes over the authenticity of 2. 558, and the Megarians' attempt to supplant the line, are further evidence against pervasive Athenian colouring (as opposed to superficial orthography).

[39] Three arguments have been prominent in recent discussions. First, a synchronism with the reintroduction of writing into Greece: I explain on p. 36 why I am not impressed by this. Secondly 'Nestor's cup', found at Ischia, is usually dated to *c*. 725, though Jeffrey (235) gives *c*. 700; for a full discussion of it, see Heubeck, 'Schrift', 109–16 (it is most accessible in R. Meiggs and D. Lewis (edd.), *A Selection of Greek Historical Inscriptions* (Oxford, 1969), no. 1). The inscription alludes no doubt to epic, but I cannot see that it must be the *Iliad* that it alludes to. For a subtle, but to me unconvincing, case, see O. Murray, 'Nestor's Cup and the Origins of the Greek *Symposium*' (forthcoming). Thirdly, Janko (*Homer, Hesiod and the Hymns*) constructs a tight argument from the rate of linguistic change and from the likely date of Hesiod's *Theogony* to arrive (231) at a date for the *Iliad* between 755 and 725 BC. This all depends, however, on the questionable validity of Janko's combined use of Homer and Hesiod.

[40] Dr C. Sourvinou-Inwood warns me that the roofing of ritual spaces was no longer a novelty by 750 BC; she agrees, however, that it was as yet far from common before the end of the century.

Delphi, at 9. 404 ff., and Agamemnon's gorgon shield, at 11. 32 ff.[41]
There is also Burkert's claim that the reference to Egyptian
Thebes at 9. 381–4 must belong long enough after 715 BC for the
Nubian kings of Dynasty XXV to have revived the fortunes of
that city, and more likely (according to him) after the sack in 663
BC.[42] This passage of Achilleus' speech may well have been worked
up late in the development of the poem, but it is far too integral
to be written off as the intrusion of an 'interpolator'—see § **2.3**,
pp. 150–1.

To move to an even rougher and more impressionistic level one
could build up a polarized picture of the eighth century and the
seventh, with the decades round the turn of the century as the
transition. The eighth-century Greek world was relatively closed
and regulated under the tight control of groups of chieftains. This
is, on the whole, the sociology and morality of Hesiod, who may,
indeed, be seen as reasserting good old values in the face of their
breakdown.[43] Geometric decoration epitomizes this relatively
stable, regulated world. The seventh century was, on the other
hand, an age of expanding horizons in almost every sense, including the broadening of social structures and the rapid development
of the *polis*. This shifting new world is reflected in the subversive
poetry of Archilochus and in the dynamic development of figured
pottery-painting and metalwork. To quote, with gratitude, from
an unpublished lecture by Robin Osborne: 'the world of the young
polis, which is certainly a world in which we are being made to

---

[41] Delphi's wealth could hardly have been 'legendary' before 700 BC—see
C. Morgan, *Athletes and Oracles* (Cambridge, 1990), esp. 106 ff., showing that 'the
Delphic sanctuary was largely the creation of the emerging states of the eighth
century'; also 194 ff. on 'the economics of dedication'. For gorgon shields, see
Burkert, *HT* 17 n. 42. Dr R. G. Osborne confirms that gorgons are clearly a motif
of orientalizing, and that, while their first appearance in the visual arts is in the
early seventh century, no gorgon shields have yet been found earlier than the
Chigi vase in mid-seventh century and even later for a gorgon surrounded by
other designs. Kirk, i. 10, is evasive on this matter.

[42] Burkert, 'Theben'. I am not impressed, on the other hand, by those passages
which are often alleged to reflect hoplite tactics, such as 12. 105, 13. 130 ff.,
16. 212 ff. These all look like descriptions of unified mass fighting which may well
be traditional rather than novel.

[43] This world is well evoked in various ways by the contributors to the Hägg
volume. It is the world of Hesiod and Geometric art, the world that Homer *grew
out of* (note his absence from most of the contributions). See also P. Millett,
'Hesiod and His World', *PCPS* 210 (1984), 84 ff. In view of Hesiod's conservatism
and Homer's radicalism, I do not necessarily conclude that Hesiod was chronolo-
gically earlier. They may well have been contemporaries.

think about possible social arrangements and their costs and consequences, and in which perhaps for the first time communities are grouping to fight wars for reasons other than the immediate gain of land: this is not an unsuitable background for the composition of poems exploring possible worlds.'

If I were to press the analogy between Homer and the visual arts, the poetry has, it seems to me, broken out of the patterned regulation of Geometric.[44] It belongs, rather, with the Trojan Horse *pithos* from Mykonos and the tripod legs from Olympia and elsewhere which show a series of juxtaposed figured scenes which include differences and surprises as well as similarities.[45] None the less, if Homer were to be conclusively dated to 725 BC or even 750, this would not, I think, affect the soundings of this book. What it might do, perhaps, is to push the crucial and explosive period of social and intellectual reassessment back into the eighth century.

Orality

Homer surely learned the art of poetry from older bards who were themselves the heirs of a long and rich tradition of oral poetry. Whatever reservations one might have about many details of his work, Milman Parry led the way to the recognition that the diction and narrative techniques of Homer are in origin and in essence oral. That remains firm whether or not his poems were touched by writing.

One unacceptable notion of Parry's, made much of by some of his successors, was that the *Iliad* as we have it *must* have been the product of a one-off improvised delivery. The complexities and long-distance correspondences—the subject of many of these soundings—are far too elaborate and well-worked-out for this model of oral composition, which owes too much to the compar-

[44] Cf. Heubeck, 'Form'. In my eyes J. M. Hurwit, *The Art and Culture of Early Greece 1100–480 BC* (Cornell, 1985), 77, has got Homer precisely wrong when he compares him with the 'Dipylon style' of c.750 BC. For references to other attempts to associate Homer with Geometric art, see n. 16 above and Holoka, *CW* 66 (1972–3), 290–92. For a sharp contrast between eighth- and seventh-century art and culture in Attica, see R. G. Osborne, *PBSA* 84 (1989), 297ff., esp. 310–12.

[45] The Trojan Horse *pithos* was excellently published by M. Ervin in *Arch. Delt.* 18 (1963), 37–75. For this and comparable developments in other arts, see R. Hampe and E. Simon, *The Birth of Greek Art* (London, 1981), 66–83; also 112–13 (tripods); 127 (armour); 212 (gold).

ison with the relatively small-scale and second-rate south-Slavic
bards. On the other hand, I do not go along with those authorities
who hold that those very complexities and the supreme structural
control of the poem demonstrate in themselves that Homer must
have exploited the aid of writing.[46] This presumption I would
label 'scripsist'. Memory has become gravely degraded in modern
Western culture, even more so with the escalating advances of
audio-visual aids and information technology. But just because
our depleted minds find it impossible to imagine such a huge and
complex feat of memory without the use of scriptural aids, that
does not mean it was impossible.

Homer may well have used *aide-mémoires* other than writing.
Although architecture has become the dominant model of mne-
monics in the Western tradition,[47] Homer's own image for the
memory-sequence of poetry seems to be the path. So he may well
have built up a mnemonic journey as the underlying shape of his
poem—for all we know, he may have mapped his poetic path in
the sand.[48] It is also important to resist the prohibition imposed
by the Parry–Lord school against the possibility that Homer
thought about his poem and worked on its shaping in between
performances.[49] If the *Iliad* is oral, then it was very likely
developed over many years, probably over the best part of a
lifetime. There would have been many performances, probably
several each year; and in between them—and no doubt during
them also—the poet would think about ways of improving the

---

[46] This view has been gaining ground during recent years. Leading exponents
have included Lesky, *RE* 698–709 and elsewhere; Schadewaldt, *Aufbau*; Lloyd-
Jones in Lloyd-Jones *et al.* (edd.), *History and Imagination: Essays in Honour of
H. Trevor-Roper* (London, 1981), 15 ff., esp. 27–9; Heubeck, introd. to *Od. Comm.*
i. 11–12, and elsewhere, cf. A. Dihle, *Homer-Probleme* (Opladen, 1970). Martin
(*The Language of Heroes*) is a strong antidote.

[47] While said to go back to Simonides, the *loci classici* are *Auct. ad Herennium*
3. 28–40; Cic. *de Or.* 2. 350–68; and Quintilian 11. 2—see H. Blum, *Die antike
Mnemotechnik* (Spudasmata, 15) (Hildesheim, 1969). The most exciting introduction to the subject is Frances Yates, *The Art of Memory* (London, 1966).

[48] For the οἴμη of song, see *Od.* 8. 74, 481; 22. 347. There is a good note on the
word in Thornton, 148f.; cf. Thalmann, 124. The notion of a song as a map and
of the drawing of song-shapes in the sand are both explored—in connection with
Australian aboriginal story-telling—in Bruce Chatwin's fascinating book *The
Songlines* (London, 1987). The shield of Achilleus might suggest a mnemonic form
of concentric circles; cf. F. Letoublon, *Poétique*, 14 (1983), 20–1.

[49] For oral poets who work on and think about their poems before and between
performances, see Finnegan, 80–3. For comparative material on 'expansion', see
Hatto, *THEP* ii. 271–2.

poem, of better incorporating novel material, of eliminating material that was not so well integrated, planting, weeding, rearranging; so finally building up the very connections and shapings which the scripsists attribute to writing. Over the years the poem is likely to have approached closer and closer towards some sort of 'finished' version. On the other hand, it is important to remember that the oral poet would never have been able to put the poem behind him, to pack it up and send it off for publication; it will have stayed with him all his life, constantly nagging for improvement.

In any case the crucial point for my purposes is not how Homer worked up the poem but how he conveyed it to his public. Not even the most zealous of the vigorous new school of scripsists would claim, I think, that Homer wrote his poem for a reading public. The important thing is that it was created to be delivered orally and to be heard.

Repertoire

Hesiod, *Works and Days* 161–6, on the heroic age of bronze is good evidence that the songs of the epic poets were dominated by stories of Thebes and of Troy. Whether the generation to which Homer was apprenticed sang songs of the length of the *Iliad* and *Odyssey* or shorter lays, more like Phemios and Demodokos, we cannot say, though I shall give some reasons for thinking the latter rather more likely. We also cannot tell whether a plot anything at all close to that of the *Iliad* had already been developed by other poets before the master-poet. I would be surprised if it had, and especially surprised if the scheme of narrative-time and the related tripartite structure were the work of anyone other than Homer.

If the generation of Homer's teachers did normally perform songs of no longer than, say, two or three hours of performance-time, then the development, whether gradual or sudden, of a far longer poem would have been all part of the lifetime's skill and thought that are called for to explain its artful complexity. Homer could still, no doubt, have provided, if called for, shorter poems from other parts of the repertoire; but it is likely that the poem of three great sessions came to dominate his offerings. As the *Iliad* grew it would have drawn in and incorporated material from elsewhere in the repertoire, such as the catalogue of ships and the

evocations of the sack of Troy—so too with, for example, the
Argo material and the Cretan stories in the *Odyssey*. On the
question whether the *Iliad* and the *Odyssey* are the work of one
and the same poet, I change my mind so often that I am reluctant
to put anything on paper. At present I am inclined to regard them
as products of the same vast mind, like the great tragedies and the
late plays of Shakespeare.[50]

If Homer's repertoire was dominated by one (or two) great
poem(s), then this would be another reason for divorcing Homer
from the model of Phemios and Demodokos. As resident poets in
Ithaka and Scherie they are expected to produce a wide variety of
entertainments, especially after dinner. For Homer to have the
opportunity to perform the *Iliad* (let alone the *Odyssey*) at all
frequently he would have needed to be more peripatetic. There
seems to be a reference to the institution of travelling bards in the
Odyssey, when Eumaios gives a list of δημιουργοί (public experts):

"τίς γὰρ δὴ ξεῖνον καλεῖ ἄλλοθεν αὐτὸς ἐπελθὼν
ἄλλον γ', εἰ μὴ τῶν οἳ δημιοεργοὶ ἔαςι,
μάντιν ἢ ἰητῆρα κακῶν ἢ τέκτονα δούρων,
ἢ καὶ θέςπιν ἀοιδόν, ὅ κεν τέρπῃςιν ἀείδων;
οὗτοι γὰρ κλητοί γε βροτῶν ἐπ' ἀπείρονα γαῖαν·"

'Who goes out of his way to invite in a stranger from elsewhere?
Not unless he is one of the public experts, a prophet or a doctor of ills
or a carpenter in wood, or an inspired poet, who delights by his poetry.
These are the people who are invited in all over the earth.'
(*Od.* 17. 382–6)[51]

On the other hand, Hesiod, if we can take him seriously (which I
seriously doubt) never crossed water from his home-territory
beneath Helikon except to perform at Chalkis (*WD* 650–60). In
later times it was commonplace for poets and performers to travel
to the places and occasions where they would be appreciated.[52]

---

[50] Cf. Heubeck, *Od. Comm.* i. 13–23 (more fully in *Der Odyssee-Dichter und die
Ilias* (Erlangen, 1954)). For a fresh assessment inclining to the view that the
Odyssey is by a separate poet who had the *Iliad* at the forefront of his mind, see
R. B. Rutherford, 'From the *Iliad* to the *Odyssey*' (forthcoming).

[51] In a sense Thamyris at *Iliad* 2. 594–600 supplies a kind of mythical precedent—and warning—for the travelling bard. He went from Thrace via Oechalia to
Dorion in the south-west Peloponnese, where the Muses stopped him.

[52] Gentili, Ch. 9 ('Intellectual Activity and Socio-Economic Situation') docu-
ments this phenomenon.

Occasion

It is possible that the *Iliad* was created to be performed through three successive nights in the banqueting-hall of a lord. We have seen Odysseus himself supplying some sort of precedent (see pp. 30–1 above); and the feast or symposium are recognized more and more as an important occasion for poetry.[53] On the other hand, the programme for such occasions would tend to be at the command of the local nobles, or to have been especially composed for that particular gathering. It is also possible, but even less plausible, that a travelling poet could on arrival impose his own programme for three long nights.

I find it hard to believe that it is coincidence that big panegyric festivals were becoming firmly established during the very period that produced the Homeric epics. At this stage these were local, though some were to become Panhellenic before long, most famously the festivals of Zeus at Olympia and Apollo at Delphi.[54] A large proportion of the local communities, often including women and children, would gather at the sanctuary and stay there for several days and nights. The time would typically be spent in sacrifice and ritual, in feasting, and in witnessing athletics and other activities in honour of the god. These activities might include poetry; and in later classical times competitions between rhapsodes were not uncommon.[55] This seems to me to be the most plausible opportunity for the three successive all-night sessions for the *Iliad* and two for the *Odyssey* which I have posited. Works of art are

---

[53] See notably R. Kannicht, 'Thalia' in W. Haug and R. Warning (edd.), *Das Fest* (Poetik und Hermeneutik, 14) (Munich, 1989), 29–52; also the contributions by E. Pollizer (177 ff.) and W. Rösler (230 ff.) in O. Murray (ed.), *Sympotica* (Oxford, 1990), and O. Murray in Hägg.

[54] See C. Rolley in Hägg, 109–14, cf. Morgan, op. cit. (n. 41 above), 61 ff., 137 ff., 161 ff. Although there were no poetic events at Olympia in classical times, perhaps it should not be ruled out as an original occasion for Homer, especially the *Odyssey*. There is much to please listeners from Sparta and Pylos—and Ithaka of course. It also seems obvious to me that Nestor's story of a four-horse chariot sent to Elis by Neleus to compete in games (*Il.* 11.698–702) must have been perceived as some sort of validating mythological forerunner of the Olympic games. It may be that too-early dating of Homer has led to the neglect of this allusion.

[55] The testimonia for rhapsodic contests are collected by Herington, app. 1 (167 ff.). A possible addition should be Dodona (I owe this to Gentili, 285, n. 3); Terpsikles the rhapsode dedicated a tripod to Zeus there in the fifth century—see M. L. Lazzarini, *Le formule delle dediche votive nella Grecia arcaica* (Rome, 1976), no. 142 on p. 198.

40   Exploratory Charts

most likely to come into existence in their particular form when
there is an audience and an occasion to receive them and to foster
them.

The most directly relevant testimony comes from the Homeric
Hymn to Apollo:

> ἀλλὰ cù Δήλωι Φοῖβε μάλιcτ' ἐπιτέρπεαι ἦτορ,
> ἔνθα τοι ἑλκεχίτωνεc Ἰάονεc ἠγερέθονται
> αὐτοῖc cùν παίδεccι καὶ αἰδοίηιc ἀλόχοιcιν.
> οἱ δέ cε πυγμαχίηι τε καὶ ὀρχηθμῶι καὶ ἀοιδῆι
> μνηcάμενοι τέρπουcιν ὅταν cτήcωνται ἀγῶνα.

But, Phoibos, your heart takes special delight in Delos, where the long-
robed Ionians congregate along with their children and respectable wives
to gratify you whenever they hold the contest in boxing and dance and
poetry. (*H. Ap.* 146–50)[56]

While ἀοιδῆι ('in poetry') fits well with my reconstruction, ἀγῶνα
('contest') does not, unless it can be taken to mean the gathering
in general rather than actual competition (as Thucydides
assumed). There can hardly have been competitions between epic
poems each of which lasted for several all-night sessions. So I
have to set Homer at non-competitive or pre-competitive festivals,
or festivals where athletics were competitive but poetry and music
were not.

Apart from the Delia as an occasion for Homer, scholars have
tended to gravitate to the Panionia, held at Mykale in honour of
Poseidon, and probably obliquely referred to in the simile at *Il.*
20. 403.[57] I have already voiced some concern, however, over the
lack of material to gratify an Ionian audience (pp. 32–3); and if

---

[56] This is the transmitted text; the passage is also quoted by Thucydides, 3. 104,
in connection with the Athenian reinstatement of prestigious contests on Delos,
probably in 426 BC. There are alarmingly many variant readings, but none directly
affects this discussion. There is also a problem with the dating of these lines and
of those soon after, which refer to Homer (165–73). Burkert ('Kynaithos', 59 ff.)
and Janko (109 ff.) have shown that in its present form (combining Pythian and
Delian Apollo) the hymn may well date from 522 BC; but the part in question is
probably much older, even contemporary with Hesiod according to Janko, 106. In
'Making', 54–6, Burkert puts forward the intriguing suggestion that in line 172 οἴκει
would have been received as imperfect οἴκει (used to live) rather than present οἰκεῖ
(lives), i.e. the poet of the poem is not claiming to be the famous bard of Chios
himself, as has been supposed by Thucydides and nearly everyone ever since, but
was a rhapsode 'advertising' the master-poet whose definitive texts he performs.

[57] In the simile a bull is sacrificed Ἑλικώνιον ἀμφὶ ἄνακτα ('around the altar of
the lord of Helike'); cf. Wade-Gery, 3–4. The allusion at *Od.* 6. 160–3 to the altar
of Apollo on Delos, seen by Odysseus himself, may well be a 'validating' reference

Homer performed several times a year he will no doubt have gone further afield. Suppose, for example, one occasion was a local panegyris at the temple of Apollo Smintheus in the Troad. The immediate locals would be pleased, especially by 1. 457–74, and so would those from many nearby cities, not least the Greeks who resettled the ruins of Ilios somewhat before 700 BC.[58] They might have included local aristocrats who claimed power by descent from Aineias as predicted at 20. 303–8. This is mere speculation; it is offered as no more than the kind of occasion that is possible and is not contrary to our evidence.

In keeping with my impressionistic sense that Homer has broken out of the relatively constrained eighth century into the more turbulent and outward-looking world of the seventh century, these burgeoning panegyric festivals would supply him with a larger, wider audience than the chieftain and his guests. This audience will have sensed their growing standing in political and social terms as the old power-structures broke up. Homer's teachers, reflected by Phemios and Demodokos, may well have normally performed poems of an hour or two at the beck and call of noble patrons. Homer, I suggest, grew out of this setting, and found in the new festivals, by a kind of symbiosis with his new public, the incentive and the occasion to expand to the epic that we have.

Recording

However it happened, it is one of the great strokes of good fortune for humanity that the *Iliad* and *Odyssey* were not only created but

to the Delian festival. Unfortunately Hesiod fr. 357 MW is too antiquarian to be authentic (it is not even sure that it goes back to Philochoros):

> ἐν Δήλωι τότε πρῶτον ἐγὼ καὶ Ὅμηρος ἀοιδοὶ
> μέλπομεν, ἐν νεαροῖς ὕμνοις ῥάψαντες ἀοιδήν,
> Φοῖβον Ἀπόλλωνα χρυσάορον, ὃν τέκε Λητώ.

Then first in Delos Homer and I, the singers,
stitching together our song in novel hymns,
glorified Phoebus Apollo, gold-sworded, Leto's child.
(Hes. *fr. dub.* 357W, tr. Herington)

As Herington says (173), 'the lines . . . seem designed to satisfy the deepest urges of any philologist: they bring together Homer and Hesiod in competition, and they triumphantly confirm the theory of the *rhaptein* school.'

[58] See Cook, 92 ff., esp. 101; for the location of Apollo Smintheus see Cook, 228 ff.

were recorded in writing. The most blatant instance of hermen-
eutic circularity in this book is the application of the working
hypothesis that the *Iliad* has been faithfully recorded in substantially the form and wording of the original master-poet: the
application of this hypothesis then leads to the discovery of so
much, such complex artistry that this 'proves' that we have a
remarkably authentic transcript of the master-poet's work. I see
no alternative but to offer these soundings with that circularity
built in.

How, then, did the *Iliad* get written down? One answer which
is attracting an increasing number of adherents is that Homer
himself learned the new Greek alphabet and realized that it was
a way of preserving his poem for the future. This cannot be ruled
out, though I find it in the highest degree implausible that the
same man who developed this great poem should also master such
a mighty technological feat.[59] And would he have been able to
make the transfer from the music and pace of oral performance
to the extremely slow labour of writing? In any case, it is totally
out of the question that Homer created the *Iliad* in order to have
it preserved in writing for future readers: the poem needs a live
audience.

If the *Iliad* was written down in Homer's own lifetime, it is far
more likely that he dictated it to someone who had become highly
proficient at the new writing. Again there is the problem, though
less severe, of abandoning the accustomed rhythm and pace of
performance. This difficulty, especially the deterioration of pros-
ody, is even recognized by Lord, the champion of the theory of
recording. On the other hand he claims that dictation provides
the time and thinking-space for oral poets to produce exceptionally
well-constructed and lengthy poems.[60] I cannot rule out the possibility that Homer's oral performances were shorter and less
highly-wrought than our *Iliad*, and that it was the process of
dictation to a scribe which brought the poem up to its exceptional

---

[59] Probably on leather scrolls at that early date: see Jeffery, 57–8; Burkert,
SHAW 1984.1, 33f.; but see also Heubeck, 'Schrift', 132–3.

[60] Lord, 124–8; cf. Hatto, *THEP* ii. 164 and 169 n. 1 for more complaints from
oral poets. The claim that dictation or tape-recording can lead to improvement
has, however, also been made from Australia and Ghana. See R. M. Bernt, *Love
Songs of Arnhem Land* (Melbourne, 1976), 46–8; J. Goody in *Classiques africains*,
20 (1980), 50–1. (I owe these references to M. Clunies Ross in *Australian Aboriginal
Studies*, 1 (1983), 16 ff., esp. 20).

length and quality. Yet I find it hard to swallow that the public which was the 'manure' for this amazing growth was a single amanuensis rather than a proper audience hearing a live performance. I am also bound to have reservations because the dictation theory cannot satisfactorily account for the huge tripartite structure which I have proposed, especially if I am right that this was synchronized with three sessions of performance.

Quite apart from the sheer technological problems of writing on this scale in the early seventh century—let alone still earlier—my instinct is to favour a means of recording Homer in performance, in full flow, with the music and pace which he had practised over the years. This means aural recording and memorization by admirers or disciples. Until now the chief modern advocate of a period of oral transmission has been G. S. Kirk. His view was, however, that the poem was transmitted by bards with poetic pretensions of their own, who changed it considerably in the process.[61] My theory is, on the contrary, that the *Iliad* was memorized from listening to performances by a 'tape-recorder' type of follower or followers, who did their very best to preserve their master's voice as perfectly as possible. The best analogy is the preservation of the 40,000 lines of the Sanskrit *Rig-Veda*, a collection of hymns and liturgies which has been passed down from generation to generation with an extraordinary accuracy that can be checked against written copies.[62]

In classical times there was a guild of rhapsodes who claimed to have done just that—the Homeridai of Chios.[63] There is no conclusive reason to deny their claim, and I suggest that it may actually have been more or less true. They would, then, have been

---

[61] Kirk, *SH* 277 ff., 316 ff. A. Parry, 'HHI' 110 ff., esp. 112–14, 128–30, rightly pointed out that the changes envisaged by Kirk would extend to every scale of composition, large and small, and that the result would be in effect that our *Iliad* is not Homer's *Iliad*, and not even close to it. In his more recent work Kirk has not argued for such substantial interpolation and tampering with the poem as was supposed in *SH* (under the influence of D. L. Page).

[62] Inevitably there is some question whether the oral transmission of the *Rig-Veda* has been completely unaided by the written copies—see Finnegan, 150–2.

[63] By the fifth century the Homeridai were caught up in various rivalries and polemics which unfortunately make the sources difficult to interpret. For discussions see T. W. Allen, *Homer: The Origins and the Transmission* (Oxford, 1927) 42–50 (credulous); Wade-Gery, 19–21; Pfeiffer, 11–12; Zs. Ritoók, *Acta Antiqua*, 18 (1970), 1–29; Burkert, 'Kynaithos', 54–8. D. Fehling in *RhM* n.s. 122 (1979), 193–9, merely shows how far, given the nature of the evidence, scepticism can be taken.

responsible for preserving the poem from Homer's own performances down until the techniques and technology of writing on
papyrus were up to the task of transcription. The undertaking also
waited for someone to feel the need of a written version, perhaps
as some kind of check on the competing claims to accuracy by
rhapsodes. That occasion may well have been the so-called 'Peisistratean recension' in Athens in the third quarter of the sixth
century. Although the testimony for this is mainly late and weak,
the widespread yet superficial Attic colouring of the dialect of our
text makes it plausible enough.[64]

However Homer was recorded, the vital fact is that he was. I
believe that this book contributes, however circularly, to the case
for holding that he was transmitted with a high degree of fidelity.
Of course, there were, before the Alexandrian standard edition,
many variations of phrases, and frequent disruption, addition, or
subtraction of one or two lines at a time, even perhaps occasionally
up to twenty lines. But this is quite different from the kind of
major interference that used to be supposed by the analysts.

1.6 *Ronsard's door*

All these speculations are offered only to give a possible setting
for these soundings. They are not, however, essential, and it may
be as well to return in the end to my central thesis: it matters to
us present readers that the *Iliad* was created to be heard in performance. Of course our reading is a very different experience,
one largely in our own heads and privacy; but it can be affected
by our awareness of what it would mean to be in the presence of,
and largely under the control of, the performing poet. My aim is,
then, to explore some ways that reading can be enriched—and
perhaps made less autistic—by this kind of awareness.

[64] Some scholars have recently made the Peisistratean recension central to the
transmission of Homer—as was supposed by Wolf and many old analysts. See
especially Jensen, *passim*, and S. West, *Od. Comm.* i. 36–9. West writes that 'this
sixth-century Athenian recension must be regarded as the archetype of all our
Homeric MSS and of the indirect tradition represented by ancient quotations and
allusions'. If this is right, it would explain how book 10 became established in its
place, since it was added, according to the T scholia on 10. 1, at this time. The
inappropriate duals in 9. 182 ff. might also have become fixed at this stage, for
whatever reason. Is it an objection to this account of the transmission that the
Alexandrian scholars do not seem to have privileged any 'Athenian text'?

Ronsard, perhaps with the instinct of a fellow-poet, arrived at a desire to read the *Iliad* right through. He even sensed the structure which I have claimed arose from the occasions when the poem first grew to its mature shape with the nourishment of its first audiences:

> Je veus lire en trois jours l'Iliade d'Homere,
> Et pour-ce, Corydon, ferme bien l'huis sur moy . . .
> Je veus trois jours entiers demeurer à requoy,
> Pour follastrer apres une sepmaine entiere.[65]

> I want to read Homer's Iliad in three days;
> So, Corydon, make sure you keep my door firmly shut . . .
> I want three whole days of peace and quiet;
> Then I can spend all next week having fun.

[65] *Continuation des Amours*, sonnet 60, 1-2 and 7-8 (1560 version) in *Œuvres complètes*, ed. P. Laumorier (Paris, 1934), 7. 182–3. But even Ronsard allows for a possible disturbance of his reading: he tells his servant Corydon that even if a god turns up he must not be interrupted—the only exception would be his mistress Cassandre. (I am grateful to David Cowling for help with Ronsard.)

2

Poetic Fieldwork

2.1 Some keys to ethical questions

Τίς τ' ἄρ σφωε θεῶν ἔριδι ξυνέηκε μάχεσθαι;
Λητοῦς καὶ Διὸς υἱός· ὁ γὰρ βασιλῆϊ χολωθεὶς
νοῦσον ἀνὰ στρατὸν ὦρσε κακήν, ὀλέκοντο δὲ λαοί,   10
οὕνεκα τὸν Χρύσην ἠτίμασεν ἀρητῆρα
Ἀτρεΐδης· ὁ γὰρ ἦλθε θοὰς ἐπὶ νῆας Ἀχαιῶν
λυσόμενός τε θύγατρα φέρων τ' ἀπερείσι' ἄποινα,
στέμματ' ἔχων ἐν χερσὶν ἑκηβόλου Ἀπόλλωνος
χρυσέωι ἀνὰ σκήπτρωι, καὶ λίσσετο πάντας Ἀχαιούς,   15
Ἀτρεΐδα δὲ μάλιστα δύω, κασμήτορε λαῶν·
"Ἀτρεΐδαι τε καὶ ἄλλοι ἐϋκνήμιδες Ἀχαιοί,
ὑμῖν μὲν θεοὶ δοῖεν Ὀλύμπια δώματ' ἔχοντες
ἐκπέρσαι Πριάμοιο πόλιν, εὖ δ' οἴκαδ' ἱκέσθαι·
παῖδα δ' ἐμοὶ λύσαιτε φίλην, τὰ δ' ἄποινα δέχεσθαι,   20
ἁζόμενοι Διὸς υἱὸν ἑκηβόλον Ἀπόλλωνα."
Ἔνθ' ἄλλοι μὲν πάντες ἐπευφήμησαν Ἀχαιοὶ
αἰδεῖσθαί θ' ἱερῆα καὶ ἀγλαὰ δέχθαι ἄποινα·
ἀλλ' οὐκ Ἀτρεΐδηι Ἀγαμέμνονι ἥνδανε θυμῶι,
ἀλλὰ κακῶς ἀφίει, κρατερὸν δ' ἐπὶ μῦθον ἔτελλε·   25
"μή σε, γέρον, κοίλησιν ἐγὼ παρὰ νηυσὶ κιχείω
ἢ νῦν δηθύνοντ' ἢ ὕστερον αὖτις ἰόντα,
μή νύ τοι οὐ χραίσμηι σκῆπτρον καὶ στέμμα θεοῖο·
τὴν δ' ἐγὼ οὐ λύσω· πρίν μιν καὶ γῆρας ἔπεισιν
ἡμετέρωι ἐνὶ οἴκωι, ἐν Ἄργεϊ, τηλόθι πάτρης,   30
ἱστὸν ἐποιχομένην καὶ ἐμὸν λέχος ἀντιόωσαν·
ἀλλ' ἴθι, μή μ' ἐρέθιζε, σαώτερος ὥς κε νέηαι."
Ὣς ἔφατ', ἔδεισεν δ' ὁ γέρων καὶ ἐπείθετο μύθωι·

Which of the gods was it who set these two to their fighting? It was
the son of Zeus and Leto. In anger at the king he raised a vile plague
throughout the army, and the people were dying, because the son of
Atreus had dishonoured Chryses, his priest. Chryses had come to the fast
ships of the Achaians to gain release for his daughter, bringing with him

unlimited ransom, and holding in his hands the sacred woollen bands of Apollo the far-shooter, wreathed on a golden staff. He began to entreat the whole body of the Achaians, but especially the two sons of Atreus, the marshals of the army. 'Sons of Atreus, and you other well-greaved Achaians, may the gods who live on Olympos grant you the sacking of Priam's city and a safe return to your homes. But release my dear child to me, and accept this ransom, in reverence for the son of Zeus, Apollo the far-shooter.' Then all the other Achaians shouted their agreement, to respect the priest's claim and take the splendid ransom. But this was not the pleasure of Agamemnon's heart, the son of Atreus. He sent him shamefully on his way, with harsh words of command: 'Old man, let me never find you by our hollow ships, either dallying here now or coming back again in future—or you will have no protection from your god's staff and sacred bands. As for the girl, I shall not release her. Before that, old age will come upon her in our house, in Argos, far from her own country, where she will work at the loom and serve my bed. No, away with you: do not provoke me, if you want to return in safety.'

So he spoke, and the old man was afraid and did as he was ordered. (1. 8–33)

This translation—like most, if not all, modern translations—takes βαcιλῆι (*basilēi*) in line 9 as 'the king'; and this clearly refers to Agamemnon. But 'one of the chiefs' might be closer to Homer (whose Greek has no definite or indefinite articles). Whatever Agamemnon's status may be, he is not 'the *basileus*', since it is clear from plenty of passages in the *Iliad* that there are many *basilēes* at Troy, with Agamemnon and Achilleus two among them. It is not clear quite how a man qualified for this status, but the existence of the comparative βαcιλεύτεροc ('more *basileus*') and superlative βαcιλεύτατοc ('most *basileus*') suggest that it was a matter of degree rather than rank.[1] Even if the context of line 9 has narrowed the possible reference of *basilēi* down to one of only two men, it is not yet clear which it refers to. Indeed, the whole run of the wording holds up the identification until the enjambement after line 11: Ἀτρεΐδηc (the son of Atreus). Those who have heard or read the poem before 'know' which *basilēi* refers to, but the

---

[1] See Taplin, 'Agamemnon', 62–70, esp. p. 63 on the famous 'one king' passage at 2. 203–6. To the works cited there (Drews, Geddes, Rihll) add Schadewaldt, *IS* 37–9; F. Gschnitzer in *Innsbrucker Beitr. zur Kulturwiss.* 11 (1965), 99 ff.; J. Halverson, *Hermes*, 113 (1985), 129 ff. (on *Od.*); P. Carlier, *La Royauté en Grèce* (Strasbourg, 1984), 136 ff.; S. West on *Od.* 1. 386–7; Collins, 64 ff.; H. van Wees, *CQ* n.s. 38 (1988), 1 ff., esp. 18–22; Morris, 98–9.

narrative still flows in a single direction, and Ἀτρείδης comes as a confirmation charged with narrative energy.

The assimilation of *basileus* to the monarch, and the assumption of Agamemnon to this sovereignty, goes back at least to the era of the Hellenistic kings, the first age of professional Homeric scholarship.[2] It may well have been to the advantage of the reception of Homer in the long run that many aspects of his mental and social structures, his 'anthropology' so to speak, have proved open to anachronistic assimilation by later ages. His adaptability to the institutions of kingship is a good illustration.[3] On the other hand, when any such anachronism is exposed as such by historical research or philology or archaeology, it is no longer possible to indulge in it unreservedly—it is time to move on. The decline of the institutions of monarchy world-wide and the questioning of absolute authority leads to a reassessment of the politics and internal anthropology of the *Iliad*. It also restores Homer more to his own time, a period when the institutions and communal bondings of society were under review, and going through momentous transition (see § 1.5).

Any venture of poetic fieldwork—that is of attempting to work out the mental and social structures of the *Iliad* by accumulating and comparing the evidence from within the poem—will find that the indications are too sparse or thin to clarify some aspects of the anthropology. On the other hand, there are many important areas where they add up to a picture, a picture which is often remarkably consistent. There may be internal contradictions, but more often there is a significant imprecision, a lack of definitive statute. It is this that leaves room for dispute, for the interplay of different views, especially of personal and political ethics, which is, I shall

---

[2] The scholia fall into giving βαϲιλεύϲ the definite article, e.g. in ΣΑ on 29, which protests, particularly absurdly, that Chryses should not have complained about his daughter bedding τῶι βαϲιλεί (with the king) (see Taplin, 'Agamemnon', 81). For Hellenistic assimilation of Homeric anthropology, see (for instance) O. Murray, 'Philodemus on the Good King according to Homer', *JRS* 55 (1965), 161 ff.

[3] I do not share the fashionable admiration for the aesthetic value or authority of the ancient scholia on Homer, voiced most persuasively by N. J. Richardson in *CQ* n.s. 30 (1980), 265 ff. and most zealously by M. Heath, *Unity in Greek Poetics* (Oxford, 1989), Ch. 8. On the whole the scholia show little sense of cultural relativity, and are often shamelessly anachronistic. A comparison of the visual arts of 200 BC with those of 700 BC makes the point that we are dealing with radically different aesthetic eras.

argue, one of the perennial strengths of the poem. Thus, Agamemnon's position, while it has an anthropological rationale, falls crucially short of final definition or official hierarchy. I explore this on pp. 57–60. If the *basileus* of line 9 were '*the* king', then the issue between him and Achilleus would be far less powerful and interesting.

The consistency of Homeric anthropology should not lead to the assumption that it directly reflects the historical reality of Homer's own day, or, even less plausibly, of some earlier age. Poetic traditions can establish their own coherent worlds. An influential but flawed methodology has used Homer selectively as a starting-point for building up a historical world; once this has been filled out by archaeological and comparative material from outside the poem, it is then reimposed on it, often at the cost of serious distortion.[4] At the same time it would be a no less distorting over-reaction to deny any connection with the realities of history and anthropology, leaving a purely invented world.[5] I do not feel competent, in the face of the ever-increasing body of archaeological material, to attempt much on the complex interaction between poem and reality, the creative transformation of the lives and experience of its audience. I do not doubt, however, that there is interesting work to be done, and I hope my textual work will help it.

The word λαοί (*lāoi*) in line 10 is an illustration of my point that internal Homeric anthropology should resist presuppositions imported from elsewhere. This word (singular or plural) is often interpreted as meaning the masses, the rank and file, the people who don't matter. But fieldwork reveals no such downgrading of *lāoi* or *lāos*:[6] they are the people as a whole, the host. This does

---

[4] The outstanding example is Finley in the *World of Odysseus*. Recently Morris, in 'The Use and Abuse of Homer', after a full and sophisticated discussion of the problems, suddenly turns, in his final section (123 ff.), to argue that the *Iliad* is, in effect, propaganda in favour of traditional *basilees*. Yet the poem, if taken as poetry, is constantly questioning the authority of *basilees*, especially that of Agamemnon. His bold assertion that 'throughout the poems, the *basileis* are glorified, and the *demos* ignored to the point of total exclusion' is simply not true. Thalmann, 115–16, enlisting comparative support from Finnegan, 242–3, makes the important point that, just because oral poetry is traditional, that does not necessarily make it politically conservative.

[5] Not even J. R. R. Tolkien or Ursula LeGuin can achieve that—or would wish to. On this subject see Morris, *passim*.

[6] Contrast the distinction at 2. 188, 198 between βαcιλῆα καὶ ἔξοχον ἄνδρα (a king or a man of importance) and δήμου ἄνδρα (a commoner); or between ἔξοχος, μεcήεις,

not seem to be exclusive even of the *basilées*,[7] though as soon as one or some or all of them are picked out, then they are necessarily no longer part of the collective *lāoi*.

There is, indeed, a significant relationship between a *basileus* and his *lāoi*, one that is very relevant to line 10. They support him, and in return he is responsible for them: it is a failure for him to bring about or fail to prevent harm to his *lāoi*. Above all, Hektor feels obliged to stand and fight Achilleus by the prospect of the reproach "*Ἕκτωρ ἧφι βίηφι πιθήсас ὤλεсε λαόν*" ('Hektor trusted in his own strength and destroyed his people') (22. 107). Even Agamemnon, though he never openly admits any fault in his treatment of Chryses, agrees to give Chryseïs back, because "*βούλομ' ἐγὼ λαὸν сῶν ἔμμεναι ἢ ἀπολέсθαι*" ('I wish my people to be saved, not to die') (1. 117). Later he will admit defeat in the Trojan expedition altogether, first in feigned despair (2. 115) and then in truth (9. 22): "*πολὺν ὤλεсα λαόν*" ('I have lost many of my people').

ἠτίμαсεν ('dishonoured') in line 11 brings in one of the few notions which is universally recognized to be central to Homeric values. While conventionally translated 'honour', poetic fieldwork shows that *τιμή* (*tīmē*) and its cognates cover the area of what is *due* to a person—recognized value, esteem, satisfaction. Every god, goddess, man, and woman wishes to have their due *tīmē*, and feels outraged to be denied it, to be *ἄτιμος* (*atīmos*). This amounts to a kind of 'code'.

Everyone agrees this much; but that is the beginning not the end of problems. *Tīmē* entails questions that are in the broadest sense 'ethical'. What does some particular one deserve *tīmē* for, and how much? Who should grant it? What form should it take? Much of the *Iliad* is, in my view, spent on disputing just such questions as these, issues of just deserts, approval, disapproval, credit, and blame. This classic assertion could, then, hardly be further from the truth:[8] 'The heroic code was complete and unambiguous, so much so that neither the poet nor his characters ever had occasion to debate it.' The characters are forever debating

and *χερειότεροс* (outstanding, middle-ranking, and lesser men) at 12. 269-70. Cf. Geddes, 21-2.

[7] For instance at 13. 105 ff. Poseidon includes in the phrase *μεθημοсύνῃсί τε λαῶν* ('through the reluctance of his people') (108) those *ἄριстοι* (leading men) (117), such as Teukros and Antilochos, whom he is addressing.

[8] Finley, 113.

ethical issues, especially when one character's estimate of his due *tīmē* is not agreed by another. That is what the audience encounters straight away in the confrontation of Agamemnon and Chryses. So, while it is never disputed that *tīmē* should be given where it is due (and denied where it is not), there is much debate between the characters over the application of this in practice. It is true that the poet does not explicitly state, let alone debate, ethical issues in his own voice, but he is the poet not the commentator.[9] Even such well-known phrases as ἀεικέα μήδετο ἔργα (he devised shameful treatment) should be seen as evaluations for the characters within the narrative, not as comments from outside. 'The evil is for the victim, not the doer.'[10] Thus in line 25 κακῶc ἀφίει (he sent him shamefully on his way) is not a condemnation by the narrator: it conveys the effect of Agamemnon's behaviour within the narrative—it is humiliating for Chryses. In Schiller's terms the *Iliad* is 'naïve' as opposed to 'sentimental'; in narratological terms, there is no moral judgement by the primary narrator-focalizer.[11]

An outstanding test-case is provided by the passage where Menelaos is seriously considering the sparing of Adrestos, and Agamemnon rebukes him with ruthless sentiments (6. 55 ff.—see further pp. 162–3). These lines follow:

> Ὥc εἰπὼν ἔτρεψεν ἀδελφειοῦ φρέναc ἥρωc,
> αἴcιμα παρειπών· ὁ δ' ἀπὸ ἔθεν ὤcατο χειρὶ
> ἥρω' Ἄδρηcτον· τὸν δὲ κρείων Ἀγαμέμνων
> οὖτα κατὰ λαπάρην·

With these words the hero turned his brother's mind, winning him with right advice. Menelaos pushed the hero Adrestos away from him with his hand, and lord Agamemnon stabbed him in the side. (6. 61–4)

I maintain that it is Menelaos, not the poet-narrator, who accepts Agamemnon's call for blood as αἴcιμα (right). Two other passages support this, which is not the usual interpretation. In the only

---

[9] This is less true, perhaps, of the *Odyssey*. I have in mind particularly the explicit attribution of blame in *Od.* 20. 394 πρότεροι γὰρ ἀεικέα μηχανόωντο (because they had been the aggressors in evil deeds)—see further pp. 98–9.

[10] Griffin, *HLD* 85, n. 9; cf. id. 'Words' (1986), 36 ff.

[11] See de Jong, *passim*, esp. 136 ff., a generally valuable discussion, though I take issue with her surprisingly perfunctory dismissal (205) of 6. 62. F. Frontisi-Ducroux, *La Cithare d'Achille: Essai sur la poétique de l'Iliade* (Rome, 1986) is also largely concerned with narratological perspectives; but see the review by H. Foley in *CPh* 84 (1989), 252–5.

other occurrence of αἴϲιμα παρειπών, at 7. 121, Agamemnon persuades Menelaos not to take on the duel with Hector: clearly his
words strike Menelaos as 'to the point'.[12] Even more clearly at
Od. 22. 45 ff. Eurymachos concedes to Odysseus "ταῦτα μὲν αἴϲιμα
εἶπαϲ" ('all you have said is right'), but still pleads that Antinoös
was the guilty instigator. αἴϲιμα conveys not moral approval, but
the recognition that a good case has been made. The narrator does
not issue moral directives.

The party which is missing from Finley's assertion is the audience. If it is conceded that the characters within the poem dispute
ethical issues, then there must necessarily be room for the audience
to consider the questions and to come to assessments independently of the characters. I would go farther and claim that a
significant element in the perennial power of Homer is the challenges of evaluation which he sets his audience. That is why the
poem begins with two scenes which provocatively demand ethical
opinion without explicitly supplying it: Agamemnon's treatment
of Chryses, and his great dispute with Achilleus. It is important
that the moral is *not* spelled out. Every generation, or rather every
reader and hearer, has to make up their own mind. I, for one, find
it impossible to remain neutral (as will emerge); yet I have to
recognize that others have seen the issues in other lights.

Yet despite the lack of direct intervention by the primary narrator-focalizer, the *Iliad* is far from objective or impersonal; it is
full of *implicit* colourings or 'focalizing'.[13] It is the different and
changing perceptions of these that open up the various interpretations. For instance, those who do not condemn Agamemnon for
his treatment of Chryses have to interpret the implicit colouring
of lines 22–3 quite differently from me. All the other Achaians
support Chryses' plea, and urge respect for the priest and acceptance of the ransom (22–3). The evaluation of this will depend on
how you see Agamemnon's status in relation to all the other
Achaians[14] (see further § 2.2), your sense of the importance of
αἰδώϲ (*aidōs*), and your assessment of its applicability to this case.

---

[12] This is also indicated by the παρα- prefix, as in παρέπεισεν in 7. 120. See
P. Chantraine, *Grammaire homérique*, ii (Paris, 1953), 120 for παρα- of persuading
or tricking.
[13] This is the thesis of de Jong. See also S. Scully in *Arethusa*, 19 (1986), 135 ff.
[14] Note πάντες ('all'). There is no further dissent when everyone approves of
Diomedes at 7. 403, 9. 50, and of Hektor at 8. 542, 18. 310.

In Homeric anthropology *aidōs* is a central concept.[15] It is essentially a sense or compunction which inhibits people from behaving badly, which is to say in a way that will attract disapproval. Or as Gould puts it of the appropriateness of *aidōs* towards suppliants:[16] 'it is characteristically of the emotional *rejection* of some line of (usually aggressive) behaviour, possible under other circumstances to another agent, that αἰδώc words are used'. It is, so far as I can see, universally assumed in Homer that *aidōs* should be felt and heeded in appropriate circumstances; and that it is a fault to lack it or to override it.

The ἄποινα (*apoina*) offered by Chryses, described as ἀπερείcια (unlimited) and ἀγλαά (splendid) (13, 20, 23, etc.), is evidently assessed as more than adequate. There are scattered references throughout to the lucrative institution by which prisoners, male or female (like the mother of Andromache at 6. 425 ff.), might be sold off as slaves or ransomed to their kin—Priam speaks of both fates for his sons captured by Achilleus (22. 44–51). The *aidōs*, however, is attached to Chryses' priesthood rather than his ransom. He has the outward symbols (14–15) and emphasizes his status at the end of his speech (21). Agamemnon makes it quite clear in line 28 that he does not care about Chryses' priesthood. His language throughout relishes his humiliation of Chryses, with its elaboration of his daughter's future subjection and disqualification from having a husband or legitimate children.[17]

However the listener may interpret the personal or religious ethics so far, the narrative has left it unclear as yet how far Agamemnon is politically entitled to settle the issue (assuming, that is, that I am right that *basilei* in 9 does not establish him as *the* sovereign). Much has yet to be revealed, including the fact that Chryseïs is his γέρας (*geras*)—see further pp. 60–2. It is, however, emphasized that Chryses makes his plea to all the Achaians (15, 17, 22); so it is significant both that not one of them speaks out against Agamemnon, and that Chryses prays for punishment not just on Agamemnon but on all the Achaians (42, cf. 10, 51, 53, 56). As the narrative unfolds, it is clear that Apollo, whose

---

[15] See S. West on *Od.* 2. 64–6 with refs., esp. Redfield, *NCI* 115–19.

[16] *JHS* 93 (1973), 170.

[17] This implicit colouring has been revealingly neglected by modern critics, perhaps in awe of the monarchy. A notable exception is J. Kakridis, *H. Rev.* 125 ff. esp. 130–1.

response is immediate and unchallenged on Olympos, regards all
the Achaians as bound up with the offence of Agamemnon.

The brief but vivid Chryses episode is a kind of miniature
'rehearsal' for the great conflict which is to follow and to shape
the poem.[18] Insult over a captured woman *geras* (Chryseïs/Briseïs)
leads to anger, which leads to a successful plea to an Olympian
for vengeance on Agamemnon and all the Achaians. The great
differences come later. Chryses' retribution is tidily called off after
reparation is made: that between Achilleus and Agamemnon will
prove harder to undo, and by the time Briseïs is returned to
Achilleus a chain of events will have been started that leads to his
own death and to the fall of Troy.

The sequence from offence to plague is very clear in the narrative. Is it clear to the characters involved? Nobody says so explicitly
before Kalchas, at 93 ff., but there may be some encouragement
to detect signs of an unspoken awareness before that. If so, it
would be an index of the possible subtlety of Homeric narrative
technique and of the indications given to the listener beneath the
explicit text. Note first that it is Achilleus, not Agamemnon, who
has to summon the ἀγορή (*agorē*) (54 ff.), and that he addresses
himself to Agamemnon at once. He takes it for granted that
everyone knows that the plague is the result of an offence against
Apollo, but he makes out that he is ignorant of the nature of the
offence (62–7). Is he posing a question to which everyone can
supply the answer? An open question perhaps at this stage. I
suggest, however, that there is complicity near the surface when
Kalchas turns to Achilleus for protection:

> "ἦ γὰρ ὀίομαι ἄνδρα χολωσέμεν, ὃς μέγα πάντων
> Ἀργείων κρατέει καί οἱ πείθονται Ἀχαιοί·"

'I think that I shall anger a man who holds great power over all the
Argives and command among the Achaians.' (1. 78–9)

Achilleus knows well whom he is referring to:

> "οὔ τις ἐμεῦ ζῶντος καὶ ἐπὶ χθονὶ δερκομένοιο
> σοὶ κοίλῃς παρὰ νηυσὶ βαρείας χεῖρας ἐποίσει
> συμπάντων Δαναῶν, οὐδ᾽ ἢν Ἀγαμέμνονα εἴπῃς,
> ὃς νῦν πολλὸν ἄριστος Ἀχαιῶν εὔχεται εἶναι."

[18] Cf. Reinhardt, *ID* 42 ff., and, recently, Rabel (this is an important contribution, even though too much concerned, for my liking, with Achilleus' psycho-
logy). For the notion of 'miniature' narratives see further pp. 87, 109, 257.

'... while I live and see the light upon earth, no man will lay violent hands on you by our hollow ships, no man among the whole number of the Danaans, even if you speak of Agamemnon, who now claims to be far the best of the Achaians.' (1. 88–91)

As often in Homer's narrative technique, a seed in the form of a passing hint or subtle implication grows, as the poem progresses, into a full-blown and explicit issue or theme.

2.2 When the understanding breaks down

Τὸν δ' ἄρ' ὑπόδρα ἰδὼν προςέφη πόδας ὠκὺς Ἀχιλλεύς·
"ὤ μοι, ἀναιδείην ἐπιειμένε, κερδαλεόφρον,
πῶς τίς τοι πρόφρων ἔπεςιν πείθηται Ἀχαιῶν   150
ἢ ὁδὸν ἐλθέμεναι ἢ ἀνδράςιν ἶφι μάχεςθαι;
οὐ γὰρ ἐγὼ Τρώων ἕνεκ' ἤλυθον αἰχμητάων
δεῦρο μαχηςόμενος, ἐπεὶ οὔ τί μοι αἴτιοί εἰςιν·
οὐ γάρ πώ ποτ' ἐμὰς βοῦς ἤλαςαν οὐδὲ μὲν ἵππους,
οὐδέ ποτ' ἐν Φθίηι ἐριβώλακι βωτιανείρηι   155
καρπὸν ἐδηλήςαντ', ἐπεὶ ἦ μάλα πολλὰ μεταξὺ
οὔρεά τε ςκιόεντα θάλαςςά τε ἠχήεςςα·
ἀλλὰ ςοί, ὦ μέγ' ἀναιδές, ἅμ' ἑςπόμεθ', ὄφρα ςὺ χαίρηις,
τιμὴν ἀρνύμενοι Μενελάωι ςοί τε, κυνῶπα,
πρὸς Τρώων· τῶν οὔ τι μετατρέπηι οὐδ' ἀλεγίζεις·   160
καὶ δή μοι γέρας αὐτὸς ἀφαιρήςεςθαι ἀπειλεῖς,
ὧι ἔπι πολλὰ μόγηςα, δόςαν δέ μοι υἶες Ἀχαιῶν.
οὐ μὲν ςοί ποτε ἶςον ἔχω γέρας, ὁππότ' Ἀχαιοὶ
Τρώων ἐκπέρςως' εὖ ναιόμενον πτολίεθρον·
ἀλλὰ τὸ μὲν πλεῖον πολυάικος πολέμοιο   165
χεῖρες ἐμαὶ διέπους'· ἀτὰρ ἤν ποτε δαςμὸς ἵκηται,
ςοὶ τὸ γέρας πολὺ μεῖζον, ἐγὼ δ' ὀλίγον τε φίλον τε
ἔρχομ' ἔχων ἐπὶ νῆας, ἐπεί κε κάμω πολεμίζων.
νῦν δ' εἶμι Φθίηνδ', ἐπεὶ ἦ πολὺ φέρτερόν ἐςτιν
οἴκαδ' ἴμεν ςὺν νηυςὶ κορωνίςιν, οὐδέ ς' ὀίω   170
ἐνθάδ' ἄτιμος ἐὼν ἄφενος καὶ πλοῦτον ἀφύξειν."

Then swift-footed Achilleus scowled at him and said: 'Oh you, your thoughts are always set on gain, and shamelessness is your very clothing! How can any of the Achaians willingly follow your orders, to go on expeditions or fight an enemy with all their strength? It was not the spearmen of Troy who caused me to come here and fight—I have no quarrel with them. They have never rustled my cows or horses, or ravaged the crops in fertile Phthia, nurse of men: because between us there lie many shadowing mountains and the roar of the sea. No, it was you, you great shameless creature, you we came with, to give you satisfaction and win requital from the Trojans for Menelaos and for you, dog-face. You have no thought or regard for this. And now you even threaten to take away my prize yourself—I laboured hard for it, and it was awarded me by the sons of the Achaians. I never have a prize equal to yours, whenever the Achaians sack some well-founded Trojan town. My hands bear the brunt of the battle's fury. But when the division comes, your prize is by far the larger, and I come back to the ships with something small but precious, when I have worn myself out in the fighting. Now I shall leave for Phthia. It is a far better thing for me to return home with my beaked ships, and I have no mind to stay here heaping up riches and treasure for you and receiving no honour myself.' (1. 148–71)

The opening scene, I have argued, has usually been received since Antiquity in the light of anachronistic models of monarchy which diminish its power and openness. In very much the same way, the confrontation between Achilleus and Agamemnon is much debilitated by the notions of military hierarchy and of patriotic service which have been assumed.

Most interpreters have supposed that there is a simple and authoritative reply to Achilleus' opening question in 150–1: why should he—why should *any* Achaian—bother to help Agamemnon at Troy? But no such response is given by Agamemnon or anyone else; and those possible replies put by Achilleus in 152 ff. are raised only to be rejected.[19] Above all, there is no claim here, nor anywhere else in the *Iliad*, that we are dealing with a Panhellenic war, undertaken under the unifying banner of patriotism against the oriental foe. This version of the Trojan war became standard in the fifth century BC, and may indeed have been invented in the wake of the Persian invasions.[20] It has usually been taken for granted ever since, not least by the ancient scholia.

Hand in hand with this Greek crusade against the barbarians goes the assumption that Agamemnon the king is the commander-in-chief of a military hierarchy. Both are alien to Homeric anthropology. Men who live in the territorial domains of Agamemnon are subject to a direct obligation;[21] but there is no suggestion of

---

[19] The γάρ ('for'—not in the translation) in 152 explains 150-1, but omits a stage in the argument: 'once I have posed this question, you cannot fob me off with any standard reason, because . . .'.

[20] This is the thesis of Hall's excellent book, esp. Ch. 1.

[21] Cf. 13. 613 ff., 23. 296 ff., and Taplin, 'Agamemnon', 68.

any social structure according to which Achilleus or any other *basileus* might be accused of mutiny or treason. There is no suggestion that Achilleus should be put on trial or sent home or communally humiliated or lynched. Whatever his relationship to Agamemnon, it is not that he is fighting for king and country. In the later Greek tradition the sanction of the unity of the expedition was the oath to Tyndareus taken by the suitors of Helen. The three allusions that there are in the *Iliad* to some sort of oath are low-key and indistinct.[22] If the story of the suitors' oath, including or not including Achilleus, predated the *Iliad*, it is not brought to bear. The plot could scarcely stand up if there were any such definitive and clear-cut arrangement.

The *Iliad* raises basic questions about the coherence of human society. Achilleus' question here exposes, and hence disturbs, the very basis of the politico-military system which holds them all at Troy. Because it opens up the possibility of the disintegration of the enterprise, the question normally lies deeply suppressed. So, why fight for Agamemnon?

Achilleus passes over the motive of simple, unprovoked acquisition of loot by implying (interestingly) that he would only attack those who are in some way αἴτιοι (*aitioi*). And he personally has no grudge against the Trojans. He sees the answer to his own question as posed in 150–1 as straightforward; and the assumptions of 158 ff. are in keeping with the evidence elsewhere for Homeric anthropology. He and his fellow *basilēes* are all at Troy to help two of their number, to help restore the damaged family *tīmē* of Menelaos and his brother—for *them* the Trojans *are aitioi*.

I suggest that the 'political' institution behind this is the gathering of a host, and that this can be coherently reconstructed by poetic fieldwork.[23] Either the 'summoners' themselves—like Agamemnon and Menelaos with Odysseus (*Od.* 24. 115 ff.)—or their agents—like Nestor and Odysseus with Achilleus and Patroklos (11. 767 ff., cf. 7. 124 ff., 9. 252 ff.)—go about recruiting. The verbs used are ἀγείρειν, κελεύειν, and ὀτρύνειν ('gather', 'urge', 'stir up'), most often with λαόν (*lāon*) as the object. The 'summoned' may in response be ready and willing (as at 11. 782) or may need a lot of persuasion (as at *Od.* 24. 118–19). It would be in keeping

---

[22] Cf. Taplin, 'Agamemnon', 68–9.
[23] Ibid. 67–70. It is often said that Agamemnon is *primus inter pares*: I do not understand what that means.

with Homeric anthropology for the summoners to appeal to past duties and obligations, and to make assurances for the future. However formal or informal the agreement might be (there is no good evidence), the summoner would, in a nutshell, offer proper honour, due esteem, *tīmē*.

Once the war is engaged, the summoned *basilēes* are committed to the supervision of the summoner, who acts as a co-ordinator and spokesman. At the same time they retain substantial independence, both off the field, where they can, for instance, call together an *agorē* or *boulē*, and on, where they lead their own men. There is a largely similar situation on the Trojan side also, where Priam is the 'summoner', though Hektor takes over on the battlefield. The term ἐπίκουροι (*epikouroi*) seems to be restricted to those aiding a defensive rather than offensive war; but, like the Achaians, the Trojan ἐπίκουροι have been prevailed on by past obligations and by promises for the future. Thus, for example, Sarpedon complains (rather like Achilleus) that he fights better than the Trojans even though he does not have possessions or relatives inside the city (5. 483–4).

This arrangement, by which one *basileus* fights for and obeys another in return for proper *tīmē*, is fine as long as it is working well. But there is bound to be within it an unclarity over when and whether it has broken down, and when and whether it should be overriden. There are circumstances when the obligation may be permissibly broken. The clearest illustration is the case of Glaukos and Diomedes. Glaukos has advanced bravely on Diomedes, who is at his most dangerous (cf. 6. 96–101); yet after Glaukos' fine speech offering the fragility of human life as all the more reason for standing out in front,[24] Diomedes' spear is fixed in the soil instead of in Glaukos' flesh (6. 212–14, contrast 20. 153). They are ξεῖνοι πατρώϊοι (ancestral guest-friends). Diomedes concludes with lines which, under more familiar national and military systems, might seem treacherous:

> "ἔγχεα δ' ἀλλήλων ἀλεώμεθα καὶ δι' ὁμίλου·
> πολλοὶ μὲν γὰρ ἐμοὶ Τρῶες κλειτοί τ' ἐπίκουροι,
> κτείνειν ὅν κε θεός γε πόρηι καὶ ποσσὶ κιχείω,
> πολλοὶ δ' αὖ σοὶ Ἀχαιοὶ ἐναιρέμεν ὅν κε δύνηαι."

'Let us keep away from each other's spears, even in the thick of the fighting. There are many of the Trojans and their famous allies for me

---

[24] See Macleod, 11–13.

Poetic Fieldwork 59

to kill, any of them that god sets in my way and my legs can catch: and
again many Achaians for you to cut down, all those you can.' (6. 226–9)

The point is that their mutual bond of ξεινία (guest-friendship) is
stronger than the obligation which either has towards his summoner. It is important that a Trojan ought not to have behaved
like Glaukos, nor ought Agamemnon or Menelaos to have behaved
like Diomedes—as has just been seen in the scene with Adrestos
(6. 37 ff., see further p. 163).

There is, however, the constant underlying possibility of a far
more drastic breakdown: when a summoned *basileus* declares that
the summoner has somehow reneged on the original agreement.
As it happens, the Lycian *epikouros* Glaukos illustrates this also.
In book 17, unaware that the body of Sarpedon has been supernaturally rescued, Glaukos reproaches Hektor with not really trying
to save him:

> "φράζεο νῦν ὅππως κε πόλιν καὶ ἄστυ caώcηιc
> οἶος cὺν λαοῖc τοὶ Ἰλίωι ἐγγεγάαcιν·
> οὐ γάρ τιc Λυκίων γε μαχηcόμενοc Δαναοῖcιν
> εἶcι περὶ πτόλιος, ἐπεὶ οὐκ ἄρα τιc χάριc ἦεν
> μάρναcθαι δηΐοιcιν ἐπ' ἀνδράcι νωλεμὲc αἰεί."

'So you must think now how to save your city and settlement by yourself,
with the people whose homeland is Ilios. No Lycian now will go out to
fight the Danaans for your city, since it appears there is no thanks if a
man fights the enemy relentlessly on and on.' (17. 144–8)[25]

This brings in the important notion of χάριc (*charis*),[26] which
underlies many Homeric social bonds, including that of 'summoner and summoned'. Achilleus may be glancing at this with
the cognate χαίρηιc ('to give you satisfaction') in 1. 158.

Glaukos makes his threat in the heat of battle and does not act
upon it. Achilleus, on the other hand, is in the official and public
setting of the *agorē*. In 1. 149 ff. he deploys cogent rhetoric to strip
down the politics of Agamemnon's war to the level of the initial
charis agreement, a level that is usually regarded as too basic to
be reopened. Achilleus' claim is that that agreement is off: his

[25] On 9. 316–17 (=17. 147–8) see further p. 68.
[26] See Hoekstra on *Od.* 15. 139. On the fundamental importance of reciprocity
in Homeric anthropology see Donlan, *passim* (though he does not pay particular
attention to χάριc). The parallels between Achilleus in 9 and Glaukos in 17 are
pointed out by C. Moulton in *Hermes*, 109 (1981), 5–8.

rightful expectation of *tīmē* has been so far disappointed that he is left *atīmos*. So there is no good reason to obey Agamemnon or to fight or even to stay at Troy. It takes a drastic breach of *charis*, such as Hektor's alleged failure to fight for Sarpedon's body, to bring things to this threat of breakdown. Part of the great challenge to the audience in this scene is to come to some assessments of its rights and wrongs. I suggest that the issue is more complicated and more 'political' than merely, as it is usually represented, an affront to personal honour. The dispute is not private and is not 'only' over a captive woman. Achilleus' immediate complaint is that Agamemnon is threatening to take away another leader's γέρας (*geras*). This particular institution, central to the whole quarrel, has not received proper attention.

A *geras* is far more than an item of booty. In addition to the general distribution of spoils when they have been taken, there is a special *geras* for some distinguished individuals, though it never emerges how they are chosen. It seems that there are *gera* whenever there has been a major haul: that is the only way to make sense of Achilleus' lines 163–8 and of the closely related passage in book 9:

"δώδεκα δὴ cὺν νηυcὶ πόλειc ἀλάπαξ' ἀνθρώπων,
πεζὸc δ' ἑνδεκά φημι κατὰ Τροίην ἐρίβωλον·
τάων ἐκ παcέων κειμήλια πολλὰ καὶ ἐcθλὰ   330
ἐξελόμην, καὶ πάντα φέρων Ἀγαμέμνονι δόcκον
Ἀτρείδῃ· ὁ δ' ὄπιcθε μένων παρὰ νηυcὶ θοῇcι
δεξάμενοc διὰ παῦρα δαcάcκετο, πολλὰ δ' ἔχεcκεν.
ἄλλα δ' ἀριcτήεccι δίδου γέρα καὶ βαcιλεῦcι,
τοῖcι μὲν ἔμπεδα κεῖται, ἐμεῦ δ' ἀπὸ μούνου Ἀχαιῶν   335
εἵλετ', ἔχει δ' ἄλοχον θυμαρέα·"

'I have sacked twelve of men's cities from my ships, and I claim eleven more by land across the fertile Troad. From all of these I took many fine treasures, and every time I brought them all and gave them to Agamemnon son of Atreus: and every time, back there by the fast ships he had never left, he would take them in, share out a few, and keep the most for himself. All the other prizes he gave to the kings and leading men stay safe with their owners. I am the only Achaian he has robbed. He has taken my wife, my heart's love—' (9. 328–36)

Two passages early in the poem which seem to imply that each leader has received only one *geras* during nine years of campaign should probably be seen as the product of rhetoric. When Agamemnon complains

> "αὐτὰρ ἐμοὶ γέρας αὐτίχ' ἑτοιμάσατ', ὄφρα μὴ οἶος
> Ἀργείων ἀγέραστος ἔω, ἐπεὶ οὐδὲ ἔοικε·
> λεύccετε γὰρ τό γε πάντεc, ὅ μοι γέρας ἔρχεται ἄλληι."

'But you must produce another prize for me without delay, so that I am not the only one of the Argives without a prize, as that would not be right—you can all see for yourselves that my own prize is leaving my hands.' (1. 118–20)

he exaggeratedly speaks as though Chryseïs were his only *geras*. Similarly his glossing of Briseïs as τὸ còν γέρας (that prize of yours) at 185 emphasizes his determination to chastise Achilleus by taking the *geras* that means most to him (hence τό (that)).

A *geras* is bestowed by the whole host; it is a communally ratified distinction. That is clear everywhere except in two passages in Achilleus' great speech to Odysseus. In 9. 334, just quoted above, δίδου implies that Agamemnon gave out the *gera*; and some later lines are explicit:

> "γέρας δέ μοι, ὅc περ ἔδωκεν
> αὖτιc ἐφυβρίζων ἔλετο κρείων Ἀγαμέμνων
> Ἀτρεΐδηc·"

'But my prize of honour—he gave it, and he, lord Agamemnon, son of Atreus, has taken it back to my insult.' (9. 367–8)

These may simply be inconsistencies; but, in view of institutions clearly set up in book 1, I am more inclined to see them as a rhetorical device to insinuate that Agamemnon uses his power arbitrarily.

Achilleus emphasizes from the start that it is the Achaian host as a whole which distributes *gera*:

> "Ἀτρεΐδη κύδιcτε, φιλοκτεανώτατε πάντων,
> πῶc γάρ τοι δώcουcι γέρας μεγάθυμοι Ἀχαιοί;
> οὐδέ τί που ἴδμεν ξυνήϊα κείμενα πολλά·
> ἀλλὰ τὰ μὲν πολίων ἐξεπράθομεν, τὰ δέδαcται,
> λαοὺc δ' οὐκ ἐπέοικε παλίλλογα ταῦτ' ἐπαγείρειν."

'Glorious son of Atreus, most acquisitive of all men, how are the great-hearted Achaians to give you a prize? We do not know of any stores of common treasure piled anywhere. What we took at the sacking of cities

has all been divided, and it is not right that the army should gather it
back again.' (1. 122–6)[27]

Agamemnon acknowledges this fact:

> "ἀλλ' εἰ μὲν δώcουcι γέραc μεγάθυμοι Ἀχαιοί,
> ἄρcαντεc κατὰ θυμόν, ὅπωc ἀντάξιον ἔcται·
> εἰ δέ κε μὴ δώωcιν,"

'No, if the great-hearted Achaians will give me a prize, suiting it to my
heart's liking, to be of equal value—then so be it. But if they will not . . .'
(1. 135–7)

Achilleus reiterates in 161–2 the complaint that Agamemnon is
threatening to take, on his own authority, the gift bestowed by all
the Achaians; and Nestor independently confirms this in his
attempt to tell them that they are both wrong—and both right:

> "μήτε cὺ τόνδ' ἀγαθόc περ ἐὼν ἀποαίρεο κούρην,
> ἀλλ' ἔα, ὥc οἱ πρῶτα δόcαν γέραc υἷεc Ἀχαιῶν·"

'You, great man though you are, do not take the girl from him, but let
her be, as the sons of the Achaians gave her to him in the beginning as
his prize.' (1. 275–6)[28]

In the opening scene with Chryses it was left open whether
Agamemnon was within his rights to answer in such personal
terms (note ἐγώ ('I') in lines 26 and 29), despite the views of all
the other Achaians. Once it emerges in 118 onwards that Chryseïs
is his *geras*, it becomes even more questionable whether he should
have retained the gift of the host against its will. Achilleus, it
seems, applies the converse of this principle: that since the whole
host, by raising no objections, goes along with Agamemnon's
seizure of Briseïs, the whole host is taking her back. That is the
point of the plural verb in his assurance in 298–9 that he will not
fight with anyone for her "ἐπεί μ' ἀφέλεcθέ γε δόντεc" ('you [plural]
gave her, and you have taken her away'). It is often held against
Achilleus that his vindictiveness against *all* the Achaians for Agamemnon's offence is selfish pride; but it is far from arbitrary. He
regards them all, by their silence, as involved in the humiliating
retraction of his *geras*. This is the explanation of his insults in

---

[27] οὐκ ἐπέοικε ('it is not right') in 126 answers Agamemnon's οὐδὲ ἔοικε ('that
would not be right') in 119. My argument is not seriously affected if λαούc in 126
should mean '[taken] from the army'.
[28] The point is still being made by Achilleus at 16. 56 and Thetis at 18. 444.

"δημοβόρος βαςιλεύς, ἐπεὶ οὐτιδανοῖςιν ἀνάςςεις·
ἦ γὰρ ἄν, Ἀτρείδη, νῦν ὕςτατα λωβήςαιο."

'. . . king who feeds fat on his people, with mere ciphers for subjects: otherwise, son of Atreus, this would now be your last outrage.' (1. 231–2)

And in his great oath enjambement emphasizes that everyone, not just Agamemnon, will miss him:

"ἦ ποτ' Ἀχιλλῆος ποθὴ ἵξεται υἶας Ἀχαιῶν
ςύμπαντας·"

'I swear now that there will come a time when the loss of Achilleus will be felt by the whole number of the sons of the Achaians.' (240–1)

So the request that he asks Thetis to take to Zeus for him is that the Achaians should suffer heavy casualties ἵνα πάντες ἐπαύρωνται βαςιλῆος (so that all may have enjoyment of their king) (410).[29] They have in effect submitted themselves to a single *basileus*, and now they must pay for his ἄτη (*ātē*). Just as the host as a whole suffered for Agamemnon's maltreatment of Chryses, so they are caught up in his offence against Achilleus.

Most interpreters over the centuries have condemned Achilleus' behaviour as egotistical and insubordinate. This is to underrate the political dimension to his case and to overrate the hierarchical standing of Agamemnon. The late eighth and early seventh century BC was not a time of unquestioned authority and social structures—such questions were open. Epic was a way of exploring political development by setting up difficult questions, questions which in real life might be intolerably confused and explosive.

At the same time, Homer subtly supplies a personal level to this dispute, implying a backlog of resentment between the two leaders 'before the poem began' so to speak. After the complicity of Achilleus and Kalchas (see above, p. 54), a long-smouldering resentment breaks into flame in the speech at 163 ff.. That is the effect of "οὐ μὲν ςοί ποτε . . . ὁππότε . . . ἀτὰρ ἦν ποτε" ('I never . . . whenever . . . but when . . .'), and of the verb of protracted labour ἀφύξειν ('heaping up'). Again in 226 ff.—(οὔτε ποτέ . . . ('never'))

---

[29] Compare the way that in the Ithakan *agorē* Mentor blames the citizens for not doing anything to stop the suitors: "νῦν δ' ἄλλωι δήμωι νεμεςίζομαι, οἷον ἅπαντες ἧςθ' ἄνεωι, ἀτὰρ οὔ τι καθαπτόμενοι ἐπέεςςι παύρους μνηςτῆρας κατερύκετε πολλοὶ ἐόντες." ('But I am indignant with the rest of the people, for the way you sit in silence; and you do nothing to complain about the suitors, even though you are many and they are few, and you could restrain them.') (*Od.* 2. 239–42).

and resumed in book 9, especially 321 ff.—the implication is that
not just now but for nine years Agamemnon has been acquisitively
inactive, while Achilleus has done all the work for inadequate
reward. A long-standing feud is also suggested by Agamemnon's
reply in

> "ἔχθιστος δέ μοί ἐσσι διοτρεφέων βασιλήων·
> αἰεὶ γάρ τοι ἔρις τε φίλη πόλεμοί τε μάχαι τε·"

'Of all the kings whom Zeus sustains you are the most hateful to me—
always your delight is in quarrelling and wars and battle.' (1. 176–7)[30]

So the political and ethical dispute is given personal colouring
and plausibility. Furthermore it is dynamic not static, developing
with the narrative as each adds further provocation. A more mag-
nanimous leader than Agamemnon might have acknowledged that
the interests of the gods are unpredictable and have accepted that
Apollo has taken away his *geras* (cf. 182). He would then not have
got angry with Kalchas (though the predictability of that may also
have an unspoken past—see further p. 86). And he would not
have added the fatal rider to the return of Chryseïs.

> "αὐτὰρ ἐμοὶ γέρας αὐτίχ' ἐτοιμάσατ', ὄφρα μὴ οἶος
> Ἀργείων ἀγέραστος ἔω, ἐπεὶ οὐδὲ ἔοικε·
> λεύσσετε γὰρ τό γε πάντες, ὅ μοι γέρας ἔρχεται ἄλληι."

'But you must produce another prize for me without delay, so that I am
not the only one of the Argives without a prize, as that would not be
right—you can all see for yourselves that my own prize is leaving my
hands.' (1. 118–20)

Whatever the ethical rights and wrongs of this claim. Agamemnon is put in a completely new situation by Achilleus' response
in 149–71. He is driven into a corner where the only way for him
to salvage his standing is to tell Achilleus that he can do without
him: let him go home and rule his relatively obscure kingdom.
After Achilleus' challenge to his very credibility as the 'summoner', he resorts to his other sanction, the last resort, bare force.
Provoked by Achilleus' suggestion that he might deserve ἴσον γέρας
(an equal prize) (163), Agamemnon concludes with a defiance
which, however ill-advised it turns out to be, is politically and
personally plausible:

---

30 Unless Aristarchos was right to reject 177 as an inapposite parallel drawn
from 5. 891? Why should Agamemnon object to Achilleus' warcraft?

"ἐγὼ δέ κ' ἄγω Βρισηΐδα καλλιπάρηιον
αὐτὸς ἰὼν κλισίηνδε, τὸ σὸν γέρας, ὄφρ' ἐὺ εἰδῆις
ὅσσον φέρτερός εἰμι σέθεν, στυγέηι δὲ καὶ ἄλλος
ἷσον ἐμοὶ φάσθαι καὶ ὁμοιωθήμεναι ἄντην."

'... so I shall take the beautiful Brisëis, your prize, going myself to fetch
her from your hut, so that you can fully realise how much I am your
superior, and others too can shrink from speaking on a level with me and
openly claiming equality.' (1. 184–7)

Agamemnon's assertion that he is φέρτερος (superior) (cf. also
324–5) is confirmed by Nestor, who produces it as his only good
reason for Achilleus to be reconciled:

"εἰ δὲ σὺ καρτερός ἐσσι, θεὰ δέ σε γείνατο μήτηρ,
ἀλλ' ὅ γε φέρτερός ἐστιν, ἐπεὶ πλεόνεσσιν ἀνάσσει."

'You may be a man of strength, with a goddess for your mother, but he
is the more powerful, because his rule is wider.' (1. 280–1)

Agamemnon thus reminds those who stay with him at Troy that,
if an issue is ever reduced to a trial of strength, then he will win.
When Achilleus seriously considers attempting to assassinate Agamemnon, at 188–91, he too faces the brute truth that in the last
resort, when social bonds fail, things come down to force.

And it *seems* to be the pragmatics of physical strength which
win the day in the agorē. In 297 ff. Achilleus concedes that, since
all the Achaians have implicitly supported Agamemnon, he will
not resist the seizure of Brisëis. By then, however, the audience
knows better, and so does Achilleus—but no one else, not even
Nestor. Contrary to the apparent triumph of Agamemnon, Achilleus has the reassurance of Athene that he will eventually get the
better of the dispute. He has even had the satisfaction of hearing
her confirm his description of Agamemnon's behaviour as ὕβρις
(arrogance). His true position of strength is soon confirmed by
the further intervention of Thetis.

Again, as in the scene with Chryses, Agamemnon is deluded in
his self-assertion. Again he is unaware, in his apparent success, of
the future trouble that he has set in motion.[31] In spurning Achilleus, Agamemnon takes comfort from the belief that Zeus esteems
him (cf. Nestor at 277–9):

---

[31] This fits well with the case made by Rabel ('Chryses and the Opening of the
Iliad') for seeing the initial Chryses scene as a kind of premonitory miniature of
the main quarrel.

"πάρ' ἔμοιγε καὶ ἄλλοι
οἵ κέ με τιμήcουcι, μάλιcτα δὲ μητίετα Ζεύc."

'I have others with me who will show me honour, and chief among them Zeus the counsellor himself.' (1. 174–5)

He is mistaken, however. By the time of book 9, Zeus will have tipped things against him so far that Nestor speaks plainly:

"cὺ δὲ cῶι μεγαλήτορι θυμῶι
εἴξαc ἄνδρα φέριcτον, ὃν ἀθάνατοί περ ἔτειcαν,
ἠτίμηcαc· ἑλὼν γὰρ ἔχειc γέραc."

'But you gave in to your heart's high passion and brought dishonour on the greatest of men, a man whom the very immortals have honoured—you have taken his prize and keep it for yourself.' (9. 109–11)

And Agamemnon himself concedes

"ὦ γέρον, οὔ τι ψεῦδοc ἐμὰc ἄταc κατέλεξαc·
ἀαcάμην, οὐδ' αὐτὸc ἀναίνομαι. ἀντί νυ πολλῶν
λαῶν ἐcτιν ἀνὴρ ὅν τε Ζεὺc κῆρι φιλήcηι,
ὡc νῦν τοῦτον ἔτειcε, δάμαccε δὲ λαὸν Ἀχαιῶν.
ἀλλ' ἐπεὶ ἀαcάμην φρεcὶ λευγαλέηιcι πιθήcαc,"

'Old man, your talk of my blindness is no lie: I was blinded, I do not deny it myself. A man loved from the heart by Zeus is worth many armies—just as now Zeus has honoured this man, and broken the army of the Achaians. But since I was blinded and listened to my heart's wretched persuasion . . .' (9. 115–19)

So Achilleus can say with some justification, when he rejects the human *timē* offered by Phoinix

"Φοῖνιξ, ἄττα γεραιέ, διοτρεφέc, οὔ τί με ταύτηc
χρεὼ τιμῆc· φρονέω δὲ τετιμῆcθαι Διὸc αἴcηι."

'Phoinix, old father, my lord, I have no need of that honour. I think I am already held in honour by the will of Zeus.' (9. 607–8)

2.3 *Paying back outrage*

"γέραc δέ μοι, ὅc περ ἔδωκεν
αὖτιc ἐφυβρίζων ἕλετο κρείων Ἀγαμέμνων
Ἀτρεΐδηc· τῶι πάντ' ἀγορευέμεν, ὡc ἐπιτέλλω,
ἀμφαδόν, ὄφρα καὶ ἄλλοι ἐπιcκύζωνται Ἀχαιοί,
εἴ τινά που Δαναῶν ἔτι ἔλπεται ἐξαπατήcειν,

370

αἰὲν ἀναιδείην ἐπιειμένος· οὐδ' ἄν ἔμοιγε
τετλαίη κύνεός περ ἐὼν εἰς ὦπα ἰδέσθαι·
οὐδέ τί οἱ βουλὰς ευμφράccομαι, οὐδὲ μὲν ἔργον·
ἐκ γὰρ δή μ' ἀπάτηcε καὶ ἤλιτεν· οὐδ' ἄν ἔτ' αὖτις   375
ἐξαπάφοιτ' ἐπέεccιν· ἅλιc δέ οἱ· ἀλλὰ ἔκηλος
ἐρρέτω· ἐκ γάρ εὖ φρέναc εἵλετο μητίετα Ζεύc.
ἐχθρὰ δέ μοι τοῦ δῶρα, τίω δέ μιν ἐν καρὸc αἴcῃ.
οὐδ' εἴ μοι δεκάκιc τε καὶ εἰκοcάκιc τόcα δοίη
ὅcca τέ οἱ νῦν ἔcτι, καὶ εἴ ποθεν ἄλλα γένοιτο,   380
οὐδ' ὅc' ἐc Ὀρχομενὸν ποτινίcεται, οὐδ' ὅcα Θήβαc
Αἰγυπτίαc, ὅθι πλεῖcτα δόμοιc ἐν κτήματα κεῖται,
αἵ θ' ἑκατόμπυλοί εἰcι, διηκόcιοι δ' ἄν ἑκάcταc
ἀνέρεc ἐξοιχνεῦcι cὺν ἵπποιcιν καὶ ὄχεcφιν·
οὐδ' εἴ μοι τόcα δοίη ὅcα ψάμαθόc τε κόνιc τε,   385
οὐδέ κεν ὡc ἔτι θυμὸν ἐμὸν πείcει' Ἀγαμέμνων,
πρίν γ' ἀπὸ πᾶcαν ἐμοὶ δόμεναι θυμαλγέα λώβην."

'But my prize of honour—he gave it, and he, lord Agamemnon, son of
Atreus, has taken it back to my insult. Tell him all that I say, and openly,
so that the rest of the Achaians can feel anger too, if he is hoping still to
cheat some other Danaan, clothed as ever in shamelessness—yet, dog
that he is, he would not dare to look me in the face. I will not join him
in plan or in action. He has cheated me and wronged me. He will not
work his cheating tongue on me again. Enough already. No, he can take
himself to ruin at his own pace—Zeus the counsellor has robbed his wits.
I abominate his gifts, I care not a splinter for the man. Not even if he
offered me ten times or twenty times all he possesses now, and others'
wealth besides, not even all the riches that pour into Orchomenos, or
Thebes in Egypt, where the houses are piled high with treasure, and the
city has a hundred gates, and through each gate two hundred men drive
out with horses and chariots: not even if he offered me gifts unnumbered
like the sand or dust—not even so could Agamemnon yet turn my mind,
until he pays me the full price for all this wrong that pains my heart.'
(9. 367–87)

The next 'confrontation' between Agamemnon and Achilleus will
take place in private not public, and Agamemnon will be represented by his delegation. The complexity of ethical considerations
has again left room for a wide range of responses and assessments.
Achilleus' rejection of the embassy has been seen as everything
from unheroic egocentricity to a magnificent stand for human
integrity. If the fieldwork arising from book 1 is at all along the

right lines, then some interpretations of book 9 will emerge as
doing far more justice than others to the poem as it is shaped.[32]

First, there is no disputing that Agamemnon more than fulfils
Athene's prediction of 1. 212–14: he is offering back Briseïs,
untouched, and a huge quantity of gifts which he catalogues in
detail, to be accurately recorded by Odysseus (9. 122–57 virtually = 264–99). Yet Achilleus' response is to spell out more
fully and vividly the same resentments as he began to formulate in
book 1.

> "οὔτ' ἔμεγ' Ἀτρεΐδην Ἀγαμέμνονα πεισέμεν οἴω
> οὔτ' ἄλλους Δαναούς, ἐπεὶ οὐκ ἄρα τις χάρις ἦεν
> μάρνασθαι δηΐοισιν ἐπ' ἀνδράσι νωλεμὲς αἰεί."

'I do not think that Agamemnon son of Atreus will win me over, nor the
rest of the Danaans, since it now appears that there is no thanks if a man
fights the enemy relentlessly on and on.' (9. 315–17)

He goes on (lines 328–36 are quoted above on p. 60) to complain,
as before, that he has done all the fighting, while Agamemnon has
taken the lion's share of the rewards. Yet he has, as the final
ingratitude, taken his *geras*, his ἄλοχον θυμαρέα ('my wife, my
heart's love') (see further § **8.2**).

How, in view of all the compensation plus Briseïs, can Achilleus
still maintain that the *charis*-compact remains spoiled or unsatis-
fied? Although his rhetoric is full of disconcertingly unpredictable
jumps, it would be quite wrong to dismiss it as incoherent rant.
Let me, for now, pull out one thread, a new and insistent complaint
against Agamemnon: that he has in some sense *deceived* him, and,
having done so once, he will not have the chance to do it again.

> "νῦν δ' ἐπεὶ ἐκ χειρῶν γέρας εἵλετο καί μ' ἀπάτησε,
> μή μευ πειράτω εὖ εἰδότος· οὐδέ με πείσει."

'Now that he has taken my prize from my hands and cheated me, let him
not try me. I known him well now—he will not persuade me.' (344–5)[33]

---

[32] The bibliography on Achilleus in book 9 is immense. Among the most helpful
contributions I have found: Owen, 94 ff.; Reinhardt, *ID* 212 ff.; D. E. Eichholz,
AJP 74 (1953), 137 ff.; Whitman, Ch. 9 (181 ff.); Motzkus, *passim*; Lohmann, Ch. 5
(213 ff.); D. B. Claus, *TAPA* 105 (1975), 13 ff.; Redfield, *NCI* 3 ff.; Schein, 104 ff.;
S. Nimis, *CW* 79 (1985–6), 217 ff.; Edwards, *HPI* 214 ff.

[33] μή μευ πειράτω ('let him not try me') suggests an awareness of Nestor's
strategy—cf. πειρᾶν ('make every effort') in 9. 181.

He returns to this in 367–78. The warning to his fellow Achaians that Agamemnon is still ἀναιδείην ἐπιειμένος (clothed as ever in shamelessness) (372, cf. 1. 149) leads into the rush of staccato, enjambed clauses which are stylistically the most extraordinary passage of his virtuoso speech.[34] "οὐδ' ἂν ἔτ' αὖτις ἐξαπάφοιτ' ἐπέεσσιν" ('he will not work his cheating tongue on me again'). There is no suggestion of any deceit about the material gifts: it is verbal. I suggest that the prelude to the embassy gives substance to Achilleus' complaint. When Nestor first proposed the mission he said

> "ἀλλ' ἔτι καὶ νῦν
> φραζώμεσθ' ὥς κέν μιν ἀρεσσάμενοι πεπίθωμεν
> δώροισίν τ' ἀγανοῖσιν ἔπεσσί τε μειλιχίοισι."

'But even at this late day let us consider how we may appease him and win him over with soothing gifts and kind persuasion.' (9. 111–13)

Agamemnon's response is strong on gifts,[35] but contains nothing whatsoever about the words to be offered to Achilleus. He avoids even naming Achilleus, and the four lines with which he concludes are hardly ἔπεα μειλίχια (kind persuasion):

> "δμηθήτω—Ἀΐδης τοι ἀμείλιχος ἠδ' ἀδάμαστος·
> τοὔνεκα καί τε βροτοῖσι θεῶν ἔχθιστος ἁπάντων—
> καί μοι ὑποστήτω, ὅσσον βασιλεύτερός εἰμι
> ἠδ' ὅσσον γενεῆι προγενέστερος εὔχομαι εἶναι."

'Let him yield—Hades is the one who never pities or yields, and for that he is of all gods the most hated by men—and let him submit to me, in that I am the greater king and can claim to be his senior in age.' (9. 158–61)

In Nestor's reply

> "δῶρα μὲν οὐκέτ' ὀνοστὰ διδοῖς Ἀχιλῆϊ ἄνακτι·
> ἀλλ' ἄγετε, κλητοὺς ὀτρύνομεν,

'. . . no-one can now find fault with the gifts you offer to lord Achilleus. Come then, let us pick men . . .' (9. 164–5)

---

[34] For something remotely comparable, see Telemachos' words of restrained anger against Antimachos at *Od.* 17. 400.

[35] Note the quantity of women: seven from Lesbos plus Briseïs herself, a choice of twenty Trojans (barring only Helen), and one of his own daughters as well. Is this *too* many to be diplomatic? In 19. 242 ff. all except Briseïs and the seven from Lesbos are quietly forgotten.

the phrasing of δῶρα μέν ... ἀλλά... ('...the gifts ... Come
then ...') makes the point that he is having to organize the verbal
and diplomatic side, since Agamemnon has failed to cover that.
The opening lines of Achilleus' reply to Odysseus go straight
to this flaw:

"διογενὲς Λαερτιάδη, πολυμήχαν' Ὀδυccεῦ,
χρὴ μέν δὴ τὸν μῦθον ἀπηλεγέωc ἀποειπεῖν,
ἦι περ δὴ φρονέω τε καὶ ὡc τετελεcμένον ἔcται,   310
ὡc μή μοι τρύζητε παρήμενοι ἄλλοθεν ἄλλοc.
ἐχθρὸc γάρ μοι κεῖνοc ὁμῶc Ἀΐδαο πύλῃcιν
ὅc χ' ἕτερον μὲν κεύθηι ἐνὶ φρεcίν, ἄλλο δὲ εἴπηι·
αὐτὰρ ἐγὼν ἐρέω ὥc μοι δοκεῖ εἶναι ἄριcτα·
οὔτ' ἔμεγ' Ἀτρεΐδην Ἀγαμέμνονα πειcέμεν οἴω   315
οὔτ' ἄλλουc Δαναούc, ἐπεὶ οὐκ ἄρα τιc χάριc ἦεν
μάρναcθαι δηΐοιcιν ἐπ' ἀνδράcι νωλεμὲc αἰεί."

'Royal son of Laertes, resourceful Odysseus, what I say I must say
outright, and tell you bluntly how I think and what will happen, so that
you do not sit here and coo your blandishments at me one after another.
I hate like the gates of Hades the man who hides one thing in his mind
and speaks another. But I will tell you what seems right to me. I do not
think that Agamemnon son of Atreus will win me over, nor the rest of
the Danaans, since it now appears that there is no thanks if a man fights
the enemy relentlessly on and on.' (9. 308–17)

In a sense the superb couplet 312–13 refers to Achilleus himself,
with γάρ ('for') explaining the general sentiment: he will exemplify
his own ethics. But in another sense κεῖνοc ('that man') has evident
reference to Odysseus, i.e. γάρ explains the ἄλλοθεν ἄλλοc ('one
after another') of 311, and αὐτὰρ ἐγών ('but I ...') is in contrast
with κεῖνοc ('that man'). So Achilleus senses a deception.

For an alert listener there is even a reference to the four lines
of Agamemnon (158–61) which Odysseus has been careful to
suppress. Hades is ἔχθιcτοc (most hated) of the gods, and the
deceiver is as ἐχθρόc (hated) as the gates of Hades. Later, even
more strikingly, Achilleus βαcιλεύτεροc ('higher king') in 392 will
contemptuously 'pick up' Agamemnon's use of the word in 160.[36]
Taken in its whole context the couplet may even have a third level
of submerged application as a parenthetical explanation referring

<hr/>

[36] For the narrative device of characters' 'knowing' something that they have
not, strictly speaking, heard, see further p. 150.

to Agamemnon.[37] His failure of *charis* (316) has to do with the lack of correspondence between what his ambassador says and what he hides in his heart.

This emphasis on verbal deceit, on the failure of words to match φρένες (mind), supports the interpretation of Achilleus' case as resting on a rejection of any simple or direct equation between *tīmē* and material goods. Achilleus is 'coming off the gold standard'. This rejection of merely material rating is often described by the catch-phrase 'breaking the heroic code'. If this implies that Achilleus puts himself clearly in the wrong, or outside the pale of his community, then I think that is mistaken. We have already seen Nestor indirectly anticipating his response; and Odysseus' speech is far from purely materialist. For 35 lines he stresses the danger posed by Hektor to the whole Achaian camp and reminds Achilleus of paternal advice, before he comes to Agamemnon's offer. He is also careful to add a dissociating coda after that:

"εἰ δέ τοι Ἀτρείδης μὲν ἀπήχθετο κηρόθι μᾶλλον,
αὐτὸς καὶ τοῦ δῶρα, σὺ δ' ἄλλους περ Παναχαιοὺς
τειρομένους ἐλέαιρε κατὰ στρατόν, οἵ σε θεὸν ὣς
τείσουσ'· ἦ γάρ κέ σφι μάλα μέγα κῦδος ἄροιο.
νῦν γάρ χ' Ἕκτορ' ἕλοις, ἐπεὶ ἂν μάλα τοι σχεδὸν ἔλθοι
λύσσαν ἔχων ὀλοήν, ἐπεὶ οὔ τινά φησιν ὁμοῖον
οἷ ἔμεναι Δαναῶν, οὓς ἐνθάδε νῆες ἔνεικαν."

'But if hatred for the son of Atreus has grown too strong in your heart, for the man and for his gifts, then still have pity on all the other Achaians of the army in their affliction, and they will honour you like a god. You could win the very greatest glory in their eyes, because now you could kill Hektor. With this fatal madness on him he would come up close to face you, since he thinks there is no match for him among all the Danaans carried here in our ships.' (9. 300–6)

Odysseus, for all his diplomacy, is too closely associated with Agamemnon to persuade Achilleus with these distinctions. Phoinix approaches him from a completely different relationship. He still, however, applies his *Litai* (Prayers) parable to the gifts of Agamemnon (515ff.), and he draws a lesson (600ff.) from the Meleagros story in terms of material *tīmē*. Aias, in by far the briefest and bluntest speech of the three, is the only one not to mention Agamemnon. He also makes a shrewd hit when he appeals to private rather than public bonds, reminding Achilleus of his undeniable warmth and hospitality towards them (narrated with full formulaic ceremony in 196 ff.)

> "cὺ δ' ἵλαον ἔνθεο θυμόν,
> αἴδεσσαι δὲ μέλαθρον· ὑπωρόφιοι δέ τοί εἰμεν
> πληθύος ἐκ Δαναῶν, μέμαμεν δέ τοι ἔξοχον ἄλλων
> κήδιστοί τ' ἔμεναι καὶ φίλτατοι, ὅσσοι Ἀχαιοί."

'Then turn your heart to kindness, remember the welcome owed by your house: we are under your roof, we have come from the whole body of the Danaans, and we trust we are beyond all others the closest and dearest to you of all the Achaians.' (9. 639–42)

He should himself be true to his φρένες (mind) without deceit.

So I do not believe that Achilleus is maintaining a view which no one else in the heroic world could understand or approve of. And even if it were true that 'the heroic code was complete and unambiguous', and even if Achilleus' attitude found no echo in any other character, this would still not necessarily alienate Homer's *audience*. I conclude that Homer's audience must have found the whole question of the 'gold standard' at the least challenging and intriguing.

The question that Homer raises for the audience, without letting Achilleus answer it too directly, is: what *would* have satisfied him? Was there any way that Agamemnon could have supplied the kind of 'true' non-material *tīmē* that Achilleus apparently demands? For a start, as Nestor implies, conciliatory words as well as material gestures would have shown good will, if not remorse.[38] Even more, he might have come in person instead of delegating to others. This prospect is momentarily evoked by Achilleus' taunt that Agamemnon could not look him in the face (373). Of course Agamemnon never considers the possibility—it would be beneath his dignity, out of character. This is the point.

It might be objected that Achilleus himself rules out even a personal embassy as inadequate in 379–87. No quantity of compensation will suffice πρίν γ' ἀπὸ πᾶσαν ἐμοὶ δόμεναι θυμαλγέα λώβην (until he pays the full price for all this wrong that pains my heart).

---

[38] At 16. 72–3 Achilleus says that he would be reconciled εἴ μοι κρείων Ἀγαμέμνων ἤπια εἰδείη (if lord Agamemnon would treat me kindly)—quite consistently with book 9, in my view.

It is usually supposed that this is a mere *adynaton*, a condition which it is utterly impossible to fulfil.[39] But the *Iliad* shows how even this apparently impossible compensation is humanly possible. Priam comes to Achilleus himself to deliver his own words. It is true that the gods tell him to go; but his first response was to want to go himself.[40] It is true that they reassure him against danger; but that does not stop the mission from being full of fear and effort in human terms—see further 9.2, 9.3. At 19. 208 Achilleus proposes that the Achaians should not eat until the evening ἐπὴν τειcαίμεθα λώβην (when we have paid back our wrong). It is clear from his treatment of the corpse of Hektor that by the time of book 24 he still does not feel that the λώβη (wrong, outrage) has been paid off. While Priam does bring *apoina*, he does not enumerate these but emphasizes the human anguish he has undergone (see further pp. 269–70):

> "ἀλλ' αἰδεῖο θεούc, Ἀχιλεῦ, αὐτόν τ' ἐλέηcον,
> μνηcάμενοc cοῦ πατρόc· ἐγὼ δ' ἐλεεινότερόc περ,
> ἔτλην δ' οἷ' οὔ πώ τιc ἐπιχθόνιοc βροτὸc ἄλλοc,
> ἀνδρὸc παιδοφόνοιο ποτὶ cτόμα χεῖρ' ὀρέγεcθαι."

'Respect the gods, then, Achilleus, and have pity on me, remembering your own father. But I am yet more pitiable than he. I have endured to do what no other mortal man on earth has done—I have brought to my lips the hands of the man who killed my child.' (24. 503–6)

This works on Achilleus, yet does not prove degrading for Priam, but ennobling rather.

Agamemnon does not do his own fighting, and he delegates all unpleasant business to others. He does not fetch Briseïs; he does not return Chryseïs; and he sends others to Achilleus while not actually feeling any change of heart. When Achilleus rejects the embassy it may not yet be clear to an audience that what he wants from Agamemnon is genuine personal regret and goodwill. By the end of the poem, however, they will have come to see the value of magnanimity and of personal suffering, which have brought Priam immortal *kleos*. In the meantime the great lord who refuses to put his heart into his own speeches, and who delegates their delivery, will have been virtually faded out of the poem.

---

[39] Especially since A. Parry's seminal essay, 'LA' (1956).
[40] See further Macleod, 21–2.

2.4 Patroklos through recurrent scenes

(a)   τὼ δ' ἀέκοντε βάτην παρὰ θῖν' ἁλὸς ἀτρυγέτοιο,
Μυρμιδόνων δ' ἐπί τε κλιcίαc καὶ νῆαc ἱκέcθην.
τὸν δ' εὗρον παρά τε κλιcίηι καὶ νηῒ μελαίνηι
ἥμενον· οὐδ' ἄρα τώ γε ἰδὼν γήθηcεν Ἀχιλλεύc.   330
τὼ μὲν ταρβήcαντε καὶ αἰδομένω βαcιλῆα
cτήτην, οὐδέ τί μιν προcεφώνεον οὐδ' ἐρέοντο·
αὐτὰρ ὁ ἔγνω ἧιcιν ἐνὶ φρεcὶ φώνηcέν τε·
"χαίρετε, κήρυκεc, Διὸc ἄγγελοι ἠδὲ καὶ ἀνδρῶν,
ἆccον ἴτ'· οὔ τί μοι ὔμμεc ἐπαίτιοι, ἀλλ' Ἀγαμέμνων,   335
ὃ cφῶϊ προΐει Βριcηΐδοc εἵνεκα κούρηc.
ἀλλ' ἄγε, διογενὲc Πατρόκλεεc, ἔξαγε κούρην
καί cφωϊν δὸc ἄγειν·"

They went reluctantly along the shore of the harvestless sea, and came
to the huts and the ships of the Myrmidons. They found him by his hut
and his black ship, sitting idle: and Achilleus had no joy in seeing them.
They stood there silent, without word or question, in fear and respect
for the king. But he understood their purpose in his mind, and spoke to
them: 'Welcome, heralds, messengers of Zeus and of men. Come closer.
It is not you I blame, but Agamemnon, who has sent you here for the
girl Briseïs. Come, lord Patroklos, bring the girl out and give her to them
for the taking.' (1. 327–38)

(b)   Τὼ δὲ βάτην παρὰ θῖνα πολυφλοίcβοιο θαλάccηc
πολλὰ μάλ' εὐχομένω γαιηόχωι ἐννοcιγαίωι
ῥηϊδίωc πεπιθεῖν μεγάλαc φρέναc Αἰακίδαο.
Μυρμιδόνων δ' ἐπί τε κλιcίαc καὶ νῆαc ἱκέcθην,   185
τὸν δ' εὗρον φρένα τερπόμενον φόρμιγγι λιγείηι,
καλῆι δαιδαλέηι, ἐπὶ δ' ἀργύρεον ζυγὸν ἦεν,
τὴν ἄρετ' ἐξ ἐνάρων πόλιν Ἠετίωνοc ὀλέccαc·
τῆι ὅ γε θυμὸν ἔτερπεν, ἄειδε δ' ἄρα κλέα ἀνδρῶν.
Πάτροκλοc δέ οἱ οἶοc ἐναντίοc ἧcτο cιωπῆι,   190
δέγμενοc Αἰακίδαο, ὁπότε λήξειεν ἀείδων.

So they went along the shore of the sounding sea, praying long to
Poseidon the encircler and shaker of the earth that it would be easy for
them to win over the great heart of Achilleus, of Aiakos' stock. They
came to the huts and the ships of the Myrmidons, and found Achilleus
giving pleasure to his heart with a clear-voiced lyre, a beautiful finely-
worked thing with a cross-piece of silver, which he had won from the
spoils when he destroyed Eëtion's city. He was delighting his heart with
this, and singing tales of men's glory. Patroklos alone sat opposite him
in silence, waiting for when Achilleus would end his singing. (9. 182–91)

γέρων δ' ἰθὺς κίεν οἴκου,
τῆι ῥ' Ἀχιλεὺς ἵζεcκε Διῒ φίλοc· ἐν δέ μιν αὐτὸν
εὗρ', ἕταροι δ' ἀπάνευθε καθήατο· τὼ δὲ δύ' οἴω,
ἥρωc Αὐτομέδων τε καὶ Ἄλκιμοc, ὄζοc Ἄρηοc,
ποίπνυον παρεόντε· νέον δ' ἀπέληγεν ἐδωδῆc   475
ἔcθων καὶ πίνων· ἔτι καὶ παρέκειτο τράπεζα.
τοὺc δ' ἔλαθ' εἰcελθὼν Πρίαμοc μέγαc, ἄγχι δ' ἄρα cτὰc
χερcὶν Ἀχιλλῆοc λάβε γούνατα καὶ κύcε χεῖραc
δεινὰc ἀνδροφόνουc, αἲ οἱ πολέαc κτάνον υἷαc.

The old man went straight for the house, where Achilleus loved of Zeus
was sitting. He found him inside, and his companions sitting apart from
him. Two only, the hero Automedon and Alkimos, branch of Ares, were
busy close by him—he had just now finished his meal and done with
eating and drinking: the table was still there beside him. Huge Priam
came in unseen, and moving close to him took Achilleus' knees in his
arms and kissed his hands, those terrible, murderous hands, which had
killed many of his sons. (24. 471–9)

The 'visit-scene' is more common in the *Odyssey* than in the *Iliad*.
At its most skeletal the sequence is: one party visits another on a
mission, is received, responded to, and finally departs. Several
more detailed elements recur quite often, and some lines or phrases
are repeated, as in these three visits to Achilleus 1. 329 = 9. 186
and is similar to 24. 472–3. These are good examples of a 'type-
scene' or 'narrative pattern', a fundamental feature of Homer's
narrative technique, derived no doubt from the oral tradition.[41]
The benefit is not so much the mnemonic aid as the way that the
recurrent scene-shapes, taken in their sequence, supply a poetic
framework on which significant similarities and differences can be
fleshed out. Moreover these recurrent scenes often narrate significant social procedures or 'rituals', where a proper observation
of—or, more important, a departure from—the norm carries further 'anthropological' meaning. The pattern, established in the
mind of the audience by the tradition, thus opens up all sorts of
possibilities which are not available to less structured, less conven-
tionalized kinds of poetry.

---

[41] Arend is always honoured as the founding father. More recently, useful work
has been done by others, esp. Lohmann; Krischer, esp. 13 ff. on *aristeia*; Fenik,
TBS and *SO*; Tsagarakis; B. Powell, *Composition by Theme in the Odyssey* (Mei-
senheim, 1977); Patzer, 26–40; Bannert, *passim*; and, not least, Edwards in a whole
series of articles (cf. *HPI* 71 ff.), esp. 'Type-scenes'. For visit-scenes in particular
see Arend, 54 ff.; Lohmann, 227–31; Edwards, 'Type-scenes', 62 ff.

Analysis of Four Visit-Scenes

	1 1. 12–43	2 1. 326–48	3 9. 173–668	4 24. 186–691
1 Agent	An old father Chryses	Two heralds	Two heralds, two leading men, and an old friend	An old father Priam, with one old herald (149, 178)
2	non-Achaian	Achaian	Achaian	non-Achaian
3	comes to the camp (journey not narrated)	come along the shore	come along the shore	come to the camp across the plain
4	on his own mission	for Agamemnon	for Agamemnon	on his own mission
5	by daylight	by daylight	at night	at night
6	under protection of Apollo		with prayers to Poseidon	at the command of the gods, with prayers and direct help of Hermes
7				(Priam leaves the herald outside)
8	to a public meeting	to the tent of Achilleus	to the tent of Achilleus	to the tent of Achilleus
9 Mission	to ransom his daughter alive.	to fetch Briseïs.	to offer conciliatory gifts.	to ransom his dead son.
10	He brings *apoina*			He brings *apoina*
11		They find A. sitting	They find A. singing poetry	he finds A. after his dinner
12		with Patroklos in attendance	with Patroklos listening	Automedon and Alkimos in waiting
13 Reception	the assembly listens	A. greets them coldly	A. welcomes them warmly	A. is amazed

Analysis of Four Visit-Scenes (continued)

	1 1. 12–43	2 1. 326–48	3 9. 173–668	4 24. 186–691
14	he addresses the assembly especially the two Atreidai.	they are silent	hospitality	Priam speaks at once
15			followed by the speeches.	followed by hospitality.
16 Response	Agamemnon rejects him	Achilleus acquiesces	Achilleus rejects them	Achilleus accepts him
17			Phoinix is bedded down	Priam and the herald are bedded down
18			Achilleus and Patroklos sleep with women	Achilleus sleeps with Briseïs
19				Priam is woken by Hermes
20 Departure	he departs in fear and prays to Apollo.	they return with Briseïs.	they return (without Phoinix) to Agamemnon and the rest.	they return with the body of Hektor.

Before trying to illustrate this from these three scenes I would add another scene which shares some narrative-shaping with Priam's visit-scene in 24: in book 1 there is another visit-scene in which a father comes to the enemy to ransom his child. This pair also share some formulae, notably 1. 12–13 and 24. 501–2.

It was on this recurrence above all that Karl Reinhardt based his principle of 'Umkehr' as an underlying law of large-scale narrative.[42] Having established the pairing of these two ransom-scenes with great detail and subtlety, he actually argued that Chryses and his scene were a poetic invention (on the analogy of Briseïs and her father Briseus from Brisa), created *after* Priam's

[42] See Reinhardt, *ID* 466–9 with 413, n. 1.

great scene had become established as a closing scene of the whole poem.[43] While this must remain a speculation, its value, regardless of the truth of the matter, is that it opens eyes to the kind of way that the poetic process may well have worked. Reinhardt's approach assumes that the *Iliad* was created by long accumulation and refinement. Once a certain feature had become fixed and important, other parts of the poem, earlier in it as well as later, might be shaped—or even invented—to fit. Oral techniques will have encouraged and helped this process of composition.

The table draws up the family resemblances between the four scenes, and in the process signals their differences. Mechanical though it is in format, it makes a helpful start. It brings out, for example, some of the extraordinary features of the Priam scene (4) by comparison with the others—see further §§ **9.3, 9.4**—for example that he is ransoming a child who is dead not alive, that the speeches are made before there is hospitality, and that the visitor stays the night before departing.

As a fuller illustration of the value of comparing recurrent scenes and of taking them in performed sequence, I shall take the role of *Patroklos* in scenes 2, 3, and 4, the three visits to Achilleus.

By the time of the first scene, at 1. 326 ff, Patroklos has received only a passing mention by his patronymic, at 1. 307. Then Achilleus tells him to bring Briseïs out to the heralds (337–8):

> Ὣς φάτο, Πάτροκλος δὲ φίλωι ἐπεπείθεθ' ἑταίρωι,
> ἐκ δ' ἄγαγε κλισίης Βρισηΐδα καλλιπάρηιον,
> δῶκε δ' ἄγειν· τὼ δ' αὖτις ἴτην παρὰ νῆας Ἀχαιῶν·
> ἡ δ' ἀέκουσ' ἅμα τοῖσι γυνὴ κίεν·

So he spoke, and Patroklos did as his dear friend told him. He brought the beautiful Briseïs out of the hut, and gave her to the heralds to take. They went back again to the ships of the Achaians, and the woman went with them, reluctant. (1. 345–8)

The more experienced the listener to the *Iliad*, the more attentively this moment will be stored up.

By the time of book 9 Patroklos has still not spoken. In fact the only intervening reference has been Zeus' almost callously terse prediction of the battle περὶ Πατρόκλοιο θανόντος (over dead Patroklos) (8. 476). His presence for the embassy scene is, however, noticed from the start. On arrival they find Achilleus singing

---

[43] Ibid. 63–8.

poetry, and Patroklos listening (9. 190–1). Achilleus tells him to arrange the hospitality, and, helped by Automedon (209), he does so with due courtesy (9. 201–20). The social 'ritual' is carried through flawlessly—hence Aias' appeal later (see pp. 71–2 above).

Achilleus later recalls him in this role, as he laments:

> "ἦ ῥά νύ μοί ποτε καὶ cύ, δυcάμμορε, φίλταθ' ἑταίρων,
> αὐτὸc ἐνὶ κλιcίηι λαρὸν παρὰ δεῖπνον ἔθηκαc
> αἶψα καὶ ὀτραλέωc"

'Oh, there was a time when you, poor ill-fated man, dearest of my companions, you yourself would set out a pleasing meal in my hut, so quick and ready . . .' (19. 315–17)

At the end of the embassy scene, after he has seen to making up the bed for Phoinix (620–2, 658–61), Patroklos is himself bedded down with what might seem gratuitous detail:

> αὐτὰρ Ἀχιλλεὺc εὗδε μυχῶι κλιcίηc εὐπήκτου·
> τῶι δ' ἄρα παρκατέλεκτο γυνή, τὴν Λεcβόθεν ἦγε,
> Φόρβαντοc θυγάτηρ, Διομήδη καλλιπάρηιοc.
> Πάτροκλοc δ' ἑτέρωθεν ἐλέξατο· πὰρ δ' ἄρα καὶ τῶι
> Ἶφιc ἐύζωνοc, τήν οἱ πόρε δῖοc Ἀχιλλεὺc
> Cκῦρον ἑλὼν αἰπεῖαν, Ἐνυῆοc πτολίεθρον.

And Achilleus slept in the interior of his well-built hut, and beside him lay a woman he had brought from Lesbos, Phorbas's daughter, beautiful Diomede. Patroklos lay down on the opposite side. He too had a woman lying beside him, the fine-girdled Iphis—Achilleus had given her to him when he took steep Skyros, the city of Enyeus. (9. 662–8)

Turning to book 24, as soon as Priam makes his astonishing entry into the tent of Achilleus, there is the digression in 471–6 (quoted above). In 9, Automedon—the man who had to take over Achilleus' horses in 17 (see further p. 190)—was Patroklos' helper, as Alkimos is his now. Now he has taken over the role of serving the feast; and so, even as Priam arrives, a frisson may be felt for the absence of Patroklos, thanks to the recurrent scene-shape.

At this early stage of the scene in 24, this might remain a merely subliminal reminder, even for the most seasoned member of Homer's audience. But, as the scene progresses, Patroklos' substitution—and hence his absence—becomes explicit:

> οὐκ οἶοc, ἅμα τῶι γε δύω θεράποντεc ἕποντο,
> ἥρωc Αὐτομέδων ἠδ' Ἄλκιμοc, οὕc ῥα μάλιcτα
> τῖ' Ἀχιλεὺc ἑτάρων μετὰ Πάτροκλόν γε θανόντα

... not alone, but two lieutenants went with him, the hero Automedon
and Alkimos, the two that Achilleus honoured most of his companions,
after Patroklos was dead. (24. 572–5)

When the hospitable meal is eventually served, after a unique
alteration of the ritual, the absence of Patroklos, killed by Priam's
son, can be deftly conveyed without being laboured:

Αὐτομέδων δ' ἄρα cῖτον ἑλὼν ἐπένειμε τραπέζηι
καλοῖc ἐν κανέοιcιν· ἀτὰρ κρέα νεῖμεν Ἀχιλλεύc·

Automedon took bread and set it out on the table in fine baskets, and
Achilleus served the meat. (24. 625–6)

This couplet is the same as 9. 216–17, but with Automedon instead
of Patroklos, the second-best replacing the best.

As the scene draws to a close, a bed is made up for Priam, as
it was for Phoinix in book 9; and there are in fact some close
similarities between 24. 643–8 and 9. 658–61. Finally

οἱ μὲν ἄρ' ἐν προδόμωι δόμου αὐτόθι κοιμήcαντο,
κῆρυξ καὶ Πρίαμοc, πυκινὰ φρεcὶ μήδε' ἔχοντεc,
αὐτὰρ Ἀχιλλεὺc εὗδε μυχῶι κλιcίηc ἐϋπήκτου·
τῶι δὲ Βρικηῒc παρελέξατο καλλιπάρηιοc.

So they then lay down in the porch of the house, the herald and Priam,
men with wise thoughts in their minds. And Achilleus slept in the interior
of his well-built hut, and the beautiful Briseïs lay beside him. (24. 673–6)

Briseïs the best replaces the second-best Diomede—but at the
price of Patroklos, who is now ashes in a golden urn. The dead
cannot make love. Though Thetis can promise her son only short
life, she urges him, in 24. 128 ff., to live that life to the full—see
further pp. 276–9. Achilleus' last active participation in the Iliad
is to assert life in the teeth of imminent death, despite even the
loss of Patroklos.

The underlying framework of the recurrent scene-shape allows
the unique variations to say a great deal without its being spelled
out. In case it seems far-fetched to claim that the couplet of
Achilleus' reunion with Briseïs in 24. 675–6 should evoke the
death of Patroklos, I should point to other links between the two
of them. The only time that Patroklos and Briseïs are seen together
is in the apparently perfunctory scene in book 1—see 1. 345–8,

quoted above.[44] There are no words, and the only colouring is
ἀέκουςα ('reluctant') in 348—though even that might be seen as
no more than the fear of those caught up in power-struggles, like
the heralds ἀέκοντε ('reluctantly') at 1. 327.
When Briseïs eventually returns to the quarters of Achilleus,
the body of Patroklos is lying, as is proper, ἀνὰ πρόθυρον (turned
towards the door) (19. 212). So they meet again in the very place
where they last parted. When the cause of the initial quarrel
laments for its unforeseen victim, the subliminal seed of ἀέκουςα
('reluctant') flowers with grief:

> "Πάτροκλέ μοι δειλῆι πλεῖcτον κεχαρicμένε θυμῶι,
> ζωὸν μέν cε ἔλειπον ἐγὼ κλιcίηθεν ἰοῦcα,
> νῦν δέ cε τεθνηῶτα κιχάνομαι, ὄρχαμε λαῶν,
> ἄψ ἀνιοῦc'· ὥc μοι δέχεται κακὸν ἐκ κακοῦ αἰεί.   290
>
> .   .   .   .
>
> οὐδὲ μὲν οὐδέ μ' ἔαcκεc, ὅτ' ἄνδρ' ἐμὸν ὠκὺc Ἀχιλλεὺc   295
> ἔκτεινεν, πέρcεν δὲ πόλιν θείοιο Μύνητοc,
> κλαίειν, ἀλλά μ' ἔφαcκεc Ἀχιλλῆοc θείοιο
> κουριδίην ἄλοχον θήcειν, ἄξειν τ' ἐνὶ νηυcὶν
> ἐc Φθίην, δαίcειν δὲ γάμον μετὰ Μυρμιδόνεccι.
> τώ c' ἄμοτον κλαίω τεθνηότα, μείλιχον αἰεί."   300

'Patroklos, more than any the pleasure of my poor heart, you were alive
when I went away from the hut and left you, and now I come back,
leader of your people, and find you dead. So it is always in my life, pain
following pain ... But when swift Achilleus killed my husband and
sacked the city of godlike Mynes, you would not let me even weep, but
you said you would make me godlike Achilleus' wedded wife, and take
me back in your ships to Phthia, and celebrate my marriage-feast among
the Myrmidons. And so I weep endlessly for your death. You were always
gentle.' (19. 287–90, 295–300)

However realistic or unrealistic her hopes (see further pp. 214–16),
the death of Patroklos means Achilleus' death at Troy. So he will
never marry Briseïs—nor any other woman—in Phthia. Briseïs
knew that Patroklos was the way to Achilleus' heart; and the way
to Patroklos' heart was through his gentleness and compassion.
Nestor knows this also, all too well (see further pp. 175–7).

---

[44] As in the name-painting of the Briseïs Painter in the British Museum. She
was a favourite with pottery painters: for this and other representations with
Agamemnon's heralds, see *LIMC* iii. 158–61. She is often present in scenes of the
ransom of Hektor, see *LIMC* iii. 162 ff.

The recurrent rituals of a visit-scene overlap with those of a hospitality-scene. These are at their clearest in the peacetime setting of the *Odyssey*—the end of the first evening that Telemachos and Peisistratos spend at Sparta in *Od.* 4 is a good example. In the closing cadence of such scenes the host and his wife, after seeing that their guest(s) are properly looked after, go to bed together themselves. So in *Od.* 4. 304-5 we have

Ἀτρείδης δὲ καθεῦδε μυχῶι δόμου ὑψηλοῖο,
πὰρ δ' Ἑλένη τανύπεπλος ἐλέξατο, δῖα γυναικῶν.[45]

But the son of Atreus slept in the interior of his high house, and beside him lay long-robed Helen.

In *Iliad* 9 the women that Achilleus and Patroklos go to bed with are explicitly concubines—these are wartime conditions. I suggest that in book 24 there is none the less an echo of the hospitality-scene at home, and that lines 675-6 are a distant and distorted echo of that wedding which Patroklos promised, the nearest that Achilleus and Briseïs will ever come to it. So the implicit connections and accumulations of this kind of poetry can convey in two lines a whole tragic world in which potential future happiness is cut short.

[45] Cf. *Od.* 3. 402-3, 7. 346-7; for further parallels, see Hainsworth on *Od.* 7. 334-7. *Il.* 24. 636, 643-6, 673 = *mutatis mutandis Od.* 4. 295, 296-300, 302.

3

The Past Beneath the Present

3.1 Before the beginning: Aulis and the Troad

"τέκνον, τί κλαίεις; τί δέ σε φρένας ἵκετο πένθος;
ἐξαύδα, μὴ κεῦθε νόωι, ἵνα εἴδομεν ἄμφω."
Τὴν δὲ βαρὺ στενάχων προσέφη πόδας ὠκὺς Ἀχιλλεύς·
"οἶσθα· τίη τοι ταῦτα ἰδυίηι πάντ' ἀγορεύω;   365
ὠιχόμεθ' ἐς Θήβην, ἱερὴν πόλιν Ἠετίωνος,
τὴν δὲ διεπράθομέν τε καὶ ἤγομεν ἐνθάδε πάντα·
καὶ τὰ μὲν εὖ δάσσαντο μετὰ σφίσιν υἷες Ἀχαιῶν,
ἐκ δ' ἕλον Ἀτρεΐδηι Χρυσηΐδα καλλιπάρηιον."

'Child, why are you crying? What pain has touched your heart? Tell me,
do not hide it inside you, so that both of us can know.'

With a heavy groan swift-footed Achilleus said to her: 'You know.
What need for me to tell you all when you know it? We had gone to
Thebe, Eëtion's sacred city. We sacked it, and brought all the spoils here.
The sons of the Achaians made proper division of all the rest among
themselves, and chose for the son of Atreus as his gift of honour the
beautiful Chryseïs.' (1. 362–9)[1]

The *Iliad* is much too good to begin at the beginning (or to end
at the end). It begins at an exact time, the day that Chryses comes
to the ships; but an extraordinary amount about the past is filled
in by piecemeal reconstruction, especially during the first three
and a half books. It is not, of course, blocked out in chronological
order; and it is conveyed by a wide variety of narrative techniques,
ranging from direct narration, to symbolic re-enactment, to passing allusions fitting the 'jig-saw' as it has been pieced together so
far. Always the poet controls the sequence and the developing
picture perceived by his hearers.

[1] For narratological approaches to this speech, see I. J. F. de Jong, *Arethusa*,
18 (1985), 5 ff.; W. F. Wyatt Jr., *CJ* 83 (1988), 289–97; also Rabel, 475–7; and
Robbins, *passim*.

Thus, as has often been observed—and sometimes complained of—the *teichoskopia* in book 3 'belongs' at the beginning of the siege, not in the tenth year. Priam should know by now who the leading Achaians are, and Helen should at least know whether or not her celebrated brothers are at Troy. Leaf (p. 117) catches the point of the narrative technique with admirable concision: 'it is enough perhaps to say that for the hearer or reader this *is* the opening of the war'.

Similarly the great catalogue of ships would come more 'logically' at the start of the expedition—and may well have been adapted from such a context. This would explain why it is a catalogue of ships, rather than of contingents; and its opening with the ships from Aulis and surrounding towns (494 ff.) may well point to the original setting. The catalogue not only enumerates the scale and personnel of the Achaian expedition; by naming and sometimes describing or evoking their homelands, it reaches back to their departures from their families, and indirectly to the years that those families have awaited the return of their men.[2]

Not all background information is conveyed in this kind of enumeration—it would become tedious in excess. Details of what has been going on for the nine long years since the Achaians arrived at Troy, for instance, are let slip here and there in passing, with very little direct narrative. They add up to a strikingly coherent picture, especially of the sacking and looting of cities in the area of Troy.[3]

The first reference is indefinite—ὁππότ' Ἀχαιοὶ Τρώων ἐκπέρςως' εὖ ναιόμενον πτολίεθρον (whenever the Achaians sack some well-founded Trojan town) (1. 163-4, see pp. 63-4 above). The elaboration that Achilleus has sacked twelve by sea and eleven overland comes at 9. 325-33. In scattered allusions you can learn that the former included Tenedos, source of Hekamede, the fine woman allotted to Nestor (11. 624-7), and Lesbos, source of seven outstandingly beautiful women offered and eventually given by Agamemnon to their captor (9. 128-30, 19. 215-16). The latter included Thebe, where Achilleus destroyed Eëtion and the rest of

---

[2] On the catalogue, see Kirk i. 168-247. It is worth noting how in two of the three entries which are adapted to fit developments since the departure from Aulis (the third is Protesilaos at 2. 895-710), the poet takes the opportunity to slip in a prediction for the future. Achilleus (681 ff.) will return to the war τάχα (soon) (674), and Philoktetes will be needed and recalled τάχα (soon) (724).

[3] See Taplin, *Chios*, with bibliog.; add Robbins, 9-13.

Andromache's family—see further p. 126—and where he captured many fine spoils, including Chryseïs, as revealed in this first reference to the place. Near to Thebe was Lyrnessos, where Achilleus captured Briseïs (2. 688–93, 19. 59–60, 291–9). Aineias had taken refuge there, but escaped (20. 89–93, 187–9 ff.; see further p. 217).

It is never explained why Chryseïs was at Thebe and not at her native city of Chryse. This has worried scholars since Antiquity— indeed explanation seems to go all the way back to the cyclic epic *Cypria*.[4] Yet there is a perfectly good explanation supplied within Homeric 'anthropology', which is, I suggest, taken for granted. Briseïs was captured from Lyrnessos, not her native Lesbos (see 19. 246), because that was the home of her husband (19. 291 ff.). Chryseïs was likewise married to a man of Thebe.[5] Just as Andromache's mother's father ransomed her after she was captured and her marital family killed (6. 425–8), so Chryseïs' father comes to ransom her.

The city of Chryse has remained unsacked, unlike another of Apollo's local cult-sites, Tenedos. The whereabouts of Chryse was disputed in Antiquity—it may have been near the famous and rich cult of Apollo Smintheus near Hamaxitos in the south-west Troad.[6] It is important that it is intact because it is the only place in the human world outside the immediate area of the Trojan plain that the *Iliad* visits at any length (the next longest is the gathering of wood on Mount Ida in 23. 110–24). The 'interlude' at 1. 430–87 has a ceremonial atmosphere;[7] and the pleasant scenes of reunion and feasting are a reminder, near the start of the poem, of the families the Achaians have left at home and of their hopes

---

[4] Fr. xix Allen = 28 Bernabé = 22 Davies. This seems a clear indication that the *Cypria* was composed as a kind of supplement to the *Iliad*, and even addressing 'Homeric problems'.

[5] It is no objection that she is referred to as κούρη (young woman) since Briseïs is also. So Kirk on 1. 366–92 is mistaken to asume that Chryseïs was only visiting Thebe; but that is not as wrong as his statement that Andromache was captured at Thebe (presumably there is some confusion with Andromache's mother).

[6] See Cook, 228–35. The title of Smintheus comes after the 'local' invocation of Apollo in 1. 37–8 (= 1. 451–2, when Chryses calls the plague off). (Compare the 'local' Trojan invocation of Zeus at 24. 290–1). These lines associate Chryse, Tenedos, and Killa (site also unknown). For Chryse and Chryseïs in later myth, see Pearson's introduction to the fragments of Sophocles' *Chryses* (ii. 327–8).

[7] For example the four lines of disembarkation beginning ἐκ δὲ ('and out . . .') (436–9), or the hieratic calling-off of the plague in 450 ff. On the scene see Reinhardt, *ID* 83–95; Edwards, 'CI' 19–23.

of return—cf. Chryses in line 19—εὖ δ' οἴκαδ' ἱκέϲθαι (and a safe return to your homes).

If there was some story about why Chryse has remained unsacked, as reported by a scholion on 1. 366, it was a local and little-known story, unlike that of the sacrifice of Iphigeneia at Aulis.[8] This is never directly alluded to in Homer, and at 9. 145 Agamemnon has a live daughter called Iphianassa. Nevertheless she provides an intriguing test-case for the extent of *inexplicit* allusion in Homer, and raises the question of how far audiences brought with them their familiarity with other tales.

After Kalchas has spoken out at the first *agorē*, Agamemnon turns on him with personal fury:

> "μάντι κακῶν, οὐ πώ ποτέ μοι τὸ κρήγυον εἶπαϲ·
> αἰεί τοι τὰ κάκ' ἐϲτὶ φίλα φρεϲὶ μαντεύεϲθαι,
> ἐϲθλὸν δ' οὔτε τί πω εἶπαϲ ἔποϲ οὔτ' ἐτέλεϲϲαϲ·"

'Prophet of evil, you have never told me anything to my liking. Always your heart's delight is to prophesy evil, and you have never spoken or brought to fulfilment any word of good.' (1. 106–8)

His rancour is explicable without recourse to the Iphigeneia story: he is characterized as easily upset, and Kalchas has foreseen an angry response (78 ff.; see above, p. 54). None the less Homer has gone out of his way to emphasize already that Kalchas has done the expedition good service (69–72); furthermore οὐ πώ ποτέ . . . αἰεί . . . οὔτε τί πω . . . ('never . . . always . . . never any . . .') suggest a past history of antagonism. If experienced hearers take this as an enriching allusion, they may then sense that this is not the first time that Kalchas has had to explain the anger of a god in a way that is not agreeable for Agamemnon.[9]

The presence of Kalchas at Aulis is explicitly recalled in a later scene, not for the sacrifice of Iphigeneia, but for his interpretation of the omen given there by Zeus. Reasserting some authority, after Agamemnon's disruption of the *agorē* in book 2, Odysseus admits (2. 291–7) that their lack of success has been wearisome. But he then takes memories vividly back to Aulis. He tells of the omen and of Kalchas' interpretation so fully in order to raise hope that the waiting will be crowned with success—τὰ δὴ νῦν πάντα τελεῖται (all is now coming to fulfilment) (330). Kalchas provided

---

[8] The long delay at Aulis was already well known to Hesiod: see *WD* 651–3.

[9] This might possibly be relevant to Poseidon's taking the form of Kalchas at 13. 95 ff., when he rallies the Achaians in terms that do Agamemnon no credit.

an important ratification of the whole expedition. That is why, when Diomedes contradicts Agamemnon's later and serious proposal to give up, he insists that he and Sthenelos will stay until Troy falls, cὺν γὰρ θεῶι εἰλήλουθμεν (since god is with us in our mission here) (9. 49). The reconstruction of the past reaches forward to the present and even into the future. The prophecy of Kalchas at Aulis in effect supplies the *Dios boulē* for the fate of Troy. For an audience with an ear for the larger narrative, its fulfilment goes beyond the immediate context of Odysseus' application, to include the shaping of the sympathies of the whole *Iliad*.[10]

In the narrative of the omen there is emotive colouring:

> "ἔνθ' ὅ γε τοὺς ἐλεεινὰ κατήcθιε τετριγῶτας,
> μήτηρ δ' ἀμφιποτᾶτο ὀδυρομένη φίλα τέκνα·
> τὴν δ' ἐλελιξάμενος πτέρυγος λάβεν ἀμφιαχυῖαν."

'Then the snake ate the chicks as they screamed pitifully, and their mother fluttered round it crying for her dear children: but the snake coiled out and caught her by the wing as she shrieked above it.' (2. 314–16)

This presages the way that in the *Iliad* both the doomed women and children of Troy and their brave defenders will be treated with sympathy and pathos. That is the attitude of the poem, but not of Odysseus and the Achaian attackers. *They* are the equivalent of the terrifying snake, and like the snake they will be ruthless in their conquest.

The fate of the snake as well as of the birds is part of the omen.

> "αὐτὰρ ἐπεὶ κατὰ τέκνα φάγε cτρουθοῖο καὶ αὐτήν,
> τὸν μὲν ἀρίζηλον θῆκεν θεός, ὅc περ ἔφηνε·
> λᾶαν γάρ μιν ἔθηκε Κρόνου πάϊc ἀγκυλομήτεω·
> ἡμεῖc δ' ἑcταότεc θαυμάζομεν οἷον ἐτύχθη."

'Then when it had eaten her children and the sparrow herself, the god who had brought the snake to light made it a miracle, plain for all to see—it was turned into stone by the son of devious-minded Kronos, and we stood there in amazement at what had happened.' (2. 317–20)[11]

---

[10] For two other examples of narratives which I claim to have a wider reflexive significance for the poem they form part of, see below on Aineias in book 5 (p. 109) and the fate of Eumelos in 23 (p. 257). Cf. Andersen.

[11] *Contra* Aristarchos, supported by Kirk, I am reading ἀρίζηλον ('conspicuous') rather than ἀίζηλον ('invisible'), and retaining line 319. Kirk says of Aulis 'there is no reason for believing that Homer's description was based on special local knowledge': I would be very surprised if the stone snake was not something visible in Homer's day, and known to at least some of his audience. This is a kind of aetiology for it.

In his interpretation Kalchas gives this marvel the phrase which he uses of the equivalent of the eventual sack of Troy—ὅου κλέος οὔ ποτ' ὀλεῖται (whose fame will never perish) (325). The fulfilment of this prophecy of *kleos* is epic poetry. Narrative song is man's nearest equivalent—at least for Homer and his audience—of Zeus' ability to create permanent landmarks. Kalchas is right about the sack of Troy: the *Iliad*, even as any one hears or reads it, is fulfilling his prediction. We (you or I) satisfy this self-referential prediction no less than Homer's own audiences.[12] So Homer makes himself and his poem part of the past at Aulis, and part of the *Dios boulē*.

3.2   The temporary constructions on the shore

"ἐννέα δὴ βεβάαςι Διὸς μεγάλου ἐνιαυτοί,
καὶ δὴ δοῦρα ϲέϲηπε νεῶν καὶ ϲπάρτα λέλυνται·   135
αἱ δέ που ἡμέτεραί τ' ἄλοχοι καὶ νήπια τέκνα
ἥατ' ἐνὶ μεγάροιϲ ποτιδέγμεναι· ἄμμι δὲ ἔργον
αὔτωϲ ἀκράαντον, οὗ εἵνεκα δεῦρ' ἱκόμεϲθα.
ἀλλ' ἄγεθ', ὡϲ ἂν ἐγὼ εἴπω, πειθώμεθα πάντεϲ·
φεύγωμεν ϲὺν νηυϲὶ φίλην ἐϲ πατρίδα γαῖαν·   140
οὐ γὰρ ἔτι Τροίην αἱρήϲομεν εὐρυάγυιαν."
   Ὣϲ φάτο, τοῖϲι δὲ θυμὸν ἐνὶ ϲτήθεϲϲιν ὄρινε
πᾶϲι μετὰ πληθύν, ὅϲοι οὐ βουλῆϲ ἐπάκουϲαν·
κινήθη δ' ἀγορὴ φὴ κύματα μακρὰ θαλάϲϲηϲ,
πόντου Ἰκαρίοιο, τὰ μέν τ' Εὖρόϲ τε Νότοϲ τε   145
ὦρορ' ἐπαΐξαϲ πατρὸϲ Διὸϲ ἐκ νεφελάων.
ὡϲ δ' ὅτε κινήϲηι Ζέφυροϲ βαθὺ λήϊον ἐλθών,
λάβροϲ ἐπαιγίζων, ἐπί τ' ἠμύει ἀϲταχύεϲϲιν,
ὣϲ τῶν πᾶϲ' ἀγορὴ κινήθη· τοὶ δ' ἀλαλητῶι
νῆαϲ ἔπ' ἐϲϲεύοντο, ποδῶν δ' ὑπένερθε κονίη   150
ἵϲτατ' ἀειρομένη· τοὶ δ' ἀλλήλοιϲι κέλευον
ἅπτεϲθαι νηῶν ἠδ' ἑλκέμεν εἰϲ ἅλα δῖαν,
οὐρούϲ τ' ἐξεκάθαιρον· αὕτη δ' οὐρανὸν ἷκεν
οἴκαδε ἱεμένων· ὑπὸ δ' ἥιρεον ἕρματα νηῶν.

'Nine years now have passed from mighty Zeus' store, and our ships' timbers have rotted and their rigging decayed. And our wives and young children are sitting in our homes, waiting for us: while the task which brought us here stands quite without completion. No, come, let us all do

---

12 For other such self-referential predictions, see below p. 243.

as I say—let us away with our ships to our own dear native land. We shall never now take the broad streets of Troy.'

So he spoke, and his words lifted the hearts of all in the mass of the army, all those who were not privy to his purpose: and the assembly was stirred like the great waves of the sea, in the deep water by Ikaria, when the east wind and the south wind rush down from father Zeus' storm-clouds and raise them high. As when the west wind stirs a deep cornfield with its coming, and the standing crop bows its ears in the fury of the blast, so the whole assembly was stirred to movement. The men swarmed cheering to the ships, and under their feet the dust rose high in a cloud. They urged each other to lay hands to the ships and drag them down to the holy sea, and they set to clearing the slipways. Their shouts reached heaven as they surged for home: and they began to pull the props from under the ships. (2. 134–54)

The setting of the Achaian ships and temporary encampments (κλιςίαι, *klisiai*) along the shore is made so familiar by ubiquitous formulae, starting with θοὰς ἐπὶ νῆας ('to the fast ships') in 1. 12, that even a hearer new to Homer would soon come to take it for granted.[13] At *Od.* 1. 61 the whole enterprise can be referred to by Ἀργείων παρὰ νηυcί ('by the ships of the Argives'). Amid such frequent and subliminal references it comes as something of a shock to be reminded—by a leap of poetic imagination—how strange the reality of such a setting would be, and how, over nine years, the timbers and equipment will have deteriorated and the launching-ramps become obscured.

Homer envisages the camp in remarkable detail. Scattered references even allow the reconstruction of a consistent 'map' of where along the line the leading Achaians are encamped. It is particularly stressed that Aias and Achilleus are at the danger points of the two wings and Odysseus in the middle (8. 222–6 = 11. 5–9); but with more or less precision a dozen or so *basilees* can be placed. From left to right, which was taken to be from east to west, they are: greater Aias, Idomeneus, Menelaos, Agamemnon, Nestor, Odysseus, Eurypylos, Diomedes, lesser Aias, Meges, (Protesilaos replaced by Podarkes), Achilleus.[14] With the exception of

---

[13] On the setting at the ships, see Schadewaldt, *IS* 67–8; Hellwig, 25–6. In general on the setting of the *Iliad*, see Elliger, 29 ff. For comparative material on the topographical setting of epic, see Hatto, ii. 215 ff.

[14] A scheme, modified from that of Cuillandre, is set out by Willcock, *Comm.* ii. 225 (cf. *Comp.* 116 f.). In later times the Greeks envisaged the camp along the shore of the Dardanelles from 'the tomb of Achilleus' at Sigeion to 'the tomb of Aias' at Rhoiteion. Any real expedition, whether in the late Bronze Age or at any

Podarkes, and perhaps, Meges, these are in fact leading Achaian *basilēes* in the *Iliad*. Their standing is established early in the poem by a variety of means.

Two—apart from Achilleus and Agamemnon—are given special portrayal early, before the troops are even armed and marshalled. Odysseus is selected for the diplomatic task of returning Chryseïs.[15] Then, when Agamemnon has so disastrously disbanded the *agorē* in book 2, it is Odysseus who is chosen by Athene to reunite it (2. 169 ff.). He takes over Agamemnon's sceptre and uses it assertively; he rallies everyone with socially appropriate sentiments; he silences Thersites[16] to the approval of all, ἀχνύμενοι (disaffected) (270) though they may be. His speech which includes the omen at Aulis (284–332) meets with great approval.

Nestor is perhaps not such an unqualified success. Though introduced as venerable, well-intentioned, and eloquent (1. 248–52),[17] he utterly fails to heal the dispute because he defers too much to Agamemnon. The false dream takes his form—τόν ῥα μάλιϲτα γερόντων τί᾽ Ἀγαμέμνων (whom Agamemnon honoured most of all the elders) (2. 21). He is the only elder to speak in the *boulē* (76 ff.), and there he once again fails to prevent a difficult development by allowing Agamemnon too much respect. After Odysseus' calm, cogent speech, Nestor supplies emotive bluster at 336–68, and Agamemnon lavishes praise on it.

After the *agorē*, while the rest of the army breakfasts, Agamemnon has along the seven γέροντας ἀριϲτῆας Παναχαιῶν (the leading

other pre-modern era, is far more likely to have camped at Beşik Bay on the Aegean coast to the south-west. This would put Achilleus at the north end, where the Lesbians founded Achilleion at Beşik Tepe. Homer himself more likely envisages this landscape as his basis in reality. This is well argued by M. Korfmann in M. J. Mellink (ed.), *Troy and the Trojan War* (Bryn Mawr, 1986), 1–28; cf. J. Latacz, *Berytus* 34 (1984), 97 ff.

[15] Perhaps it is not coincidence that he is connected with the one and only *nostos* (that of Chryseïs) in the *Iliad*? On Odysseus in the *Iliad*, see the inaugural lecture of K. Borthwick, *Odyssean Elements in the Iliad* (Edinburgh, 1985); also Martin, 120–4.

[16] What Thersites says is far from despicable; but Odysseus takes the opportunity to stop an unsuitable person from saying it at an unsuitable time. For an interesting recent study of Thersites, see W. G. Thalmann in *TAPA* 11 (1988), 1–28.

[17] This introduction is honorific—it is out of the question that Nestor might have been an unfamiliar figure. About half the occurrences of the formula ὅ ϲφιν εὐφρονέων ἀγορήϲατο ('in all good will he spoke to them') (first at 1. 253) are applied to him. On Nestor the speaker, see Martin, 101 ff.

elders of the Panachaians) for roast beef (2. 404–8). This gathering of the eight leading Achaians (barring Achilleus of course) illustrates the *Iliad*'s clear and consistent grasp on 'prosopography' and on the 'pecking order' of the leading heroes. Nestor comes πρώτιστα (first of all); Odysseus comes sixth but is given a whole line. So is Menelaos, who has yet to speak or otherwise contribute to the *Iliad*—he comes αὐτόματος (without need for summons).[18] Idomeneus and the greater Aias have been named before (1. 138, 148); and Aias will be singled out as the best warrior, in the absence of Achilleus, in a sort of appendix to the catalogue at 2. 760 ff. This is the first mention of Diomedes and of the other Aias (whether this is Teukros or the Locrian Aias). The only person in this eight who might be 'lucky' to be included is the other Aias—Eurypylos might dispute his ranking.

In the opening kills of the first great battle, at 4. 457–5. 8—an obvious place for a roll of honour—these eight are all there except the other Aias, and of course old Nestor. Antilochos is, in fact, put first, then come Aias and Odysseus, then Thoas, then Diomedes, Agamemnon, Idomeneus and Menelaos, Meges and Eurypylos. Similarly five of our eight are the first to volunteer for single combat, at 7. 161 ff. (Nestor and Menelaos are ruled out); then come Meriones, Eurypylos, Thoas, and last Odysseus. When there is an Achaian resurgence at 8. 253 ff., apart from Nestor and Odysseus, who are off the field, the other six are there, followed by Meriones and Eurypylos, and perhaps for the first time in such company Teukros, who has a brief moment of glory. And so on through the *Iliad*.

Agamemnon himself is always there among the front fighters, though seldom outstanding. The passages where the narrative gives him most prominence and respect are probably the marshalling of the host at 2. 441 ff. (cf. 579–80) and the *teichoskopia* (3. 166 ff.). I have argued, however, that the opening scenes put him in a poor light (above, § **2.2**). It seems to me that he comes across as a highly ambivalent figure in the opening scenes of book 2 as well, especially for the way he misjudges the spirit of the *lāos*. After their communal passivity in book 1 (see pp. 61–2 above), it is Agamemnon who spurs them into activity. Through that miscalculation

---

[18] Line 409 is very likely an interpolation.

the poet reveals to the audience the state that their morale has reached after all these years at Troy.

It is clearly not a regular or easy task to arm the Achaians for battle. The dream that advises Agamemnon to do this (θωρῆξαι (arm) 2. 11, cf. 28, 65, 72, 83) is in any case a false one—νήπιος, οὐδὲ τὰ ἤιδη ἅ ῥα Ζεὺς μήδετο ἔργα (poor fool, he knew nothing of Zeus' design) (38). Despite this, he adds a proposal of his own, which is highlighted by the triple repetition of the 'proper' message before he appends it in 73–5.[19]

"πρῶτα δ᾽ ἐγὼν ἔπεσιν πειρήσομαι, ἣ θέμις ἐστί,
καὶ φεύγειν σὺν νηυσὶ πολυκλήϊσι κελεύσω·
ὑμεῖς δ᾽ ἄλλοθεν ἄλλος ἐρητύειν ἐπέεσσιν."

'But first, as is the proper way, I shall test them with an address, and tell them to make for home with their many-benched ships: and you must try to restrain them with your orders, each from his own position.' (2. 73–5)

When he puts this to the army, they enthusiastically set about departure for home without hesitation or contradiction.

One reason why Agamemnon's speech in 110–41 reveals the low morale of the army all too effectively and counter-productively is that, while it is meant to be deceitful, it contains much that is true. Some of these truths are known to Agamemnon, some are ironically unintended. For instance, Zeus has indeed bound him with *ātē* (111), more than he knows: by the time of 9. 115–20 he will be admitting that his treatment of Achilleus was *ātē* from Zeus (see further p. 207). Zeus has, as he says, devised a κακὴν ἀπάτην (vile deception) (114): Agamemnon thinks that he is himself devising one, without realizing that the dream was false. When he admits "πολὺν ὤλεσα λαόν" ('I have lost many of my people') (115), this is a truth which would better have been left untrumpeted. So too with the numerical inferiority of the Trojans and the great help they have had from their *epikouroi* (130–3)—both these demoralizing truths are confirmed later in the poem.

At this stage, while he does not realize the folly of his treatment of Achilleus, Agamemnon feigns despair with sentiments

---

[19] This used to be one of the analyst complaints against the scene; but the use of large-scale repetition to bring out an important variation can be seen elsewhere, e.g. Odysseus' omission of Agamemnon's four lines of message in 9. 158–61—see p. 70 above. For a powerful and wide-ranging defence of this whole scene against analytical attacks see Reinhardt, *ID* 107–20.

unworthy of the great sceptre on which he leans. But by the time of his speech in 9. 17–28 he is in earnest. His lines there are made up of partial repetition of the speech in book 2.[20] Both speeches gravely miscalculate the mood of the men. The earlier false speech is met with enthusiastic acceptance: the true speech in 9 is met with silence and grief (29–30), and is eventually contradicted by Diomedes to general approval. There will even be a third occasion where Agamemnon counsels despair, though this time in front of only Nestor, Odysseus, and Diomedes, not the whole *agorē* (14. 65–81).[21] This time he also includes practical proposals for hasty escape, and concludes with highly unheroic clichés. That is perhaps Agamemnon's lowest low point in the poem. His proposals, which would be strategically disastrous, are perfunctorily dismissed by Odysseus (82–102), and it is Diomedes again who gives encouragement (109–34).

So we see early what is confirmed later: Agamemnon does not himself have the good judgement or determination to keep his expedition at Troy. He needs Odysseus and others to repair the confusions and demoralizations he inspires. After the troops have been restored to order by Odysseus and Nestor, and Agamemnon is put in a better light, he is still credulously overconfident. He prays to Zeus that he may kill Hektor and sack Troy on this very day.

Ὣς ἔφατ', οὐδ' ἄρα πώ οἱ ἐπεκραίαινε Κρονίων,
ἀλλ' ὅ γε δέκτο μὲν ἱρά, πόνον δ' ἀμέγαρτον ὄφελλεν.

So he spoke, but the son of Kronos would not yet grant his prayer—he took the sacrifice, but heaped higher their joyless hardship. (2. 419–20)

By the time night falls on this day in book 7, Troy is still intact, there will have been heavy casualties, and Hektor will be on the eve of two days of triumphant attack.

Of all the things in Agamemnon's speech which are disturbing for his audience, the collocation of the deteriorating condition of their ships with the reminder of their families at home is the most painful. The ships are their only means of returning home. The fact that they are no longer in good trim makes the men all the more eager to get them launched.

---

[20] 9. 17–25, 26–8 = 2. 110–19, 139–41.
[21] 14. 69 and 14. 74 are repeated yet again (= 2. 116, 9. 23, and = 2. 139, 9. 26).

3.3 *The well-walled city and its landmarks*

Ὡς ἔφαθ', Ἕκτωρ δ' οὔ τι θεᾶς ἔπος ἠγνοίησεν,
αἶψα δὲ λῦσ' ἀγορήν· ἐπὶ τεύχεα δ' ἐσσεύοντο·
πᾶσαι δ' ὠΐγνυντο πύλαι, ἐκ δ' ἔσσυτο λαός,
πεζοί θ' ἱππῆές τε· πολὺς δ' ὀρυμαγδὸς ὀρώρει.   810
Ἔστι δέ τις προπάροιθε πόλιος αἰπεῖα κολώνη,
ἐν πεδίωι ἀπάνευθε, περίδρομος ἔνθα καὶ ἔνθα,
τὴν ἤτοι ἄνδρες Βατίειαν κικλήσκουσιν,
ἀθάνατοι δέ τε σῆμα πολυσκάρθμοιο Μυρίνης·
ἔνθα τότε Τρῶές τε διέκριθεν ἠδ' ἐπίκουροι.   815

So she spoke: Hektor did not fail to hear the goddess speaking, and immediately broke up the assembly. They rushed to their arms. All the gates were opened and the army streamed out, foot-soldiers and horsemen, and the din rose loud.

In front of the city there is a steep mound, standing alone in the plain with open space around it on all sides: men's name for it is Batieia, but the immortals call it the barrow of dancing Myrine. It was here that the Trojans and their allies then formed into their divisions. (2. 807–15)

Troy is a great stone-built city, many generations old, with many well-known permanent features and landmarks. The Achaian camp could hardly be in greater contrast. It is an improvised, wooden world, peopled by soldiers and their captured women. The camp does not even have a wall (and that built later in the poem will be obliterated after the war, see further pp. 138–40). It has no temples, no long-term landmarks or formalized social spaces. It is not a proper place.

Moreover, the Achaian camp is highly inflammable. If the ships were to burn, the Achaians would be trapped. The very idea of setting fire to the ships has never occurred to anyone during the nine years of siege so far. Until now the Trojans have scarcely ventured outside their gates, as is pointed out by Athene at 5. 788–91 and Achilleus at 9. 352–4. This fiery ambition comes to Hektor as a kind of inspiration at 8. 180–3, and is eventually achieved at the height of his day of glory—see further pp. 172–3.

The wooden camp and the stone city are the two bases between which the armies fight. They will fight until one or the other goes up in flames. As Hektor sees, Zeus will prolong the fighting

"εἰς ὅ κεν ἢ ὑμεῖς Τροίην εὔπυργον ἕλητε,
ἢ αὐτοὶ παρὰ νηυσὶ δαμήετε ποντοπόροισιν."

'until either you capture the strong walls of Troy or are yourselves beaten down beside your seafaring ships.' (7. 71–2)

Aias defies Hektor with his opposing hopes:

> "ἦ θήν πού τοι θυμὸς ἐέλπεται ἐξαλαπάξειν
> νῆας· ἄφαρ δέ τε χεῖρες ἀμύνειν εἰcὶ καὶ ἡμῖν.
> ἦ κε πολὺ φθαίη εὖ ναιομένη πόλιc ὑμὴ
> χερcὶν ὑφ' ἡμετέρηιcιν ἁλοῦcά τε περθομένη τε."

'I suppose your heart must be hoping to destroy our ships. But we have hands too, ready at a moment to defend them. Much sooner than that our hands will have taken and sacked your well-founded city.' (13. 813–16)[22]

The crucial imbalance is that Troy is the proper home for many people, men and women, young and old. There are constant reminders, both through particular allusions and through the subliminal effect of formulae, of the broad paved streets, fine ashlar buildings, furniture, clothing. Around all are the mighty defences, built by Poseidon and Apollo, and in them the great symbol of defence and vulnerability, the Skaian gate.[23] Inside, as well as houses, there are, for example, the meeting-place before Priam's house and the Pergamos where Athene and Apollo have temples.

Outside the city there are the great local features such as the rivers Skamandros and Simoeis and Mount Ida, whose peak is associated with Zeus. There are also landmarks on a smaller, human scale, the kind of fixed points which help to articulate the doings of everyday life. One example out of many is the oak tree.[24] When the Achaians need a turning-point for the chariot race, it is telling that they have to use a Trojan landmark which they cannot identify (23. 326–33, 358–61).

The *Iliad* is 1,400 lines old (over two hours) when it moves rather abruptly, at 2. 786, to be in the presence of the Trojans for the first time. As with the Achaians, they are stimulated by a message from Zeus to hold an *agorē*, and to move on to an armed muster. But in their case the message is more straightforward and more honest (cf. 2. 807).

---

[22] Note ἐξαλαπάξειν νῆας ('to destroy our ships'). All eight other occurrences of the verb are used of the sack of a city (all except 4. 40 of Troy).

[23] On the question of whether this is the same as the Dardanian gate see Kirk on 3. 145.

[24] Refs. at 6. 237, 9. 359, 11. 170; also probably 5. 693, 7. 22, 7. 60, 21. 549.

It is no mere epic padding that there are two named landmarks in this brief scene. At 793 there is a reference to the tomb of Aisyëtes; and then at 811 ff. the troops gather at a particular place before the city, one which is a *cĥμα* (*sēma*) even for the gods. Troy is established as a place that has been lived in and died in for many generations. Here people have gone about their business of life, and they have named the features of their familiar landscape. These landmarks are, then, one of many ways to which Troy, far from being merely 'the enemy', becomes a place that the audience care about.

3.4 Helen and blame for war

Ὣς ἄρ' ἔφαν, Πρίαμος δ' Ἑλένην ἐκαλέσσατο φωνῆι·
"δεῦρο πάροιθ' ἐλθοῦσα, φίλον τέκος, ἵζευ ἐμεῖο,
ὄφρα ἴδηι πρότερόν τε πόςιν πηούς τε φίλους τε—
οὔ τί μοι αἰτίη ἐςςί, θεοί νύ μοι αἴτιοί εἰςιν,
οἵ μοι ἐφώρμησαν πόλεμον πολύδακρυν Ἀχαιῶν—   165
ὥς μοι καὶ τόνδ' ἄνδρα πελώριον ἐξονομήνηις,
ὅς τις ὅδ' ἐςτὶν Ἀχαιὸς ἀνὴρ ἠΰς τε μέγας τε.
ἤτοι μὲν κεφαλῆι καὶ μείζονες ἄλλοι ἔαςι,
καλὸν δ' οὕτω ἐγὼν οὔ πω ἴδον ὀφθαλμοῖςιν,
οὐδ' οὕτω γεραρόν· βαςιλῆϊ γὰρ ἀνδρὶ ἔοικε."   170
Τὸν δ' Ἑλένη μύθοιςιν ἀμείβετο, δῖα γυναικῶν·
"αἰδοῖός τέ μοί ἐςςι, φίλε ἑκυρέ, δεινός τε·
ὡς ὄφελεν θάνατός μοι ἀδεῖν κακὸς ὁππότε δεῦρο
υἱέϊ ςῶι ἑπόμην, θάλαμον γνωτούς τε λιποῦςα
παῖδά τε τηλυγέτην καὶ ὁμηλικίην ἐρατεινήν."   175

That is what they said, but Priam called out to Helen: 'Come here, dear child, and sit in front of me, so you can see your former husband and your relatives and friends. It is not you I blame—I blame the gods, who brought on me the misery of war with the Achaians. Sit here, so you can tell me the name of that huge man there—who is he, this tall and manly Achaian? There are others of greater stature, but I have never yet set eyes on a man so fine-looking or so dignified: he has the look of a king.'

Helen, queen among women, answered him with these words: 'Dear father-in-law, you are a man I honour and revere. Oh, if only vile death had been my choice when I came here with your son, leaving behind the house of my marriage, and my family and my darling child and the sweet company of friends!' (3. 161–75)

The armies have been marshalled and are advancing to meet each other by 3. 15 ff.; yet it is another 900 lines before they actually clash and the slaughter begins. First a kind of primal story-pattern urges that a duel should be fought in the presence of the beautiful princess whose hand is to be the prize. *"τῶι δέ κε νικήcαντι φίλη κεκλήcηι ἄκοιτιc"* ('and you will be called the dear wife of the man who wins'), as Iris tells Helen (3. 138). But in this case the contenders are already competing husbands. Which should win? Both sides pray to Zeus to strike down *ὁππότεροc τάδε ἔργα μετ' ἀμφοτέροιcιν ἔθηκε* (whichever of the two it was that brought these troubles on our peoples) (321): but is that the wife-stealer or the warmonger? This part of the *Iliad* is much concerned with apportioning blame, and with denying it. Who started it? Is Helen the cause of the war?

From her very first participation Helen is established as an exceptional person, far more than merely a sex-object or a *femme fatale*.[25] She belongs to both sides, yet to neither; she is *μέccωι ἀμφοτέρων* (in the middle of both sides) in Aphrodite's phrase (3. 416). She is at the centre of the war, yet she has the detachment to be its observer. She belongs both to the present, and to the future long after they are all dead. So Iris finds her—and the poem first finds her—

> τὴν δ' εὗρ' ἐν μεγάρωι· ἡ δὲ μέγαν ἱcτὸν ὕφαινε,
> δίπλακα πορφυρέην, πολέαc δ' ἐνέπαccεν ἀέθλουc
> Τρώων θ' ἱπποδάμων καὶ Ἀχαιῶν χαλκοχιτώνων,
> οὓc ἕθεν εἵνεκ' ἔπαcχον ὑπ' Ἄρηοc παλαμάων·

Iris found Helen in her room, working at a great web of purple cloth for a double cloak, and in it she was weaving many scenes of the conflict between the horse-taming Trojans and the bronze-clad Achaians, which they were enduring for her sake at the hands of Ares. (3. 125–8)[26]

This gives her a special affinity with the poet and his audience. She shows the same kind of self-awareness when she explains to Hector that she and Paris have brought suffering

> "ὡc καὶ ὀπίccω
> ἀνθρώποιcι πελώμεθ' ἀοίδιμοι ἐccομένοιcι."

---

[25] There is a fine study of Helen in Kakridis, *H. Rev.* 25 ff. Her special perspective is marked by the self-referentiality of her weaving: cf. A. Bergren, *Helios*, 7 (1979–80), 19 ff.; Thalmann, 153; Collins, 42–3.

[26] Line 127 is used of the 'real' war almost immediately at 131 and again at 251.

'so that in time to come we can be themes of song for men of future generations.' (6. 357–8)

The war that Helen weaves is being fought ἔθεν εἵνεκα (for her sake). Does this imply that she is to blame for it? Although the matter has been controversial, it seems to me clear beyond dispute that the characters of the *Iliad* and *Odyssey* are much concerned with responsibility. This makes such issues of interest to the audience also, though they will not necessarily concur with the assessments of the participants. The *Odyssey*'s concern with such issues is, indeed, established at the very start by Zeus' so-called 'programme':

> "ὦ πόποι, οἷον δή νυ θεοὺς βροτοὶ αἰτιόωνται.
> ἐξ ἡμέων γάρ φασι κάκ' ἔμμεναι, οἱ δὲ καὶ αὐτοὶ
> cφῆιcιν ἀταcθαλίηιcιν ὑπὲρ μόρον ἄλγε' ἔχουcιν."

'O the way these mortals blame the gods! They say that their troubles come from us, and yet they also bring excessive sorrow upon themselves through their own wrongheaded will.' (*Od.* 1. 32–4)

In the *Iliad* such questions surface most openly in the scenes surrounding the duel of Paris and Menelaos, a good context to start up the whole question of the rights and wrongs of the Trojan war. Homer is too fine an observer of the complexities of human affairs to make the issue black and white. The question of the guilt—or innocence—of Helen is so posed that it has had an enduring fascination for the ancient Greeks and ever since.

This calls for a more general discussion of blame and innocence and responsibility in Homer and of how such issues usually involve the extrapolation of the past. Within the range of language for disputing blame ἔνεκα with the genitive ('for the sake of') is at the weaker end, and much depends on its context. The implication is clear in, for instance, Achilleus' exoneration of the Trojans:

> "οὐ γὰρ ἐγὼ Τρώων ἔνεκ' ἤλυθον αἰχμητάων
> δεῦρο μαχηcόμενοc, ἐπεὶ οὔ τί μοι αἴτιοί εἰcιν·"

'It was not the spearmen of Troy who caused me to come here and fight—I have no quarrel with them.' (1. 152–3)

But there is little or no acknowledgement of blame in Hector's description of Paris, τοῦ εἵνεκα νεῖκοc ὄρωρεν (the man who gave rise to our quarrel) (3. 87). Naturally Menelaos is less neutral: both sides have suffered, he says, εἵνεκ' ἐμῆc ἔριδοc καὶ Ἀλεξάνδρου ἔνεκ' ἀρχῆς (because of my quarrel and Alexandros who began it) (3. 100). ἀρχῆς ('beginning') here clearly attributes blame.[27] In the same way, it is crucial to establish which side, if the oath is broken, broke it πρότερος—see 3. 299, 351; 4. 72, 271, and further below.

The clearest blame/innocence language has been surprisingly neglected by scholars: the use of αἴτιος (*aitios*), αἰτιάομαι, and related words.[28] Two clear examples will be enough. Achilleus says that the Trojans are not *aitioi* as far as he is concerned (as opposed to Menelaos)—see 1. 153, quoted above. And when the heralds come for Briseïs, he reassures them,

"οὔ τί μοι ὔμμες ἐπαίτιοι, ἀλλ' Ἀγαμέμνων,
ὅ cφῶϊ προΐει Βρισηΐδος εἵνεκα κούρης."

'It is not you I blame, but Agamemnon, who has sent you here for the girl Briseïs.' (1. 335–6)

The most direct way to clear one party is to blame another—in that case Agamemnon. But the most ready-to-hand third party tends to be the gods—they are, after all, inscrutable and powerful, and they are known to bring suffering to humans. Thus, for example, Idomeneus protests at 13. 222 ff. that no man is *aitios* for the Achaian defeat, it must be Zeus; at *Od.* 1. 346 ff. Telemachos defends Phemios on the grounds that it is Zeus not the bard who is *aitios* for the suffering of mortals.

The trouble with such excuses is that they attempt to override the 'double motivation' or 'over-determination' which is the standard model in Homer (see pp. 104–5 below on Pandaros).[29] To give two relatively straightforward illustrations: at 9. 701–3 Diomedes predicts that Achilleus will fight ὁππότε κέν μιν θυμὸς ἐνὶ cτήθεccιν ἀνώγηι καὶ θεὸς ὄρcηι (when the heart in his breast urges him and god sets him to it); and at *Od.* 14. 389 Eumaios tells the

---

[27] For ἀρχῆς ('beginning') here rather than ἄτης ('madness'), see Macleod on 24. 27 *contra* Kirk on 3. 100. For the importance of establishing who began the trouble, and of revenge, see J. Gould, *Herodotus* (London, 1989), esp. Chs. 3 and 4 (42–85). At 5. 63 the narrator calls Paris' ships ἀρχεκάκους, a memorable formation echoed by Herodotus' description of the ships sent to help the Ionian revolt as ἀρχὴ κακῶν (the beginning of trouble) (5. 97).

[28] For interesting examples, see *Il.* 13. 111, 13. 222, 13. 775, 19. 410, 20. 297, 21. 275; *Od.* 1. 348, 11. 559, 20. 131, 22. 48, 22. 356; see further pp. 207–9. (I am grateful to Dr C. Pelling for drawing my attention to some of these passages.)

[29] Fundamental contributions on this subject were provided by Lesky, 'Motivation', and Dodds.

stranger that he will look after him Δία ξένιον δείcαc αὐτόν τ' ἐλεαίρων (because I reverence the patron of strangers, Zeus, and because I pity you for your own sake). According to this model, then, there is divine prompting and collaboration, but at the same time the human acts for himself or herself. By the same token the human is entitled to at least some credit, or liable for at least some blame. So putting *all* the blame on the gods is, in effect, an attempt to reduce the double motivation to single. Those well-disposed may be inclined to go along with this, those ill-disposed disinclined.

All this bears on Helen and Priam. He is kindly disposed to her—ἑκυρὸc δὲ πατὴρ ὡc ἤπιος αἰεί (though your father was always kind to me as a real father), as she acknowledges at 24. 770 (a notable consistency). It is characteristic of Helen, however, that she does not accept his well-intentioned palliation. Her response in 173–5 (cf. 3. 180, 242) is a clear acceptance of her side of any double determination. She should have chosen death rather than have chosen to desert her marriage-home.

Instead of leaving the issue there, Homer actually narrates a scene between Helen and Aphrodite after the battle which fascinatingly explores the extent of her self-motivation. It is clear without statement that the two of them are intimate: Helen recognizes Aphrodite easily (396–8); the goddess carries a footstool for the mortal (424–6—ἀπρεπέc (improper) in the eyes of Zenodotos). Helen's language in 399–412 is bold and shrewish, more like that bandied about among the immortals on Olympos. A comparison with Diomedes to Aphrodite at 5. 348–51 or Achilleus to Apollo at 22. 15–20 brings out its courage—or effrontery—as she attempts to assert independent human will. Her extraordinary lines

> "ἧcο παρ' αὐτὸν ἰοῦcα, θεῶν δ' ἀπόεικε κελεύθον,
> μηδ' ἔτι coῖcι πόδεccιν ὑποcτρέψειας Ὄλυμπον,
> ἀλλ' αἰεὶ περὶ κεῖνον ὀΐζυε καί ἑ φύλαccε,
> εἰc ὅ κέ c' ἢ ἄλοχον ποιήcεται, ἢ ὅ γε δούλην."

'. . . and sit by him yourself—abandon the paths of the gods, never again turn your feet back to Olympos: no, stay with him, for ever whimpering round him and watching over him, until he makes you his wife—or else his slave' (3. 406–9)

are a challenge to the god to imagine what it is like to be mortal, shamed and abused by fellow-mortals. Aphrodite in response sharply reminds Helen that she can make life hell for her. She gives in in silence, follows (420), and is sat down in obedience (425).

It is part of the subtlety of the scene—and part of the reason for its enduring fascination—that it is impossible to pin down definitively the degree to which Aphrodite is an outside compulsion and the degree to which she is an externalization of Helen's own mixed feelings. Consider her words to Paris:

> "ἀλλ' ἴθι νῦν προκάλεccαι ἀρηΐφιλον Μενέλαον
> ἐξαῦτιc μαχέcαcθαι ἐναντίον· ἀλλά c' ἔγωγε
> παύεcθαι κέλομαι, μηδὲ ξανθῶι Μενελάωι
> ἀντίβιον πόλεμον πολεμίζειν ἠδὲ μάχεcθαι
> ἀφραδέωc, μή πωc τάχ' ὑπ' αὐτοῦ δουρὶ δαμήηιc."

'Well, go now, challenge the warrior Menelaos to fight you again face to face. No, I would advise you to stop now, and not pit yourself against fair-haired Menelaos in warfare or combat without thinking—you might well be brought down by his spear.' (3. 432–6)

Some audiences may hear this as straight sarcastic hostility (thus Kirk, for example), but others may detect her love despite herself for Paris. I find myself, like Helen herself perhaps, caught between hearing a wish for his death and a desire to have him alive. Paris' following words are full of sweet seduction, and when he goes to the bed ἅμα δ' εἵπετ' ἄκοιτιc (his wife followed) (447). So despite Iris' line 138 (quoted on p. 97) she remains the ἄκοιτιc (wife) of the loser—or rather of the military loser. Paris has been none the less the conqueror over her shame and self-respect.

With her powerful sexuality and her keen self-reproach, Helen remains a deeply ambivalent and mysterious figure (one who can sustain the role of delivering the final lament for Hektor—see pp. 119–20). Paris on the other hand has no regrets. Many have seen him as a mere dandy or libertine. But he can fight effectively on occasion;[30] and, when set against the earnestness, however admirable, of Hektor or Menelaos, he has, some may feel, an attractive panache and fluency, typified by his leopard-skin as he cavorts out in front at 3. 15 ff. He is not a coward: he accepts Hektor's rebukes with bravado (3. 59 = 6. 333); and he himself proposes the single combat without frivolity or evasion (3. 67 ff.).

---

[30] Esp. in books 11 and 13; cf. Fenik, *TBS* 96.

This will put him in serious danger—he was, as Zeus observes, διόμενον θανέεcθαι (he thought his death had come) (4. 12). Menelaos is the superior warrior. He also has a strong sense of holding the ethical higher ground. He will not trust the *sons* of Priam to solemnize the oath, since they are ὑπερφίαλοι καὶ ἄπιcτοι (violent men and not to be trusted) (3. 106). Paris makes no prayer before he casts: Menelaos is full of righteous indignation:

"Ζεῦ ἄνα, δὸc τείcαcθαι ὅ με πρότεροc κάκ' ἔοργε,
δῖον Ἀλέξανδρον, καὶ ἐμῆιc ὑπὸ χερcὶ δάμαccον,
ὄφρα τιc ἐρρίγηιcι καὶ ὀψιγόνων ἀνθρώπων
ξεινοδόκον κακὰ ῥέξαι, ὅ κεν φιλότητα παράcχηι."

'Zeus, lord, grant me vengeance on the man who did me first wrong, godlike Alexandros, and bring him low under my hands, so that even among generations yet to be born a man may shrink from doing wrong to a host who gives him hospitality.' (3. 351–4)

He sees the issue as black and white, and is impatient with Zeus for not settling the war more quickly. His sense of injury is forthright at 3. 365–8, and at 13. 620 ff. where he cannot understand "οἷον δὴ ἄνδρεccι χαρίζεαι ὑβριcτῆιcι" (the way you [Zeus] favour these men of violence) (633)—see further pp. 169–70.

But for all Menelaos' 'moral victory', it is Paris who keeps and enjoys Helen. Hektor may rebuke him that, if he loses,

"οὐκ ἄν τοι χραίcμηι κίθαριc τά τε δῶρ' Ἀφροδίτηc,
ἥ τε κόμη τό τε εἶδοc, ὅτ' ἐν κονίηιcι μιγείηc."

'There would be no help then in your lyre-playing and the gifts of Aphrodite, your long hair and your looks, when you have your union with the dust.' (3. 54–5)[31]

But Paris stands up to him:

"μή μοι δῶρ' ἐρατὰ πρόφερε χρυcέηc Ἀφροδίτηc·
οὔ τοι ἀπόβλητ' ἐcτὶ θεῶν ἐρικυδέα δῶρα,
ὅccα κεν αὐτοὶ δῶcιν, ἑκὼν δ' οὐκ ἄν τιc ἕλοιτο."

'. . . but do not charge against me golden Aphrodite's lovely gifts: there is no discarding the glorious gifts that come of the gods' own giving, though a man would not take them of his choice.' (3. 64–6)

And he is right: as he says to Helen, πάρα γὰρ θεοί εἰcι καὶ ἡμῖν (there are gods on our side too) (3. 440). Aphrodite has rescued

---

[31] μιγείηc ('you have your union') (55) bitterly echoes the sexual μιχθείc ('mingled with') in 48.

him ῥεῖα μάλ᾽ ὥϲ τε θεός (with the ease of a god) (381), instantly refreshed and clothed him, and fetched Helen, all while no one else knows what on earth is going on (420 ff., 448 ff.) Their palace is fine, with a scented, high *thalamos*, where Paris lies on the bed in fresh clothes. All this is in stark contrast with the plain outside the walls.

> Τὼ μὲν ἄρ᾽ ἐν τρητοῖϲι κατεύναϲθεν λεχέεϲϲιν,
> Ἀτρεΐδηϲ δ᾽ ἀν᾽ ὅμιλον ἐφοίτα θηρὶ ἐοικώϲ,
> εἴ που ἐϲαθρήϲειεν Ἀλέξανδρον θεοειδέα.
> ἀλλ᾽ οὔ τιϲ δύνατο Τρώων κλειτῶν τ᾽ ἐπικούρων
> δεῖξαι Ἀλέξανδρον τότ᾽ ἀρηϊφίλωι Μενελάωι·
> οὐ μὲν γὰρ φιλότητί γ᾽ ἐκεύθανον, εἴ τιϲ ἴδοιτο·
> ἶϲον γάρ ϲφιν πᾶϲιν ἀπήχθετο κηρὶ μελαίνηι.

They then lay down together on the fretted bed. But the son of Atreus went ranging up and down the mass of troops like a wild beast, looking for a sight of godlike Alexandros. But none of the Trojans or their famous allies could then point out Alexandros to the warrior Menelaos: certainly they were not trying to conceal him out of friendship, if any were to have seen him—he was hated by all of them like black death. (3. 448–54)

The Trojans are no more pleased than Menelaos. Yet the word φιλότητι ('out of friendship/love') in 453 reminds us that Paris has the better of them all: just before in lines 441 and 445, and in fifteen out of sixteen other occurrences in the *Iliad*, this dative form refers to sexual intercourse.

And this is how it has been for the past nine years. Paris has kept Helen, and all the other Trojans, for all their distaste, have not prevented him—see further pp. 106–7. Meanwhile the Achaians have been frustrated of success. Menelaos has been outside in the plain in his armour, while Paris has been inside his palace on his double-bed. Menelaos may have 'won' the dispute (3. 457, cf. 439, 4. 13), but Paris possesses Helen's lovely body. With a nice touch of humour this moment encapsulates the war so far.

3.5 *The re-enactment of Paris' guilt*

> "ἦ ῥά νύ μοί τι πίθοιο, Λυκάονοϲ υἱὲ δαΐφρον.
> τλαίηϲ κεν Μενελάωι ἐπιπροέμεν ταχὺν ἰόν,

πᾶcι δέ κε Τρώεccι χάριν καὶ κῦδοc ἄροιο,   95
ἐκ πάντων δὲ μάλιcτα Ἀλεξάνδρωι βαcιλῆϊ.
τοῦ κεν δὴ πάμπρωτα παρ' ἀγλαὰ δῶρα φέροιο,
αἴ κεν ἴδηι Μενέλαον ἀρήϊον Ἀτρέοc υἱὸν
cῶι βέλεϊ δμηθέντα πυρῆc ἐπιβάντ' ἀλεγεινῆc.
ἀλλ' ἄγ' ὀΐcτευcον Μενελάου κυδαλίμοιο,   100
εὔχεο δ' Ἀπόλλωνι Λυκηγενέϊ κλυτοτόξωι
ἀρνῶν πρωτογόνων ῥέξειν κλειτὴν ἑκατόμβην
οἴκαδε νοcτήcαc ἱερῆc εἰc ἄcτυ Ζελείηc."
Ὣc φάτ' Ἀθηναίη, τῶι δὲ φρέναc ἄφρονι πεῖθεν·

'Do something now that I tell you, warlike son of Lykaon. You could bring yourself to shoot a quick-flying arrow at Menelaos, and then you would gain gratitude and glory among all the Trojans, and most of all with prince Alexandros. From him before all others you would win splendid gifts, if he sees Menelaos, Atreus' warrior son, brought down by your arrow and set on the pyre of sorrow. Come then, shoot at glorious Menelaos: and vow to Apollo the Lycian-born, the archer, to make him a splendid sacrifice of first-born lambs on your return home to the town of holy Zeleia.'

So Athene spoke, and persuaded his foolish mind. (4. 93–104)

For the time being, then, Paris is 'sitting pretty'. But there follows immediately a kind of re-enactment of his original outrage, and this is followed in due course by the death of the culprit. I offer this sequence of crime and punishment as a prime example of the way that the *Iliad* prefers implicit rather than explicit ethical colouring. It is also a nice illustration of subtle narrative technique in sequence and linkage.

Pandaros,[32] like Paris, offends against one of Zeus' most basic protectorates: oaths look above all to Zeus for sanction. Like Paris, he has the encouragement of a god—but that does not exculpate him. Hera proposes, and Zeus agrees, that Athene should renew the strife

"πειρᾶν δ' ὥc κε Τρῶεc ὑπερκύδανταc Ἀχαιοὺc
ἄρξωcι πρότεροι ὑπὲρ ὅρκια δηλήcαcθαι."

'and try to make the Trojans first to break the oaths and do harm to the triumphant Achaians.' (4. 66–7 = 71–2)

Taking the form of Laodokos she finds the right man to do it— the gods 'tend to work on what they find in the human heart,

---

[32] He is the fifth to be named in the catalogue of Trojans at 2. 824–7.

The Past Beneath the Present

impulses or plans or scruples'.[33] As well as offering fame and wealth, especially from Paris, she flatters his bowmanship and his hope for the favour of Apollo.[34] It is important, however, that Athene does not coerce him, she does not manipulate his muscles or interfere with his nervous system. She simply says the right kind of thing to the right kind of man—τῶι δὲ φρένας ἄφρονι πεῖθεν (and she persuaded his foolish mind).

αὐτίκα δ' ἔρρεεν αἷμα κελαινεφὲς ἐξ ὠτειλῆς (and immediately dark blood trickled from the wound) (4. 140): 2,089 lines (well over 3 hours) into the poem this is the first blood to flow in the *Iliad*. It is the blood of the man who has been wronged by Paris, wronged again by one who acted πρότερος (first). Menelaos' blood draws from Agamemnon a powerful speech in 155–82, which is both bitter and triumphant as it tries to say two things at once. On the one hand he is righteously confident that Troy must be doomed for breaking the truce:

"εὖ γὰρ ἐγὼ τόδε οἶδα κατὰ φρένα καὶ κατὰ θυμόν·
ἔσσεται ἦμαρ ὅτ' ἄν ποτ' ὀλώληι Ἴλιος ἱρὴ
καὶ Πρίαμος καὶ λαὸς ἐϋμμελίω Πριάμοιο,
Ζεὺς δέ σφι Κρονίδης ὑψίζυγος, αἰθέρι ναίων,
αὐτὸς ἐπισσείηισιν ἐρεμνὴν αἰγίδα πᾶσι
τῆσδ' ἀπάτης κοτέων· τὰ μὲν ἔσσεται οὐκ ἀτέλεστα·"

'One thing I know well in my heart and in my mind. The day will come when sacred Ilios shall be destroyed, and Priam, and the people of Priam of the fine ash spear, and Zeus the son of Kronos who sits on high and dwells in heaven shall himself shake the darkness of his aegis against them all, in anger for this betrayal. These things shall not fail of fulfilment.' (4. 163–8)[35]

On the other hand the war is for the *tīmē* of Menelaos: so if he dies, as Agamemnon fears, the whole expedition will have to disband ignominiously.

The audience knows from the interventions of Athene at 129 ff. and 151 ff. that the wound is not fatal. So they can share Agamemnon's belief that the crime of Pandaros has reconfirmed the doom

---

[33] Macleod, 22.

[34] At 2. 827 the bow is reported to have been the gift of Apollo. Since the armour of Peleus and the new armour of Achilleus are literally gifts of the gods, I do not go along with the standard view (e.g. Schein, 56–7) that gifts like this should be taken figuratively.

[35] On the repetition of 163–5 in the mouth of Hektor in book 6, see p. 123.

on Troy. He goes on to stress the sureness of divine punishment when he encourages the troops at 234 ff.—"οἵ περ πρότεροι ὑπὲρ ὅρκια δηλήcαντο" ('they were the first to break the oaths and do us harm'). Idomeneus reflects the same righteous optimism (4. 268–71). On the other side, Hektor at 7. 69 ff. will make light of the oath-breaking as simply 'the will of Zeus'.[36] But at the Trojan assembly at the end of the day Antenor advocates the surrender of Helen:

"νῦν δ' ὅρκια πιcτὰ
ψευcάμενοι μαχόμεcθα· τῶ οὔ νύ τι κέρδιον ἡμῖν
ἔλπομαι ἐκτελέεcθαι, ἵνα μὴ ῥέξομεν ὧδε."

'We are fighting now with our sworn oaths broken: so I can see no good coming for us, unless we act as I say.' (7. 351–3)

Antenor is overruled by Paris, and the *agorē* confirms the protection of Paris and his continued possession of Helen. Homer leaves the constitutional position here obscure, deliberately no doubt.[37] What matters is that Paris is able to overturn a proposal couched in the first-person plural by a contradiction in the first-person singular (7. 362). Priam tamely ratifies this, latching on to the compromise that Paris is willing to make material compensation. The upshot is that Troy's guilty association is publicly renewed.

This is the context for the Achaian rejection of the Trojan terms in book 7. They respond to Diomedes' confidence:

"μήτ' ἄρ τιc νῦν κτήματ' Ἀλεξάνδροιο δεχέcθω
μήθ' Ἑλένην· γνωτὸν δὲ καὶ ὃc μάλα νήπιός ἐcτιν,
ὡc ἤδη Τρώεccιν ὀλέθρου πείρατ' ἐφῆπται."

'Let no-one now accept possessions from Alexandros, nor Helen either. Even a very fool can see that now the threads of death are fastened on the Trojans.' (7. 400–2)

Analyst complaints about this coming so soon after the Achaian despondency the previous evening (7. 323 ff.) fail to take proper account of the narrative sequence and its effect on the audience.[38]

To return to the earlier narrative, battle is finally joined at

---

[36] Leaf (291) objects to this as 'almost cynical'. But in the context Hektor is in an assertive and optimistic mood.

[37] Cf. Schadewaldt, *IS* 155. Note that no mention whatsoever of Hektor is made in this scene.

[38] The Trojan herald Idaios virtually admits their guilt (7. 388, 390, 393). They know that Paris is in the wrong; yet they have done nothing about him.

4. 446 ff., and is more or less continuous until 6. 72, dominated, though not throughout (see above), by Diomedes. Much blood is shed, yet there are only two really important deaths: Adrestos at the hands of the Atreidai (see pp. 162–3) and Pandaros at the hands of Diomedes at 5. 310. This is some 700 lines (over an hour) after his perfidious arrow-shot at Menelaos. No explicit link is made between the two events. Homer's narrative technique is far above the kind of prosaic and heavy underlining that many critics seem to require.

First, at 5. 95 ff., Pandaros shoots an arrow at Diomedes from a safe distance. As with Menelaos, he hits him but does not wound him seriously. Diomedes prays to Athene

"δὸς δέ τέ μ' ἄνδρα ἑλεῖν καὶ ἐς ὁρμὴν ἔγχεος ἐλθεῖν,
ὅς μ' ἔβαλε φθάμενος καὶ ἐπεύχεται"

'Grant that I may kill this man, that he comes within my spear's throw, the man who shot me before I saw him and is now triumphing over me . . .' (5. 118–19)

She responds and promises him special powers. Homer is too good a poet to have her spell out in so many words 'I will help you to kill the treacherous Pandaros'—the audience must infer that.

Next, at 166 ff. Aineias finds Pandaros and asks him why he does not shoot at the unidentified Achaian who is doing so much damage—

"εἰ μή τις θεός ἐστι κοτεσσάμενος Τρώεσσιν
ἱρῶν μηνίσας· χαλεπὴ δὲ θεοῦ ἔπι μῆνις."

'unless it is some god working his fury on the Trojans, in anger at sacrifice missed, and a god's anger lies hard on us.' (5. 177–8)[39]

Pandaros identifies Diomedes and comes very close to making a connection between Diomedes' likely divine aid and the failure of his own bowmanship:

"εἰ δ' ὅ γ' ἀνὴρ ὅν φημι, δαΐφρων Τυδέος υἱός,
οὐχ ὅ γ' ἄνευθε θεοῦ τάδε μαίνεται, ἀλλά τις ἄγχι
ἕστηκ' ἀθανάτων, νεφέληι εἰλυμένος ὤμους,
ὃς τούτου βέλος ὠκὺ κιχήμενον ἔτραπεν ἄλληι.
ἤδη γάρ οἱ ἐφῆκα βέλος, καί μιν βάλον ὦμον

[39] Is Aineias obliquely referring to the breaking of the truce? That would be like the technique suggested for 1. 62 on p. 54 above.

δεξιὸν ἀντικρὺ διὰ θώρηκος γυάλοιο·
καί μιν ἔγωγ' ἐφάμην Ἀϊδωνῆϊ προϊάψειν,
ἔμπης δ' οὐκ ἐδάμασσα· θεός νύ τίς ἐστι κοτήεις."

'But if he is the man I think, Tydeus' warrior son, then this rampage of his cannot be without a god's help, but one of the immortals is standing by him, with mist wrapped round his shoulders, and turned aside the sharp arrow that was finding its mark in him—I have already let fly an arrow at him, and struck him in the right shoulder, straight through the corselet's front-piece. And I thought that I would send him on his way to Hades, but for all that I did not bring him down—so this must be some god in anger.' (5. 184–91)

He goes on to regret having left his chariot at home, coming to Troy with his bow instead:

"ὣς λίπον, αὐτὰρ πεζὸς ἐς Ἴλιον εἰλήλουθα
τόξοισιν πίσυνος· τὰ δέ μ' οὐκ ἄρ' ἔμελλον ὀνήσειν.
ἤδη γὰρ δοιοῖσιν ἀριστήεσσιν ἐφῆκα,
Τυδεΐδηι τε καὶ Ἀτρεΐδηι, ἐκ δ' ἀμφοτέροιιν
ἀτρεκὲς αἷμ' ἔσσευα βαλών, ἤγειρα δὲ μᾶλλον.
τῶ ῥα κακῆι αἴσηι ἀπὸ πασσάλου ἀγκύλα τόξα
ἤματι τῶι ἑλόμην ὅτε Ἴλιον εἰς ἐρατεινὴν
ἡγεόμην Τρώεσσι, φέρων χάριν Ἕκτορι δίωι."

'So I left them, and came on foot to Ilios, relying on my bow, which it seems was to do me no good. I have already shot at two leading fighters, the son of Tydeus and the son of Atreus, and I set the blood running from both with a plain hit, but only roused them to greater fury. So it was under a cross fate that I took my curved bow from its peg on that day when I led my Trojans to lovely Ilios, as a service of friendship to godlike Hektor.' (5. 204–11)

An alert audience will appreciate the irony.

Diomedes has yet, however, to get Pandaros in his clutches, as he prayed in line 118. Pandaros fulfils this voluntarily and characteristically in a carefully plotted sequence. Aineias asks Pandaros to take over his horses so that he can confront Diomedes (217 ff.); Pandaros replies that he will himself fight while Aineias controls the horses (229 ff.); Diomedes resolves to take on both of them (241 ff.). Now that they are within hearing distance, Pandaros proclaims (276 ff.) that he was the unidentified bowman; then he throws and prematurely boasts. Now at last Athene guides Diomedes' spear to the fulfilment of his prayer.[40]

---

[40] There may be poetic justice in the (physiologically impossible) death-wound which chops out the oath-breaker's tongue.

None of the Trojans even criticizes Pandaros for truce-breaking, let alone attempts to disown or punish him. He continues to fight among them, and Aineias positively encourages and helps him. Aineias is also, I suggest, caught up in the implicit sequence of crime and punishment. This is not directly through his wound, which is quickly cured, but through the opportunity that this gives Sthenelos and Diomedes, in the meantime, to capture his horses. Diomedes had foreseen this possibility, and told Sthenelos at length how exceptionally fine these horses are, thanks to their pedigree from a stallion given to Tros by Zeus (259–73). This reputation is twice confirmed in practice later in the poem. At 8. 80 ff. Nestor is in some trouble when Diomedes rescues him and offers him a 'ride' with these horses captured from Aineias (note 8. 105–7 = 5. 221–3). And these are the very horses which will take Diomedes to victory in the main event of the funeral games of Patroklos. When he rises to the challenge, their history is recalled:

> ἵππους δὲ Τρωιοὺς ὕπαγε ζυγόν, οὕς ποτ' ἀπηύρα
> Αἰνείαν, ἀτὰρ αὐτὸν ὑπεξεςάωςεν Ἀπόλλων.

. . . and brought under the yoke those horses of Tros' stock which he had taken that time from Aineias, though Apollo rescued their master. (23. 291–2)

Aineias loses these wonderful beasts as a result of pairing up with Pandaros. The narrative connection is direct; the ethical connection is left implicit.

As Pandaros' crime is a kind of re-enactment of the hospitality-breaking deed of Paris, so Aineias is the equivalent of the Trojans in the larger story. They go on with Paris in their midst, and they fail to renounce him. They are guilty by association; and in due course they will pay for it.

4

Troy from the Inside

4.1 Not 'us' against 'them'

ὣс τότ' ἐπαссύτεραι Δαναῶν κίνυντο φάλαγγεс
νωλεμέωс πόλεμόνδε· κέλευε δὲ οἶсιν ἕκαстοс
ἡγεμόνων· οἱ δ' ἄλλοι ἀκὴν ἴсαν, οὐδέ κε φαίηс
τόссον λαὸν ἔπεсθαι ἔχοντ' ἐν стήθεсιν αὐδήν,   430
сιγῆι δειδιότεс сημάντοραс· ἀμφὶ δὲ πᾶсι
τεύχεα ποικίλ' ἔλαμπε, τὰ εἱμένοι ἐстιχόωντο.
Τρῶεс δ', ὥс τ' ὄϊεс πολυπάμονοс ἀνδρὸс ἐν αὐλῆι
μυρίαι ἑстήκαсιν ἀμελγόμεναι γάλα λευκόν,
ἀζηχὲс μεμακυῖαι ἀκούουсαι ὄπα ἀρνῶν,   435
ὣс Τρώων ἀλαλητὸс ἀνὰ стρατὸν εὐρὺν ὀρώρει·
οὐ γὰρ πάντων ἦεν ὁμὸс θρόοс οὐδ' ἴα γῆρυс,
ἀλλὰ γλῶсс' ἐμέμικτο, πολύκλητοι δ' ἔсαν ἄνδρεс.

So then, rank after rank, the Danaan battalions moved in ceaseless advance to war. Each of the leaders gave commands to his men: and the rest of the army moved in silence, and you would not think that so many men with voices in their chests were marching behind them, as they went silently, in fear of their commanders: and round each of them as they marched was the gleam of the beaten armour they wore. But the Trojans, like ewes standing innumerable in a rich man's farmyard, ready to give their white milk, and bleating incessantly as they hear their lambs' voices—so hubbub rose from the Trojans throughout the breadth of the army: since there was no common speech or single language shared by all, but a mixture of tongues, and men called from many different lands.
(4. 427–38)

From the fifth century BC onwards the Trojans became equated with the alien East, and the *Iliad* became a nationalist Hellenic epic. This view is ubiquitous in the scholia and still common among modern critics.[1] Yet it has very little basis in the poem; and it has often led to perversely one-eyed interpretations. A pair of illustrations happen to occur close together at the end of book 8. Hektor ends his jubilant speech persuading the Trojans to stay out in the plain:

> "εἰ γὰρ ἐγὼν ὣc
> εἴην ἀθάνατοc καὶ ἀγήρωc ἤματα πάντα,
> τιοίμην δ' ὣc τίετ' Ἀθηναίη καὶ Ἀπόλλων,
> ὣc νῦν ἡμέρη ἥδε κακὸν φέρει Ἀργείοιcιν."

'Oh, if only I could be deathless and ageless for all time, and honoured as Athene and Apollo are honoured, as surely as this coming day brings disaster to the Argives!' (8. 538–41)

Willcock speaks for most commentators when he says 'even to consider such a possibility shows dangerous presumption in a human being. Hektor often displays this sort of lack of judgement'.[2] But Hektor is *not* considering the possibility: as Leaf illustrates with plentiful parallels (to which add 9. 445–6, 12. 323 ff.), this is an *adynaton*. The wish is as impossible as the prediction is sure—the sentiment would lose its point if the wish were a real possibility.

After this comes the simile likening the Trojan camp-fires to the stars at night, and including the clause γέγηθε δέ τε φρένα ποιμήν (and the shepherd's heart is glad) (559). Adam Parry excused what he took to be an inappropriate touch as the pressure of the oral tradition: 'the imminent disaster of the Achaeans is embodied in those very fires. Yet Homer pauses in the dramatic trajectory of his narrative to represent not the horror of the fires, but their glory.' Michael Reeve, taking issue, does not question the inappropriateness of the glad shepherd, but explains that 'Homer elaborates his similes without regard to the narrative'.[3] What neither even considers is that the shepherd is glad because the Trojans

---

[1] As in the opening pages of Griffin, *HLD*, for instance, or Edwards, *HPI* 173, 'a mighty Greek achievement against a foreign foe'. Gorgias' *Palamedes* (82 B 11a, 7 *DK*) already assumes that the Trojans are βάρβαροι (barbarians) and speak a foreign language.

[2] Willcock, *Comp.* 92 (cf., for different reasons, Nagy, 148–50). F. Combellack, *AJP* 102 (1981), 115 ff. shares my view.

[3] Parry, 'LA' 1 ff. (quote from p. 2), M. Reeve, *CQ* 23 (1973), 1 ff. Lines 557–8 in the simile have been questioned. 557 seems to me a fine observation, above question. 558 makes different and less good sense than 16. 300: the lucidity of the atmosphere is, it seems, envisaged as breaking out from the distant heavens.

are glad, contributing to the simile-picture the same feeling as the watch-fires give the Trojans. The simile at 9. 4–7 correspondingly reflects the Achaians' mood. The previous seventy lines have all been from the Trojan point of view, yet Parry and Reeve both speak as though this never happened, as though the audience is invariably Achaian-minded.

So far as I can see, the Trojans in the *Iliad* are not presented as alien. This should inhibit the assumption that any audience automatically sides with the Achaians. Edith Hall's new book saves me from labouring the point that 'ethnographically' the Trojans are virtually indistinguishable from the Achaians. In all those areas which characterize ethnic difference they are the same: political and social structures, kinship institutions, and funeral customs, for instance. On a more mundane level, consider housing, clothing, agriculture, food, furniture, and armour.[4] Even Priam's polygamy is not clearly different from the Achaian fathering of νόθοι. The only passage that gives him (unlike any other Trojan) more than one full-status wife is at 22. 46 ff., where Laothoë, daughter of Altes, seems to be more than merely one of ἐνὶ μεγάροιϲι γυναῖκεϲ (the women in my house) (24. 497).

Of all ethnic differentia the two most prominent, and most likely to lead to conflict, are surely religion and language. So it is important that the Achaians and Trojans share exactly the same gods and cult-practices. Athene favours the Achaians, but she still has her temple in Troy;[5] Apollo favours the Trojans, but he is also, for example, the patron of Kalchas (1. 86 ff.). Troy is generally a pious and god-favoured city, with a past which had seen close contact with the Olympians such as through Laomedon and Ganymedes. Zeus is reluctant to see battle joined at all, for as he says:

> "ἐγὼ coì δῶκα ἑκὼν ἀέκοντί γε θυμῶι·
> αἳ γὰρ ὑπ' ἠελίωι τε καὶ οὐρανῶι ἀϲτερόεντι
> ναιετάουϲι πόληεϲ ἐπιχθονίων ἀνθρώπων,
> τάων μοι περὶ κῆρι τιέϲκετο Ἴλιοϲ ἱρὴ
> καὶ Πρίαμοϲ καὶ λαὸϲ ἐϋμμελίω Πριάμοιο.
> οὐ γάρ μοί ποτε βωμὸϲ ἐδεύετο δαιτὸϲ ἐΐϲηϲ,
> λοιβῆϲ τε κνίϲηϲ τε· τὸ γὰρ λάχομεν γέραϲ ἡμεῖϲ."

---

[4] In the later Greek iconographic tradition Trojans (equated with Phrygians) are clearly differentiated by clothing.
[5] The Palladion is never referred to in the *Iliad*.

'I have agreed to grant you this of my own will, though not my heart's will. Of all the cities of earthly men that lie beneath the sun and the starry heaven, the most cherished in my heart was sacred Ilios, and Priam and the people of Priam of the fine ash spear. My altar there was never without a share of the feasting, libation of wine and the smoke of sacrifice, which is our rightful honour.' (4. 44–9)

As for language, there is no suggestion at all that the Trojans speak a language different from the Achaians. The epithet of the Carians in the catalogue—βαρβαροφώνων (whose speech is foreign) (2. 867)—implies that this would not be applicable to the Trojans or to most of their allies.[6] There are, however, some allusions early in the poem to the linguistic diversity of the Trojan *epikouroi*; and these are perhaps the best evidence there is for any pro-Achaian/anti-Trojan colouring. When Iris, in the form of Polites, first appears to the Trojans, she tells Hektor to organize the troops:

"πολλοὶ γὰρ κατὰ ἄςτυ μέγα Πριάμου ἐπίκουροι,
ἄλλη δ' ἄλλων γλῶςςα πολυςπερέων ἀνθρώπων·
τοῖςιν ἕκαςτος ἀνὴρ ςημαινέτω οἷςί περ ἄρχει,
τῶν δ' ἐξηγείςθω κοςμηςάμενος πολιήτας."

'There are many allies with us in Priam's great city, but they are men from far and wide and each speaks a different tongue. Have each leader give his orders to the men he commands, and have him marshal his own countrymen and lead them out to battle.' (2. 803–6)

Soon after, at 3. 1–9, the Trojans advance noisily while the Achaians (οἱ δέ . . .) march in silence. And then, most prominently, there is the passage at 4. 422 ff. as the two armies close for the first actual clash. But this contrast-motif is not repeated again, and it is not consistently maintained. At 11. 50 and 13. 169, for instance, it is the Achaians who are noisy; at 13. 39–44 it is the Trojans who are silent; and at 14. 400 both are clamorous.

Lines such as these in this context might well be taken as preparation for a massacre of the ill-disciplined aliens. So it is interesting that this is not fulfilled. In the first round the battle follows a 'chain reaction',[7] and casualties are more or less even,

---

[6] It is curious that geographically these Carians come from the heartland of Ionia. Greeks had been there for at least 200 years before Homer, and in Miletos since Mycenaean times. I find it hard to believe Kirk, ad loc., that these barbarophones are a conscientious evasion of anachronism. Hall, 9 and n. 30, wonders whether the epithet is a post-Homeric intrusion.

[7] Cf. Fenik, *TBS* 10.

as is brought out by the repetition of ἐν κονίῃcι παρ' ἀλλήλοιcι
τετάcθην ('they lay stretched in the dust side by side') in 4. 536
and 544. Indeed the first day of battle as a whole is bad for both
sides (see further p. 137). It is true that during Diomedes' successes the Trojans are in trouble, but Achaian success is to be
expected after the breach of the truce. This is the 'normal' tendency, and it makes the Trojan successes later all the more
impressive.[8]

Throughout the *Iliad* Trojan casualties are generally heavier
than Achaian. Typically, ten out of forty-four Achaians named in
the catalogue are killed in the course of the poem, while seventeen
out of twenty-seven named Trojans and allies come to grief.[9] This
does not, however, demonstrate the alleged chauvinism. The
apparent national bias may be partly explained by a bias so ten-
aciously built into the poetic tradition that it was impossible to
purge.[10] At the same time the usual patterns of Achaian success,
which are constantly tending to reassert themselves, accentuate
the extraordinary Trojan successes during the span of the poem,
especially in books 8 to 17. Yet beneath the reverses of the *Iliad*
the audience can still perceive the long-term military superiority
which will culminate in the fall of Troy. The Achaians will be
victorious; the Trojans are doomed by Paris. And yet the poem
is not one-sided. This is very far from the triumph of the righteous
compatriots over the alien infidel.

While the Trojan *epikouroi* supply linguistic variety, they too
are not treated as foreign or as barbarous. On the contrary, the
Lycian leaders, Sarpedon and Glaukos (cousins, see 6. 196 ff.)
stand out from both sides for their nobility and chivalry as well
as their unfailing martial courage. On several occasions, indeed,
they inspire a rally, reminding Hektor and the Trojans of their
heroic calling.[11]

Glaukos' first action in the *Iliad* is at 6. 119 ff., where he bravely
faces Diomedes (see above p. 58). Sarpedon's is to rally Hektor,
at 5. 471 ff. Not long after this he has a prominent and exciting
encounter with Tlepolemos—a son of Zeus against a grandson of

    [8] Cf. Owen, 45–6.
    [9] Note the predictions in 2. 832–4, 859–61, 872–5. The figures are derived
from Willcock, *Comp.* 34, 38.
    [10] This is proposed in the justly classic essay "Ἀεὶ φιλέλλην ὁ Ποιητής;" ('Is the
Poet always pro-Greek?') by Kakridis, *H. Rev.* 54–67.
    [11] See Fenik, *TBS* 49–53 for this typical sequence.

Zeus (5. 627–98). Yet Sarpedon's victory is darkened by clear
hints that he himself has not long to live. He is wounded, πατὴρ
δ' ἔτι λοιγὸν ἄμυνεν (but his father kept destruction from him for
the time) (662). When Odysseus decides not to assail the wounded
man, we are told that it was not μόρcιμον ('fated') for him to kill
him (674 ff.). Sarpedon's plea to Hektor for rescue at 684–8 foreshadows the plea he will make to Glaukos in deadly earnest at
16. 492–501. As this sympathetic leader recalls in his introductory
speech, he has left a wife and young son at home (480, cf. 688).
Clearly Sarpedon is in some ways a double and a foil for Hektor.
And they are both to die within days.

4.2 Hektor's fatal kindness

εὖτε πύλας ἵκανε διερχόμενος μέγα ἄςτυ
Cκαιάς, τῆι ἄρ' ἔμελλε διεξίμεναι πεδίονδε,
ἔνθ' ἄλοχος πολύδωρος ἐναντίη ἦλθε θέουσα
Ἀνδρομάχη, θυγάτηρ μεγαλήτορος Ἠετίωνος,   395
Ἠετίων, ὃς ἔναιεν ὑπὸ Πλάκωι ὑληέσσηι,
Θήβηι Ὑποπλακίηι, Κιλίκεσς' ἄνδρεσσιν ἀνάσσων·
τοῦ περ δὴ θυγάτηρ ἔχεθ' Ἕκτορι χαλκοκορυστῆι.
ἥ οἱ ἔπειτ' ἤντης', ἅμα δ' ἀμφίπολος κίεν αὐτῆι
παῖδ' ἐπὶ κόλπωι ἔχους' ἀταλάφρονα, νήπιον αὔτως,   400
Ἑκτορίδην ἀγαπητόν, ἀλίγκιον ἀστέρι καλῶι,
τόν ῥ' Ἕκτωρ καλέεσκε Cκαμάνδριον, αὐτὰρ οἱ ἄλλοι
Ἀστυάνακτ'· οἶος γὰρ ἐρύετο Ἴλιον Ἕκτωρ.
ἤτοι ὁ μὲν μείδησεν ἰδὼν ἐς παῖδα σιωπῆι·
Ἀνδρομάχη δέ οἱ ἄγχι παρίστατο δάκρυ χέουσα,   405
ἔν τ' ἄρα οἱ φῦ χειρὶ ἔπος τ' ἔφατ' ἔκ τ' ὀνόμαζε·
"δαιμόνιε, φθίσει σε τὸ σὸν μένος, οὐδ' ἐλεαίρεις
παῖδά τε νηπίαχον καὶ ἔμ' ἄμμορον, ἣ τάχα χήρη
cεῦ ἔσομαι·"

When he had crossed the great city and reached the Skaian gates, where
he would make his way out to the plain, there came running to meet him
his dowered wife Andromache, daughter of great-hearted Eëtion—
Eëtion, who had lived under wooded Plakos, in Thebe-under-Plakos,
ruling over his people the Kilikes: he it was whose daughter was wife to
Hektor of the bronze helmet. She then came up to him, and with her
there went a maid carrying at her breast their innocent child, no more
than a baby, Hektor's only beloved son, shining lovely as a star. Hektor's
name for him was Skamandrios, but the others called him Astyanax,

Lord of the City, because Hektor was Ilios' sole protection. Hektor looked
at his son and smiled in silence. Andromache came close to him with her
tears falling, and took his hand and spoke to him: 'Poor dear man, your
own brave spirit will destroy you, and you have no pity for your baby
son and for me your doomed wife, who will soon be your widow.'
(6. 392–409)

Hektor, from his first mention at 1. 242 f. (already with the epithet
ἀνδροφόνοιο (murderous)) until he goes into Troy in book 6, is seen
externally in his role as figurehead. He rebukes Paris, fights hard,
rallies the Trojans, and even alarms Diomedes (5. 596–606)—all
this establishes him as the special protector of Troy. It is surprising perhaps that there is only one place where a clear connection
is made between Hektor's name and the various forms of ἔχειν
('have', 'hold'). This is in Sarpedon's complaint at 5. 472 ff:

> "Ἕκτορ, πῆι δή τοι μένος οἴχεται ὃ πρὶν ἔχεσκες;
> φῆς που ἄτερ λαῶν πόλιν ἐξέμεν ἠδ' ἐπικούρων
> οἶος, σὺν γαμβροῖσι κασιγνήτοισί τε σοῖσι.
> τῶν νῦν οὔ τιν' ἐγὼ ἰδέειν δύναμ' οὐδὲ νοῆσαι"

'Hektor, where has that strength gone that *you had* before? You used to
say—did you not?—that you *could hold* this city alone, without help from
your people or allies, just you and your brothers and brothers-in-law. I
cannot now catch sight or glimpse of any of them . . .' (5. 472–5)

There does, however, seem to be another oblique allusion near
the end of the poem in Andromache's comment:

> "ἦ γὰρ ὄλωλας ἐπίσκοπος, ὅς τέ μιν αὐτὴν
> ῥύσκευ, ἔχες δ' ἀλόχους κεδνὰς καὶ νήπια τέκνα,"

'you used to protect the city, and *keep safe* her loved wives and little
children.' (24. 729–30)

It is possible that the 'etymology' is to be regarded as too obvious
to be laboured.[12]

The episode of Hektor in Troy (6. 237–7. 7, prepared by
6. 73–118) is, however, revealing not only for Hektor himself, but
for the whole picture of Troy—'so far from being a mere interlude,

---

[12] I should perhaps dissociate this kind of conscious etymology (however falla-
cious) from the school led by Nagy (*The Best of the Achaeans*), which regards
alleged etymologies from the distant linguistic past to be some kind of key to
Homeric epic.

[it] creates a tension which sustains the poem to its end'.[13] On his
first arrival Hektor is seen in his civic aspect: he comes to the
public landmarks of the oak tree and Skaian gates (6. 237, see
p. 95 above), and is immediately surrounded by women:

> Ἕκτωρ δ' ὡς Cκαιάς τε πύλας καὶ φηγὸν ἵκανεν,
> ἀμφ' ἄρα μιν Τρώων ἄλοχοι θέον ἠδὲ θύγατρες
> εἰρόμεναι παῖδάς τε κασιγνήτους τε ἔτας τε
> καὶ πόσιας· ὁ δ' ἔπειτα θεοῖς εὔχεσθαι ἀνώγει
> πάσας ἐξείης· πολλῇσι δὲ κήδε' ἐφῆπτο.

Now when Hektor came to the Skaian gates and the oak tree, the wives
and daughters of the Trojans came running to surround him, asking after
their sons and brothers and kinsmen and husbands. He told each one of
them to pray to the gods: but sorrow was there in store for many.
(6. 237–41)

The city is full of dependent women (cf. 6. 81–2, 8. 57, etc.), and
moreover they form a network of marital and kinship relationships.

This leads by association of thought as well as topography to the
great palace of Priam (6. 242–50) with its θάλαμοι (*thalamoi*), which
house all the γαμβροί and κασίγνητοι (brothers and brothers-in-law)
that Sarpedon alluded to. The fine building is the breeding-ground
of a great dynasty[14]—as is promptly illustrated. Hektor finds
Hekabe accompanied by her beautiful daughter Laodike (252),
who presumably sleeps in one of the twelve *thalamoi* of 247–50
with her husband Helikaon, son of Antenor (3. 121–4). In other
words she is a daughter-in-law of Theano, the priestess of Athene,
and a sister-in-law of Helenos, who first proposed that Hektor
should go to the city and speak μητέρι σῇι καὶ ἐμῆι (to your mother
and mine) (6. 87), i.e. to Hekabe and Theano.

It is only with Andromache that a clearly valedictory element

---

[13] Macleod, 149. On Hektor's role in general, see Erbse, 'HI'; W. Schadewaldt,
Hellas und Hesperien (Zürich, 1970), i. 21 ff. (first publ. 1956); Redfield, *NCI*
passim, esp. Ch. 4. Of the many discussions of Hektor in Troy I have found among
the most helpful: Schadewaldt, *HWW* 227 ff.; G. Brocchia, *RFIC* 92 (1964),
385–96; H. Herter, *Grazer Beitr.* 1 (1973), 157 ff.; Redfield, *NCI* 119–23; M. B.
Arthur in H. Foley (ed.), *Reflections of Women in Antiquity* (New York, 1981),
19 ff.; Schein, 173 ff.; Edwards, *HPI* 206–13; Lohmann, 96 ff.; id., *Die Andromache-
Szenen der Ilias* (Hildesheim, 1988).
[14] At home in Sparta Menelaos recalls the sack of Troy: "ἐπεὶ μάλα πολλὰ πάθον,
καὶ ἀπώλεσα οἶκον/εὖ μάλα ναιετάοντα, κεχανδότα πολλὰ καὶ ἐσθλά." ('I have suffered
much and have destroyed a fine dwelling full of good things.') (*Od.* 4. 95–6). Other
'dynasties' alluded to in the *Iliad* are those of Eëtion (6. 421 ff.), Neleus (11. 691 ff.),
and, through scattered references, Antenor.

comes into the episode; but before that there are signs of the associative guilt and the inescapable fate in which Hektor is implicated. This also gives the 'personal' narrative a 'political' dimension. Above all, when Hekabe goes to the store-room to select the finest cloth of all[15] for Athene:

> αὐτὴ δ' ἐc θάλαμον κατεβήcετο κηώεντα,
> ἔνθ' ἔcαν οἱ πέπλοι παμποίκιλα ἔργα γυναικῶν
> Cιδονίων, τὰc αὐτὸc Ἀλέξανδρος θεοειδὴc
> ἤγαγε Cιδονίηθεν, ἐπιπλὼc εὐρέα πόντον,
> τὴν ὁδὸν ἣν Ἑλένην περ ἀνήγαγεν εὐπατέρειαν·
> τῶν ἕν' ἀειραμένη Ἑκάβη φέρε δῶρον Ἀθήνηι,
> ὃc κάλλιcτοc ἔην ποικίλμαcιν ἠδὲ μέγιcτοc,
> ἀcτὴρ δ' ὣc ἀπέλαμπεν· ἔκειτο δὲ νείατοc ἄλλων.

She herself went down into the sweet-smelling storeroom where her robes were kept—the intricate work of Sidonian women, who had been brought from Sidon by godlike Alexandros himself, as he sailed over the breadth of the sea on that same voyage which carried back Helen, daughter of a noble house. Hekabe lifted out one of the robes and took it as a gift for Athene—it was the finest in its woven decoration and the largest, gleaming like a star, and it lay beneath all the others. (6. 288–95)

Like the cloth, Troy is magnificent but tainted. Athene's response is doubly inevitable: ἀνένευε δὲ Παλλὰc Ἀθήνη (but Pallas Athene shook her head in refusal) (311).

Again the train of thought as well as the topography leads to the next location. Paris' house is ἐγγύθι τε Πριάμοιο καὶ Ἕκτοροc, ἐν πόλει ἄκρηι (close to Priam and Hektor, on the city's height) (317)—which is also where the temple of Athene is (297). It is that very proximity which, so to speak, infects Hektor and Priam. This luxurious and childless mansion was the very first Trojan dwelling entered by the poem, back in book 3. Yet, even here, it would be over-simple to moralize in black and white. Paris is the same man as before—vain, languid, yet charming and willing to make an effort under reproach. And Helen is still the same half-wife in a half-home with a man whom she half-loves and half-wishes would go out and get killed. She also still combines self-reproach with a special awareness of their suffering as the stuff of future song:

"οἷcιν ἐπὶ Ζεὺc θῆκε κακὸν μόρον, ὡc καὶ ὀπίccω
ἀνθρώποιcι πελώμεθ᾽ ἀοίδιμοι ἐccομένοιcι."

'On us two Zeus has set a doom of misery, so that in time to come we
can be themes of song for men of future generations.' (6. 357–8)

Even though it is a κακὸν μόρον (doom of misery), she does offer
Hektor a future in poetry.

Helen speaks intimately to Hektor, and he replies kindly to her.
As with Hekabe and Andromache, he has to refuse her plea to
stay.[16] The way is prepared here for a masterstroke at the very
end of the poem. The third and last and most personal lament for
Hektor is given to her:

"Ἕκτορ, ἐμῶι θυμῶι δαέρων πολὺ φίλτατε πάντων,
ἦ μέν μοι πόcιc ἐcτὶν Ἀλέξανδρος θεοειδής,
ὅc μ᾽ ἄγαγε Τροίηνδ᾽· ὡc πρὶν ὤφελλον ὀλέcθαι.
ἤδη γὰρ νῦν μοι τόδ᾽ ἐεικοcτὸν ἔτος ἐcτὶν   765
ἐξ οὗ κεῖθεν ἔβην καὶ ἐμῆc ἀπελήλυθα πάτρηc·
ἀλλ᾽ οὔ πω cεῦ ἄκουcα κακὸν ἔπος οὐδ᾽ ἀcύφηλον·
ἀλλ᾽ εἴ τίc με καὶ ἄλλος ἐνὶ μεγάροιcιν ἐνίπτοι
δαέρων ἢ γαλόων ἢ εἰνατέρων εὐπέπλων,
ἢ ἑκυρή—ἑκυρὸc δὲ πατὴρ ὡc ἤπιος αἰεί—,   770
ἀλλὰ cὺ τὸν ἐπέεccι παραιφάμενος κατέρυκες,
cῆι τ᾽ ἀγανοφροcύνηι καὶ cοῖc ἀγανοῖc ἐπέεccι.
τῶ cέ θ᾽ ἅμα κλαίω καὶ ἔμ᾽ ἄμμορον ἀχνυμένη κῆρ·
οὐ γάρ τίc μοι ἔτ᾽ ἄλλος ἐνὶ Τροίηι εὐρείηι
ἤπιος οὐδὲ φίλος, πάντες δέ με πεφρίκαcιν."   775

'Hektor, dearest to my heart by far of all my husband's brothers—my
husband is godlike Alexandros: he brought me to Troy, and how I wish
that I had died before that! This is now the twentieth year since I came
from there and left my own native land. But in all that time I have never
heard a hard word from you or any rudeness. But if anyone spoke harshly
to me in the house—one of your brothers or sisters or your brothers'
fine-dressed wives, or your mother (though your father was always kind
to me as a real father)—then you would speak winning words to them
and stop them, through your own gentle-hearted way and your gentle
words. And so I weep in anguish of heart both for you and for my own
ill-fated self. There is no-one else now in the broad land of Troy to be

---

[16] Cf. Kakridis, *H. Rev.* 68 ff., where he acutely observes 'it is the chief function
of woman in the *Iliad* to exercise consciously restricting power over men'. He
does not, however, note the exception which proves the rule: Helen with Paris—
see 6. 337–8.

kind to me and a friend, but they all shudder with loathing for me.'
(24. 762–75)

The beauty of her lines owes much to the ambivalence of her role.[17] The reason why all the other members of the house of Priam have been so unpleasant to her is because her presence has been the cause of all their troubles. Her union with Paris is the 'rotten apple' which corrupts all the rest of Troy. Rather as it was Patroklos' gentleness and compassion which led to his death (cf. p. 213 on 19. 287 ff.), so it is, in a sense, Hektor's kindness to Helen that destroys him. The others might well complain that it is his complaisance, his foolish indulgence to the slut, that spells destruction for the whole city—if only he (and Priam) had got rid of Helen, then he would not be lying dead for her to lament him.

Yet such is the subtlety of the *Iliad*'s portrayal of Helen, that it would be a rare member of the audience who would share the attitudes of Helen's other in-laws. Most would surely warm to Hektor's ἀγανοφροσύνη (gentle-heartedness). The poem does not have a straightforward morality of crime and punishment; its ethics are blurred and made controversial and perennially interesting by human sympathy and complexity.

The great scene between Hektor and Andromache is held between opposing forces: optimism and pessimism, fear and bravery, union and separation, laughter and tears (δακρυόεν γελάcαcα (smiling with tears in her eyes) 484[18]), male and female. An initial signal of the narrative place of this scene, caught in the middle, is the trouble that the poet takes to set it at the borderline between home and battlefield.

4.3   *The union of misfortunes*

Ὣc εἰπὼν οὗ παιδὸc ὀρέξατο φαίδιμοc Ἕκτωρ·
ἂψ δ' ὁ πάϊc πρὸc κόλπον ἐϋζώνοιο τιθήνηc

---

[17] See Macleod's fine note on 24. 771–2. There is a comparable but different beauty to the words of the shade of Odysseus' mother: "ἀλλά με cόc τε πόθοc cά τε μήδεα, φαίδιμ' Ὀδυccεῦ, cή τ' ἀγανοφροcύνη μελιηδέα θυμὸν ἀπηύρα" ('It was longing for you, my pride Odysseus—for you with your wisdom and gentle ways—that parted me from a life still sweet') (tr. Shewring).

[18] The nearest comparable conflict of emotions I have found in Homer is that of Eurykleia at *Od.* 19. 471, τὴν δ' ἅμα χάρμα καὶ ἄλγοc ἕλε φρένα (joy and sorrow seized on her heart at once).

ἐκλίνθη ἰάχων, πατρὸς φίλου ὄψιν ἀτυχθείς,
ταρβήσας χαλκόν τε ἰδὲ λόφον ἱππιοχαίτην,
δεινὸν ἀπ' ἀκροτάτης κόρυθος νεύοντα νοήσας.   470
ἐκ δὲ γέλασσε πατήρ τε φίλος καὶ πότνια μήτηρ·
αὐτίκ' ἀπὸ κρατὸς κόρυθ' εἵλετο φαίδιμος Ἕκτωρ,
καὶ τὴν μὲν κατέθηκεν ἐπὶ χθονὶ παμφανόωσαν·
αὐτὰρ ὅ γ' ὃν φίλον υἱὸν ἐπεὶ κύσε πῆλέ τε χερσίν,
εἶπε δ' ἐπευξάμενος Διί τ' ἄλλοισίν τε θεοῖσι·   475
"Ζεῦ ἄλλοι τε θεοί, δότε δὴ καὶ τόνδε γενέσθαι
παῖδ' ἐμόν, ὡς καὶ ἐγώ περ, ἀριπρεπέα Τρώεσσιν,
ὧδε βίην τ' ἀγαθόν, καὶ Ἰλίου ἶφι ἀνάσσειν·
καί ποτέ τις εἴποι 'πατρός γ' ὅδε πολλὸν ἀμείνων'
ἐκ πολέμου ἀνιόντα· φέροι δ' ἔναρα βροτόεντα   480
κτείνας δήϊον ἄνδρα, χαρείη δὲ φρένα μήτηρ."

So speaking glorious Hektor reached out to take his son. But the child shrank back crying against the breast of his girdled nurse, terrified at the sight of his own father, frightened by the bronze and the crest of horse-hair, as he saw it nodding dreadfully from the top of the helmet. His dear father and his honoured mother laughed aloud at this, and glorious Hektor took the helmet straight from his head and laid it gleaming bright on the ground. Then he kissed his dear son and dandled him in his arms, and said in prayer to Zeus and the other gods: 'Zeus and you other gods, grant that this my son may become, as I have been, preeminent among the Trojans, as strong and brave as I, and may he rule in strength over Ilios. And let people say, as he returns from the fighting: "This man is better by far than his father." May he carry home the bloody spoils of the enemy he has killed, and bring joy to his mother's heart.' (6. 466–81)[19]

The baby boy is also caught and dandled between two worlds, reflected in his two names, one taken from the river of Troy's peacetime fertility, the other from his father's role in war. On the one side is the sweet-scented, soft embrace against caring breasts (400, 467, 483): on the other the armed warrior spattered with gore (266–8), and wearing the helmet which terrifies his infant. For all his tenderness, Hektor's prayer for his son is not for a future of peace and pleasure. He prays solemnly that he may ruthlessly destroy the sons and husbands and fathers of many other families. If his hopes are fulfilled, the δήϊον ἄνδρα (the enemy) will suffer the fate that Andromache fears on his own behalf: if,

[19] Line 474 gives the only kisses of affection in the *Iliad* (there are plenty in the *Odyssey*). Note, however, that πάλλω ('brandish', 'dandle') is common in battle contexts. Hektor's epithet κορυθαίολος ('of the glistening helmet') (thirty-eight times of him, once of Ares) is present, unspoken, through this scene.

on the other hand, the enemy succeeds, it is Hektor who will
supply the ἔναρα βροτόεντα (bloody spoils). This is the quintessence
of 'the Homeric paradox': that victory is matched by the necessary
corollary of defeat. Ironically Hektor is praying for the death of
Astyanax, a fate which will have come much closer by the end of
the poem.[20] In her final laments, Andromache foresees a life of
slavery for her son, or alternatively:

> "ἤ τις Ἀχαιῶν
> ῥίψει χειρὸς ἑλὼν ἀπὸ πύργου, λυγρὸν ὄλεθρον,
> χωόμενος, ὧι δή που ἀδελφεὸν ἔκτανεν Ἕκτωρ
> ἢ πατέρ', ἠὲ καὶ υἱόν, ἐπεὶ μάλα πολλοὶ Ἀχαιῶν
> Ἕκτορος ἐν παλάμηισιν ὀδὰξ ἕλον ἄσπετον οὖδας."

'Or some Achaian will catch you by the arm and fling you from the walls
to a miserable death, in his anger because Hektor killed his brother, it
may be, or his father or perhaps his son—there were very many of the
Achaians who sank their teeth in the broad earth, brought down at
Hektor's hands.' (24. 734–8)

Andromache begs Hektor to stay out of battle since he stands
for all her kin. There is a poignant balance within his rejection of
her plea, since he explains that the prospect of her enslavement
hurts him more than any other consequence of the fall of Troy.
They have a unique place for each other, even though they fail to
save each other.

> "ἦ καὶ ἐμοὶ τάδε πάντα μέλει, γύναι· ἀλλὰ μάλ' αἰνῶς
> αἰδέομαι Τρῶας καὶ Τρωιάδας ἑλκεσιπέπλους,
> αἴ κε κακὸς ὣς νόσφιν ἀλυσκάζω πολέμοιο·
> οὐδέ με θυμὸς ἄνωγεν, ἐπεὶ μάθον ἔμμεναι ἐσθλὸς
> αἰεὶ καὶ πρώτοισι μετὰ Τρώεσσι μάχεσθαι,
> ἀρνύμενος πατρός τε μέγα κλέος ἠδ' ἐμὸν αὐτοῦ."

'Wife, all that you say is surely in my mind also. But I would feel terrible
shame before the men of Troy and the women of Troy with their trailing
dresses, if like a coward I skulk away from the fighting. Nor is that what
my own heart urges, because I have learnt always to be brave and to fight
in the forefront of the Trojans, winning great glory for my father and for
myself.' (6. 441–6)

The prospect of facing the Trojans if he went against this lesson
is unbearable. This is the same strong sense of *aidōs* that keeps

---

[20] It may be, as Macleod, 42 suggests, that the lack of any divine response at
the end of Hektor's prayer is ominous.

Hektor outside the gates to face Achilleus (6. 442 = 22. 105, see p. 234). Lines 444–6 are a noble version of the heroic ideal to set beside Sarpedon's formulation at 12. 310 ff.[21] They even begin to sound like some unquestionable 'code' until the flow reaches the three lines that Hektor adds:

"εὖ γὰρ ἐγὼ τόδε οἶδα κατὰ φρένα καὶ κατὰ θυμόν·
ἔσσεται ἦμαρ ὅτ' ἄν ποτ' ὀλώληι Ἴλιος ἱρὴ
καὶ Πρίαμος καὶ λαὸς ἐϋμμελίω Πριάμοιο."

'One thing I know well in my heart and in my mind: the day will come when sacred Ilios shall be destroyed, and Priam, and the people of Priam of the fine ash spear.' (6. 447–9)[22]

Why the pessimism just here?

Despite this deep-seated intuition and the vivid predictions of the fall of Troy that follow, Hektor still prays, only 30 lines later, for a glorious future for his son; and in his last speech to Andromache, at 486–93, he maintains that, while death may be his αἶσα (fate), it may not be. By the time that Paris joins him he is talking of victory (526–9), and the κρητῆρα ... ἐλεύθερον (the feasting-bowl of freedom) counterbalances his predictions of slavery in 455 and 463. This should not be written off as merely the kind of contradiction which has to be excused in oral poetry. The scene as a whole contains conflicting hopes and fears which make sense in human terms. Hektor fears he will fail but hopes he will not. Lines 447–9 are not an oracle; and, though they cast a deep shadow, they do not blot out any possibility of a future for Troy and Astyanax. There is room for optimism to squeeze back in: while there's life, there's hope.

The point of coming to such hard grips with the prospect of defeat is that it becomes a compelling reason for Hektor to go out and win *kleos*. The lines are connected to what precedes by γάρ ('because'): not 'I must fight *even though* Troy is bound to fall' but 'I must fight *because* Troy is bound to fall'. This is different

---

[21] See further p. 166 and Fenik, *TBS* 31.

[22] 6. 447–9 = 4. 163–5. It is almost as though Homer is testing the degree of difference in meaning that context can impart to repeated lines. Agamemnon's vindictive bitterness could hardly be further from Hektor's elegiac determination. Macleod, 43: 'the repetition of these impressive lines allows us to view the fall of the city through both Greek and Trojan eyes, as a just punishment for wrongdoing, and as unquestioned but inexplicable suffering: both viewpoints are essential to the whole poem.'

from Odysseus at 11.408ff.—οἶδα γὰρ ὅττι ... (for I know that)—since there his heroic knowledge simply dissolves his dilemma whether to stand or flee. Hektor's premonition, however, somehow explains why his knowledge is urgently applicable at this moment.[23] Sarpedon's exhortation to Glaukos is much closer: it is mortality which makes it essential to risk your life boldly, because death ever threatens to snuff a man out without trace (νῦν δ' ἔμπης γὰρ κῆρες ἐφεστᾶσιν ... (but *since* as it is, whatever we do the fates of death stand over us ...) 12. 326). The threat of death is a prerequisite for making battle κυδιάνειρα (where men win glory) (12. 325), a place where a man strives to make his mark. So Hektor must win μέγα κλέος (great glory) while he can, *because* he knows that Troy will fall.

The sense that this is going to be a farewell scene is introduced as soon as Hektor first raises the idea of a visit to his wife and child:

"καὶ γὰρ ἐγὼν οἶκόνδε ἐλεύσομαι, ὄφρα ἴδωμαι
οἰκῆας ἄλοχόν τε φίλην καὶ νήπιον υἱόν.
οὐ γὰρ οἶδ' εἰ ἔτι σφιν ὑπότροπος ἵξομαι αὖτις,
ἢ ἤδη μ' ὑπὸ χερσὶ θεοὶ δαμόωσιν Ἀχαιῶν."

'I am going now to my own home, to see my servants and my dear wife and baby son. I cannot know whether I shall ever return again and come back to them, or it is now that the gods bring me down at the hands of the Achaians.' (6. 365–8)

At the end of the scene Andromache departs ἐντροπαλιζομένη (turning often) (496); and Paris finds Hektor lingering at their meeting place (6. 515–16). When Andromache gets home,

κιχήσατο δ' ἔνδοθι πολλὰς
ἀμφιπόλους, τῆισιν δὲ γόον πάσηισιν ἐνῶρσεν.
αἱ μὲν ἔτι ζωὸν γόον Ἕκτορα ὧι ἐνὶ οἴκωι·
οὐ γάρ μιν ἔτ' ἔφαντο ὑπότροπον ἐκ πολέμοιο
ἵξεσθαι, προφυγόντα μένος καὶ χεῖρας Ἀχαιῶν.

all the many servant-women she found inside she set to lamentation. So they mourned Hektor, while he still lived, in his own house: because they thought he would never again return from the fighting, and escape the fury of the Achaians' hands. (6. 498–502)

---

[23] Cf. Schadewaldt, *IS* 62–3.

So he is lamented in the very place where there should be most hope for his survival.²⁴ Despite this, he *is* still alive, and in the scene with Paris, Homer shows how there is still hope.

Homer is careful to preserve this sense of final farewell from book 6 by avoiding any allusion to Andromache or to Hektor when the Trojans return to the city at the end of the day's battle. Hektor is kept out of the guilty debate at 7. 365 ff. (see above p. 106) and is not mentioned at all between 7. 310 and 8. 88. Andromache is indeed mentioned only twice in the poem all the way from book 6 to book 22, both times recalling book 6. One allusion takes advantage of Hektor's having no close ἑταῖρος (*hetairos*) or charioteer: at a high moment he calls to his horses,

"Ξάνθε τε καὶ cύ, Πόδαργε, καὶ Αἴθων Λάμπε τε δῖε,
νῦν μοι τὴν κομιδὴν ἀποτίνετον, ἣν μάλα πολλὴν
Ἀνδρομάχη θυγάτηρ μεγαλήτορος Ἠετίωνος
ὑμῖν πὰρ προτέροιcι μελίφρονα πυρὸν ἔθηκεν
οἶνόν τ' ἐγκεράcαcα πιεῖν, ὅτε θυμὸς ἀνώγοι,
ἢ ἐμοί, ὅc πέρ οἱ θαλερὸς πόcιc εὔχομαι εἶναι."

'Come, Xanthos, and you, Podargos, and Aithon and splendid Lampos! Now you can repay me for your keep, all the care that Andromache, daughter of great-hearted Eëtion, has given you, serving you with heartening wheat, and mixing wine for you to drink at your will—and all before feeding me, her own strong husband.' (8. 185–90)²⁵

Secondly, as Hektor puts on the captured armour of Achilleus, Zeus pities him:

"ἀτάρ τοι νῦν γε μέγα κράτος ἐγγυαλίξω,
τῶν ποινὴν ὅ τοι οὔ τι μάχης ἐκ νοcτήcαντι
δέξεται Ἀνδρομάχη κλυτὰ τεύχεα Πηλεΐωνος."

'But for the moment I shall grant you great power, in recompense for what will happen—you will never return home from the fighting, for Andromache to take from you the famous armour of the son of Peleus.' (17. 206–8 (see further pp. 186–8))

Andromache will never again receive spoils from her husband, let alone, as he had prayed, from her son.

Andromache is the type of widowhood in the *Iliad*. All three of her great speeches are in effect laments for Hektor, the first while

---

²⁴ Compare and contrast 24. 327–8, where the Trojans lament Priam's departure as though he is going to his death.
²⁵ Note the echo of 6. 430, θαλερὸς παράκοιτιc (my strong husband).

he is still alive, the second at his death, and the last at his funeral.
All five occurrences of χήρη ('widow') (first at 6. 408) are hers.
When, at 22. 437 ff., the narrative returns to find her at her loom
in obedience to Hektor's command in 6. 490, there are recollec-
tions of the farewell scene. She fears that his courage (ἀγηνορέη
22. 457, cf. the premonitory simile at 12. 46) may have brought
him to grief, as she had feared at 6. 407 (μένος (brave spirit)). In
her alarm she rushes to the walls μαινάδι ἴςη (like a woman in a
frenzy) (22. 460), as she did μαινομένηι ἐϊκυῖα (like a woman in a
frenzy) (6. 389). But on the later occasion Hektor's shining helmet
is off, and his hair is dragged in the dust.

The ground for the lament in 22 is well prepared in 6. Her first
introduction by the narrator, in 6. 395–8 (quoted fully on p. 115),
might seem rather laboured, yet there is even more in her speech
at 414–28 about how Achilleus sacked Thebe, killed Eëtion and
all her seven brothers, and in effect her mother. Thebe was a fine
city and source of fine spoils, and Andromache begs Hektor not
to turn Troy into another Thebe.[26]

A member of the audience who has stored the allusions to Thebe
and its fate from book 6 will find the scene when Andromache
sees Hektor dead before Troy in 22 greatly enriched. Lines which
stand firm enough in their own right are given a whole extra
dimension by Andromache's accumulated life-story. Her gesture
of throwing off her head-dress brings the account of her past back
into vivid presence:

> . . . ὅ ῥά οἱ δῶκε χρυςέη Ἀφροδίτη
> ἤματι τῶι ὅτε μιν κορυθαίολος ἠγάγεθ' Ἕκτωρ
> ἐκ δόμου Ἠετίωνος, ἐπεὶ πόρε μυρία ἕδνα.

. . . that golden Aphrodite had given her on the day when Hektor of the

---

[26] On Thebe cf. Taplin, *Chios*, 18–19; P. Easterling, 'Holy Thebe' (forthcoming); Robbins, 9–11. I think it is more than possible that lines 433–9 have been
added from some other poem where they were more in place—the lines were
rejected by Aristarchos, though for different reasons. I have in mind these considerations: (1) 429–32 form a climax to Andromache's speech and a ring-composition
with 407–9. (2) The strategic details are less appropriate here than to a context
after Achilleus is dead (hence his omission), and when the *lāos* is inside the city,
not out in the field. Considerations in the other direction include: (1) λαὸν δὲ cτῆcον
(433) ('have the army take up position') connects with αὐτοῦ μίμνε ('stay here') in
431. (2) The implicit reference to the sack of Troy in 434 leads into Hektor's open
talk of it in 484 ff. (3) Hektor's contrast between warcraft and housework is a sort
of 'answer' to these lines.

glinting helmet led her as his wife from Eëtion's house, when he had given a countless bride-price for her. (22. 470–2)

Her lament then begins:

> "Ἕκτορ, ἐγὼ δύστηνος· ἰῆι ἄρα γιγνόμεθ᾽ αἴςηι
> ἀμφότεροι, cὺ μὲν ἐν Τροίηι Πριάμου κατὰ δῶμα,
> αὐτὰρ ἐγὼ Θήβηιcιν ὑπὸ Πλάκωι ὑληέccηι
> ἐν δόμωι Ἠετίωνος, ὅ μ᾽ ἔτρεφε τυτθὸν ἐοῦcαν,
> δύcμορος αἰνόμορον· ὡc μὴ ὤφελλε τεκέcθαι.
> νῦν δὲ cὺ μὲν Ἀΐδαο δόμουc ὑπὸ κεύθεcι γαίηc
> ἔρχεαι, αὐτὰρ ἐμὲ cτυγερῶι ἐνὶ πένθεϊ λείπειc
> χήρην ἐν μεγάροιcι· πάϊc δ᾽ ἔτι νήπιος αὔτωc,
> ὅν τέκομεν cύ τ᾽ ἐγώ τε δυcάμμοροι·"

'Hektor, my life is misery! So both of us were born under the same fate, you in Troy in Priam's house, and I in Thebe under wooded Plakos in the house of Eëtion, who brought me up when I was small, doomed father and doomed child—how I wish he had never fathered me! Now you are going down to the house of Hades in the cellars of the earth, and leaving me behind in hateful mourning, a widow in your house. And our child is still only a baby, the son that was born to you and me, ill-fated parents.' (22. 477–85)

It is part of the *Iliad*'s greatness, and one of the ways it rewards an attentive audience, that such detailed and powerful connections are made across such huge narrative distances.

5

Olympian Athanatology

5.1 Immortals and the balance of power

Τὴν δ' ἀπαμειβόμενος προσέφη νεφεληγερέτα Ζεύς· 560
"δαιμονίη, αἰεὶ μὲν ὀίεαι, οὐδέ σε λήθω·
πρῆξαι δ' ἔμπης οὔ τι δυνήσεαι, ἀλλ' ἀπὸ θυμοῦ
μᾶλλον ἐμοὶ ἔσεαι· τὸ δέ τοι καὶ ῥίγιον ἔσται.
εἰ δ' οὕτω τοῦτ' ἐστίν, ἐμοὶ μέλλει φίλον εἶναι·
ἀλλ' ἀκέουσα κάθησο, ἐμῶι δ' ἐπιπείθεο μύθωι, 565
μή νύ τοι οὐ χραίσμωσιν ὅσοι θεοί εἰσ' ἐν Ὀλύμπωι
ἆσσον ἰόνθ', ὅτε κέν τοι ἀάπτους χεῖρας ἐφείω."
Ὣς ἔφατ', ἔδεισεν δὲ βοῶπις πότνια Ἥρη,
καί ῥ' ἀκέουσα καθῆστο, ἐπιγνάμψασα φίλον κῆρ·
ὄχθησαν δ' ἀνὰ δῶμα Διὸς θεοὶ Οὐρανίωνες· 570
τοῖσιν δ' Ἥφαιστος κλυτοτέχνης ἦρχ' ἀγορεύειν,
μητρὶ φίληι ἐπὶ ἦρα φέρων, λευκωλένωι Ἥρηι·
"ἦ δὴ λοίγια ἔργα τάδ' ἔσσεται οὐδ' ἔτ' ἀνεκτά,
εἰ δὴ σφὼ ἕνεκα θνητῶν ἐριδαίνετον ὧδε,
ἐν δὲ θεοῖσι κολωιὸν ἐλαύνετον· οὐδέ τι δαιτὸς 575
ἐσθλῆς ἔσσεται ἦδος, ἐπεὶ τὰ χερείονα νικᾶι.
μητρὶ δ' ἐγὼ παράφημι, καὶ αὐτῆι περ νοεούσηι,
πατρὶ φίλωι ἐπὶ ἦρα φέρειν Διί, ὄφρα μὴ αὖτε
νεικείηισι πατήρ, σὺν δ' ἡμῖν δαῖτα ταράξηι.
εἴ περ γάρ κ' ἐθέλησιν Ὀλύμπιος ἀστεροπητὴς 580
ἐξ ἑδέων στυφελίξαι· ὁ γὰρ πολὺ φέρτατός ἐστιν·
ἀλλὰ σὺ τόν γ' ἐπέεσσι καθάπτεσθαι μαλακοῖσιν·
αὐτίκ' ἔπειθ' ἵλαος Ὀλύμπιος ἔσσεται ἡμῖν."

Zeus the cloud-gatherer answered her: 'My dear wife, you are always suspecting, and no action of mine can escape you. But even so there is nothing you can do, except to put yourself yet further from my heart—and that will be the worse for you. If the matter is as you say, then that must be how I wish it. No, sit still and be quiet, and do as I tell you, or all the gods in Olympos will be no help to you, when I come close and lay my invincible hands on you.'

So he spoke, and the ox-eyed queen Hera was afraid, and sat in silence, bending her heart to obey. There was uproar among the heavenly gods in Zeus' house. But Hephaistos the famous craftsman began to speak to them, anxious to do service to his dear mother, white-armed Hera: 'This will be a grievous business, and beyond endurance, if you two are to quarrel in this way over mortal men, and set the gods to wrangling: and we shall have no pleasure in the excellent feast, since unworthy things will be foremost. I urge my mother—though she knows it herself—to make her peace with our dear father Zeus, so that the father does not scold her again and spoil our feasting. If the Olympian lord of the lightning is minded to dash us from our seats—well, he is far stronger than all of us. No, you should approach him with soft words, and then the Olympian will be kindly to us again.' (1. 560–83)

Apollo can terrify with his plague, Hephaistos raise laughter by his bustling. The Iliadic gods are a mixture of awesome power and quarrelsome pettiness, reflected in ethics by their mixture of roles as guarantors of justice and as amoral self-seekers. Just as one can reconstruct an 'anthropology' from within the poem (see Chapter 2), so it is possible to piece together a theology, or, as I would rather call it to avoid misleading associations, an 'athanatology'. As with the anthropology, this will not necessarily be consistent throughout, and it is not obvious how far it corresponds to the religion of 'real life'.[1]

The wilful and the moral, the trivial and the awesome are deeply intermixed. For instance the grand *Dios boulē* of 1. 5 turns out to be in response to Thetis' personal request. This is granted partly on personal grounds: Thetis has claims on Zeus in return for past benefits (1. 393–412, cf. 503–4, 514–16); Achilleus is the child of a god (cf. Hera at 24. 56–61); and he has special claims because of the certainty of his short life. Thetis urges Zeus

> "τίμησόν μοι υἱόν, ὃς ὠκυμορώτατος ἄλλων
> ἔπλετ'· ἀτάρ μιν νῦν γε ἄναξ ἀνδρῶν Ἀγαμέμνων
> ἠτίμησεν· ἑλὼν γὰρ ἔχει γέρας, αὐτὸς ἀπούρας.
> ἀλλὰ σύ πέρ μιν τεῖσον, Ὀλύμπιε μητίετα Ζεῦ·"

'Show honour to my son, who is short-lived beyond all other men. Now Agamemnon, lord of men, has dishonoured him: he has taken his prize with his own hands, and keeps it for himself. But you now show him honour, Zeus, counsellor, Olympian lord.' (1. 505–8, cf. 352–6 and p. 195 below)

---

[1] Subject of a good discussion by Kirk (ii. 1–14).

But it is also clear that Achilleus and Thetis expect Zeus to do something to redress the *atīmia* because it is an ethical issue. Hence the emphasis of ἀλλὰ cύ πέρ ... ('but you now ...') in 508, and the γάρ ('for') in 355. Zeus' hesitation arises not from the rights and wrongs of the case, which he does not dispute, but from his reluctance to give even more offence to Hera, the implacable enemy of Troy.

The Olympian scene at the end of book 1 illustrates well an important feature of athanatology—the balance of power among the gods. This divine 'politics' is generally confirmed and filled out throughout the poem by poetic fieldwork. It is of the essence that all the Homeric gods have their own interests, often conflicting interests; and that, if they possibly can, they will get their own way, by words or by deeds, by fair means or foul. The chief limitation or inhibition on this 'selfish' motivation is that there has been strife and violence among the gods in the past,[2] and that they do not want any return to that sort of unpleasantness. There is a certain, no doubt purposeful, vagueness over just what would happen if this balance of power broke down. Though it is never clearly formulated, there may be some sense that disharmony on Olympos would entail some kind of vast cosmic disturbance.[3]

The balance of power is particularly destabilized by Zeus' sleep and his awakening to find that on the battlefield his will has been reversed. He reminds Hera of the time that he hung her from Olympos and threw off the other gods (15. 18–33). Soon after, Ares wants to intervene, despite Zeus, to avenge his son Askalaphos,[4] but Athene—πᾶcι περιδείcαcα θεοῖcιν (in fear for all the gods) (123)—dissuades him:

"ἦ ἐθέλειc αὐτὸc μὲν ἀναπλήcαc κακὰ πολλὰ
ἂψ ἴμεν Οὔλυμπόνδε καὶ ἀχνύμενόc περ ἀνάγκηι,

[2] See e.g. Schadewaldt, *IS* 118; Schein, 50. Note Hephaistos' diplomacy at 1. 586 ff., when he tells of his own fall from Olympos rather than alluding directly to the ordeal of Hera which is recalled at 15. 18 ff.

[3] There is perhaps a suggestion of this at 20. 61 ff., where Hades fears that Poseidon will break open the earth and reveal the realms below to the light.

[4] The death of Askalaphos was carefully planted in the midst of the slaughter at 13. 561 ff., and attention was drawn to Ares' ignorance of it, in obedience to Zeus' prohibition (13. 521–5—note the figurative use of 'Ares' nearby in 13. 444, 569). By the way, Askalaphos, despite his paternity, has no martial distinction and is only hit because Deïphobos yet again (καὶ τότε 13. 518) misses Idomeneus.

αὐτὰρ τοῖc ἄλλοιcι κακὸν μέγα πᾶcι φυτεῦcαι;
αὐτίκα γὰρ Τρῶαc μὲν ὑπερθύμουc καὶ Ἀχαιοὺc 135
λείψει, ὁ δ' ἡμέαc εἶcι κυδοιμήcων ἐc Ὄλυμπον,
μάρψει δ' ἑξείηc ὅc τ' αἴτιοc ὅc τε καὶ οὐκί.
τῶ c' αὖ νῦν κέλομαι μεθέμεν χόλον υἷοc ἑῆοc·
ἤδη γάρ τιc τοῦ γε βίην καὶ χεῖραc ἀμείνων
ἢ πέφατ', ἢ καὶ ἔπειτα πεφήcεται· ἀργαλέον δὲ 140
πάντων ἀνθρώπων ῥῦcθαι γενεήν τε τόκον τε."

'Or do you want to have your fill of suffering and then be forced back to Olympos however reluctant, and at the same time sow the seeds of great trouble for all the rest of us? Because Zeus will immediately leave the proud Trojans and the Achaians, and come back to Olympos to beat us about, and he will lay hands on each of us in turn, guilty and innocent alike. So I tell you now to leave your anger for your son. Better men than he in the strength of their hands have already been killed, and will be killed yet. It is impossible for us to save everyone's family and children.' (15. 132–41)[5]

And when Zeus sends Iris down to Poseidon to tell him to leave the battlefield, he complies under protest, asserting the principle of the balance of power:

"ἀλλ' ἤτοι νῦν μέν κε νεμεccηθεὶc ὑποείξω·
ἄλλο δέ τοι ἐρέω, καὶ ἀπειλήcω τό γε θυμῶι·
αἴ κεν ἄνευ ἐμέθεν καὶ Ἀθηναίηc ἀγελείηc,
Ἥρηc Ἑρμείω τε καὶ Ἡφαίcτοιο ἄνακτοc,
Ἰλίου αἰπεινῆc πεφιδήcεται, οὐδ' ἐθελήcει
ἐκπέρcαι, δοῦναι δὲ μέγα κράτοc Ἀργείοιcιν,
ἴcτω τοῦθ', ὅτι νῶϊν ἀνήκεcτοc χόλοc ἔcται."

'Well, for this time I shall hold myself back and give in to him. But I tell you something else, a threat I make in my heart. If in spite of me and Athene, goddess of spoil, and Hera and Hermes and lord Hephaistos, Zeus spares steep Ilios, and will not sack it and grant a great victory to the Argives, let him be sure of this, that there will be anger without healing between us.' (15. 211–17)

On the anthropological level it is only rarely exposed that brute violence is the ultimate sanction, as in the *agorē* in book 1 — see pp. 64–5 above. In athanatology this threat is raised more openly and more often. It is clear that, if it came to it, Zeus would be

---

[5] Coming so soon after Zeus' outline of his *boulē* in 15. 49 ff., there is some poignancy in this last line, since he has lined up his own son Sarpedon for death — and Patroklos, and Hektor.

stronger than all the rest put together: this is epitomized by the parable of the golden chain, at 8. 17–27. Zeus *could* have his own way on everything; he could even annul something long-fated, even perhaps his own *boulē*. But the repercussions would be so disagreeable that it would not be worth it. "ἔρδε", 'Go on, do it', other gods cry when Zeus contemplates going back on something that was settled. "ἀτὰρ οὔ τοι πάντες ἐπαινέομεν θεοὶ ἄλλοι" ('but we other gods will not all applaud you') (4. 29 = 16. 443 = 22. 181). Clearly this threatens something far worse than merely witholding praise.

"αἰνότατε Κρονίδη, ποῖον τὸν μῦθον ἔειπες·
πῶς ἐθέλεις ἅλιον θεῖναι πόνον ἠδ' ἀτέλεστον,
ἱδρῶ θ' ὃν ἵδρωσα μόγωι, καμέτην δέ μοι ἵπποι
λαὸν ἀγειρούσηι, Πριάμωι κακὰ τοῖό τε παιςίν.
ἔρδ'· ἀτὰρ οὔ τοι πάντες ἐπαινέομεν θεοὶ ἄλλοι."

'Dread son of Kronos, what is this you are saying? How can you intend to make empty and fruitless all my labours, and the sweat that I sweated in my exertions, and the weariness of my horses as I gathered together an army of doom to Priam and his children? Do it, then: but we other gods will not all applaud you.' (4. 25–9)

This is Hera's response when Zeus seems to propose peace, and to reopen the question of whether the war should continue or whether the truce of book 3 should be prolonged into a treaty (4. 14–19). Yet Zeus does not seriously mean this—he only says it to annoy Hera:

αὐτίκ' ἐπειρᾶτο Κρονίδης ἐρεθιζέμεν Ἥρην
κερτομίοις ἐπέεσσι, παραβλήδην ἀγορεύων·

Soon the son of Kronos set himself to provoke Hera with a taunting speech, and there was devious purpose in his words . . . (4. 5–6)

He certainly succeeds; but when he asks her why she hates Priam and his city so ruthlessly (31 ff.), she does not even deign to explain: she simply offers her three favourite cities—Argos, Sparta, and Mykene—in return for the destruction of Troy (51 ff.). On one level the answer is 'the Judgement of Paris', but this is left unspoken.[6] In human terms, in terms that might satisfy Homer's audience, there is no sufficient reason.

The whole scene is 'a nightmare picture for men'.[7] When Athene

---

[6] Subject of Reinhardt's classic essay 'Das Parisurteil'.
[7] Griffin, *HLD* 197.

descends comet-like to stir up hostilities, the humans, sitting unarmed on the ground (3. 326–7) do not know which way things will turn:

θάμβος δ' ἔχεν εἰcορόωνταc,
Τρῶάc θ' ἱπποδάμουc καὶ ἐϋκνήμιδαc Ἀχαιούc·
ὧδε δέ τιc εἴπεcκεν ἰδὼν ἐc πληcίον ἄλλον·
"ἦ ῥ' αὖτιc πόλεμόc τε κακὸc καὶ φύλοπιc αἰνὴ
ἔccεται, ἢ φιλότητα μετ' ἀμφοτέροιcι τίθηcι
Ζεύc, ὅc τ' ἀνθρώπων ταμίηc πολέμοιο τέτυκται."

The horse-taming Trojans and the well-greaved Achaians looked on in wonder: and one would glance at his neighbour and say, 'There will surely be grim war again and the horror of battle—or else Zeus who holds the issue of men's fighting is setting friendship between the two sides.' (4. 79–84)

Longed-for peace is glimpsed, only to be swept aside by the gods for reasons that are not explained. Athanatology mimics anthropology, yet observes a power politics that is shallow in human terms.

The amusing diplomacy of Hephaistos in 1. 573 ff. is a good illustration. The experienced inner ear will hear echoes of Nestor in the *agorē*: the conciliatory advice, the similarity of 1. 581 to 1. 281, the warning that Zeus is πολὺ φέρτατος (far stronger) just as Agamemnon was φέρτερος (stronger). And there are other ways in which the divine scene echoes that in the Achaian camp:[8] the verbal abuse (note 519, 539 f., 574 f.); the issue of *tīmē* (516, 558); the long-standing wrangle (520, 541); the threats of force (567, 580–4, 589 ff.); the issue of strength as a last resort. The mimicry, parody almost, brings out the way that Hephaistos has a far easier task than Nestor. Nestor has to try to disarm a dispute that could lead to irreparable disaster and death—and he fails. Hephaistos merely persuades Hera to a temporary conciliation: Olympian pleasures are more important than mortal affairs.

Humans in the *Iliad* are interesting because they are—like the audience—mortal. They live under the pressure of time and the threat of obliteration. The immortals, by contrast, lack tragic potential; they have endless time to be carefree, whatever the passing, temporary disturbances. The closing scenes of book 1 on Olympos introduce those aspects of divine relationships and 'politics' which, set against human life, seem somewhat frivolous.

[8] Cf. Reinhardt, *ID* 74, n. 15.

But remember that this all comes after the first two divine participations in the poem: the terrifying Apollo, and the Athene who so crucially alters the whole shape of Achilleus' confrontation in the *agorē*. Even on Olympos, for all the laughter and feasting, Zeus is determined to fulfil his undertaking to Thetis, even though that will mean terrible suffering at Troy.

Zeus is never entirely frivolous. It may be related to this that he never participates *in propria persona* in battle, unlike the other gods. It is not in fact until the second half of book 5 that there is a concentration of supernatural interference in the field, with Athene and Hera on one side and Apollo and Ares on the other.[9] As in the *theomachia* in 21, the gods' activities are grand and amazing, but they are at the same time coloured by the ease and humour of immortality. Only once does a god directly kill a mortal. That is Ares with Periphas at 5. 842 ff.—and what is the point of a god's stripping a mortal's armour? This may be one reason why Athene is so keen to get at Ares (835 ff.); as Hera complains (757–61), Ares' killing is, μάψ, ἀτὰρ οὐ κατὰ κόσμον (reckless and unjustified).[10] Yet Ares is not on the whole as belligerent as Zeus' unsympathetic words at 5. 889 ff. suggest. And even he is quickly cured and restored to dignity (5. 899 ff.).

The god who fights most actively is undoubtedly Athene. This is clear and prominent in her help to Diomedes. She not only helps him (5. 1 ff., 121 ff.), she enables him to see the gods, and warns him not to fight with any but Aphrodite (124–32). When he tries to attack Aineias, despite his protection by Apollo, the god warns him:

> "φράζεο, Τυδεΐδη, καὶ χάζεο, μηδὲ θεοῖσιν
> ἶσ' ἔθελε φρονέειν, ἐπεὶ οὔ ποτε φῦλον ὁμοῖον
> ἀθανάτων τε θεῶν χαμαὶ ἐρχομένων τ' ἀνθρώπων."

'Think, son of Tydeus, and shrink back! Never think yourself gods' equal—since there can be no likeness ever between the race of immortal gods and of men who walk on the ground.' (5. 440–2)

Diomedes yields and survives—as Patroklos at 16. 702 ff. does not (see further p. 183). There has already been a touch of burlesque about his clash with Aphrodite (327 ff.); and Diomedes even taunts the wounded goddess in the satirical style that the Olympians

---

[9] Good observations in Fenik, *TBS* 36–77, esp. 39, 77.
[10] The same phrase is used of the speech of Thersites at 2. 214.

enjoy using against each other (348 ff. cf. 421 ff.). Dione comforts Aphrodite with illustrations of the gods' suffering pain at the hands of mortals (382 ff.), and foresees Diomedes' coming to grief (406 ff.). Yet her portentous illustrations of divine pain have more in common with Demodokos' tale of Ares and Aphrodite than with the sufferings of the *Iliad*.[11] Diomedes is carefully chosen for battle with the gods in book 5. Despite Dione's warning, we know of no unhappy future for him; he fights the gods and lives to tell the tale. Yet fighting the immortals is not, in the end, as serious or impressive as fighting other men. Diomedes, despite this distinction, does not achieve the stature of Achilleus or Hektor.[12] He seems to enjoy a charmed immunity to real, deep suffering. He has a straightforward drive to do what is γενναῖον (noble) (5. 253), and he straightforwardly succeeds. Note, for example, how he does not join in the general flight at 8. 78 ff.—contrast Odysseus (8. 92–8)!

Diomedes is Achilleus without the complications, and his stature in the *Iliad* is to a large extent made possible by the vacuum left by Achilleus. They are both young and valiant; both fight Aineias until he is rescued; they are both given special help and encouragement by Athene; and they are both caught up in *theomachiai*. Yet they are also contrasting foils. This is clearly brought out by an incident during the *epipōlēsis* (4. 223–421) before battle is even joined, when Agamemnon goes about on foot 'inspecting' the Achaian lines. After a generous enough start, he is quite unjustifiably rude to Odysseus, showing a haste and discourtesy like that in book 1. When contradicted by Odysseus, he manages to repair his error (4. 327–63); but this does not stop him going on to censure Diomedes (365 ff.; cf. νείκεccεν (abused) in 336 and 368). Again the complaint is groundless, though this time he adds some anecdote to show that Tydeus was a better man than his son. Diomedes' response is remarkable:

> Ὣc φάτο, τὸν δ' οὔ τι προcέφη κρατερὸc Διομήδηc,
> αἰδεcθεὶc βαcιλῆοc ἐνιπὴν αἰδοίοιο·

So he spoke, and strong Diomedes made no answer, silenced by respect for the king and his rebuke. (4. 401–2)

---

[11] As Macleod (133) observes, she offers a witty divine reversal of the grim human consolation that the gods inflict suffering on mankind, even the greatest.

[12] Cf. Owen, 52–3 (and Sheppard quoted there); Whitman, 165–9; Erbse, 'Betr.' 5; and Ø. Andersen, *Die Diomedesgestalt in der* Ilias (Symb. Osl. Suppl. 25; Oslo, 1978), *passim*, esp. 48 ff.

Even when Sthenelos answers back, Diomedes virtually defends Agamemnon:

"τέττα, cιωπῆι ἧcο, ἐμῶι δ᾽ ἐπιπείθεο μύθωι·
οὐ γὰρ ἐγὼ νεμεcῶ Ἀγαμέμνονι, ποιμένι λαῶν,
ὀτρύνοντι μάχεcθαι ἐϋκνήμιδαc Ἀχαιούc·
τούτωι μὲν γὰρ κῦδοc ἅμ᾽ ἕψεται, εἴ κεν Ἀχαιοὶ
Τρῶαc δηιώcωcιν ἕλωcί τε Ἴλιον ἱρήν,
τούτωι δ᾽ αὖ μέγα πένθοc Ἀχαιῶν δηιωθέντων.
ἀλλ᾽ ἄγε δὴ καὶ νῶϊ μεδώμεθα θούριδοc ἀλκῆc."

'Friend, stay still and be quiet, and do as I tell you.

I do not resent Agamemnon, shepherd of the people, for urging the well-greaved Achaians into battle: because his will be the glory that follows if the Achaians slaughter the Trojans and capture sacred Ilios, but his again the depth of grief if the Achaians are slaughtered. Come then, let us too recall our fighting spirit.' (4. 412–18)

This makes a striking contrast with Achilleus.

So it is fitting that Diomedes should have a straightforward relationship with the gods, far 'cleaner' than that of Achilleus or Hektor or Agamemnon. It is this that makes him the right man to assert an authoritative confidence in eventual divine retribution on Troy at 7. 400–2 (see p. 106 above). His confidence is such that he declares his intention to stay at Troy even if everyone else runs away—cὺν γὰρ θεῶι εἰλήλουθμεν (since god is with us in our mission here) (9. 49—see p. 87 above).

5.2 Reassertions of the Dios boulē

"ἠοῦc δὴ καὶ μᾶλλον ὑπερμενέα Κρονίωνα   470
ὄψεαι, αἴ κ᾽ ἐθέληιcθα, βοῶπιc πότνια Ἥρη,
ὀλλύντ᾽ Ἀργείων πουλὺν cτρατὸν αἰχμητάων·
οὐ γὰρ πρὶν πολέμου ἀποπαύcεται ὄβριμοc Ἕκτωρ,
πρὶν ὄρθαι παρὰ ναῦφι ποδώκεα Πηλεΐωνα,
ἤματι τῶι ὅτ᾽ ἂν οἱ μὲν ἐπὶ πρύμνηιcι μάχωνται   475
cτείνει ἐν αἰνοτάτωι περὶ Πατρόκλοιο θανόντοc,
ὡc γὰρ θέcφατόν ἐcτι"

'In the morning, ox-eyed queen Hera, if you have the mind for it, you will see the son of Kronos in yet greater power, destroying the Argive spearmen in great numbers. Because mighty Hektor will not cease from his fighting before the swift-footed son of Peleus is roused to action beside the ships, on that day when they will fight in desperate confinement by the sterns over dead Patroklos—this is the way of fate.' (8. 470–7)

The Achaians as a whole do not by any means always keep on the right side of the gods. There is, for instance, the wall which they hastily build after the first, far from successful, day of battle. Although Diomedes has dominated the fighting, the Trojans have met with unusual success, including the last kills of the day, at 7. 8–16. After the fighting there are four assemblies, two on each side (though the fourth is only perfunctorily narrated, at 7. 414–17). It is at the first that Nestor advises the Achaians to build the wall, since the Trojans might now actually threaten the camp and ships (323–44). This, it is implied, is unprecedented in all the previous years, as is confirmed by Achilleus later:

"ἦ μὲν δὴ μάλα πολλὰ πονήcατο νόcφιν ἐμεῖο,
καὶ δὴ τεῖχος ἔδειμε, καὶ ἤλαce τάφρον ἐπ' αὐτῶι
εὐρεῖαν μεγάλην, ἐν δὲ cκόλοπαc κατέπηξεν·
ἀλλ' οὐδ' ὡc δύναται cθένοc Ἕκτοροc ἀνδροφόνοιο
ἴcχειν· ὄφρα δ' ἐγὼ μετ' Ἀχαιοῖcιν πολέμιζον
οὐκ ἐθέλεcκε μάχην ἀπὸ τείχεοc ὀρνύμεν Ἕκτωρ,
ἀλλ' ὅcον ἐc Cκαιάc τε πύλαc καὶ φηγὸν ἴκανεν·
ἔνθα ποτ' οἶον ἔμιμνε, μόγιc δέ μευ ἔκφυγεν ὁρμήν."

'Oh, he has laboured hard in my absence, and built a wall, and run a ditch in front, large and wide, and fixed stakes in it. Yet even so he cannot hold back the strength of murderous Hektor. But while I was fighting with the Achaians, Hektor was never willing to push the battle away from the wall, but would come out no further than the Skaian gates and the oak-tree. There he once stood up to me alone, and barely escaped my attack.' (9. 348–55)

The assemblies take place on the evening of the battle and on the next morning; the rest of that next day (7. 421–32) is devoted to burning the dead. It is only on the day after that, which dawns with 7. 433, that the dead are buried, and that the Achaians construct their wall and ditch. This takes them the whole day: δύcετο δ' ἠέλιοc, τετέλεcτο δὲ ἔργον Ἀχαιῶν (and the sun set and the Achaians' work was done) (7. 465). In counterpoint with this hurried human activity, the brief diversion to Olympos in 7. 442–63 gives the larger perspective of Zeus and the other gods.[13] Poseidon complains both that this new wall will outshine in fame the one which he and Apollo built round Troy for Laomedon, and that the Achaians have failed to make due offerings to the

---

[13] Cf. Owen, 79–81.

gods. Zeus replies that in the long run there is no threat to the *kleos* of the gods as opposed to that of humans (7. 458, answering 451): after the Achaians have gone away, he is welcome to obliterate their puny earthworks.

This longer perspective, shared by gods and audience, but not by the characters,[14] is further explored in the unique and rather disturbing digression in 12. 1–35. There, again, there is emphasis on the Achaians' failure to win divine favour:

> οὐδ' ἄρ' ἔμελλε
> τάφρος ἔτι cχήcειν Δαναῶν καὶ τεῖχος ὕπερθεν
> εὐρύ, τὸ ποιήcαντο νεῶν ὕπερ, ἀμφὶ δὲ τάφρον
> ἤλαcαν, οὐδὲ θεοῖcι δόcαν κλειτὰc ἑκατόμβαc,
> ὄφρα cφιν νῆάc τε θοὰc καὶ ληΐδα πολλὴν
> ἐντὸc ἔχον ῥύοιτο· θεῶν δ' ἀέκητι τέτυκτο
> ἀθανάτων· τὸ καὶ οὔ τι πολὺν χρόνον ἔμπεδον ἦεν.

And the Danaans' ditch was not going to hold longer, or the broad wall rising above it, which they had made round their ships and driven the ditch along its length, without offering splendid hecatombs to the gods. They had made it to protect their fast ships and the mass of booty it held behind it: but it was built without the immortal gods' sanction, and therefore it did not stand long. (12. 3–9)

By that time the wall has been fully worked into the narrative.[15] It has held up the anticipated Trojan attack (8. 177 ff., 213 ff., 255, 336 ff.), and guarded the Achaians during the night of crisis (9. 68, 87, 233; 10. 180 ff., cf. 10. 564). On the next day the Achaians have issued from it (11. 48 ff.), and at the time of the digression are about to be driven back to it, crowding in through the gates (12. 118 ff.), while the Trojans come to the ditch-edge (12. 49 ff.). Their breaking through the ditch/walls and gate forms a well-defined section of narrative at 12. 35–471.

The digression has an unusual detachment through taking a standpoint in time long after the end of the war:

> ὄφρα μὲν Ἕκτωρ ζωὸς ἔην καὶ μήνι' Ἀχιλλεὺς   10
> καὶ Πριάμοιο ἄνακτος ἀπόρθητος πόλις ἔπλεν,

---

[14] Cf. de Jong, 88.

[15] 'The wall is built in order to be fought over', M. L. West, *CR* 19 (1969), 93, replying, effectively, to D. Page, *History and the Homeric Iliad* (Berkeley, Calif., 1959), 315 ff. I shall not go into the analytical objections to the Achaian wall which mainly arose from treating the *Iliad* as though it should be real history. (It is interesting, however, that 7. 334–5, which are surely interpolated, were probably added in the mid-fifth century at the earliest.)

τόφρα δὲ καὶ μέγα τεῖχος Ἀχαιῶν ἔμπεδον ἦεν.
αὐτὰρ ἐπεὶ κατὰ μὲν Τρώων θάνον ὅccοι ἄριcτοι,
πολλοὶ δ᾽ Ἀργείων οἱ μὲν δάμεν, οἱ δὲ λίποντο,
πέρθετο δὲ Πριάμοιο πόλιc δεκάτωι ἐνιαυτῶι,   15
Ἀργεῖοι δ᾽ ἐν νηυcὶ φίλην ἐc πατρίδ᾽ ἔβηcαν,
δὴ τότε μητιόωντο Ποcειδάων καὶ Ἀπόλλων
τεῖχοc ἀμαλδῦναι, ποταμῶν μένοc εἰcαγαγόντεc.
ὅccοι ἀπ᾽ Ἰδαίων ὀρέων ἅλαδε προρέουcι,
Ῥῆcόc θ᾽ Ἑπτάποροc τε Κάρηcόc τε Ῥοδίοc τε   20
Γρήνικόc τε καὶ Αἴcηποc δῖόc τε Cκάμανδροc
καὶ Cιμόειc, ὅθι πολλὰ βοάγρια καὶ τρυφάλειαι
κάππεcον ἐν κονίηιcι καὶ ἡμιθέων γένοc ἀνδρῶν·

For as long as Hektor was alive and Achilleus kept up his anger, and the city of king Priam remained unsacked, the great wall of the Achaians also stood firm. But when all the leading men of the Trojans had been killed, and many of the Argives brought down, while others survived, and the city of Priam was sacked in the tenth year, and the Argives had left in their ships for their dear native land, then Poseidon and Apollo planned the destruction of the wall, turning the power of the rivers against it, all the rivers that flow out to the sea from the mountains of Ida, Rhesos and Heptaporos and Karesos and Rhodios and Grenikos and Aisepos, and holy Skamandros and Simoeis, where many ox-hide shields and helmets and a race of men half-divine had fallen in the dust. (12. 10–23)

There is an almost archaeological observation about the buried bodies and armour of the heroic past. This is accentuated by the unique occurrence in Homer of the word ἡμίθεοc ('half-divine'). This is not the usual internal anthropology; it is more the perspective of Hesiod, who looks back on the past bronze age of heroes in *WD* 159–60:

ἀνδρῶν ἡρώων θεῖον γένοc, οἳ καλέονται
ἡμίθεοι, προτέρη γενεὴ κατ᾽ ἀπείρονα γαῖαν.[16]

a god-like race of hero men, who are called half-divine, the era before our own through the boundless earth.

It is also emphasized that the wall and ditch will be wiped out without trace:

τῶν πάντων ὁμόcε cτόματ᾽ ἔτραπε Φοῖβοc Ἀπόλλων,
ἐννῆμαρ δ᾽ ἐc τεῖχοc ἵει ῥόον· ὗε δ᾽ ἄρα Ζεὺc   25
cυνεχέc, ὄφρα κε θᾶccον ἁλίπλοα τείχεα θείη.

---

[16] See M. L. West, ad loc.; Reinhardt, *ID* 207–8; cf. also R. Scodel in *HSCP* 86 (1982), 33 ff.

αὐτὸc δ' ἐννοcίγαιοc ἔχων χείρεccι τρίαιναν
ἡγεῖτ', ἐκ δ' ἄρα πάντα θεμείλια κύμαcι πέμπε
φιτρῶν καὶ λάων, τὰ θέcαν μογέοντεc Ἀχαιοί,
λεῖα δ' ἐποίηcεν παρ' ἀγάρροον Ἑλλήcποντον,　　　30
αὖτιc δ' ἠϊόνα μεγάλην ψαμάθοιcι κάλυψε,
τεῖχοc ἀμαλδύναc· ποταμοὺc δ' ἔτρεψε νέεcθαι
κὰρ ῥόον, ᾗι περ πρόcθεν ἵεν καλλίρροον ὕδωρ.

Phoibos Apollo turned all these rivers to join at one mouth, and for nine
days he hurled their waters at the wall: and Zeus rained without ceasing,
to wash the wall the sooner into the sea. The Earth-shaker himself took
the foremost part, his trident in his hands, and carried away in his waves
all the foundations of logs and stones that the Achaians had laboured to
set, and made all smooth beside the strong flow of the Hellespont, and
covered the deep shore once more with sand, after obliterating the wall:
and he turned the rivers to run in the course where their lovely waters
had flowed before. (12. 24–33)

For all the hard work put into it by the Achaians (μογέοντεc, 'had
laboured'), the works of human strength are, in the face of time
and of the power of the gods, temporary, perishable.[17]

The perspective of the digression also makes a point about
poetry. The reason why we, the audience, know about the wall,
despite its total obliteration, is that it is preserved in poetry. Poetry
is imperishable, provided that—unlike the wall—it has attracted
divine favour. The poet prompts the thought that it is significant
that the gods have not obliterated the *Iliad*.

After their rather lavish and random interventions during the
first great day of battle, the gods frame the next, the relatively
brief battle of 8. 53–349,[18] with a substantial prologue and epilogue. Zeus makes it clear from the start (1–27)[19] that he is now
taking over sole control of the battle:

"μήτε τιc οὖν θήλεια θεὸc τό γε μήτε τιc ἄρcην
πειράτω διακέρcαι ἐμὸν ἔποc, ἀλλ' ἅμα πάντεc
αἰνεῖτ', ὄφρα τάχιcτα τελευτήcω τάδε ἔργα."

---

[17] Compare, even within the narrative, the ease with which Apollo, at 15. 355 ff.,
flattens some of the bank of the ditch—πολὺν κάματον καὶ ὀϊζὺν cύγχεαc Ἀργείων
(you smashed all the work the Argives had laboured at with much pain)—like a
boy with his sandcastles.
[18] This used to be a favourite plaything for the analysts; but it has been
comprehensively defended by Schadewaldt, *IS* 96–127, and Reinhardt, *ID*
138–211.
[19] Lines 28–40 may well be an interpolation.

'Now let no female god or male either attempt to frustrate my stated will, but I want agreement from all of you, so I can bring this business to a speedy end.' (8. 7–9)

From his vantage-point on Ida, κύδεϊ γαίων (glorying in his splendour) (51), he reinforces the turning-point at midday (66 ff.), symbolized by his golden scales,[20] with thunder and lightning which demoralize the Achaians.[21] Diomedes, reluctant to take the advice of his unlikely charioteer, Nestor, is stopped in his tracks by a thunderbolt (133 ff.) and repeatedly warned by Zeus' thunder (167–75). Hektor, on his side, can also interpret the signs (175 ff., see further p. 147).

Hera inspires a slight Achaian rally, though even then against Poseidon's advice (198–219). But when she and Athene attempt a more substantial intervention, something more like that of 5. 733 ff., Zeus sends a warning message, and then comes back to Olympos in person to voice his fury. The scene from 350 to 468 shows the gods in their least sublime aspect, squabbling for power and free with insults and taunts. For example, Athene complains against Zeus:

"νῦν δ' ἐμὲ μὲν στυγέει, Θέτιδος δ' ἐξήνυσε βουλάς,
ἥ οἱ γούνατ' ἔκυσσε καὶ ἔλλαβε χειρὶ γενείου,
λισσομένη τιμῆσαι Ἀχιλλῆα πτολίπορθον.
ἔσται μὰν ὅτ' ἂν αὖτε φίλην γλαυκώπιδα εἴπῃ."

'But now Zeus hates me, and has brought about the designs of Thetis, who kissed his knees and took his chin in her hand, begging him to show honour to Achilleus, sacker of cities. But the time will come when he calls me his darling Bright Eyes once again.' (8. 370–3)[22]

It is a spiteful exaggeration of Thetis' supplication to say that she kissed Zeus' knees.[23] And Zeus soon answers his daughter's petulant complaint about being called γλαυκῶπις (bright-eyed): the

---

[20] It is extraordinary how many commentators have spoken as though the scales offer a fifty-fifty outcome; and as though some third party—Fate or something—determines which scale will go down. But in Homeric athanatology 'Fate' is not a metaphysical power separate from Zeus, and it does not make sense to ask which is superior. Here in 8 there is no question but that the Trojans will have the better of the day. The scales do not decide this; they mark a crisis in the narrative. In some passages, indeed, they become a purely figurative way of indicating a turning-point, e.g. in 16. 658, 19. 223.

[21] Untypical according to Fenik, *TBS* 220; cf. *TBS* 222 on 133 ff.

[22] στυγέει ('hates') is a word play with Στυγὸς ('of Styx') in 369.

[23] Compare Odysseus (fictionally) grovelling to the king of Egypt at *Od.* 14. 279.

purpose of his warning message is ὄφρα ἰδῆι γλαυκῶπις ὅτ' ἄν ὧι πατρὶ μάχηται (so that the bright-eyed goddess can learn what it is to fight with her father) (406); and Iris adapts this to the (unique) vocative γλαυκῶπι (bright-eyed) in 420.[24] After these peevish exchanges, and followed by the bluster of 479–83, Zeus' stark predictions in 470 ff. have a piercing hardness. This is θέςφατον (the way of fate), and its direct harshness is accentuated by all the preceding squabbles. In book 1 Zeus had said to Hera

"Ἥρη, μὴ δὴ πάντας ἐμοὺς ἐπιέλπεο μύθους
ἐιδήςειν· χαλεποί τοι ἔςοντ' ἀλόχωι περ ἐούςηι·
ἀλλ' ὃν μέν κ' ἐπιεικὲς ἀκουέμεν, οὔ τις ἔπειτα
οὔτε θεῶν πρότερος τόν γ' εἴςεται οὔτ' ἀνθρώπων·"

'Hera, do not expect to know of all my thoughts—they will be hard for you, even though you are my wife. When it is right for you to hear my thought, no-one, god or man, will know of it before you do.' (1. 545–8)

It is now, after she has in fact provoked him by thwarting him, that he sets out a sequence of his *boulē* for the future.[25] His brief revelations do not exactly correspond to the full narrative when it unfolds. Even more, they do not in any way convey the human struggle and suffering which will fulfil them. 'The detail of what is to come is not dully pre-empted, and that also faithfully represents the interplay of destiny and decision in human affairs.[26]

These same features are even clearer in Zeus' fuller declaration of his *boulē* in book 15, which is a kind of resumption, almost a second start, concluding with explicit allusion back to his undertakings at the start of the poem:

"τὸ πρὶν δ' οὔτ' ἄρ' ἐγὼ παύω χόλον οὔτε τιν' ἄλλον
ἀθανάτων Δαναοῖςιν ἀμυνέμεν ἐνθάδ' ἐάςω,
πρίν γε τὸ Πηλεΐδαο τελευτηθῆναι ἐέλδωρ,
ὥς οἱ ὑπέςτην πρῶτον, ἐμῶι δ' ἐπένευςα κάρητι,
ἤματι τῶι ὅτ' ἐμεῖο θεὰ Θέτις ἥψατο γούνων,
λιςςομένη τιμῆςαι Ἀχιλλῆα πτολίπορθον."

'But I shall not cease my anger or allow any other of the immortals to give help here to the Danaans, until the son of Peleus' desire has been

---

[24] Actually, when he is being affectionate Zeus calls her Τριτογένεια, φίλον τέκος (Tritogeneia, dear child) (e.g. at 8. 39, 22. 183).

[25] Cf. Schein, 36.

[26] Macleod, 28, n. 1; see also the important discussion in Schadewaldt, *IS* 110–13, esp. 111, n. 2.

fulfilled, as I promised him at the beginning and nodded agreement with my head, on that day when the goddess Thetis took hold of my knees, begging me to show honour to Achilleus, sacker of cities.' (15. 72–7)

At the site of her deceitful love-making, Zeus tells Hera both of his immediate intentions (15. 53–64) and of the longer term. Tersely and dispassionately he checks off events which will mean heavy ordeals for their human enactors. Some are already well known; others are new, most notably the death of Sarpedon and Achilleus' anger against Hektor; others are not quite accurate, for instance Achilleus does not exactly 'rouse' Patroklos. And some important events are not included, such as the ransom of Hektor's body, and, above all, the death of Achilleus.

So in some ways the audience is given a privileged insight into athanatology by the poet, an eavesdropping on divine behaviour, motivation, and relationships. In other ways the narrative alienates the gods from the human perspective, since in their immortality, they cannot live through pressures and agonies of human life.

6

Plotting Time

6.1 The evening before the central day

"κέκλυτέ μευ, Τρῶες καὶ Δάρδανοι ἠδ' ἐπίκουροι·
νῦν ἐφάμην νῆάς τ' ὀλέσας καὶ πάντας Ἀχαιοὺς
ἂψ ἀπονοστήςειν προτὶ Ἴλιον ἠνεμόεςςαν·
ἀλλὰ πρὶν κνέφας ἦλθε, τὸ νῦν ἐςάωςε μάλιστα   500
Ἀργείους καὶ νῆας ἐπὶ ῥηγμῖνι θαλάςςης.
ἀλλ' ἤτοι νῦν μὲν πειθώμεθα νυκτὶ μελαίνηι
δόρπα τ' ἐφοπλιςόμεςθα· ἀτὰρ καλλίτριχας ἵππους
λύςαθ' ὑπὲξ ὀχέων, παρὰ δέ ςφιςι βάλλετ' ἐδωδήν·
ἐκ πόλιος δ' ἄξεςθε βόας καὶ ἴφια μῆλα   505
καρπαλίμως, οἶνον δὲ μελίφρονα οἰνίζεςθε
ςῖτόν τ' ἐκ μεγάρων, ἐπὶ δὲ ξύλα πολλὰ λέγεςθε,
ὥς κεν παννύχιοι μέςφ' ἠοῦς ἠριγενείης
καίωμεν πυρὰ πολλά, ςέλας δ' εἰς οὐρανὸν ἵκηι,
μή πως καὶ διὰ νύκτα κάρη κομόωντες Ἀχαιοὶ   510
φεύγειν ὁρμήςωνται ἐπ' εὐρέα νῶτα θαλάςςης.
.   .   .   .
κήρυκες δ' ἀνὰ ἄςτυ Διῒ φίλοι ἀγγελλόντων
παῖδας πρωθήβας πολιοκροτάφους τε γέροντας
λέξαςθαι περὶ ἄςτυ θεοδμήτων ἐπὶ πύργων·
θηλύτεραι δὲ γυναῖκες ἐνὶ μεγάροιςιν ἑκάςτη   520
πῦρ μέγα καιόντων· φυλακὴ δέ τις ἔμπεδος ἔςτω,
μὴ λόχος εἰςέλθηιςι πόλιν λαῶν ἀπεόντων.
ὧδ' ἔςτω, Τρῶες μεγαλήτορες, ὡς ἀγορεύω·
μῦθος δ' ὃς μὲν νῦν ὑγιὴς εἰρημένος ἔςτω,
τὸν δ' ἠοῦς Τρώεςςι μεθ' ἱπποδάμοις ἀγορεύςω.   525
.   .   .   .
ἀλλ' ἤτοι ἐπὶ νυκτὶ φυλάξομεν ἡμέας αὐτούς,
πρῶϊ δ' ὑπηοῖοι ςὺν τεύχεςι θωρηχθέντες   530
νηυςὶν ἔπι γλαφυρῆιςιν ἐγείρομεν ὀξὺν Ἄρηα.
εἴςομαι εἴ κέ μ' ὁ Τυδεΐδης κρατερὸς Διομήδης
πὰρ νηῶν πρὸς τεῖχος ἀπώςεται, ἦ κεν ἐγὼ τὸν
χαλκῶι δηιώςας ἔναρα βροτόεντα φέρωμαι.

αὔριον ἦν ἀρετὴν διαείσεται, εἴ κ' ἐμὸν ἔγχος   535
μείνηι ἐπερχόμενον· ἀλλ' ἐν πρώτοιcιν, ὀίω,
κείcεται οὐτηθείc, πολέεc δ' ἀμφ' αὐτὸν ἑταῖροι,
ἠελίου ἀνιόντοc ἐc αὔριον· εἰ γὰρ ἐγὼν ὣc
εἴην ἀθάνατοc καὶ ἀγήρωc ἤματα πάντα,
τιοίμην δ' ὡc τίετ' Ἀθηναίη καὶ Ἀπόλλων,   540
ὡc νῦν ἡμέρη ἥδε κακὸν φέρει Ἀργείοιcιν."

'Listen to me, Trojans and Dardanians and allies. Today I thought that
I would return to windy Ilios with the ships and all the Achaians
destroyed—but before that darkness came, and it is that above all which
has now saved the Argives and their ships on the shore. Well, for the
present we should give way to dark night and prepare our supper. Unyoke
your lovely-maned horses from your chariots and throw fodder by them.
And bring oxen and sturdy sheep from the city quickly, and take cheering
wine and bread from your houses, and gather piles of wood as well, so
that we can burn many fires all night long until the early-born dawn, and
their light can strike up to the sky—in case the long-haired Achaians
perhaps try to escape during the night over the sea's broad back . . . And
let the heralds, loved of Zeus, proclaim throughout the city that the boys
in their early youth and the grey-headed old men should camp on the
god-built walls around the city. And as for the womenfolk, let each man's
wife burn a great fire in the house: and there must be a constant watch,
so that no enemy band can enter the city while the fighting men are away.
Let these things be done, great-hearted men of Troy, as I tell you. So
much for my orders to suit the present need. Now I will give you horse-
taming Trojans some words for the morrow . . . So for the night we must
keep guard on our position. But early in the morning, before the showing
of dawn, let us arm in our weapons and wake war's anger by the hollow
ships. And I shall know whether Tydeus' son, strong Diomedes, will
drive me back from the ships to the wall, or whether I will cut him down
with the bronze and carry away my bloody spoils. Tomorrow we shall
come to know his courage, whether he can stand against the onslaught
of my spear—but I think he will lie there stabbed among the first to die,
and many companions round him, as the sun rises for tomorrow. Oh, if
only I could be deathless and ageless for all time, and honoured as Athene
and Apollo are honoured, as surely as this coming day brings disaster to
the Argives!' (8. 497–511, 517–25, 529–42)[1]

[1] On this speech as a whole, see Schadewaldt, *IS* 101, n. 3. Encouraged by the
scholiasts' reports of the complaints of the Alexandrian scholars, modern commentators, including Kirk, have made heavy weather of the second half of Hektor's
speech. Given the run of the sense and the emphasis on tomorrow, most of the
objections seem pedantic. (1) τὸν δ' ἠοῦc in 525 means 'the second part of my
speech, which concerns tomorrow'. It is essential to pick up the ἠοῦc of Zeus only
55 lines earlier (470). (2) 535–7 may well be an interpolation expanding 532–4,

The framework of narrative-time is crucial for the structuring of the *Iliad*, as I hope to have shown in the introductory chapter. Skilful use of temporal markers and calibration of the passage of days and nights give the audience a grasp on the shaping of events. The daring decision to make the whole central part of the poem into a single day of battle has consequences in narrative technique which come into effect long before it is reached.

The audience is acclimatized to the long narrative day by the one which begins before dawn with Agamemnon's dream in book 2 and does not set till book 7 (though battle is not joined until well on in book 4, almost exactly half way through in performance-time). By the time Hektor returns to the field with Paris, it is well advanced; and not long after, Athene and Apollo agree to end the mass battle for today (σήμερον, 7. 30) with Hektor's challenge to single combat. Nightfall is used as the reason for ending that with a satisfactory draw:[2]

> "μηκέτι, παῖδε φίλω, πολεμίζετε μηδὲ μάχεςθον·
> ἀμφοτέρω γὰρ ςφῶϊ φιλεῖ νεφεληγερέτα Ζεύς,
> ἄμφω δ' αἰχμητά· τό γε δὴ καὶ ἴδμεν ἄπαντες.
> νὺξ δ' ἤδη τελέθει· ἀγαθὸν καὶ νυκτὶ πιθέςθαι."

'Stop your fighting now, dear children—no more battle. Zeus the cloud-gatherer has love for both of you, and both are fine fighters—we all know this. And night is coming on now. It is good to give way to the night.' (7. 279–82)

The feasting, assemblies, and so forth that follow in the next 200 lines are in effect, a tailpiece to this first bloody day of battle.

The next day of battle, the κόλος μάχη (short battlè), is far briefer in performance-time, and has a far simpler narrative direction. Despite brief rallies by Diomedes and Teukros, Zeus ensures that it is an overwhelming success for the Trojans. At its height, when he realizes how far things are tipping his way, Hektor

---

though it is a pity to lose αὔριον ('tomorrow') in 535. (3) ἐc αὔριον in 538 means 'when the sun rises to bring in tomorrow'. (4) ἡμέρη ἤδε ('this day') in 541 is fine as a vivid anticipation of the next day. It is possible that line 540 has been interpolated from 13. 827. (5) on the *adynaton* in 538–41 see p. 111 above.

[2] The appropriateness of this outcome, anticipated at 7. 200–5, is brought out by the use of duals, reinforced by the pleasure given to both sides. For example εὐφρήνῃς ('you can bring gladness') of Aias in 294, εὐφρανέω ('I shall bring gladness') of Hektor in 297, ἐχάρηcαν ('they were overjoyed') of the Trojans in 307, and κεχαρηότα νίκῃ ('with the joy of victory') of Aias in 312. Cf. de Jong, 101–2.

conceives an ambition which will prove to be an important narrative motif:[3]

"γιγνώcκω δ' ὅτι μοι πρόφρων κατένευce Κρονίων
νίκην καὶ μέγα κῦδοc, ἀτὰρ Δαναοίcί γε πῆμα·
νήπιοι, οἳ ἄρα δὴ τάδε τείχεα μηχανόωντο
ἀβλήχρ' οὐδενόcωρα· τὰ δ' οὐ μένοc ἁμὸν ἐρύξει·
ἵπποι δὲ ῥέα τάφρον ὑπερθορέονται ὀρυκτήν.
ἀλλ' ὅτε κεν δὴ νηυcὶν ἔπι γλαφυρῆιcι γένωμαι,
μνημοcύνη τιc ἔπειτα πυρὸc δηΐοιο γενέcθω,
ὡc πυρὶ νῆαc ἐνιπρήcω, κτείνω δὲ καὶ αὐτοὺc
Ἀργείουc παρὰ νηυcὶν ἀτυζομένουc ὑπὸ καπνοῦ."

'I can see that the son of Kronos has willed and granted me the victory and great glory—and to the Danaans disaster. Poor fools, they have contrived this wall of theirs, a feeble thing of no account—it will not keep back my fury: my horses will easily leap over the ditch they have dug. And when I am there by their hollow ships, then let me have you mindful of the fire to consume them, so that I can set fire to the ships and cut down the Argives as they panic in the smoke.' (8. 175–83)

The firing of the ships becomes Hektor's great goal and his great glory. The threat is reinforced throughout book 8 (217, 235, 498, 554 ff.), and is seen by the Achaians as the great danger for them (9. 242f., cf. 346–7; 435–6; 601–2, cf. 652–3). The motif becomes a more general one during the first part of the central day (11. 557, 665; 12. 198, 441; 13. 319, 629; 14. 47); but, as the battle of book 15 progresses, the reality of flaming timber comes closer and closer, as will be traced in due course—see pp. 172–4 below.

When the narrative leaves the battlefield at 8. 349 Hektor is threatening the fortifications. It never returns to him before nightfall:

ἐν δ' ἔπεc' Ὠκεανῶι λαμπρὸν φάοc ἠελίοιο,
ἕλκον νύκτα μέλαιναν ἐπὶ ζείδωρον ἄρουραν.
Τρωcὶν μέν ῥ' ἀέκουcιν ἔδυ φάοc, αὐτὰρ Ἀχαιοῖc
ἀcπαcίη τρίλλιcτοc ἐπήλυθε νὺξ ἐρεβεννή.

And the bright light of the sun sank into Ocean, drawing black night over the grain-giving ploughland. The Trojans were sorry to see the daylight set, but for the Achaians the coming of night's welcome darkness was their most fervent prayer. (8. 485–8)

---

[3] For the motif of the threat to the ships, see Schadewaldt, *IS* 67–8 (esp. 67, n. 3) and 121.

The meantime is taken up by the interchanges on Olympos. These culminate in Zeus' declaration of his *boulē* (see above). It is important that his very first word is ἠοῦς (quoted on p. 136): Zeus himself begins the anticipation of what will prove to be the great central day, and he does so even before the sun has set on the previous one.

After a day's battle there is the standard sequence as both sides respond in 'post-mortem' scenes—see pp. 22–5. This time it is the Trojans' *agorē* which is recounted first, and at some length (8. 489–565). They meet out in the field, and Hektor, who is the only speaker, leans on his spear rather than on a sceptre. His speech is full of temporal markers which place it crucially between the two days of battle. He refers first to the frustration of nightfall and moves on to his plan for the night. It is important to appreciate that the Trojans have scarcely issued from the gates during the previous years of the siege (see p. 137 above). These are unprecedented and exhilarating tactics. In the last part of the speech, where he looks forward, the anticipations of tomorrow come thick and fast (too much so for the taste of some critics). The Trojans roar assent, and the closing description of them around their fires μέγα φρονέοντες (with high thoughts in their minds) (553) also conveys tense anticipation of the next day. They have high hopes that the flames of their watch-fires will be taken right to the ships themselves (on the simile at 555 ff. see p. 111 above). The scene closes with attention to the horses, who are also experiencing unaccustomed tactics (prepared by 503–4, 543–4):

ἵπποι δὲ κρῖ λευκὸν ἐρεπτόμενοι καὶ ὀλύρας
ἑσταότες παρ' ὄχεσφιν ἐύθρονον Ἠῶ μίμνον.

And the horses stood beside their chariots munching their white barley and wheat, and waiting for the throned dawn. (8. 564–5)

The Achaians meet in a very different mood. Contrast their simile at 9. 4–7 with the Trojan one at 8. 555–61. Agamemnon's counsel of despair (see p. 93) meets with silence and grief (29–30): contrast the response to Hektor. It is Diomedes who speaks up— appropriately, not only because he has been the most successful Achaian warrior, but also to redress Agamemnon's unjustified attack on him in the *epipōlēsis*—pp. 135–6 above. He takes the opportunity to set the record straight in public:

"ἀλκὴν μέν μοι πρῶτον ὀνείδιcαc ἐν Δαναοῖcι,
φὰc ἔμεν ἀπτόλεμον καὶ ἀνάλκιδα· ταῦτα δὲ πάντα
ἴcαc' Ἀργείων ἠμὲν νέοι ἠδὲ γέροντεc.''

'It was my courage you decried before now in front of the Danaans,
saying I was a coward and a weakling—all this is known by the Achaians,
young and old alike.' (9. 34–6)

Skilfully picking up these reproaches later in his speech (39, 41),
and turning Agamemnon's advice back on him (47 = 27), he wins
the approval of everyone, including Nestor. Nestor believes, however, that he knows better (53–78), and discreetly proposes a
meeting and feasting of the *gerontes*. With a good practical sense
of the strategic crisis (lacking in Agamemnon), he also proposes
an efficient system of watches (carried out in 80–8), concluding
with a powerful line which presses on all that follows: νὺξ δ' ἥδ'
ἠὲ διαρραίcει cτρατὸν ἠὲ cαώcει (this night will prove the shattering
of our army or its saving) (9. 78).

The threat of the Trojans and their confident anticipation is
kept vivid and urgent by the device of having Odysseus tell Achilleus about it, almost as though he had been at the Trojans' *agorē*
himself, and indeed as though he had heard Hektor's incendiary
hopes at 8. 180–3.

"ἐν δοιῆι δὲ cαώcεμεν ἢ ἀπολέcθαι   230
νῆαc ἐϋccέλμουc, εἰ μὴ cύ γε δύcεαι ἀλκήν.
ἐγγὺc γὰρ νηῶν καὶ τείχεοc αὖλιν ἔθεντο
Τρῶεc ὑπέρθυμοι τηλεκλειτοί τ' ἐπίκουροι,
κηάμενοι πυρὰ πολλὰ κατὰ cτρατόν, οὐδ' ἔτι φαcὶ
cχήcεcθ', ἀλλ' ἐν νηυcὶ μελαίνηιcιν πεcέεcθαι.   235
Ζεὺc δέ cφι Κρονίδηc ἐνδέξια cήματα φαίνων
ἀcτράπτει· Ἕκτωρ δὲ μέγα cθένεϊ βλεμεαίνων
μαίνεται ἐκπάγλωc, πίcυνοc Διί, οὐδέ τι τίει
ἀνέραc οὐδὲ θεούc· κρατερὴ δέ ἑ λύccα δέδυκεν.
ἀρᾶται δὲ τάχιcτα φανήμεναι Ἠῶ δῖαν·   240
cτεῦται γὰρ νηῶν ἀποκόψειν ἄκρα κόρυμβα
αὐτάc τ' ἐμπρήcειν μαλεροῦ πυρόc, αὐτὰρ Ἀχαιοὺc
δηιώcειν παρὰ τῆιcιν ὀρινομένουc ὑπὸ καπνοῦ.''

'There is doubt whether we can save our well-benched ships or they are
lost, if you do not clothe yourself in your fighting power. The high-
hearted Trojans and their far-famed allies have made camp right close to
our ships and the wall, they have lit countless fires throughout their army,
and they think there will be no holding them now, but they will hurl

themselves on our black ships. And Zeus the son of Kronos is showing
them signs of his favour with lightning on the right. Hektor is revelling
high in his strength and raging hideously, with his trust in Zeus and no
thought for men or gods—a mighty madness has entered him. He is
praying for holy dawn to come quickly, as he threatens to cut the poop-
ends from our ships, then burn the ships themselves with devouring fire
and cut the Achaians down beside them as the smoke drives them madding
in confusion.' (9. 230–43)

Homer makes good use of this narrative technique by which
characters come to know what the audience already knows,
although in strict accuracy they had no opportunity to do so.[4]
Odysseus returns to Hektor again at the end of his speech (λύσσαν,
'madness', 305 ~ λύςςα, 239); and he is quite right that Achilleus
has a flattering opportunity to catch him in his state of unguarded
confidence.

Although the sharpest points of Achilleus' reply are aimed
elsewhere (see § **2.3**, pp. 196–7, 214–15), he has perceptively registered the arguments about Hektor and the damage that he
threatens for the next day. Previously Hektor was contained, he
points out (346 ff.), even without a wall,

"νῦν δ' ἐπεὶ οὐκ ἐθέλω πολεμιζέμεν Ἕκτορι δίωι,
αὔριον ἱρὰ Διὶ ῥέξας καὶ πᾶςι θεοῖςι,
νηήςας εὖ νῆας, ἐπὴν ἅλαδε προερύςςω,
ὄψεαι, αἴ κ' ἐθέληιςθα καὶ αἴ κέν τοι τὰ μεμήληι,
ἦρι μάλ' Ἑλλήςποντον ἐπ' ἰχθυόεντα πλεούςας
νῆας ἐμάς, ἐν δ' ἄνδρας ἐρεςςέμεναι μεμαῶτας·"

'But now, since I do not wish to fight with godlike Hektor, tomorrow I
shall make sacrifice to Zeus and the other gods, I shall load my ships full,
I shall drag them down to the water—and you will see, if you wish, if
you have the mind for it, in the early morning you will see my ships
sailing out over the fish-filled Hellespont, and men in them eager at their
oars.' (9. 356–61)

---

[4] Some other illustrations: Achilleus knows of Chryses' prayer to Apollo
(1. 380–1); Agamemnon at 14. 44–7 speaks as though he had heard Hektor in 8;
at 17. 241 Aias fears that Hektor will maltreat Patroklos, as he in fact threatened
at 17. 126; at 18. 261 ff. Poulydamas knows that Achilleus' fury against Agamemnon
is over; at 24. 203–5 Hekabe speaks as though she heard Zeus at 24. 148, 177.
Achilleus' 'intuition' of the words of Agamemnon which are omitted by Odysseus
is related to this narrative technique but has more point. See further Schadewaldt,
IS 122; Bowra in *CH* 70; Macleod on 24. 203–5; Robbins, 3–9.

This picks up Hektor's refrain all too well: tomorrow, when he is burning the other ships, Achilleus will be safely at sea. He harks back to this at the end of the speech, when he gives Phoinix the choice of whether to return home with him (αὔριον, 'tomorrow', 428–9). It is, however, on this very issue, his immediate departure, that Phoinix urges him to change his position; and in his brief reply Achilleus, while he does not concede that he will stay, does say

<blockquote>

"ἅμα δ' ἠοῖ φαινομένηφι
φρασσόμεθ' ἤ κε νεώμεθ' ἐφ' ἡμέτερ' ἤ κε μένωμεν."
</blockquote>

'Then with the showing of dawn we shall consider whether to return to our own land or to stay.' (9. 618–19)

He makes a further concession to Aias, but when the ambassadors (minus Phoinix) arrive back with the *gerontes*, who have remained in session throughout, Odysseus reports the worst possible account, emphasizing ἅμ' ἠοῖ φαινομένηφι (with the showing of dawn) (682, cf. 692).[5] It is Diomedes who eventually rallies the meeting, exhorting them to get on with the war without Achilleus. This was, in fact, his stance at 9. 32 ff., before Nestor rather patronizingly capped his proposals. Diomedes is quite right, both that Zeus' will is too complex for them to understand, and that Achilleus will eventually fight. In the meantime they must face the immediate pressure of night and day, and be practical:

<blockquote>

"αὐτὰρ ἐπεί κε φανῆι καλὴ ῥοδοδάκτυλος Ἠώς,
καρπαλίμως πρὸ νεῶν ἐχέμεν λαόν τε καὶ ἵππους
ὀτρύνων, καὶ δ' αὐτὸς ἐνὶ πρώτοισι μάχεσθαι."
</blockquote>

Ὣς ἔφαθ', οἱ δ' ἄρα πάντες ἐπήινησαν βασιλῆες,
μῦθον ἀγασσάμενοι Διομήδεος ἱπποδάμοιο.
καὶ τότε δὴ σπείσαντες ἔβαν κλισίηνδε ἕκαστος,
ἔνθα δὲ κοιμήσαντο καὶ ὕπνου δῶρον ἕλοντο.

'Then when rosy-fingered dawn appears in her beauty, you, Agamemnon, should quickly draw up your forces, men and chariots, in front of the ships and urge them on, then fight yourself among the leaders.'
So he spoke, and all the kings applauded his proposal, delighted at the speech of Diomedes the horse-tamer. And then after libations they went

---

[5] Scodel ('The Word of Achilleus') makes the interesting suggestion that it is significant for the plot, esp. in book 16, that Odysseus fails to report back the last version of Achilleus' position. Line 694 must surely, by the way, be a marginal 'concordance' intrusion drawn from 9. 431—otherwise it is parody.

each to his own hut. There they lay down and took the benison of sleep.
(9. 707–13)

So, as argued in § **1.4**, there is a conclusive closure for the night
on both sides, but with confident anticipation of their great opportunity in the morning for the Trojans, while at the end of 9 the
Achaians look forward with anxiety but determination. Whether
or not there is anything to my theory of the coincidence of narrative-time and performance-time, this is a great juncture in the *Iliad*
which achieves a closing cadence combined with keen suspense.
This is perhaps the greatest single objection to the *Doloneia*, which
utterly disrupts this artful construction.

The closures send both sides to bed to be refreshed before the
demands of the dawn (Ἠώ, 8. 565, Ἠώς, 9. 707). The *Doloneia*
reawakes both sides for assemblies to send out a spy. The two
volunteer with the same line: ἔμ' ὀτρύνει κραδίη καὶ θυμὸς ἀγήνωρ . . .
(my heart and proud spirit urge me . . .) (10. 220 = 319). There
the similarities cease, and a pro-Greek chauvinism enters which
is not characteristic of the *Iliad* as a whole (see § **4.1**).

The Achaian assembly is courageous and chivalrous (194–271):
the shorter Trojan meeting verges on stupidity (299–332). Diomedes' reward is to be some sheep, along with ὑπουράνιον κλέος (glory
under heaven) (212); and Odysseus goes along out of sheer loyalty
and bravery. The Trojan volunteer is offered the finest Achaian
horses and chariot (303 ff.), and Dolon specifies no less than those
of Achilleus. Out in the dark it is a very unequal contest between
the cowardly amateur and the two consummate professionals. The
story is exciting but blatantly slanted. They are alert and hear
Dolon (338 ff.): he is incautious—ἀφραδίῃσιν (in his ignorance)
(350). They trap him skilfully (344 ff.), and Diomedes petrifies
him with a well-judged near-miss (372 ff.). Odysseus presses him
hard with questions (385–9, 406–11, 424–5); and Dolon pours out
answers without concealment or compunction. He goes far beyond
what is demanded when he draws attention to the defencelessness
of the *epikouroi* (420 ff.), eagerly pointing out the special opportunity provided by Rhesos and the Thracians (432 ff.). It is hard to
feel any objection to his ignoble dispatch. He shares his death line
φθεγγομένου δ' ἄρα τοῦ γε κάρη κονίῃσιν ἐμίχθη ('he was beginning
to speak as his head dropped in the dust') (457) with the dis-
credited seer Leodes at *Od.* 22. 329.

Odysseus and Diomedes set out as spies but end up as horse-rustlers. In a kind of efficient conveyor-belt, Diomedes butchers each sleeping Thracian while Odysseus hauls the corpse by the feet to clear a pathway for the horses: there is a macabre humour verging on sadism in the treatment of the Thracians as mere traffic-hazards. Odysseus' use of his bow as a whip (500–1) is typical of the jolly jape, as is the dispatch of Rhesos, who never gains any personality.[6]

Our daring Greek 'heroes' are presented as stars: their opponents are stupid and cowardly. The atmosphere of manly high-spirits is sustained to the end. They wash off their sweat in the sea, have a hot bath in a tub (the only ἀcάμινθοc of the *Iliad*), and settle down for a meal—for Odysseus the third that night. Dawn now arrives without their having had any proper sleep.

Points such as these all confirm the basic objection arising from structural technique and the calibration of time to isolate the *Doloneia* as an intrusion into an *Iliad* complete without it. The *Doloneia* has undoubtedly been fashioned to fit its setting within the *Iliad*, for example the Trojan fires in the plain at 10. 12 ff. But I can see no sign that the rest of the *Iliad* has been in any way fashioned to include the *Doloneia*. It could be omitted without trace. I am not aware of any other substantial section of the *Iliad* of which this would be true. Even the standard defence of its place in the plot—that Achaian morale needs a boost before their new assertion in book 11—seems to me untrue: that is precisely the function of Diomedes' rallying call at the end of book 9.[7]

6.2 The central day until evening

(a)   "βάcκ' ἴθι, Ἶρι ταχεῖα, τὸν Ἕκτορι μῦθον ἐνίcπεc·
         ὄφρ' ἂν μέν κεν ὁρᾶι Ἀγαμέμνονα, ποιμένα λαῶν,
         θύνοντ' ἐν προμάχοιcιν, ἐναίροντα cτίχαc ἀνδρῶν,

---

[6] The most interesting thing about Rhesos is his dream in 494–7. Does he heave because he is in his death-throes, i.e. Diomedes is only figuratively a bad dream? Or is he having a nightmare about being killed in a peculiar doubling of literal and figurative? Either way he is the victim of a macabre humour which is highly uncharacteristic of Homer, because it is conveyed through the eye of the narrator, not put in the direct-speech taunt of a character.

[7] Diomedes conclusively settled the issue in favour of battle rather than flight, yet this is contradicted by Nestor at 10. 146–7.

τόφρ' ἀναχωρείτω, τὸν δ' ἄλλον λαὸν ἀνώχθω
μάρνασθαι δηΐοιcι κατὰ κρατερὴν ὑcμίνην.   190
αὐτὰρ ἐπεί κ' ἢ δουρὶ τυπεὶc ἢ βλήμενοc ἰῶι
εἰc ἵππουc ἅλεται, τότε οἱ κράτοc ἐγγυαλίξω
κτείνειν, εἰc ὅ κε νῆαc ἐϋccέλμουc ἀφίκηται
δύηι τ' ἠέλιοc καὶ ἐπὶ κνέφαc ἱερὸν ἔλθηι."

'Away with you, swift Iris, and tell what I say to Hektor. As long as he
can see Agamemnon, shepherd of the people, raging among the front-
fighters and cutting down the ranks of men, he should keep back and
urge the rest of his army to fight against the enemy in the battle's fury.
But when a spear-hit or arrow-shot sends Agamemnon to mount his
chariot, then I shall grant Hektor the power to go on killing until he
reaches the well-benched ships and the sun sets and the holy darkness
comes on.' (11. 186–94)

(b)   'Ἥλιον δ' ἀκάμαντα βοῶπιc πότνια Ἥρη
πέμψεν ἐπ' Ὠκεανοῖο ῥοὰc ἀέκοντα νέεcθαι·
ἠέλιοc μὲν ἔδυ, παύcαντο δὲ δῖοι Ἀχαιοὶ
φυλόπιδοc κρατερῆc καὶ ὁμοιΐου πολέμοιο.

Now the ox-eyed queen Hera sent the tireless sun hurrying down
against his will to the stream of Ocean. So the sun set, and the godlike
Achaians could stop the furious struggle of levelling war. (18. 239–42)

It is my belief that the opening of book 11,

'Ἠὼc δ' ἐκ λεχέων παρ' ἀγαυοῦ Τιθωνοῖο
ὄρνυθ', ἵν' ἀθανάτοιcι φόωc φέροι ἠδὲ βροτοῖcι·
Ζεὺc δ' Ἔριδα προΐαλλε θοὰc ἐπὶ νῆαc Ἀχαιῶν
ἀργαλέην, πολέμοιο τέραc μετὰ χερcὶν ἔχουcαν.

Dawn now rose from her bed beside lordly Tithonos, to bring light to
deathless gods and mortal men. And Zeus sent Strife down to the fast
ships of the Achaians, the cruel goddess, holding in her hands a sign of
war. (11. 1–4)

was the beginning of one of the three great sessions of performance, and that the previous session had ended with Diomedes'
brave exhortation for the following dawn in 9. 707–9 (quoted
above). Whether or not these theses are true, the great day when
it comes is dominated—even though with set-backs—by Zeus'
supervision of the Trojan triumph, as he gave notice in 8. 470 ff.
(see above). He acts in despite of the other gods, who stay on
Olympus (11. 74 ff.)

τῶν μὲν ἄρ' οὐκ ἀλέγιζε πατήρ· ὁ δὲ νόσφι λιασθεὶς
τῶν ἄλλων ἀπάνευθε καθέζετο κύδεϊ γαίων,
εἰςορόων Τρώων τε πόλιν καὶ νῆας Ἀχαιῶν
χαλκοῦ τε ςτεροπήν, ὀλλύντας τ' ὀλλυμένους τε.

But the Father cared nothing for the gods: he drew away from the others
and sat down apart, glorying in his splendour, and looking out over the
Trojans' city and the ships of the Achaians, at the flash of bronze and
men killing and being killed. (11. 80–3)

Though he sends Eris down to stir up the Achaians, and though
they are eager for war, the tendency of his portents is clear enough
for the audience:

ἐν δὲ κυδοιμὸν
ὦρce κακὸν Κρονίδης, κατὰ δ' ὑψόθεν ἧκεν ἐέρcac
αἵματι μυδαλέας ἐξ αἰθέρος, οὕνεκ' ἔμελλε
πολλὰς ἰφθίμους κεφαλὰς Ἄϊδι προϊάψειν.

And the son of Kronos started a troubled commotion among them, and
from the height of the sky he rained down over them drops of blood,
since it was his intention to hurl down to Hades many mighty heads of
heroes. (11. 52–5)

The echo in 11. 55 of the third line of the poem[8] is a disturbing
warning that the greatest slaughter arising from the *Dios boulē* is
about to begin.

Until the mid-morning (84–9)[9] the honours are equal. Agamemnon then has his hour; but this initial success is calculatedly
'misleading', in that it accentuates the extent of the reverse which
is to follow. His *aristeia* is interrupted by Zeus' message to Hektor
(181–217), and not long after that he has to retire wounded—see
further pp. 162–4. The message, passed on verbatim by Iris, sustains Hektor's efforts throughout the day. He first acknowledges
it as soon as Agamemnon is wounded—"ἐμοὶ δὲ μέγ' εὖχος ἔδωκε
Ζεὺς Κρονίδης" ('Zeus the son of Kronos has granted me great
glory') (11. 288–9). He refers to Zeus' promise at 12. 235–6, when
he rejects Poulydamas' warning, and at 13. 153–4, when he rallies
the Trojans. His wish at 13. 825 ff. echoes that at 8. 538 ff. (see
above), but now ἡμέρη ἥδε means 'this present day' rather than
'this coming day'. As the moment of triumph grows closer, after

---

[8] The only other remotely similar wording is at 5. 190 and 6. 487.
[9] δεῖπνον seems to be a mid-morning meal: the woodcutter's first shift is finished
(cf. Schadewaldt, *IS* 44, n. 2).

the reverses of the *Dios apatē*, Hektor once again refers to Zeus'
assurance to rally his men:

"οἴcετε πῦρ, ἅμα δ' αὐτοὶ ἀολλέεc ὄρνυτ' ἀϋτήν·
νῦν ἡμῖν πάντων Ζεὺc ἄξιον ἦμαρ ἔδωκε,
νῆαc ἐλεῖν, αἳ δεῦρο θεῶν ἀέκητι μολοῦcαι
ἡμῖν πήματα πολλὰ θέcαν"

'Bring fire, and raise the war-cry all together. Now Zeus has given us a
day that repays us for all—the capture of the ships, which came here
against the gods' will and have brought much pain on us . . .' (15. 718–21)

—if he can only take full advantage of the day that Zeus has given
him, it might outweigh nine years of oppressive siege.
Hektor's day of glory is well-advanced by the time that he sets
fire to a ship. And when Patroklos is at his height, it is signalled
that late afternoon has been reached (16. 777–9). Even so, there
is still some daylight left when Hektor puts on the armour of
Achilleus, and Zeus confirms his favour for the time being—*"ἀτάρ*
τοι νῦν γε μέγα κράτοc ἐγγυαλίξω . . ." ('but for the moment I shall
grant you great power . . .') (17. 206, see further pp. 185–7). And
when he decides to rescue Achilleus' horses, Zeus repeats his
undertaking for one last time:

"ἔτι γάρ cφιcι κῦδοc ὀρέξω,
κτείνειν, εἰc ὅ κε νῆαc ἐϋccέλμουc ἀφίκωνται
δύῃ τ' ἠέλιοc καὶ ἐπὶ κνέφαc ἱερὸν ἔλθῃ."

'. . . because I shall still give the Trojans glory, to keep on killing until
they reach the well-benched ships and the sun sets and the holy darkness
comes on.' (17. 453–5)

The sun does not actually set until after Achilleus has been
aroused.[10] There is then the standard scene-sequence of the 'post-
mortem scenes', but given special variations, to great effect. As at
8. 489ff. the Trojan *agorē* is narrated first, but this time there is
a very different mood, since they have been alarmed by the appearance of Achilleus (246–8). The previous evening only Hektor
spoke, but this time

---

[10] Is the sun reluctant (18. 240) as a foil to Hera's eagerness to end a day of
Achaian defeat? Owen, 183, suggests, characteristically, that the sun reflects the
audience's fears for Hektor. Note, by the way, how the simile at 18. 207ff. anticipates the sunset: the city is embattled all day until, *ἅμα ἠελίωι καταδύντι* (with the
setting of the sun), the beacons shine out for help.

τοῖcι δὲ Πουλυδάμαc πεπνυμένοc ἦρχ' ἀγορεύειν
Πανθοΐδηc· ὁ γὰρ οἶοc ὅρα πρόccω καὶ ὀπίccω·
Ἕκτορι δ' ἦεν ἑταῖροc, ἰῆι δ' ἐν νυκτὶ γένοντο,
ἀλλ' ὁ μὲν ἄρ μύθοιcιν, ὁ δ' ἔγχεϊ πολλὸν ἐνίκα·
ὅ cφιν ἐϋφρονέων ἀγορήcατο καὶ μετέειπεν·

The first to speak was Poulydamas in his wisdom, the son of Panthoös,
the only man among them with eyes for both past and future. He was a
companion of Hektor, the two of them born in the same night, but
Poulydamas was far the better with words, as Hektor was better with the
spear. In all good will he spoke and addressed the assembly . . .
(18. 249–53)

Poulydamas' 'biography' might suggest that he has been invented,
or at least first made prominent, for this occasion. In any case his
contribution here has been skilfully prepared for through the
preceding day.[11] He is first named at 11. 57, and proves to be no mean warrior
on several occasions through the central books. He first speaks at
12. 61 ff. The Trojan leaders' horses have baulked at the ditch,
and Poulydamas is quick with strategic advice on dismounting,
which Hektor accepts, and which proves effective (see further
p. 165). At 12. 200 ff., however, when they are about to cross the
ditch, he gives a cautious interpretation of the omen of the eagle
and snake. Hektor rejects him vehemently, starting with the same
line as he will use in book 18—"Πουλυδάμα, cὺ μὲν οὐκέτ' ἐμοὶ φίλα
ταῦτ' ἀγορεύειc" ('Poulydamas, what you say now is not to my
liking') (12. 231 = 18. 284). In book 12 Hektor's confident rejection
of caution is far from clearly foolish or blasphemous.[12] Thirdly,
when the Trojan assault becomes disorganized, at 13. 674 ff.,
Poulydamas advises the caution of rallying the leaders together,
good advice that Hektor follows. Poulydamas concludes

"ἦ γὰρ ἔγωγε
δείδω μὴ τὸ χθιζὸν ἀποcτήcωνται Ἀχαιοὶ

[11] On Poulydamas, see esp. Schadewaldt, *IS* 105–7; Reinhardt, *ID* 272–7;
Lohmann, 31–3, 119–20; Redfield, *NCI* 143–7; Bannert, 71–81.
[12] Defences of Hektor (cf. de Jong, 215): (1) there is room to doubt the genuineness of a portent—see Poulydamas himself at 217—especially a bird portent
(see 239–40) (on later Greek attitudes, see A. D. Nock, *Essays on Religion and the
Ancient World* (Oxford, 1972), ii. 534 ff.). (2) Zeus himself gives clear indications
to the contrary (see 235–6, 241–2); and his dust-storm heartens the Trojans. (3)
Hektor's sentiments are admirable, especially the much-quoted line 243 (cf.
15. 496–7). (4) Poulydamas' fears are actually not fulfilled until much later, at
16. 364 ff.; and even then they do not prove disastrous.

χρεῖος, ἐπεὶ παρὰ νηυςὶν ἀνὴρ ἄτος πολέμοιο
μίμνει, ὃν οὐκέτι πάγχυ μάχης cχήcεcθαι ὀίω."

'For my part I fear that the Achaians may pay us back their debt of
yesterday, as there is waiting by their ships a man who is greedy for war,
and I do not think he will keep right out of the fighting any longer.'
(13. 744–7)

(an impressive temporal back-reference to Hektor's victories in
8). This is premature. But when Poulydamas next speaks, which
is at 18. 254 ff., the premonition will have come true.

Poulydamas' advice in 18 is to retreat inside the walls in order
to pre-empt any possibility of a rout at the hands of Achilleus
while they are retreating before him across the plain.[13] He fears
exactly what does happen. He explicitly contrasts the situation
with the justified confidence of the *agorē* the previous evening:

"ἀμφὶ μάλα φράζεcθε, φίλοι· κέλομαι γὰρ ἔγωγε
ἄcτυδε νῦν ἰέναι, μὴ μίμνειν ἠῶ δῖαν   255
ἐν πεδίωι παρὰ νηυcίν· ἑκὰc δ' ἀπὸ τείχεόc εἰμεν.
ὄφρα μὲν οὗτοc ἀνὴρ Ἀγαμέμνονι μήνιε δίωι,
τόφρα δὲ ῥηΐτεροι πολεμίζειν ἦcαν Ἀχαιοί·
χαίρεcκον γὰρ ἔγωγε θοῆιc ἐπὶ νηυcὶν ἰαύων
ἐλπόμενοc νῆαc αἱρηcέμεν ἀμφιελίccαc.   260
νῦν δ' αἰνῶc δείδοικα ποδώκεα Πηλεΐωνα·

. . . .

ἀλλ' ἴομεν προτὶ ἄcτυ, πίθεcθέ μοι· ὧδε γὰρ ἔcται·
νῦν μὲν νὺξ ἀπέπαυcε ποδώκεα Πηλεΐωνα
ἀμβροcίη· εἰ δ' ἄμμε κιχήcεται ἐνθάδ' ἐόνταc
αὔριον ὁρμηθεὶc cὺν τεύχεcιν, εὖ νύ τιc αὐτὸν
γνώcεται· ἀcπαcίωc γὰρ ἀφίξεται Ἴλιον ἱρὴν   270
ὅc κε φύγηι"

'Think very carefully, friends. I advise you to return to the city now, and
not wait for the holy dawn out here in the plain by the ships, this far
from our city-wall. As long as this man kept up his anger against godlike
Agamemnon, the Achaians were easier to fight—and I too was glad to
be camping close by their fast fleet in the hope of capturing the balanced
ships. But now I am terribly afraid of the swift-footed son of Peleus . . .
No, let us go back to the city. Believe me, it will be as I say. For the
moment immortal night has stopped the swift-footed son of Peleus. But
if he catches us out here tomorrow and comes against us in armed

---

[13] Strictly speaking he does not have direct evidence that Achilleus has given
up his anger—though the audience has. For this narrative technique, see p. 150
above.

strength, then no-one will fail to be aware of him: we will be glad to reach sacred Ilios, those of us who escape . . .' (18. 254–61, 266–71)

The motif of tomorrow and of waiting for the dawn is, in effect, a citation of Hektor's speech of twenty-four hours earlier (in performance-time as well as narrative-time, if my theory is right). If they avoid the danger by spending the night inside the city, then

"πρῶϊ δ' ὑπηοῖοι cὺν τεύχεcι θωρηχθέντεc
cτηcόμεθ' ἂμ πύργουc· τῶι δ' ἄλγιον, αἴ κ' ἐθέληιcιν
ἐλθὼν ἐκ νηῶν περὶ τείχεοc ἄμμι μάχεcθαι."

'early in the morning, before the showing of dawn, we will arm in our weapons and take posts along the walls. Then it will be the worse for Achilleus if he comes out from the ships and tries to fight us for the wall.' (18. 277–9)

Hektor's reply, implying that Poulydamas' real motive is cowardly avarice, works in some pointed ripostes. He caps what he has said about tomorrow:

"πρῶϊ δ' ὑπηοῖοι cὺν τεύχεcι θωρηχθέντεc
νηυcὶν ἔπι γλαφυρῆιcιν ἐγείρομεν ὀξὺν Ἄρηα.
εἰ δ' ἐτεὸν παρὰ ναῦφιν ἀνέcτη δῖοc Ἀχιλλεύc,
ἄλγιον, αἴ κ' ἐθέληιcι, τῶι ἔccεται."

'Then early in the morning, before the showing of dawn, let us arm in our weapons and wake war's anger by the hollow ships. And if it is true that godlike Achilleus has stirred from the ships, then yes, it will be the worse for him if that is what he tries!' (18. 303–6)

The folly of Hektor's over-confidence and of its endorsement by the Trojans, as on the previous evening (18. 310 = 8. 542), is spelt out by the narrator with untypical explicitness:

ὣc Ἕκτωρ ἀγόρευ', ἐπὶ δὲ Τρῶεc κελάδηcαν,
νήπιοι· ἐκ γάρ cφεων φρένac εἵλετο Παλλὰc Ἀθήνη.
Ἕκτορι μὲν γὰρ ἐπῄνηcαν κακὰ μητιόωντι,
Πουλυδάμαντι δ' ἄρ' οὔ τιc, ὃc ἐcθλὴν φράζετο βουλήν.

So Hektor spoke, and the Trojans roared in approval—the fools: Pallas Athene had taken away their wits. They applauded Hektor and his disastrous plan, and not one of them supported Poulydamas, who had given them good advice. (18. 310–13)

It is not just that Hektor has failed to see the sense of Poulydamas' strategic arguments; he has failed to remember the message of

Zeus. The calibration of time and the placing of this speech so soon after the sunset accentuate his failure of *mētis* when he alludes to Zeus' favour:

> "νῦν δ' ὅτε πέρ μοι ἔδωκε Κρόνου πάϊς ἀγκυλομήτεω
> κῦδος ἀρέςθ' ἐπὶ νηυςί, θαλάςςῃ τ' ἔλςαι Ἀχαιούς,
> νήπιε, μηκέτι ταῦτα νοήματα φαῖν' ἐνὶ δήμωι·"

'But now when the son of devious-minded Kronos has granted me glory won by the ships, and the Achaians penned back against the sea, this is no time, fool, to put these thoughts of yours before the people.' (18. 293–5)

Hektor's day is over, and his over-confidence and vulnerability are captured in this mistake of timing, his misuse of νῦν δέ ('but now'). This is a supreme example of the way that Homer's use of his framework of narrative-time is more than merely a structuring mechanism. Though Hektor does not realize it, an alert audience can see that he is in fact choosing to die tomorrow (see further p. 200).

The anticipation of tomorrow in book 18 is in fact raised by a divinity and before the sunset (cf. Zeus at 8. 470). Thetis tells Achilleus,

> "ἀλλὰ cὺ μὲν μή πω καταδύcεο μῶλον Ἄρηος,
> πρίν γ' ἐμὲ δεῦρ' ἐλθοῦcαν ἐν ὀφθαλμοῖcιν ἴδηαι·
> ἠῶθεν γὰρ νεῦμαι ἅμ' ἠελίωι ἀνιόντι
> τεύχεα καλὰ φέρουcα παρ' Ἡφαίcτοιο ἄνακτοс."

'No, you must not enter the fray of war until you see me returned to you here—in the morning, at the sun's rising, I shall come bringing you beautiful armour from lord Hephaistos.' (18. 134–7)

When the sun does set, there is no kind of *agorē* on the Achaian side, in contrast with book 9: the scene is overshadowed by the lamentation over the body of Patroklos, led by Achilleus (314–53). The big *agorē* is postponed till the next morning (the opening of part III), which enables it to correspond to, and to cancel, that of book 1 as well as that of book 9.

During the mourning-scene there is no explicit reference to tomorrow. Achilleus' undertaking, however—

> "οὔ cε πρὶν κτεριῶ, πρίν γ' Ἕκτορος ἐνθάδ' ἐνεῖκαι
> τεύχεα καὶ κεφαλήν, μεγαθύμου coῖο φονῆοс·"

'I shall not give you burial until I have brought here the armour and the head of Hektor, the great man who murdered you.' (18. 334–5)

—will in fact be fulfilled on the following evening. They lament for Patroklos παννύχιοι (all night long) (315), which implies until morning. This is picked up again in

> παννύχιοι μὲν ἔπειτα πόδας ταχὺν ἀμφ' Ἀχιλῆα
> Μυρμιδόνες Πάτροκλον ἀνεστενάχοντο γοῶντες·
> Ζεὺς δ' Ἥρην προσέειπε κασιγνήτην ἄλοχόν τε·

Then all night long the Myrmidons gathered round swift-footed Achilleus and mourned in lamentation for Patroklos. And Zeus spoke to Hera, his sister and wife . . . (18. 354–6)

These are, according to me, the opening lines of part III. The obvious calibration—to end one part with bed and to begin the next with dawn, as I believe happened at 9/11—is here bridged by Thetis' fetching of the new armour, an incident which takes all the night.

6.3 Hektor and Sarpedon break through

> cτῆ δὲ μάλ' ἐγγὺς ἰών, καὶ ἐρεισάμενος βάλε μέccαc,
> εὖ διαβάc, ἵνα μή οἱ ἀφαυρότερον βέλος εἴη,
> ῥῆξε δ' ἀπ' ἀμφοτέρους θαιρούς· πέce δὲ λίθος εἴcω
> βριθοcύνηι, μέγα δ' ἀμφὶ πύλαι μύκον, οὐδ' ἄρ' ὀχῆες   460
> ἐcχεθέτην, cανίδες δὲ διέτμαγεν ἄλλυδιc ἄλλη
> λᾶος ὑπὸ ῥιπῆς· ὁ δ' ἄρ' ἔcθορε φαίδιμος Ἕκτωρ
> νυκτὶ θοῆι ἀτάλαντος ὑπώπια· λάμπε δὲ χαλκῶι
> cμερδαλέωι, τὸν ἔεcτο περὶ χροΐ, δοιὰ δὲ χερcὶ
> δοῦρ' ἔχεν· οὔ κέν τίc μιν ἐρύκακεν ἀντιβολήcαc   465
> νόcφι θεῶν, ὅτ' ἐcᾶλτο πύλαc· πυρὶ δ' ὄccε δεδήει.
> κέκλετο δὲ Τρώεccιν ἑλιξάμενος καθ' ὅμιλον
> τεῖχος ὑπερβαίνειν· τοὶ δ' ὀτρύνοντι πίθοντο.
> αὐτίκα δ' οἱ μὲν τεῖχος ὑπέρβαcαν, οἱ δὲ κατ' αὐτὰc
> ποιητὰc ἐcέχυντο πύλαc· Δαναοὶ δὲ φόβηθεν   470
> νῆαc ἀνὰ γλαφυράc, ὅμαδος δ' ἀλίαcτος ἐτύχθη.

Hektor went in and stopped close, then taking a firm stance he hurled the rock at the centre of the doors, spreading his legs well apart to give more power to his cast, and he smashed off the hinges on either side—its own weight carried the stone on inside, and the gates groaned loud and the bars could not hold: and the doors were shattered in flying fragments under the impact of the rock. Then glorious Hektor leapt inside, his face like the rush of night. He shone with the fearful bronze that covered his body, and there were two spears in his hands. None but the gods could have faced and stopped him when he leapt through the gates: and his eyes blazed with fire. He swung round and shouted to the mass of Trojans to cross over the wall, and they followed his command. At once some climbed over the wall, and the others poured in through the strong-built gateway itself. The Danaans were sent running in panic among their hollow ships, and the din rose unceasing. (12. 457–71)

In between the dawn of the great central day and the crucial synchronism of the burning of a ship with the arousal of Patroklos at 16. 112–29 (see § **6.4** below) there are some 3,500 lines, perhaps 6 hours of performance-time. These are largely taken up with battle which, though to and fro, tends necessarily in Hektor's favour.

With all its fighting, this is not the part of the *Iliad* which appeals most obviously to modern taste. It does help, however, to appreciate the extent of the large-scale narrative strategies, as this sets the events into the shaping of the poem as a whole. First of all, for example, Agamemnon, Diomedes, and Odysseus are all off the field by 11. 600—as indeed are Eurypylos and Machaon. The separate incidents combine to form a narrative shape.

Agamemnon's so-called *aristeia* is not very long, compared with those of Achilleus, Diomedes, Patroklos, or, indeed, Hektor; in fact Agamemnon's scene of battle success lasts from 11. 91 to 180. There is, however, no shortage of blood in it.[14] After disposing of a pair of sons of Priam, whom Achilleus had previously spared and ransomed, he is supplicated by Peisandros and Hippolochos, sons of Antimachos. According to the anthropology of the battle-field supplication-scene, the captured man appeals both to pity and to the prospect of *apoina* from a kinsman. The captor not only gains the *apoina*, but gives out some κῆδος (concern); and so a *charis*-relationship is set up (see p. 59). Hence the recurrent line τῶν κέν τοι χαρίσαιτο πατὴρ ἀπερείσι᾽ ἄποινα (my father would favour you with unlimited ransom) (6. 49 = 10. 380 = 11. 134). It is in keeping with the character of Menelaos that he should relent before the plea of Adrestos at 6. 45–53. Agamemnon comes up, however, with an equally characteristic response:

"ὦ πέπον, ὦ Μενέλαε, τίη δὲ σὺ κήδεαι οὕτως
ἀνδρῶν; ἦ σοὶ ἄριστα πεποίηται κατὰ οἶκον

---

[14] Cf. Reinhardt, *ID* 251–3; Whitman, 158–9. On his alarming shield as suitable preparation, see Armstrong, 345.

πρὸς Τρώων; τῶν μή τιc ὑπεκφύγοι αἰπὺν ὄλεθρον
χεῖράc θ' ἡμετέραc, μηδ' ὅν τινα γαcτέρι μήτηρ
κοῦρον ἐόντα φέροι, μηδ' ὃc φύγοι, ἀλλ' ἅμα πάντεc
Ἰλίου ἐξαπολοίατ' ἀκήδεcτοι καὶ ἄφαντοι."

'Menelaos, dear brother, why this concern for men's lives? Did you get the very best treatment from the Trojans in your house? Not one of them must escape stark destruction at our hands, even the boys still carried in their mothers' wombs—not even they must escape, but all be extinguished together, wiped from Ilios without sight or ceremony.' (6. 55–60)

His objection is that, since it is Menelaos' quarrel that has brought them there, it is inappropriate for him to grant any κῆδοc—contrast the situation of Glaukos and Diomedes soon after, see pp. 58–9. His argument has some validity—and Menelaos accepts it as αἴcιμα, see pp. 51–2. None the less no one else in the *Iliad* extends the violence of war as far as hacking the bellies of pregnant women in case they carry male children.[15] So too with Peisandros and Hippolochos. Agamemnon prefers blood to gold, ironically turning Antimachos' ill-gotten wealth into the reason for his sons' death rather than their survival.[16] The bizarre mutilation of the corpse of Hippolochos (145–7) may also be in keeping with the portrayal of Agamemnon, who seems to specialize in grisly slayings, as do Meriones and the lesser Aias.[17]

Once the narrative rejoins Agamemnon after Zeus' message to Hektor (181–217, see above), the prediction of his wounding hangs over him. So the grand invocation of the Muses in 218 ff. asks, in effect, which Trojan it was who wounded Agamemnon. First Iphidamas, son of Antenor and Theano—venerable and much-bereaved parents—nearly wounds him; then his eldest brother Koön, in revenge for him, does pierce Agamemnon's arm—and seriously enough to put him out of action—before Agamemnon decapitates him. Koön's moment of glory, but not his nasty death, is recalled at 19. 53. The audience, since it knows Zeus' message to Hektor, should be able to hear more than the participants

---

[15] Some, e.g. C. Moulton, *Similes in the Homeric Poems* (Göttingen, 1977), 98–9, find the simile likening Agamemnon's wound to a woman's labour pains at 11. 269–72 pointed in connection with his sentiments in book 6; but any connection is extremely remote.

[16] The story may be an invention for this moment, cf. Schadewaldt, *IS* 48; Willcock, *HSCP* 81 (1977), 46.

[17] Cf. Schadewaldt, *IS* 47; Fenik, *TBS* 15, 84; Taplin, 'Agamemnon', 72.

themselves can in Agamemnon's words as he leaves the battlefield
for the last time in the *Iliad*:

> "ὦ φίλοι, Ἀργείων ἡγήτορες ἠδὲ μέδοντες,
> ὑμεῖς μὲν νῦν νηυσὶν ἀμύνετε ποντοπόροισι
> φύλοπιν ἀργαλέην, ἐπεὶ οὐκ ἐμὲ μητίετα Ζεὺς
> εἴασε Τρώεσσι πανημέριον πολεμίζειν."

'Friends, leaders and lords of the Argives, now it is you who must keep
the grim battle from our sea-going ships, since Zeus the counsellor has
not allowed me to fight the whole day long against the Trojans.'
(11. 276–9)

Diomedes and Odysseus manage to hold up Hektor's ensuing
rally, and Diomedes even stuns him temporarily (349–67); but he
can see well enough which side Zeus is favouring (317–19). Before
long, Paris wounds Diomedes in the foot with an arrow: for all
his scorn and abuse, the fact remains that Diomedes has to leave
the field and that he is off for the rest of the *Iliad* (though not the
Funeral Games). The scholiast (on 369–72), taking his cue from
Diomedes, has been followed by many critics: 'even standing by
the tomb of his ancestor, he can do nothing worthy'. Yet Paris is
no mean warrior on occasion, and the use of the ancestral landmark
to steady his aim may be seen as a way of enhancing this significant
hit rather than diminishing it.[18]

Odysseus is now isolated, and before long (428 ff.) is wounded
by Sokos, whom he kills (like Agamemnon with Koön). In
response to his calls, the only two remaining first-rung Achaians,
Aias and Menelaos, come to the rescue. Again and again through
the day, the image recurs of Aias fighting a rearguard action and
doggedly protecting his comrades.[19] At this stage, when Hektor
has succeeded on the left with the help of Paris (497 ff.), he turns
against Aias (521 ff.), who slowly retreats like a lion from spears
and firebrands:

> ὣς Αἴας τότ' ἀπὸ Τρώων τετιημένος ἦτορ
> ἤϊε πόλλ' ἀέκων· περὶ γὰρ δίε νηυσὶν Ἀχαιῶν.

So then Aias went back from the Trojans, distressed at heart and much
against his will, as he was fearful for the Achaians' ships. (11. 556–7)

---

[18] Obviously it anticipates the death of Achilleus. I agree with Fenik (*TBS* 234)
that this does not entail neo-analytic theories about the *Aethiopis*. The tomb of
Ilos, by the way, also crops up at 10. 415, 11. 166, 24. 239. Ilos was great-grandson
of Dardanos and grandfather of Priam (20. 215–40). For Trojan landmarks, see
§ 3.3 above.

[19] On Aias, see Schadewaldt, *IS* 69–70; Whitman, 169–75.

He is fierce and heroic like the lion; and at the same time he is stubborn and unpretentious like the donkey, the second simile at 558 ff.

At this stage the narrative leaves the battlefield for 250 lines to set Patroklos off on the path to his death—see pp. 175–6 below. On return at 12. 35 ff., Hektor is by now attacking the newly built wall. When the ditch proves a problem for their chariots, Pouly-damas' advice proves useful (see above). Asios, however, rashly pushes forward for immediate advantage—the point is spelt out at once:

νήπιος, οὐδ' ἄρ' ἔμελλε κακὰς ὑπὸ κῆρας ἀλύξας
ἵπποισιν καὶ ὄχεσφιν ἀγαλλόμενος παρὰ νηῶν
ἂψ ἀπονοστήσειν προτὶ Ἴλιον ἠνεμόεσσαν·
πρόσθεν γάρ μιν μοῖρα δυσώνυμος ἀμφεκάλυψεν
ἔγχεϊ Ἰδομενῆος, ἀγαυοῦ Δευκαλίδαο.

... poor fool, he was not to escape the vile fates of death and make his return back from the ships to windy Ilios in all the glory of his horses and chariot: before that accursed doom unfolded him by the spear of Idomeneus, proud son of Deukalion. (12. 113–17)

Asios soon regrets his strategy (164 ff.), but he is not actually killed until 13. 383–9, and then in quite different circumstances. The poet, with the kind of detail that he is capable of on occasion, names five of Asios' followers in 12. 139–40, and then makes sure that all five come to grief in the course of the next 1,000 lines.[20] So the first man to reject the advice of Poulydamas meets disaster, as Hektor will—and so do his followers, as the Trojans will.

By the stage of 12. 256 ff., Hektor and his men are trying to demolish the wall, though they meet with resistance led by the Aiantes. There follows, in 12. 270–414, something of an *aristeia* for Sarpedon.

Οὐδ' ἄν πω τότε γε Τρῶες καὶ φαίδιμος Ἕκτωρ
τείχεος ἐρρήξαντο πύλας καὶ μακρὸν ὀχῆα,
εἰ μὴ ἄρ' υἱὸν ἑὸν Σαρπηδόνα μητίετα Ζεὺς
ὦρσεν ἐπ' Ἀργείοισι, λέονθ' ὣς βουσὶν ἕλιξιν.

And even then the Trojans and glorious Hektor would not yet have broken through the gate of the wall and its long cross-bar, if Zeus the

[20] Iamenos and Orestes are soon killed, at 12. 193–4. The rest do not die as a direct result of this strategic mistake: Oinomaos is killed by Idomeneus at 13. 506. Thoön by Antilochos at 13. 545, and lastly Asios' own son Adamas is brought down by Meriones at 13. 560–75.

counsellor had not set his own son Sarpedon at the Argives, like a lion on twist-horned cattle. (12. 290–3)

Although his assaults on the wall run into resistance (333–91, 406–37), he is none the less the first to make a passable breach in the battlements—πολέεccι δὲ θῆκε κέλευθον (and he had opened a passage for many) (399). At 16. 558 Patroklos will boast that he has killed the man ὃc πρῶτοc ἐcήλατο τεῖχοc Ἀχαιῶν (who was the first to break through the Achaian wall).

As well as his deeds, Sarpedon is given his great speech to Glaukos at 310–28, carefully placed as a kind of commentary on Hektor's advance. Far from being a statement of the heroic obvious, the lines are a superbly fresh vision grasped on the verge of their speaker's finest hour. Sarpedon's insight is to see not only that a leader should properly deserve *tīmē* and *kleos*, but that the pressure of death is a spur—not to survive, but to risk your life boldly. The formulaic epithet in μάχην ἐc κυδιάνειραν (328) carries particular force in the context. Far from showing the unquestioned unanimity of 'the heroic code', these lines show how the motivation to dare death is subject to constant scrutiny. 'It is not unreflective or unselfconscious heroism that drives men on. Facing death, they see both the obligation and the terror, and their speech reflects the totality of their situation and their response.'[21]

The battle over the Achaian wall understandably takes on some of the characteristics of a siege narrative, drawing, no doubt, on the traditional elements of siege-poems. Hence the emphasis on the gates.[22] After the simile of the widow's scales (433 ff.) there is, despite all the Achaian resistance, a turning-point—or a scale-tipping—which leads to Hektor's dramatic breakthrough. It is as though the motif of the scales spreads over from the simile into the narrative. While Hektor's armour and eyes flash brightly, his swoop through the gates is like nightfall, conveying the impression

---

[21] Griffin, *HLD* 73, cf. 92–3.
[22] At 12. 120 ff. they are still held open to receive fugitives, like Troy at 21. 530 ff. They recur at 175 ff., 223–4, 291, and 340, where they are now closed. I believe, by the way, that ancient critics were right to take 12. 175–81 to be interpolated: the multiplicity of gates there, the fire (reserved in the *Iliad* for the threat to the ships), and the masonry ramparts all belong to another poem with a more substantial siege. The casual self-reference of με in 176 is also un-Homeric.

of the turn of events as seen by the Argives.[23] The figure of speech in 465–6 prepares for the imminent actual intervention of Poseidon, at 13. 10 ff. It is his and Hera's interference with the plan of Zeus that stand between Hektor's breach of the gates and his next objective—the firing of the ships.

6.4 Fire nears the ships

Τρῶες δὲ λείουσιν ἐοικότες ὠμοφάγοισι
νηυσὶν ἐπεσσεύοντο, Διὸς δὲ τέλειον ἐφετμάς,
ὅ σφισιν αἰὲν ἔγειρε μένος μέγα, θέλγε δὲ θυμὸν
Ἀργείων καὶ κῦδος ἀπαίνυτο, τοὺς δ' ὀρόθυνεν.   595
Ἕκτορι γάρ οἱ θυμὸς ἐβούλετο κῦδος ὀρέξαι
Πριαμίδηι, ἵνα νηυσὶ κορωνίσι θεσπιδαὲς πῦρ
ἐμβάλοι ἀκάματον, Θέτιδος δ' ἐξαίσιον ἀρὴν
πᾶσαν ἐπικρήνειε· τὸ γὰρ μένε μητίετα Ζεύς,
νηὸς καιομένης σέλας ὀφθαλμοῖσιν ἰδέσθαι.   600

Now the Trojans swept on at the ships like lions who eat raw flesh. They were effecting the will of Zeus, who constantly roused the spirit strong in them, and bewildered the hearts of the Argives and denied them glory, while spurring on the Trojans. His heart wished to give the glory to Hektor, son of Priam, so he could throw the untiring power of monstrous fire on the beaked ships, and thus the fatal prayer of Thetis could be granted in full. Zeus the counsellor was waiting for his eyes to see the blaze of a ship alight. (15. 592–600)

Hektor's great triumph is long-delayed. Once he has broken through the gates, Zeus turns his attention elsewhere:

οὐ γὰρ ὅ γ' ἀθανάτων τινὰ ἔλπετο ὃν κατὰ θυμὸν
ἐλθόντ' ἢ Τρώεσσιν ἀρηξέμεν ἢ Δαναοῖσιν.

he did not think in his heart that any of the immortals would come to bring help to either Trojans or Danaans. (13. 8–9)

This miscalculation, compounded by the *Dios apatē*, opens the way for some 1,750 lines of 'retardation' (perhaps some three hours of performance). This is taken up with a great deal of back-and-forth battle which is strategically insignificant in that by

---

[23] I am rather baffled by ὑπώπια ('face') in 463, however. It is impossible to take it with νυκτί ('night') or with λάμπε ('shone') without emendation. For the combination of light and dark cf. 17. 591 ff. and Griffin, *HLD* 171.

15. 405 Hektor has brought the struggle back to much the same point of advantage he had reached at the end of book 12. This 'retardation' gives a brief prominence to several relatively minor characters, such as Idomeneus, Meriones, and Deïphobos, and it gives scope for abundant bloodshed, gruesome details, and battlefield 'humour', the macabre human counterpart of the goings-on on Olympos. Yet the struggle and the deaths never become merely perfunctory, they are consistently real. And the cruelty and waste of war are not taken for granted:

> μάλα κεν θρασυκάρδιος είη
> ὃς τότε γηθήςειεν ἰδὼν πόνον οὐδ' ἀκάχοιτο.

It would be a hard-hearted man indeed who could take pleasure in that sight and not be struck with horror. (13. 343–4)[24]

The whole situation is much less clear than when Zeus had control over it. For example, when the leading Achaians form a kind of armoured wall (13. 125 ff.),[25] Hektor calls confidently to his troops

> "Τρῶες καὶ Λύκιοι καὶ Δάρδανοι ἀγχιμαχηταί,
> παρμένετ'· οὔ τοι δηρὸν ἐμὲ cχήcουcιν Ἀχαιοί,
> καὶ μάλα πυργηδὸν cφέαc αὐτοὺc ἀρτύναντεc,
> ἀλλ', ὀίω, χάccονται ὑπ' ἔγχεοc, εἰ ἐτεόν με
> ὦρcε θεῶν ὦριcτοc, ἐρίγδουποc πόcιc Ἥρηc."

'Trojans and Lycians and close-fighting Dardanians, stand by me! The Achaians will not hold me for long, even though they have formed themselves into a wall against me—no, I think they will give way under my spear, if it was indeed the greatest of gods that inspired my attack, the loud-thundering husband of Hera.' (13. 150–4)

This is true, but not straightforwardly so; and Hektor's exhortation produces no immediate result. What follows is typical of this part of the *Iliad*: an indecisive clash between Deïphobos and Meriones (157f.), more melée (169–205), and then, following from a further intervention by Poseidon (206–39), the arousal of Idomeneus.

---

[24] There are many good observations on book 13 in C. Michel, *Erläuterungen zum N der Ilias* (Heidelberg, 1971). On 13–15, see also C. H. Whitman and R. Scodel in *HSCP* 85 (1981), 1–16.

[25] These unusual tactics are inspired by a god—cf. Reinhardt, *ID* 281–2. They are a peculiar attempt to form an armoured barrier, so they are not necessarily influenced by the development of hoplite ranks; cf. O. Murray, *Early Greece* (London, 1980), 127–8; *contra* e.g. M. L. West, Hesiod, *Th.* 46, n. 2.

The battle in the centre, which is dominated by Hektor and the Aiantes, is left by the narrator from 13.205 to 13.674. Once Idomeneus and Meriones join the battle on the left at 330 ff., there follow 300 particularly slaughter-crammed lines, scarcely relieved by the departure of Idomeneus at 515 and of his particular foe Deïphobos at 539. The touches of humour intensify rather than relieve the gruesomeness of the slaughter—as, for example, with Idomeneus' black-humour 'stage direction' over Othryoneus, Kassandra's suitor, at 13.361 ff., especially 381–4. A kind of macabre contest of vaunting is set up. Asios (and his charioteer) die trying to retrieve the corpse of Othryoneus (384 ff.); Deïphobos, seeking revenge for them, hits Hyperenor and boasts

"οὐ μὰν αὖτ' ἄτιτος κεῖτ' Ἄcιος, ἀλλά ἕ φημι
εἰς Ἀϊδός περ ἰόντα πυλάρταο κρατεροῖο
γηθήσειν κατὰ θυμόν, ἐπεί ῥά οἱ ὤπαсα πομπόν."

'So now Asios does not lie there unavenged—even on his journey down to Hades the strong Keeper of the Gate, I think he will be happy at heart, now I have given him a guide.' (13.414–16)[26]

Idomeneus, when he kills Alkathoös, taunts Deïphobos instead of the corpse directly:

"Δηΐφοβ', ἦ ἄρα δή τι ἐΐcκομεν ἄξιον εἶναι
τρεῖς ἑνὸς ἀντὶ πεφάσθαι;"

'Deïphobos, are we then to reckon it a fair bargain yet, three men killed for one?' (13.446–7)[27]

Major characters are on the whole kept out of this part of the *Iliad*. Aineias only figures at 13.458–544, for example, Paris at 13.765 ff., and Menelaos at 13.581–642. Menelaos delivers a homily on κόρος (satiety) (13.620–39), which has been generally slighted;[28] but it is characteristic of him, especially in such a blood-

---

[26] The humour is not, however, the kind of breezy relish worked up by E. Vermeule, *Aspects of Death in Early Greek Art* (Berkeley, Calif., 1979), Ch. 3. On the importance of minor warriors for the poem as a whole see G. Strasburger. In 423, by the way, we must read cτενάχοντε ('the two of them groaning') with Aristarchos and against the *paradosis*, which has been corrupted by formulaic influence. Hypsenor is dead and cannot be groaning.

[27] There is far more pathos in the marriage of Alkathoös (427 ff.) than in the hopes of Othryoneus; cf. Griffin, *HLD* 131–2; Willcock, *Comp.* on 13.428.

[28] Older commentators such as Leaf used to blame incompetent interpolation. Fenik (*TBS* 147) blames the power of traditional technique for 'Menelaus' unhappy excursus'. On Menelaos and his 'special relationship' with the narrator, see A. Parry, *LCH* 317–24; cf. Willcock in *BOP* 189–90.

filled context. His train of thought is that the Trojans first behaved villainously by abducting Helen in despite of Zeus ὅρκιος (of the oath), and yet now (αὖτε, 628) they are adding insult to injury by attacking the very ships that bring their retribution. It is understandable that he should rebuke Zeus for supporting the side which he believes to be so utterly in the wrong (ἄνδρεσσι ὑβριστῆισι (men of violence) 633).

Indeed Menelaos' attitude might well be taken as the view of warfare which the *Iliad* implicitly shares with many of its audience: war is evil, but there are times when it is a necessary evil. No one in his right senses would prefer war to the delights of peace. The sympathetic Menelaos works in a very Homeric list of such delights:

"πάντων μὲν κόρος ἐστί, καὶ ὕπνου καὶ φιλότητος
μολπῆς τε γλυκερῆς καὶ ἀμύμονος ὀρχηθμοῖο,
τῶν πέρ τις καὶ μᾶλλον ἐέλδεται ἐξ ἔρον εἶναι
ἢ πολέμου· Τρῶες δὲ μάχης ἀκόρητοι ἔασιν."

'Men reach their fill of all things, even of sleep and love and sweet music and the delightful dance, things in which a man would rather slake his pleasure than in war: but the Trojans cannot have their fill of battle.' (13. 636–9)

The last event of this long stretch of battle is an exchange of provocative words between Hektor and Aias (13. 802–32). This is eventually resumed, at 14. 361 ff., by a marshalling of the hosts and the long-anticipated clash of these two heroes. In between comes a continuation of the return of Patroklos, followed by a meeting of Achaian leaders off the field (14. 1 ff.), and then the *Dios apatē* (14. 153–360). Fenik (*TBS* 156–8) has shown how all this is an unparalleled disruption of a typical sequence. His claim that 'something has gone seriously wrong here' and his recourse to the ways of old-style analysis seem tendentious, however.[29] Just because many battle-scenes in the *Iliad* follow typical patterns, that does not mean that all have to (though I do not deny the relatively poor quality of some of this, especially of 14. 135–52 and 368–83).

The scene of divine dalliance, with all its beauty and light-heartedness, stands in extreme contrast with the grim masses of toil and slaughter before and after it. Its humour—for example

---

[29] Cf. Whitman and Scodel, op. cit. (n. 24 above). On the meeting of the Achaian leaders, see R. M. Frazer, *Hermes*, 113 (1985), 1–7.

Hera's devious raising of the topic of love-making between estranged partners (14. 305–6), or Zeus' Leporello-style catalogue of past conquests—is tellingly set against the deadly jests of the battlefield. At least two elements verge on 'parody' of mortal warfare. Hera girds herself for 'battle' with items of toilet that play on an arming scene (14. 175–86).[30] These culminate with Aphrodite's ἱμάc (band), which, like a shield or baldric with its terrifying motifs, is ornamented appropriately for its function:

ἔνθ' ἔνι μὲν φιλότηc, ἐν δ' ἵμεροc, ἐν δ' ὀαριcτύc
πάρφαcιc, ἥ ρ' ἔκλεψε νόον πύκα περ φρονεόντων.

Here there was love, and desire, and the sweet allurement of whispered talk, which seduces the heart even in those of good sense. (14. 216–17)

And in the end Zeus is reduced to deep sleep on his particular 'territory' of Ida with a description which comes close to mocking the language of death in battle:

Ὥc ὁ μὲν ἀτρέμαc εὗδε πατὴρ ἀνὰ Γαργάρωι ἄκρωι,
ὕπνωι καὶ φιλότητι δαμείc, ἔχε δ' ἀγκὰc ἄκοιτιν·

So the father slept unmoving on the height of Gargaron, overcome by sleep and love, holding his wife in his arms. (14. 352–3)

Events now move fast: once Aias has put Hektor out of action (402–39), there is a sequence of bloody tit-for-tat[31] until the Trojans take to their heels (14. 508–22, 15. 1–4). Zeus reawakens at 15. 4, but it takes him all the way until 15. 262 to restore his authority on Olympos and replace Poseidon with Apollo on the battlefield. The next 130 lines are spent getting Hektor and the Trojans back to where they were at the end of the book 12, except that, while the ditch posed a serious obstacle earlier (especially at 12. 49–87), Apollo now pushes down the banks to make a causeway for their horses. This brings the Trojans right to the ships for the first time, and sets up the strange (quixotic?) picture of chariots fighting against hulks.

There is considerable invention in the details of the tactics and weaponry adapted to these unusual circumstances.[32] Lykophron

---

[30] Cf. Reinhardt, *ID* 291; Edwards, *HPI* 247 ff.

[31] Typified by Ilioneus, an only child and favourite of Hermes, who is killed by Peneleos in revenge for Promachos (486 ff.). He is singled out, however, for the degradation of decapitation, his head held up on a spear 'like a poppy-head'.

[32] Earlier, at 14. 409–11, Aias picked up one of the ἔχματα νηῶν (chocks (?) for the ships), but it is not clear just what they were.

does not simply fall to the ground, for example, but νηὸς ἄπο πρύμνης (15. 435). The Achaians make use of the weapons lying to hand, the long glued ξυστοί intended for sea battles. At 674 ff. Aias fights an extraordinary rearguard action with one of these pikes, δυωκαιεικοσίπηχυ (a length of 22 cubits) (678), leaping from ship to ship like some circus-performer. He eventually has to give way θρῆνυν ἐφ' ἑπταπόδην (to the seven-foot bridge) (729): there he takes his stand, jabbing at the flame-bearing attackers.

The great confrontation between Hektor and Aias has been building up ever since their duel in book 7. While Zeus slept, Aias put Hektor out of action, but eventually a balance between them is restored:

> τὼ δὲ μιῆς περὶ νηὸς ἔχον πόνον, οὐδὲ δύναντο
> οὔθ' ὁ τὸν ἐξελάcαι καὶ ἐνιπρῆcαι πυρὶ νῆα
> οὔθ' ὁ τὸν ἂψ ὤcαcθαι, ἐπεί ῥ' ἐπέλαccέ γε δαίμων.

These two then struggled over a single ship: Hektor could not drive Aias away and set fire to the ship, and Aias could not push Hektor back, now that god had brought him that far. (15. 416–18)

During the following 450 lines Hektor will steadily get the better of the struggle and Aias reluctantly give way. Their 'dialogue' of exhortations may be 'typical generals' exhortations . . . the obvious arguments . . .',[33] but it includes such memorable turns of phrase as Hektor's call that it is οὐ . . . ἀεικέc (no shame) to die for your country (15. 485 ff.), and Ajax's appeal to *aidōs* both before the enemy and in front of your own fellow fighters (15. 502 ff., 561–4). This is no dance that Hektor has invited them to, he insists; the ships are at stake and that means their hopes of ever returning home:

> "ἦ ἔλπεcθ', ἢν νῆας ἕληι κορυθαίολος Ἕκτωρ,
> ἐμβαδὸν ἵξεcθαι ἢν πατρίδα γαῖαν ἕκαcτος;
> ἦ οὐκ ὀτρύνοντος ἀκούετε λαὸν ἅπαντα
> Ἕκτορος, ὃc δὴ νῆας ἐνιπρῆcαι μενεαίνει;"

'Or do you think, if Hektor of the glinting helmet takes our ships, each of us will be able to walk back to his native land? Do you not hear Hektor urging on his whole army? His aim now is to fire the ships.' (15. 504–7)

The glorious idea of burning the ships amid a massacre on the beach came to Hektor first at 8. 180 ff.—see p. 147 above—and it is during this battle that the ambition becomes a possibility. The growing imminence of this moment is well plotted. It is Hektor's aim at 417 (quoted above); and when his cousin Kaletor is brought down by Aias at 419 ff. he is carrying a blazing torch, the first actual flame. Zeus' undertaking to Thetis becomes expressly linked to Hektor's firing of the ships. He urgently wills this climax, impatient actually to *see* the flames. Aias puts up a great defence. Yet, stage by stage, he has to give way. At 704 ff. Hektor actually gets a grip on the ship of Protesilaos,[34] and calls out on the verge of triumph (15. 718–19, quoted on p. 156). Aias fully expects to die (728), but rallies the Achaians one more time with the hard facts of strategic topography:

> "ὦ φίλοι ἥρωες Δαναοί, θεράποντες Ἄρηος,
> ἀνέρες ἔστε, φίλοι, μνήσασθε δὲ θούριδος ἀλκῆς.
> ἠέ τινάς φαμεν εἶναι ἀοσσητῆρας ὀπίσσω,   735
> ἦέ τι τεῖχος ἄρειον, ὅ κ' ἀνδράσι λοιγὸν ἀμύναι;
> οὐ μέν τι σχεδόν ἐστι πόλις πύργοις ἀραρυῖα,
> ἧι κ' ἀπαμυναίμεσθ' ἑτεραλκέα δῆμον ἔχοντες·
> ἀλλ' ἐν γὰρ Τρώων πεδίωι πύκα θωρηκτάων
> πόντωι κεκλιμένοι ἑκὰς ἥμεθα πατρίδος αἴης·   740
> τῶ ἐν χερσὶ φόως, οὐ μειλιχίηι πολέμοιο."
> Ἦ, καὶ μαιμώων ἔφεπ' ἔγχεϊ ὀξυόεντι.
> ὅς τις δὲ Τρώων κοίληις ἐπὶ νηυσὶ φέροιτο
> σὺν πυρὶ κηλείωι, χάριν Ἕκτορος ὀτρύναντος,
> τὸν δ' Αἴας οὔτασκε δεδεγμένος ἔγχεϊ μακρῶι·   745
> δώδεκα δὲ προπάροιθε νεῶν αὐτοσχεδὸν οὖτα.

'Friends, Danaan heroes, Ares' men-at-arms—be men, my friends, and fill your minds with fighting spirit. Or do we think there are men behind us to come to our aid, or some stronger wall which could save men from disaster? We have no city near us ringed with battlements, where we could defend ourselves and raise more troops to turn the battle. No, we find ourselves here in the plain held by the heavy-armoured Trojans, pressed back against the sea, and far from our native land. So salvation is in the strength of our hands, not courtesy in battle.'

So he spoke, and laid about him furiously with his sharp pike. When any Trojan came up against the hollow ships with blazing fire, hoping to serve Hektor's command, Aias was watching for him and stabbed him

---

[34] This is carefully prepared for at 13. 673 ff., where Hektor fights for the ground where he first broke through ἔνθ' ἔσαν Αἴαντός τε νέες καὶ Πρωτεσιλάου (where the ships of Aias [the Lesser] and Protesilaos were pulled up). Since Protesilaos can never return home anyway, is Hektor's triumph undercut by burning a ship without a captain?

with the long pike: and there were twelve that he wounded in front of the ships with a stab straight from his hand (15. 733–46)

The Trojans have burning torches in their hands: the only 'light' that the Achaians have is their fighting spirit. At this point Patroklos arrives back from the mission that Achilleus sent him on in book 11.

6.5   *The fatal link of pity*

<blockquote>

"Ἔσπετε νῦν μοι, Μοῦσαι Ὀλύμπια δώματ' ἔχουσαι,
ὅππως δὴ πρῶτον πῦρ ἔμπεσε νηυσὶν Ἀχαιῶν.
Ἕκτωρ Αἴαντος δόρυ μείλινον ἄγχι παραστὰς
πλῆξ' ἄορι μεγάλωι, αἰχμῆς παρὰ καυλὸν ὄπισθεν,   115
ἀντικρὺ δ' ἀπάραξε· τὸ μὲν Τελαμώνιος Αἴας
πῆλ' αὔτως ἐν χειρὶ κόλον δόρυ, τῆλε δ' ἀπ' αὐτοῦ
αἰχμὴ χαλκείη χαμάδις βόμβησε πεσοῦσα.
γνῶ δ' Αἴας κατὰ θυμὸν ἀμύμονα, ῥίγησέν τε,
ἔργα θεῶν, ὅ ῥα πάγχυ μάχης ἐπὶ μήδεα κεῖρε   120
Ζεὺς ὑψιβρεμέτης, Τρώεσσι δὲ βούλετο νίκην·
χάζετο δ' ἐκ βελέων. τοὶ δ' ἔμβαλον ἀκάματον πῦρ
νηὶ θοῆι· τῆς δ' αἶψα κατ' ἀσβέστη κέχυτο φλόξ.
ὣς τὴν μὲν πρύμνην πῦρ ἄμφεπεν· αὐτὰρ Ἀχιλλεὺς
μηρὼ πληξάμενος Πατροκλῆα προσέειπεν·   125
"ὄρσεο, διογενὲς Πατρόκλεες, ἱπποκέλευθε·
λεύσσω δὴ παρὰ νηυσὶ πυρὸς δηΐοιο ἰωήν·
μὴ δὴ νῆας ἕλωσι καὶ οὐκέτι φυκτὰ πέλωνται·
δύσεο τεύχεα θᾶσσον, ἐγὼ δέ κε λαὸν ἀγείρω."

</blockquote>

Tell me now, you Muses who have your homes on Olympos, how it was that fire was first thrown on the ships of the Achaians.

Hektor came close and struck at Aias' ash spear with his great sword, hitting by the socket behind the spear-head, and sheared it clean off. So Aias, son of Telamon, was left with just a docked spear quivering in his hand, and the bronze head spun far away and thudded to the ground. Aias' noble heart shuddered to recognise the hand of the gods, how Zeus the high-thunderer was wholly frustrating the skill of his fighting, and willing victory for the Trojans: and he fell back out of range of the weapons. Then the Trojans threw untiring fire on the fast ship, and immediately unquenchable flame poured over it. So the fire worked on the stern of the ship: and Achilleus struck his thighs and spoke to Patroklos: 'Up now, lord Patroklos, driver of horses! I can see the rush of destroying fire by the ships. They must not take our ships and then there be no more chance of escape. Put your armour on quickly, while I gather our men.' (16. 112–29)

Patroklos sets off to battle in book 16. He does not even speak at all before book 11, i.e. on my theory during part I. His first words would be an apparently innocuous question, but for the warning half-line that precedes them:

αἶψα δ' ἑταῖρον ἑὸν Πατροκλῆα προσέειπε,
φθεγξάμενος παρὰ νηός· ὁ δὲ κλισίηθεν ἀκούσας
ἔκμολεν ἶσος Ἄρηϊ, κακοῦ δ' ἄρα οἱ πέλεν ἀρχή.
τὸν πρότερος προσέειπε Μενοιτίου ἄλκιμος υἱός·
"τίπτέ με κικλήσκεις, Ἀχιλεῦ; τί δέ σε χρεὼ ἐμεῖο;"

Quickly he spoke to his companion Patroklos, calling from the ship. Patroklos heard him inside the hut, and came out looking like Ares the god of war: and this was to be the beginning of his doom. The brave son of Menoitios spoke first: 'Why do you call me, Achilleus? What do you want of me?' (11. 602–6)

The answer to this turns into a narrative thread which runs through the central battle, leading up to the point of the great synchronism of Hektor's firing a ship and Achilleus' command. In another sense the answer to Patroklos' question is: 'your life'.

The key intermediary in this skilful and extended interweaving of narratives is Nestor. His departure from the battlefield with the wounded Machaon at 11. 520 ff. brings the narrative off behind it to spend 250 lines in a private scene. In response to Achilleus' instruction to find out about the wounded man, Patroklos makes it clear to Nestor that he is in a hurry (11. 648 ff.). Nestor will not, however, allow him to return hastily, and retains him with one of the longest speeches in the *Iliad* (147 lines), a speech whose apparent aimlessness has, in fact, a purpose crucial to the whole plot.[35] The shrewd old man quickly realizes that Patroklos' surprise arrival has given him an unexpected opportunity to try to move Achilleus after the failure of the previous night. He knows Patroklos and works on his susceptibilities. After giving a full picture of traditional heroic endeavours to contrast with Achilleus' present behaviour (cf. 762–4), he comes to the recent yet still

---

[35] Cf. Owen, 115; Reinhardt, *ID* 263 f.; R. von Scheliha, *Patroklos* (Basle, 1943), 233 ff.; also cf. A. Parry, *LCH* 312–17 on Patroklos' 'softness', and H. Erbse, *Hermes*, 111 (1983), 1–15, who argues that the Patrokleia is an invention of Homer's own.

heroic past when Achilleus and Patroklos were sent off to war by
their fathers. Odysseus used the same motif; and recalled the very
same occasion at 9. 252 ff.—in fact 9. 259 = 11. 790 ὡς ἐπέτελλ' ὁ
γέρων, cὺ δὲ λήθεαι (that was the old man's advice, and you are
forgetting it). But Odysseus is not Nestor, and Patroklos is not
Achilleus. Nestor's ploy is to set up a kind of emotional chain-reaction as
a route of access to Achilleus. He starts with a sarcastic question:

> "τίπτε τ' ἄρ' ὧδ' Ἀχιλεὺς ὀλοφύρεται υἶας Ἀχαιῶν,
> ὅccοι δὴ βέλεcιν βεβλήαται;"

'Now why does Achilleus show such concern for those sons of the Achaians who have been wounded by flying weapons?' (11. 656–7)

Yet the fact that Achilleus has shown curiosity at all means that
he is not totally impervious. Nestor succeeds in moving
Patroklos—τῶι δ' ἄρα θυμὸν ἐνὶ cτήθεccιν ὄρινε (and he moved the
heart in his breast) (804). On his way back to Achilleus in this
heightened emotional state he is confronted with Eurypylos,
wounded at 11. 574–94 with careful narrative preparation as the
last of Paris' three hits. He feels compassion—ὤικτιρε (felt pity)
814, ὀλοφυρόμενος (in distress) 815—which gives Nestor's effect
on him a further charge of energy. Despite the urgency of his
mission, Patroklos is not the man to refuse a plea for medical aid:

> "ἔρχομαι, ὄφρ' Ἀχιλῆϊ δαΐφρονι μῦθον ἐνίσπω,
> ὃν Νέcτωρ ἐπέτελλε Γερήνιος, οὖρος Ἀχαιῶν·
> ἀλλ' οὐδ' ὥc περ cεῖο μεθήcω τειρομένοιο."

'I am on my way to speak to the warrior Achilleus as Gerenian Nestor,
warden of the Achaians, has urged me. But even so I will not desert you
in your trouble.' (11. 839–41)

Trouble is taken to build up the picture of the person who can
affect Achilleus as no one else can.

The narrative then leaves Patroklos throughout the battle over
the wall and the great retardation, returning to him only at
15. 390–405, when a new stage of the battle has been reached,
with the Trojans pouring into the Achaian camp in their chariots
to attack the very ships. He is still tending Eurypylos and the
thread is briefly but carefully picked up. As he leaves to try to
arouse Achilleus he actually takes over Nestor's couplet of
11. 792–3:

"τίc δ' οἶδ' εἴ κέν οἱ cὺν δαίμονι θυμὸν ὀρίνω
παρειπών; ἀγαθὴ δὲ παραίφαcίc ἐcτιν ἑταίρου."

'Who knows if, with god's help, I might move his heart with my persuasion? There is power in a friend's persuasion.' (15. 403–4)

By the time that Patroklos arrives back, at 16. 2 ff., the situation
in the battle has become even more desperate (see above—the
book-division between 15 and 16 spoils the narrative structure).
In extreme contrast, an intimate and emotional atmosphere is
immediately established (reinforced by the mother–daughter simile at 16. 7 ff.), unlike anything yet encountered in the poem, except
perhaps Hektor and Andromache. Achilleus is immediately
touched (τὸν δὲ ἰδὼν ὤικτιρε (he felt pity when he saw him) 16. 5 =
11. 814, Patroklos' response to Eurypylos). Though he asks what
is the matter, he knows well. A large part of Patroklos' reply in
21–45 is taken over from Nestor (16. 23–8, 36–45 = 11. 658–62,
794–802), including the proposal that he should fight by himself
yet wearing Achilleus' armour.

Ὣc φάτο λιccόμενοc μέγα νήπιοc· ἦ γὰρ ἔμελλεν
οἷ αὐτῶι θάνατόν τε κακὸν καὶ κῆρα λιτέcθαι.

So he spoke in entreaty, the poor fool—what he was begging would
be a wretched death for himself and his own destruction. (16. 46–7)

It is the current of compassion, set in movement by Nestor, that
sends Patroklos to his death. In the *Iliad*, pity advances suffering
as well as to some extent redeeming it.[36]

Achilleus' response in 16. 49–100 still has much in common
with the position he took up in book 9: things would be quite
different εἴ μοι κρείων Ἀγαμέμνων ἤπια εἰδείη (if lord Agamemnon
would treat me kindly) (16. 72–3)—see above, p. 72.[37] He did,
however, concede to Aias that he would not fight until Hektor
threatened his own ships with fire. Now Patroklos' plea, including
Nestor's idea about Achilleus' armour, which he presents as his
own, tips the balance so that the undertaking to Aias is half-
fulfilled and half-evaded. Achilleus makes it clear, however, that

[36] This makes me think of the old shepherd in Sophocles' *Oedipus Tyrannus*,
who, when asked why he preserved the baby Oedipus, replies "κατοικτίcαc, ὦ
δέcποτα . . ." ('in pity for you, master') (*OT* 1178).
[37] Cf. Motzkus, 126–33; Macleod, 24–5; Schein, 117–20; Scodel, 91–3. Lines
85–6 are, I think, a real problem and possibly should be athetized—unless the
emphasis is on πάντων ('everyone'), i.e. including Agamemnon?

he wants Patroklos to join the battle only briefly, long enough to repel the fire.[38] Any more than this would render him ἀτιμότερον (reduced in worth) (90). It is the thought of *tīmē* which leads to the 'wild and wonderful fantasy'[39] at the end of the speech (97–100). The irony is that, far from being the only two left alive at the sack, they will both be dead.

Achilleus and Patroklos are unaware how desperate a stage has been reached in Aias' battle against Hektor and the fire-bearing Trojans. It now takes only 23 lines of battle-narrative, at 16. 101–24, to bring the long struggle to its conclusion with the dramatic monosyllables which close lines 122 and 123.[40] The turning-point, marked by the invocation of the Muses in 112–13, is interwoven with the Patroklos–Achilleus narrative, so that that also reaches a turning-point as Achilleus urges his companion on his way.

[38] This is an ironic reversal of Nestor's picture at 11. 782 ff., where it was Patroklos' role to restrain Achilleus.

[39] Macleod, 24.

[40] It is significant that the weapon that Hektor renders useless is the extraordinary 22-cubit pike that Aias has been wielding with such skill (see p. 172). Cf. R. M. Frazer, *CPh* 78 (1983), 127–30.

7

Turnings Towards Death

7.1 Patroklos' failure to listen

"Πάτροκλ', ἦ που ἔφηςθα πόλιν κεραϊξέμεν ἀμήν,   830
Τρωϊάδας δὲ γυναῖκας ἐλεύθερον ἦμαρ ἀπούρας
ἄξειν ἐν νήεσσι φίλην ἐς πατρίδα γαῖαν,
νήπιε· τάων δὲ πρόςθ' Ἕκτορος ὠκέες ἵπποι
ποςςὶν ὀρωρέχαται πολεμίζειν· ἔγχεϊ δ' αὐτὸς
Τρωςὶ φιλοπτολέμοιςι μεταπρέπω, ὅ ςφιν ἀμύνω   835
ἦμαρ ἀναγκαῖον· ςὲ δέ τ' ἐνθάδε γῦπες ἔδονται.
ἆ δείλ', οὐδέ τοι ἐςθλὸς ἐὼν χραίςμηςεν Ἀχιλλεύς,
ὅς πού τοι μάλα πολλὰ μένων ἐπετέλλετ' ἰόντι·
'μή μοι πρὶν ἰέναι, Πατρόκλεες ἱπποκέλευθε,
νῆας ἔπι γλαφυράς, πρὶν Ἕκτορος ἀνδροφόνοιο   840
αἱματόεντα χιτῶνα περὶ ςτήθεςςι δαΐξαι.'
ὣς πού ςε προςέφη, ςοὶ δὲ φρένας ἄφρονι πεῖθε."
    Τὸν δ' ὀλιγοδρανέων προςέφης, Πατρόκλεες ἱππεῦ·
"ἤδη νῦν, Ἕκτορ, μεγάλ' εὔχεο· ςοὶ γὰρ ἔδωκε
νίκην Ζεὺς Κρονίδης καὶ Ἀπόλλων, οἵ με δάμαςςαν   845
ῥηιδίως· αὐτοὶ γὰρ ἀπ' ὤμων τεύχε' ἕλοντο.
τοιοῦτοι δ' εἴ πέρ μοι ἐείκοςιν ἀντεβόληςαν,
πάντες κ' αὐτόθ' ὄλοντο ἐμῶι ὑπὸ δουρὶ δαμέντες.
ἀλλά με μοῖρ' ὀλοὴ καὶ Λητοῦς ἔκτανεν υἱός,
ἀνδρῶν δ' Εὔφορβος· ςὺ δέ με τρίτος ἐξεναρίζεις.   850
ἄλλο δέ τοι ἐρέω, ςὺ δ' ἐνὶ φρεςὶ βάλλεο ςῆιςιν·
οὔ θην οὐδ' αὐτὸς δηρὸν βέῃι, ἀλλά τοι ἤδη
ἄγχι παρέςτηκεν θάνατος καὶ μοῖρα κραταιή,
χερςὶ δαμέντ' Ἀχιλῆος ἀμύμονος Αἰακίδαο."
    Ὣς ἄρα μιν εἰπόντα τέλος θανάτοιο κάλυψε·   855
ψυχὴ δ' ἐκ ῥεθέων πταμένη Ἄϊδόςδε βεβήκει,
ὃν πότμον γοόωςα, λιποῦς' ἀνδροτῆτα καὶ ἥβην.
τὸν καὶ τεθνηῶτα προςηύδα φαίδιμος Ἕκτωρ·
"Πατρόκλεις, τί νύ μοι μαντεύεαι αἰπὺν ὄλεθρον;
τίς δ' οἶδ' εἴ κ' Ἀχιλεύς, Θέτιδος πάϊς ἠϋκόμοιο,   860
φθήηι ἐμῶι ὑπὸ δουρὶ τυπεὶς ἀπὸ θυμὸν ὀλέςςαι;"

'Patroklos, you must have thought that you would sack our city, and take the day of freedom from the women of Troy and carry them off in your ships to your own native land—poor fool! In their defence Hektor's swift horses speed into battle, and I am renowned for my spear among all the war-loving Trojans, for keeping the day of compulsion from them—but you, the vultures will eat you here. Poor wretch, not even Achilleus, for all his greatness, could help you. He must have given you firm instructions when he stayed behind and sent you out, saying, "Let me not see you back at the hollow ships, horseman Patroklos, until you have ripped and bloodied murderous Hektor's tunic on his chest." That is what he will have said, and swayed your foolish heart.'

Then with the strength low in you, horseman Patroklos, you said to him: 'Yes, make your great boasts now, Hektor. You were given the victory by Zeus the son of Kronos and Apollo—it was they who overpowered me with ease: they took the armour from my shoulders. But if twenty such men as you had come against me, they would all have died where they stood, brought down under my spear. No, it is cruel fate and Leto's son that have killed me, and of men Euphorbos—you are the third in my killing. I tell you another thing, and you mark it well in your mind. You yourself, you too will not live long, but already now death and strong fate are standing close beside you, to bring you down at the hands of Achilleus, great son of Aiakos' stock.'

As he spoke the end of death enfolded him: and his spirit flitted from his body and went on the way to Hades, weeping for its fate, and the youth and manhood it must leave. Then glorious Hektor spoke to him, dead though he was: 'Patroklos, why make me this prophecy of grim death? Who knows if Achilleus, son of lovely-haired Thetis, might be struck by my spear first, and lose his life before me?' (16. 830–61)

There has been no shortage of deaths by the time that Patroklos sets out to battle. Many have been coloured with a touch of pathos, but the only character to die who has been given a sustained individuality and motivation is Pandaros. He largely deserved his fate (see § **3.5** above): the series of deaths which begin with Sarpedon's are different. The audience is inspired to pity and to a helpless reluctance as the narration lines them up in a horribly inevitable sequence.

Patroklos is perhaps the most amiable character in the poem, yet imminent death hangs over his participation. There have been the two terse predictions of Zeus at 8. 476–7 and 15. 64–77 (see pp. 136, 142–3), and the two direct 'comments' by the narrator at 11. 604 and 16. 46–7 (see pp. 175–7). Achilleus himself is apprehensive:

"μηδ' ἐπαγαλλόμενος πολέμωι καὶ δηϊοτῆτι,
Τρῶας ἐναιρόμενος, προτὶ Ἴλιον ἡγεμονεύειν,
μή τις ἀπ' Οὐλύμποιο θεῶν αἰειγενετάων
ἐμβήηι· μάλα τούς γε φιλεῖ ἑκάεργος Ἀπόλλων·
ἀλλὰ πάλιν τρωπᾶσθαι, ἐπὴν φάος ἐν νήεσσι
θήηις, τοὺς δ' ἔτ' ἐᾶν πεδίον κάτα δηριάασθαι."

'And do not lead your men on towards Ilios, slaughtering Trojans, in the delight of battle with the enemy, or one of the ever-living gods from Olympos might come against you—Apollo the far-worker has much love for the Trojans. No, turn back again once you have brought saving light to the ships, and let the others fight on over the plain.' (16. 91–6)

His warnings are there, in effect, to be broken. Once Patroklos and the Myrmidons have mustered, Achilleus' separation from them is marked by his going inside to pray to Zeus (16. 220ff.). He is asking for an additional rider to his successful prayer back in book 1:[1]

Ὣς ἔφατ' εὐχόμενος, τοῦ δ' ἔκλυε μητίετα Ζεύς.
τῶι δ' ἕτερον μὲν δῶκε πατήρ, ἕτερον δ' ἀνένευσε·
νηῶν μέν οἱ ἀπώσασθαι πόλεμόν τε μάχην τε
δῶκε, σόον δ' ἀνένευσε μάχης ἐξ ἀπονέεσθαι.

So he spoke in prayer, and Zeus the counsellor heard him. Half of the prayer the father granted him, and half he refused. He granted that Patroklos should push the battle back from the ships, but refused his safe return from the fighting. (16. 249–52)

Patroklos is a pale reflection of Achilleus' own fate: Zeus will grant him the *kūdos* (241) of success in battle, but at the same time will deny him his safe return.

When Patroklos takes the divine armour of a greater man, this marks him out as a vulnerable surrogate. Two particular premonitory notes are sounded.[2] First, he is unable to manage Achilleus' great ash spear (139–44). Secondly, Automedon adds Pedasos, who was captured from ill-fated Thebe (see p. 126), as a trace-horse to run with Xanthos and Balios—ὃς καὶ θνητὸς ἐὼν ἔπεθ' ἵπποις ἀθανάτοισι (mortal though he was, he ran with the immortal

---

[1] 16. 236–8 = 1. 453–5: this is, in a sense, a follow-up prayer like that of Chryses. But Achilleus is not simply cancelling, he is making additions.

[2] Cf. Armstrong, 346–8; Reinhardt, *ID* 314; Patzer, 29 f. The armour used to be an analytic starting-point: this provoked some fine refutation from Reinhardt, *ID* 308–29. On Patroklos in 16 see also L. Leinieks, *CJ* 69 (1973), 102 ff.; Thalmann, 45 ff.

horses) (154). Like Patroklos, Pedasos will play a brave part, but will die (by the spear of Sarpedon, at 16. 466ff.). Patroklos is a kind of trace-horse to Achilleus—as Achilleus, in his turn, is a kind of trace-horse to the immortals on Olympos.

The stages by which Patroklos goes too far and meets his death are skilfully articulated. He has a series of 'chances', and at each he is plausibly stimulated to press on.[3] Achilleus recognizes his susceptibility before he ever sets off; and he recalls his warnings just before he hears the news of his end:

> "ἦ μάλα δὴ τέθνηκε Μενοιτίου ἄλκιμος υἱός,
> σχέτλιος· ἦ τ' ἐκέλευον ἀπωσάμενον δήϊον πῦρ
> ἄψ ἐπὶ νῆας ἴμεν, μηδ' Ἕκτορι ἶφι μάχεσθαι."

'It must surely be that the brave son of Menoitios is now dead—obstinate man! I told him to come back to the ships once he had driven away the enemy fire, and not face Hektor in full fight.' (18. 12–14)

At first, when the ships have been—almost perfunctorily—cleared of fire (see 16. 293–6), and the Trojans eventually turned to flight, Patroklos does not press on across the plain, but stays to cut off the vulnerable fugitives (394ff.). Even this may exceed Achilleus' instructions of 83ff., but at least it does not go against the chief warning not to assault Troy. Next Sarpedon nobly comes to the aid of his comrades; this leads to his death; which leads to the fierce struggle over his corpse (508–644), the first battle of this sort in the *Iliad*. Eventually his friends retreat and Patroklos strips the armour of the son of Zeus (657ff.). It is this triumph that stimulates him to press on and to turn his advantage into a rout.

Zeus pays close attention to the fight over his son, and he links Patroklos' triumph closely with his death. He even considers having him killed in the fight over Sarpedon (644ff.), but decides to let him kill more Trojans and to win yet more glory in his last hour. So Patroklos' final victories are distinctly darkened by his approaching death:

> Πάτροκλος δ' ἵπποισι καὶ Αὐτομέδοντι κελεύσας
> Τρῶας καὶ Λυκίους μετεκίαθε, καὶ μέγ' ἀάσθη   685
> νήπιος· εἰ δὲ ἔπος Πηληϊάδαο φύλαξεν,
> ἦ τ' ἂν ὑπέκφυγε κῆρα κακὴν μέλανος θανάτοιο.

---

[3] Cf. Schadewaldt, *IS* 42; Reinhardt, *ID* 339; Fenik, *TBS* 201.

ἀλλ' αἰεί τε Διὸς κρείccων νόος ἠέ περ ἀνδρῶν·
ὅc τε καὶ ἄλκιμον ἄνδρα φοβεῖ καὶ ἀφείλετο νίκην
ῥηϊδίωc, ὅτε δ' αὐτὸc ἐποτρύνηιcι μάχεcθαι·   690
ὅc οἱ καὶ τότε θυμὸν ἐνὶ cτήθεccιν ἀνῆκεν.

Ἔνθα τίνα πρῶτον, τίνα δ' ὕcτατον ἐξενάριξαc,
Πατρόκλειc, ὅτε δή cε θεοὶ θάνατόνδε κάλεccαν;

But Patroklos called to his horses and Automedon and went in pursuit
of the Trojans and Lycians, and this was a fatal error, poor fool—if he
had kept to the instruction of the son of Peleus, he would have escaped
the vile doom of black death. But Zeus' mind is always stronger than the
mind of men—he can bring terror on even the brave man and easily rob
him of victory: and then again he himself will spur a man to fight. And
it was Zeus then who put the urge in Patroklos' heart.

Then who was the first, and who the last that you killed, Patroklos,
when the gods now called you to your death? (16. 684–93)

This massacre inspires him actually to assault the walls of Troy,
though he gives way when Apollo beats him back thrice, with the
warning that Troy will not fall even to Achilles (698–711). There
is no longer, however, any thought of returning to the ships; and
soon Hektor is renewing the challenge (726 ff.). In similar circumstances Diomedes managed to keep on the right side of powerful
gods (5. 431 ff., see p. 134 above); but Patroklos, after his final
triumph over Kebriones, goes on the offensive once more:

τρὶc μὲν ἔπειτ' ἐπόρουcε θοῶι ἀτάλαντοc Ἄρηϊ,
cμερδαλέα ἰάχων, τρὶc δ' ἐννέα φῶταc ἔπεφνεν.
ἀλλ' ὅτε δὴ τὸ τέταρτον ἐπέccυτο δαίμονι ἶcοc,
ἔνθ' ἄρα τοι, Πάτροκλε, φάνη βιότοιο τελευτή·

Three times then he charged like the swift war-god himself, shouting
fearfully, and three times he killed nine men. But when for the fourth
time he flung himself on like a god, then, Patroklos, the ending of your
life was revealed. (16. 784–7)

The intimacy of the narrator's plain vocative somehow accentuates
his nearness to death. Now Apollo is ruthless as he deprives
Patroklos of the armour which he so eagerly took up before the
battle,[4] the fatal armour which will soon pass on to Hektor—see
below, § 7.2.

Hektor and Patroklos, the most sympathetic figures on either
side and the most prominent to fall during the narrative, are paired

---

[4] Cf. Reinhardt, *ID* 319 (*contra* Fenik, *TBS* 191, who calls this 'overly subtle').

in many ways. The multiple doublings reach their acme with their actual deaths and their parallel sets of death-speeches—see further § 8.5. Sarpedon's rallying of Glaukos and the Lycians round his corpse (16. 492 ff.) is the first of only three sets of death-speeches in the *Iliad* and prepares for the dying-scene of Patroklos.[5] The device brings out the way that Hektor, like Patroklos, is ignorant and over-confident: his inability to pull back will similarly lead to his death. Hektor begins in 16. 830–3 with a true perception of the state of mind that has brought Patroklos to his death. He goes on, however, to speculate, in 837–42, about the scene when Patroklos left Achilleus to set out: this scene was directly narrated in 64–100 and 124–253, and the audience knows clearly how far it really was from Hektor's imaginings. Achilleus, far from saying 'don't come back until . . .', actually said 'come back as soon as . . .'. Hektor's optimistic ignorance will be epitomized by his hope in the next speech (859–61) that he might kill Achilleus— see further pp. 246–7.

The focus on men who have taken a fatal turning towards death is maintained by removing Hektor from the narrative from 16. 864 to 17. 69 as he sets off in vain pursuit of Achilleus' horses. This clears the scene for Euphorbos. He is not even mentioned until his wounding of Patroklos, at 16. 806 ff. But his nomination by the dying Patroklos (16. 850 ff.) and his bold defiance of Menelaos (17. 33 ff.) mark him out for death.[6]

Euphorbos' death is a consequence of, but not obviously a punishment for, the death of Patroklos. He thus functions as a foreshadowing and reflection of the fate of Hektor. He was the first to stab Patroklos, while Hektor dealt the death-blow. He stands out bravely for *kleos* (17. 16) and for vengeance; and he defies the more experienced Menelaos in a fashion which, while foolhardy, is also admirably noble. This may help to mould an audience's response to Hektor. He will similarly stand up to

---

[5] All three share ὡς ἄρα μιν εἰπόντα τέλος θανάτοιο κάλυψε ('as he spoke, the end of death covered him over') 16. 502 = 16. 855 = 22. 361.

[6] I see no justification for Griffin's association of effeminacy with Euphorbos (*HLD* 4). His speech to Menelaos was called by Pope 'one of the finest answers in all Homer'. It is worth noting that, while Menelaos did indeed kill Hyperenor at 14. 516–19, there was at the time no reference to his parentage. The painting which is very possibly the earliest surviving work of art directly inspired by the *Iliad* shows Euphorbos' last battle with Menelaos. The Rhodian plate of *c*.600 to which I am referring has been widely reproduced (British Museum A749).

Achilleus, however 'foolishly', in an attempt to win vengeance—
in his case, for those Trojans who have been killed under his
leadership (see § **8.4**).

7.2 Armour of death, immortal horses

cτὰc δ' ἀπάνευθε μάχηc πολυδακρύου ἔντε' ἄμειβεν·
ἤτοι ὁ μὲν τὰ ἃ δῶκε φέρειν προτὶ Ἴλιον ἱρὴν
Τρωcὶ φιλοπτολέμοιcιν, ὁ δ' ἄμβροτα τεύχεα δῦνε
Πηλείδεω Ἀχιλῆος, ἅ οἱ θεοὶ Οὐρανίωνεc   195
πατρὶ φίλωι ἔπορον· ὁ δ' ἄρα ὧι παιδὶ ὄπαccε
γηράc· ἀλλ' οὐχ υἱὸc ἐν ἔντεcι πατρὸc ἐγήρα.
   Τὸν δ' ὡc οὖν ἀπάνευθεν ἴδεν νεφεληγερέτα Ζεὺc
τεύχεcι Πηλείδαο κορυccόμενον θείοιο,
κινήcαc ῥα κάρη προτὶ ὃν μυθήcατο θυμόν·   200
"ἃ δείλ', οὐδέ τί τοι θάνατοc καταθύμιόc ἐcτιν,
ὃc δή τοι cχεδὸν εἶcι· cὺ δ' ἄμβροτα τεύχεα δύνειc
ἀνδρὸc ἀριcτῆοc, τόν τε τρομέουcι καὶ ἄλλοι·
τοῦ δὴ ἑταῖρον ἔπεφνεc ἐνηέα τε κρατερόν τε,
τεύχεα δ' οὐ κατὰ κόcμον ἀπὸ κρατόc τε καὶ ὤμων   205
εἴλευ· ἀτάρ τοι νῦν γε μέγα κράτοc ἐγγυαλίξω,
τῶν ποινὴν ὅ τοι οὔ τι μάχηc ἐκ νοcτήcαντι
δέξεται Ἀνδρομάχη κλυτὰ τεύχεα Πηλείωνοc."
   Ἦ, καὶ κυανέηιcιν ἐπ' ὀφρύcι νεῦcε Κρονίων.
Ἕκτορι δ' ἥρμοcε τεύχε' ἐπὶ χροΐ, δῦ δέ μιν Ἄρηc   210
δεινὸc ἐννάλιοc, πλῆcθεν δ' ἄρα οἱ μέλε' ἐντὸc
ἀλκῆc καὶ cθένεοc·

Then, standing at a distance from the battle's misery, he exchanged
armour. He gave his own to the war-loving Trojans to take back to sacred
Ilios, and put on the immortal armour of Achilleus son of Peleus, which
the heavenly gods had given to Achilleus' dear father: and when he was
old he gave it to his son—but the son was not to grow old in his father's
armour.

Now when Zeus the cloud-gatherer saw Hektor away from the battle
arming himself in the armour of the godlike son of Peleus, he shook his
head and said to his own heart: 'Poor wretch, death is not in your thought
at all, and it is now coming close to you. You are dressing in the immortal
armour of the best of men, a man all others fear. And you have now
killed this man's friend, who was kind and strong, and you have taken
the armour from his head and shoulders, wrongly. But for the moment
I shall grant you great power, in recompense for what will happen—you

will never return home from the fighting, for Andromache to take from you the famous armour of the son of Peleus.'
So the son of Kronos spoke, and nodded his dark brows. And the armour fitted close to Hektor's body, and the fearful war-god Ares entered into him, and inside him his body was filled with courage and strength. (17. 192–212)

Hektor will die wearing the same armour as Patroklos. The motif of his approaching death accumulates during his last day of victory, reaching a peak in Zeus' commentary on the exchange of armour. There have been earlier warnings: the 'cautionary tale' of Asios (see p. 165 above); the narrow escape from Diomedes at 11.349ff.; the blow from Aias at 14.409ff.; and, perhaps, the simile at 12. 41 ff., where it is said of the lion which refuses to flee ἀγηνορίη δέ μιν ἔκτα (and it is his courage that kills him).[7] Hektor's death is explicitly laid down by Zeus at 15. 68, and, as his triumph with the fire approaches, Zeus' interest in his mortal prowess is directly narrated:

αὐτὸς γάρ οἱ ἀπ' αἰθέρος ἦεν ἀμύντωρ
Ζεύς, ὅς μιν πλεόνεσσι μετ' ἀνδράσι μοῦνον ἐόντα
τίμα καὶ κύδαινε. μινυνθάδιος γὰρ ἔμελλεν
ἔσσεσθ'· ἤδη γάρ οἱ ἐπώρνυε μόρσιμον ἦμαρ
Παλλὰς Ἀθηναίη ὑπὸ Πηλεΐδαο βίηφιν.

... because his ally was Zeus himself in the sky above, who was giving honour and glory to this one man among the multitude of others, as he would live only a short time: already Pallas Athene was advancing the day of his fate, at the hands of the strong son of Peleus. (15. 610–14)[8]

As Patroklos' 'usurpation' of Achilleus' armour marked him out for death, so Hektor's donning of it on the battlefield is signalled as a turning on his road to Hades. It may be that the story of how this armour was a gift from the gods to Peleus at his wedding was so well known that the audience was supposed to take it for granted. For any audience not familiar with this story the information is revealed in a piecemeal way. The first allusion to it is the spear that Patroklos *cannot* handle—

τὸ μὲν οὐ δύνατ' ἄλλος Ἀχαιῶν
πάλλειν, ἀλλά μιν οἶος ἐπίστατο πῆλαι Ἀχιλλεύς,

[7] For other similes premonitory of death see 12. 299 ff. (Sarpedon) and 16. 752 f. (Patroklos).
[8] Leaf's case for interpolation ('there are real difficulties', Griffin *HLD* 128, n. 42) seems weak to me—cf. Willcock, *Comm.* ad loc.

Πηλιάδα μελίην, τὴν πατρὶ φίλωι πόρε Χείρων
Πηλίου ἐκ κορυφῆς, φόνον ἔμμεναι ἡρώεσσιν.

which no other Achaian could wield, but Achilleus alone had the skill to
handle it, the spear of Pelian ash from the height of Pelion, which Cheiron
had given to his dear father to be the death of fighting men. (16. 141–4)[9]

The narrator spells the history out clearly at 17. 194–6 as preparation for Zeus' contemplations; and Achilleus is explicit at 18. 82–5.
This may help to explain Zeus' οὐ κατὰ κόςμον ('wrongly') in
17. 205: to capture ordinary armour is κατὰ κόςμον ('right'), but to
seize the gifts of the immortals is not. Furthermore the maltreatment of Achilleus' armour has already been implicitly connected
with the death of Hektor. Apollo knocked the helmet from
Patroklos' head and the narrator adds:

ἡ δὲ κυλινδομένη καναχὴν ἔχε ποccὶν ὑφ' ἵππων
αὐλῶπιc τρυφάλεια, μιάνθηcαν δὲ ἔθειραι
αἵματι καὶ κονίηιcι· πάροc γε μὲν οὐ θέμιc ἦεν
ἱππόκομον πήληκα μιαίνεcθαι κονίηιcιν,
ἀλλ' ἀνδρὸc θείοιο κάρη χαρίεν τε μέτωπον
ῥύετ' Ἀχιλλῆοc· τότε δὲ Ζεὺc Ἕκτορι δῶκεν
ἧι κεφαλῆι φορέειν, cχεδόθεν δέ οἱ ἦεν ὄλεθροc.

and the great masking helmet rolled clattering under the horses' feet, and
the hair of its crest was sullied with blood and dust. Before now it was
not permitted for this horse-crested helmet to be sullied in the dust, but
it guarded the head and fine brow of a godlike man, Achilleus: and now
Zeus allowed Hektor to wear it on his head, as his death was close upon
him. (16. 794–800)

The simple connective δέ ('and') in 800 shows how surely Hektor
will die as a consequence of the death of Patroklos.

Homer has, in fact, to go to considerable trouble to manage the
highly unusual change of armour on the battlefield.[10] When at
17. 124 ff. Menelaos returns with Aias to protect the corpse of
Patroklos, Hektor gives the captured armour to his companions
for safe keeping, which is the usual procedure.[11] Yet he himself
climbs into his chariot (130). This suggests that he intends to

---

[9] The word-play πάλλειν. . .πῆλαι. . .Πηλιάδα. . .Πηλίου might be alluding to a
well-known story. The scholia are clear that in the *Cypria* the spear was Cheiron's
wedding-present. On Homer's use of the gifts, see also Wilson.

[10] Note the vagueness at 6. 230–6 over how the exchange between Glaukos and
Diomedes was actually managed.

[11] ἀπηύρα in 17. 125 is too vague to justify all the old analytic furore.

leave the field (cf. 11. 273, 399); and it is this that provokes
Glaukos' bitter reproaches in 140 ff. Stung by these, Hektor
instead catches up his companions, who had begun on their way
(189–91), and puts the newly captured armour on. It is not clear
whether this is because it is the best way to keep it safe, now that
return has been postponed, or whether it is simply an unexplained
fancy. Either way it is ill-omened.

Hektor's final exploits and his death will now follow so soon
that he will never again return to Troy alive. Zeus' speech on this
occasion is not a cold command, but has personal colour. He links
the pathos of the companion of Achilleus—ἐνηέα τε κρατερόν τε
(who was kind and strong) (204, see further p. 192)—with the fate
of the husband of Andromache. He nods his head to his *boulē* with
the same line (209 = 1. 528) as 'his original agreement with Thetis.

There will be one more reminder of the significance of the
usurped armour before this central day is over (for the next day
see p. 242). When Thetis tells her son about the capture of his
armour, she is able to provide a divine perspective, personally
coloured though it is:

> "ἀλλά τοι ἔντεα καλὰ μετὰ Τρώεccιν ἔχονται,
> χάλκεα μαρμαίροντα· τὰ μὲν κορυθαίολος "Εκτωρ
> αὐτὸς ἔχων ὤμοιcιν ἀγάλλεται· οὐδέ ἔ φημι
> δηρὸν ἐπαγλαϊεῖcθαι, ἐπεὶ φόνος ἐγγύθεν αὐτῶι."

'But think, your fine armour of gleaming bronze is in the Trojans'
possession: and Hektor of the glinting helmet is glorying to wear it on
his own shoulders—but I do not think that he will have his pride in it
for long, as his own death is close on him.' (18. 130–3)

Not long after this, Hektor fatally rejects the advice of
Poulydamas.

During the first two-thirds of the central day there is little
thought of Achilleus, or at least little direct attention. Once he
has sent out Patroklos, it is very different; and once Patroklos is
dead, there is a narrative undercurrent pulling the audience's mind
back towards him. None the less, the struggle over the body is
protracted, and what we know as book 17 intervenes. Over 100
lines are spent, for instance, on Achilleus' immortal horses and
their exploits with Automedon, their temporary charioteer selected
by their usual charioteer Patroklos (as carefully prepared for at
16. 145 ff., 218–20, 472, 684, 864).

These horses are little more than mentioned before they take to
the field, merely as a sort of afterthought to the Achaian catalogue
(2. 772) (and as the reward promised to Dolon—10. 322-3, 330,
392-3, 401-4). They are properly introduced when they are prepared for battle at 16. 145ff.; and they serve Patroklos well
throughout his hour of glory. As soon as he has killed Patroklos,
Hektor goes after them, not the armour (16. 864-7).[12] He is dis-
tracted by this chase throughout the Euphorbos scene, until Apollo
recalls him at 17.71 ff.:

> "Ἕκτορ, νῦν cὺ μὲν ὧδε θέεις ἀκίχητα διώκων
> ἵππους Αἰακίδαο δαΐφρονος· οἱ δ' ἀλεγεινοὶ
> ἀνδράcι γε θνητοῖcι δαμήμεναι ἠδ' ὀχέεcθαι,
> ἄλλωι γ' ἢ Ἀχιλῆϊ, τὸν ἀθανάτη τέκε μήτηρ."

'Hektor, all this time you have been running after fierce Achilleus' horses,
chasing what can never be caught. Those horses are hard for any mortal
man to control or drive, except for Achilleus, and he is the son of an
immortal mother.' (17. 75-8)

Like the armour, they were a gift from the gods of Peleus' wedding
(Poseidon is specified at 23. 277-8); but unlike the armour they
will not fall into Hektor's hands.

When the narrative returns to the horses, at 17. 426ff., an extraordinary verbal portrait of them is painted:

> τὼ δ' οὔτ' ἂψ ἐπὶ νῆας ἐπὶ πλατὺν Ἑλλήcποντον
> ἠθελέτην ἰέναι οὔτ' ἐc πόλεμον μετ' Ἀχαιούc,
> ἀλλ' ὥc τε cτήλη μένει ἔμπεδον, ἥ τ' ἐπὶ τύμβωι
> ἀνέρος ἑcτήκηι τεθνηότος ἠὲ γυναικός,
> ὣc μένον ἀcφαλέωc περικαλλέα δίφρον ἔχοντες,
> οὔδει ἐνιcκίμψαντε καρήατα· δάκρυα δέ cφι
> θερμὰ κατὰ βλεφάρων χαμάδιc ῥέε μυρομένοιcιν
> ἡνιόχοιο πόθωι· θαλερὴ δ' ἐμιαίνετο χαίτη
> ζεύγληc ἐξεριποῦcα παρὰ ζυγὸν ἀμφοτέρωθεν.

... but the two horses would not move, either back to the ships by the
broad Hellespont or to join the Achaians in the battle, but as a grave-
stone stands unmoving, set on the mound of a man or a woman who has
died, so they stood there holding the beautiful chariot motionless, hanging
their heads to the ground. Warm tears ran down from their eyes to the
earth as they mourned for the loss of their charioteer: and their thick
manes were dirtied where they spilled down from under the yoke-pad on
either side of the yoke. (17. 432-40)

---

[12] Cf. Wilson. I am assuming that 16. 381 is interpolated from 16. 867.

Only Thetis is more anomalously and more wretchedly caught between the divine and human worlds. Zeus himself reflects on their plight and emphasizes how far superior immortal horses are to mortal men:

> "ἆ δειλώ, τί cφῶϊ δόμεν Πηλῆϊ ἄνακτι
> θνητῶι, ὑμεῖc δ' ἐcτὸν ἀγήρω τ' ἀθανάτω τε.
> ἦ ἵνα δυcτήνοιcι μετ' ἀνδράcιν ἄλγε' ἔχητον;   445
> οὐ μὲν γάρ τί πού ἐcτιν ὀϊζυρώτερον ἀνδρὸc
> πάντων ὅccα τε γαῖαν ἔπι πνείει τε καὶ ἕρπει.
> ἀλλ' οὐ μὰν ὑμῖν γε καὶ ἅρμαcι δαιδαλέοιcιν
> Ἕκτωρ Πριαμίδηc ἐποχήcεται· οὐ γὰρ ἐάcω.
> ἦ οὐχ ἅλιc ὡc καὶ τεύχε' ἔχει καὶ ἐπεύχεται αὔτωc;   450
> cφῶϊν δ' ἐν γούνεccι βαλῶ μένοc ἠδ' ἐνὶ θυμῶι,
> ὄφρα καὶ Αὐτομέδοντα caώcετον ἐκ πολέμοιο
> νῆαc ἔπι γλαφυράc·"

'Poor wretches, why did we give you to lord Peleus, a mortal man, when you are ageless and immortal? Was it for you to share the pain of unhappy mankind? Since there is nothing more miserable than man among all the creatures that breathe and move on earth. But at least Hektor son of Priam will not be carried by you and your crafted chariot: I shall not allow it. Is it not enough that he has the armour, and glories in that? But I shall put strength in your knees and your hearts, so that you can bring Automedon safe out of the fighting back to the hollow ships.' (17. 443–53)

Yet this is fulfilled only after all-too-human diversions, as if to show the gap between the simplicity of divine rule and the confusion of human effort. First (456 ff.) Automedon makes solo dashes in among the Trojans, even though he cannot actually attack them. Then with the help of Alkimedon and others he is eventually able to kill and despoil Aretos:

> τεύχεά τ' ἐξενάριξε καὶ εὐχόμενοc ἔποc ηὔδα·
> "ἦ δὴ μὰν ὀλίγον γε Μενοιτιάδαο θανόντοc
> κῆρ ἄχεοc μεθέηκα χερείονά περ καταπεφνών."

...he stripped him of his armour and spoke in triumph over him: 'Now my heart is relieved of a little of the pain for Patroklos' death, though the man I have killed is less than his equal.' (17. 537–9)

His actual return to the ships is not directly narrated; but it calls for no comment when next day he is Achilleus' charioteer (19. 392 ff.)

Meanwhile, on either side of the Automedon diversion, the

struggle over the body of Patroklos goes on in a dense fog of dark. The narrative achieves an almost gothic effect at 366 ff., when it is described as seen from the clear, bright daylight outside it. The battle-cloud is uniquely sustained and grim.[13] Zeus first creates it at 268 ff. to preserve the body of Patroklos.[14] Yet, despite the sterling efforts of Menelaos and Aias, the battle generally tips in Hektor's favour; and the darkness frustrates both tactical planning and the recruitment of a runner to take the news to Achilleus. In desperation Aias turns (asyndetically) from Menelaos to Zeus:

"ἀλλ' οὔ πηι δύναμαι ἰδέειν τοιοῦτον Ἀχαιῶν·
ἠέρι γὰρ κατέχονται ὁμῶc αὐτοί τε καὶ ἵπποι.
Ζεῦ πάτερ, ἀλλὰ cὺ ῥῦcαι ὑπ' ἠέροc υἷαc Ἀχαιῶν,
ποίηcον δ' αἴθρην, δὸc δ' ὀφθαλμοῖcιν ἰδέcθαι·
ἐν δὲ φάει καὶ ὄλεccον, ἐπεί νύ τοι εὔαδεν οὕτωc."
Ὣc φάτο, τὸν δὲ πατὴρ ὀλοφύρατο δάκρυ χέοντα·
αὐτίκα δ' ἠέρα μὲν cκέδαcεν καὶ ἀπῶcεν ὀμίχλην,
ἠέλιοc δ' ἐπέλαμψε, μάχη δ' ἐπὶ πᾶcα φαάνθη·

'But I cannot see anywhere an Achaian who could do this—they are all covered in fog, men and horses alike. Father Zeus, save the sons of the Achaians from this fog, make the sky clear, and give us light for our eyes—kill us in daylight, if you will, since this is your pleasure.'
So he spoke, and the Father pitied his tears. Immediately he scattered the fog and dispelled the darkness, and the sun shone out over them, and the whole battle was clearly seen. (17. 643–50)

It is indeed a dazzling moment when Zeus takes pity on the ignorant armies that clash by night.[15]

Menelaos feels a particular responsibility for Patroklos. At 17. 91 f. he is most reluctant to desert the man ὅc κεῖται ἐμῆc ἕνεκ' ἐνθάδε τιμῆc (who lies here killed for my avenging); and at 123 ff. he takes his stand with Aias μέγα πένθοc ἐνὶ cτήθεccιν ἀέξων (the grief swelling strong in his heart) (139—a unique expression). Later he inspires a rally (543 ff.) and tells Athene (in the guise of Phoinix) how strongly he wants to defend him μάλα γάρ με θανὼν ἐcεμάccατο θυμόν (since his death has touched right to my heart)

---

[13] Fenik, *TBS* 52 f., has been able to fit even clouds into a typical battle-sequence.

[14] μίcηcεν ('he hated') in 272 is, by the way, the only occurrence of any form of that verb in Homer.

[15] I am inclined to go along with Schadewaldt's tendency (*IS* 117) to regard this as symbolic of the human condition, beyond its immediate context, despite Willcock's common sense (*Comp.* 199).

(564). So it is πόλλ' ἀέκων (with great reluctance) (666) that he leaves Patroklos to find Antilochos. When he returns, he and Meriones pick up the body while the Aiantes defend their retreat— a dangerous tactic (see 730 ff.). Menelaos is characterized elsewhere as a man of sensibility with no love of violence for its own sake—see pp. 169–70. So his particular affinity with Patroklos is appropriate, as is the striking reason he gives when he rallies his comrades round:

"Αἴαντ', Ἀργείων ἡγήτορε, Μηριόνη τε,
νῦν τις ἐνηείης Πατροκλῆος δειλοῖο
μνηcάcθω· πᾶcιν γὰρ ἐπίcτατο μείλιχος εἶναι
ζωὸς ἐών· νῦν αὖ θάνατος καὶ μοῖρα κιχάνει."

'Aiantes, leaders of the Argives, and Meriones, think now of poor Patroklos and remember his kindness. His way was to be gentle to all men, when he was alive: but now death and fate have overtaken him.' (17. 669–72)

This is a reminder that, for all his martial feats in his last battle, Patroklos was brought back into the fighting by his susceptibility to compassion—see pp. 176–7 above. The epithet ἐνηήc ('kind') is especially his. Zeus himself first uses it in what amounts to an oxymoron: ἑταῖρον ... ἐνηέα τε κρατερόν τε (friend ... who was kind and strong) (204); it will also be used of him by Lykaon at 21. 91 (see p. 223) and of his funeral ashes at 23. 253.[16]

Antilochos is also particularly suitable for his role in this context. A relationship has already been built up between him and Menelaos which makes him an appropriate choice,[17] though he is at first touchingly struck by ἀμφαcίη ἐπέων (speechlessness) (17. 695). The scene with Achilleus is conveyed with the utmost brevity. Antilochos speaks only four lines (18. 18–21), and Achilleus, who senses the truth before he is told (18. 4ff.), does not reply.[18]

---

[16] On the one use of the epithet applied to someone else—Nestor at 23. 648— see further p. 254 n. 7.

[17] See 5. 561 ff., 15. 568 ff., and, more generally, Willcock, 'Antilochus' and in *BOP* 189–91.

[18] αὖτε ('once more') in 18. 6 refers back to the end of book 15. As at 16. 2 ff., the messenger comes, weeping, to an Achilleus who can tell no more than that the battle is going against the Achaians.

7.3   Anger displaces anger

Τὸν δ' αὖτε προσέειπε Θέτις κατὰ δάκρυ χέουσα·
"ὠκύμορος δή μοι, τέκος, ἔσσεαι, οἷ' ἀγορεύεις·   95
αὐτίκα γάρ τοι ἔπειτα μεθ' Ἕκτορα πότμος ἑτοῖμος."

Τὴν δὲ μέγ' ὀχθήσας προσέφη πόδας ὠκὺς Ἀχιλλεύς·
"αὐτίκα τεθναίην, ἐπεὶ οὐκ ἄρ' ἔμελλον ἑταίρωι
κτεινομένωι ἐπαμῦναι· ὁ μὲν μάλα τηλόθι πάτρης
ἔφθιτ', ἐμεῖο δὲ δῆσεν ἀρῆς ἀλκτῆρα γενέσθαι.   100
νῦν δ' ἐπεὶ οὐ νέομαί γε φίλην ἐς πατρίδα γαῖαν,
οὐδέ τι Πατρόκλωι γενόμην φάος οὐδ' ἑτάροισι
τοῖς ἄλλοις, οἳ δὴ πολέες δάμεν Ἕκτορι δίωι,
ἀλλ' ἧμαι παρὰ νηυσὶν ἐτώσιον ἄχθος ἀρούρης,
τοῖος ἐὼν οἷος οὔ τις Ἀχαιῶν χαλκοχιτώνων   105
ἐν πολέμωι· ἀγορῆι δέ τ' ἀμείνονές εἰσι καὶ ἄλλοι.
ὡς ἔρις ἔκ τε θεῶν ἔκ τ' ἀνθρώπων ἀπόλοιτο,
καὶ χόλος, ὅς τ' ἐφέηκε πολύφρονά περ χαλεπῆναι,
ὅς τε πολὺ γλυκίων μέλιτος καταλειβομένοιο
ἀνδρῶν ἐν στήθεσσιν ἀέξεται ἠΰτε καπνός·   110
ὡς ἐμὲ νῦν ἐχόλωσεν ἄναξ ἀνδρῶν Ἀγαμέμνων.
ἀλλὰ τὰ μὲν προτετύχθαι ἐάσομεν ἀχνύμενοί περ,
θυμὸν ἐνὶ στήθεσσι φίλον δαμάσαντες ἀνάγκηι·
νῦν δ' εἶμ', ὄφρα φίλης κεφαλῆς ὀλετῆρα κιχείω,
Ἕκτορα· κῆρα δ' ἐγὼ τότε δέξομαι, ὁππότε κεν δὴ   115
Ζεὺς ἐθέληι τελέσαι ἠδ' ἀθάνατοι θεοὶ ἄλλοι.
οὐδὲ γὰρ οὐδὲ βίη Ἡρακλῆος φύγε κῆρα,
ὅς περ φίλτατος ἔσκε Διὶ Κρονίωνι ἄνακτι·
ἀλλά ἑ μοῖρα δάμασσε καὶ ἀργαλέος χόλος Ἥρης.
ὡς καὶ ἐγών, εἰ δή μοι ὁμοίη μοῖρα τέτυκται,   120
κείσομ' ἐπεί κε θάνω· νῦν δὲ κλέος ἐσθλὸν ἀροίμην,
καί τινα Τρωϊάδων καὶ Δαρδανίδων βαθυκόλπων
ἀμφοτέρηισιν χερσὶ παρειάων ἀπαλάων
δάκρυ' ὀμορξαμένην ἁδινὸν στοναχῆσαι ἐφείην,
γνοῖεν δ' ὡς δὴ δηρον ἐγὼ πολέμοιο πέπαυμαι·   125
μηδέ μ' ἔρυκε μάχης φιλέουσά περ· οὐδέ με πείσεις."

Then Thetis said to him with her tears falling: 'Then, child, I must
lose you to an early death, for what you are saying: since directly after
Hektor dies your own doom is certain.'

Swift-footed Achilleus answered her in great passion: 'Then let me die
directly, since I was not to help my friend at his killing—he has died far
away from his native land, and did not have me there to protect him from
destruction. So now, since I shall not return to my dear native land, since
I have not been a saving light to Patroklos or my many other companions

who have been brought down by godlike Hektor, but sit here by the ships, a useless burden on the earth—I, a man without equal among the bronze-clad Achaians in war, though there are others better skilled at speaking—oh, that quarrels should vanish from gods and men, and resentment, which drives even a man of good sense to anger! It is far sweeter to men than trickling honey, and swells to fill their hearts like smoke—such is the anger that Agamemnon, lord of men, has caused me now. But all this is past and we should let it be, for all our pain, forcing down the passion in our hearts. And now I shall go, to find the destroyer of that dear life, Hektor—and I shall take my own death at whatever time Zeus and the other immortal gods wish to bring it on me. Even the mighty Herakles could not escape death, and he was the dearest of men to lord Zeus, son of Kronos: but fate conquered him, and the cruel enmity of Hera. So I too, if the same fate is there for me, will lie finished when I die. But now my wish is to win great glory, to make some of the deep-breasted Trojan and Dardanian women wipe the tears with both hands from their soft cheeks and set them wailing loud, and have them learn that I have stayed too long now out of the fighting. And do not try to keep me from battle, though you love me—you will not persuade me.' (18. 94–126)[19]

The scene between Achilleus and Thetis at 18. 67–144 is crucial to the entire poem, and marks his irrevocable turning towards death.[20] On my analysis it signals the closing sequence of part II, which makes structural sense of its strong connections with book 1 and with book 9. Thetis herself has not participated since her first involvement. Although she is not especially summoned this time, she is still the immortal so entangled with the mortal world as to vitiate the long-term carefreeness which is only to be expected for an immortal: and this is again marked by her coming from her strange habitation, which is neither Olympos above nor Peleus' palace in Phthia—ἄκουσε δὲ πότνια μήτηρ ἡμένη ἐν βένθεσσιν ἁλὸς παρὰ πατρὶ γέροντι (his honoured mother heard him where she sat by the side of her old father in the depths of the sea) (18. 35–6 = 1. 357–8).

"τέκνον τί κλαίεις; τί δέ σε φρένας ἵκετο πένθος; ἐξαύδα, μὴ κεῦθε." ('Child, why are you crying? What pain has touched your heart? Tell me, do not hide it.') (18. 73–4 = 1. 362–3). Again their talk is almost frighteningly frank, above all on the subject of the brevity

---

[19] Line 106 looks like a pedantic footnote. Its excision might be an improvement.
[20] On the motif of Achilleus' impending death, see, among others, Schadewaldt, *HWW* 250ff.; Kullmann, 308–13, 320–5; Schein, esp. Ch. 3; Rutherford, 145–6.

of Achilleus' life. Their relationship is infused by this shared awareness from the very start. There is something chilling about the choice of the very first words in the poem that Achilleus speaks to his immortal mother:

πολλὰ δὲ μητρὶ φίληι ἠρήcατο χεῖραc ὀρεγνύc·
"μῆτερ, ἐπεί μ' ἔτεκέc γε μινυνθάδιόν περ ἐόντα,
τιμήν πέρ μοι ὄφελλεν 'Ολύμπιοc ἐγγυαλίξαι
Ζεὺc ὑψιβρεμέτηc· νῦν δ' οὐδέ με τυτθὸν ἔτειcεν·"

He stretched out his hands, and prayed long to his dear mother: 'Mother, since it was you that bore me, if only to a life doomed to shortness, surely honour should have been granted to me by Olympian Zeus, the high-thunderer. But now he has shown me not even the slightest honour.' (1. 351-4)

It is well known between them that he is μινυνθάδιοc (doomed to a short life), and Thetis does not herself contest or protest against it:

"ὤ μοι τέκνον ἐμόν, τί νύ c' ἔτρεφον αἰνὰ τεκοῦcα;
αἴθ' ὄφελεc παρὰ νηυcὶν ἀδάκρυτοc καὶ ἀπήμων
ἧcθαι, ἐπεί νύ τοι αἶcα μίνυνθά περ, οὔ τι μάλα δήν·
νῦν δ' ἅμα τ' ὠκύμοροc καὶ ὀϊζυρὸc περὶ πάντων
ἔπλεο· τῶι cε κακῆι αἴcηι τέκον ἐν μεγάροιcι.
τοῦτο δέ τοι ἐρέουcα ἔποc Διὶ τερπικεραύνωι
εἶμ' αὐτὴ πρὸς "Ολυμπον ἀγάννιφον, αἴ κε πίθηται."

'Oh my child, what did I rear you for, after the pain of your birth? If only you could sit by your ships without tears or sorrow—because your fate is of short span, not at all long. But now you are both short-lived and miserable as well beyond all others: so it was a cruel fate under which I bore you in our house. But I shall go myself to snow-capped Olympos and make this appeal to Zeus who delights in thunder, in the hope that he will grant it.' (1. 414-20)[21]

The connection between Achilleus' short life and his claims on tīmē from Zeus are taken by Thetis to Olympos—"τίμηcόν μοι υἱόν, ὃc ὠκυμορώτατοc ἄλλων ἔπλετο" ('show honour to my son, who is short-lived beyond all other men') (1. 505-6).

There is then a conspicuous reminder of the early death of Achilleus and of its association with Thetis towards the end of

---

[21] αἰνὰ τεκοῦcα ('with the pain of your birth') becomes transformed to the amazing word-formation δυcαριcτοτόκεια ('unhappy in the best of birth') in 18. 54. (Δύcπαρι, εἶδοc ἄριcτε ('Badparis, good for looks') (3. 39, 13. 769) is perhaps the nearest thing to it.)

part I. After the main part of his reply to Odysseus in book 9, in
which he insists on Agamemnon's inability to give proper *tīmē*,
he brings together the combination of possible outcomes which
every hero has to consider and to balance up when going into
battle. These are, in effect, material gain, glory, and death. These
are the considerations behind Sarpedon's celebrated speech to
Glaukos, where he makes the classic case in favour of risking death
for the sake of the other two. But for other mortals the risk is
unpredictable: when Achilleus weighs up the combination, it is
different.

First, however, he establishes the point that there is a crucial
asymmetry between life on the one hand and material gains,
however great, on the other—an imbalance that is normally left
unspoken or even unrecognized. In 9. 388 ff. he says that he will
find a bride at home, rather than a daughter of Agamemnon, for
(γάρ) no amount of wealth is equivalent to his life,

> "οὐ γὰρ ἐμοὶ ψυχῆς ἀντάξιον οὐδ' ὅσα φασὶν
> Ἴλιον ἐκτῆcθαι, εὖ ναιόμενον πτολίεθρον"

'Because nothing equals the worth of my life—not even all the riches
they say were held by the well-founded city of Ilios . . .' (9. 401–2)

for (γάρ) possessions are a two-way traffic, unlike life:

> "ληϊcτοὶ μὲν γάρ τε βόεc καὶ ἴφια μῆλα,
> κτητοὶ δὲ τρίποδέc τε καὶ ἵππων ξανθὰ κάρηνα·
> ἀνδρὸc δὲ ψυχὴ πάλιν ἐλθεῖν οὔτε λεϊcτὴ
> οὔθ' ἑλετή, ἐπεὶ ἄρ κεν ἀμείψεται ἕρκοc ὀδόντων."

'Men can raid catttle and sturdy sheep, and men can win tripods and bay
horses by the head—but there is no raiding or winning a man's life back
again, when once it has passed the guard of his teeth.' (9. 406–9)[22]

While it is undeniable that material compensations are not much
use to a dead man, there is still, as Sarpedon points out, another
promise held out to those who risk their lives in battle: *kleos*,

---

[22] Achilleus' vivid formulation is, I suggest, given an extra pungency by the
new life he gives to the dead metaphor of ἕρκοc ὀδόντων ('the guard of the teeth').
ποῖόν cε ἔποc φύγεν ἕρκοc ὀδόντων; ('what is this you have let slip the guard of your
teeth?') is formulaic; but, since a ἕρκοc is literally the pen which contains cattle—
at least as long as they do not become ληϊcτοί (raided)—the phrase is given a new
twist: a life, once raided from the pen of the teeth, can never be recovered. There
seems to be a comparably sardonic word-play in τὸ γὰρ γέραc ἐcτὶ γερόντων ('such
is the *geras* of *gerontes*') in 9. 422 (which, as used by Nestor at 3. 323, seems to be
Polonian joke).

immortal fame. Death is a serious threat but it is not certain; the fortunate man may win glory and get safe home. That is the equation for other mortals. Achilleus' further argumentative γάρ marks him out as an exception:

"μήτηρ γάρ τέ μέ φησι θεὰ Θέτις ἀργυρόπεζα   410
διχθαδίας κῆρας φερέμεν θανάτοιο τέλοςδε.
εἰ μέν κ' αὖθι μένων Τρώων πόλιν ἀμφιμάχωμαι,
ὤλετο μέν μοι νόστος, ἀτὰρ κλέος ἄφθιτον ἔσται·
εἰ δέ κεν οἴκαδ' ἴκωμι φίλην ἐς πατρίδα γαῖαν,
ὤλετό μοι κλέος ἐσθλόν, ἐπὶ δηρὸν δέ μοι αἰών."   415

'For my mother, the silver-footed goddess Thetis, says that I have two fates that could carry me to the end of death. If I stay here and fight on round the Trojans' city, then gone is my home-coming, but my glory will never die: and if I come back to my dear native land, then gone is my great glory, but my life will stretch long.' (9. 410–15)[23]

This choice, phrased with the balance and authority of an oracle, has not been mentioned earlier. This is because it is only here that Achilleus really follows through the case in favour of a total withdrawal, a *nostos*. This is the right moment in the unfolding of the narrative to reveal that, if he fights for Agamemnon, then he will not only be *risking* his life, like all the others, he will be certain to *lose* it. He has questioned whether Agamemnon's cause is good enough to fight for, and hence, perhaps, whether the *kleos* it might win would be ἐσθλόν (great, good). He implies at this stage that he will choose *nostos* and life rather than *kleos* and death. The choice set out here hangs over all that follows, above all over the meeting with Thetis in 18.[24] An explicit restatement is not needed. There is a muted allusion, I suggest, in Achilleus' prediction that Thetis will never welcome him οἴκαδε νοστήσαντα (back to his home) (90, cf. 101), and an unmistakable allusion for well-tuned ears in line 121: νῦν δὲ κλέος ἐσθλὸν ἀροίμην (but now my wish is to win great glory).

In between 9 and 18 the only clear reference to the early death of Achilleus is indirect—but closely connected with the death of

---

[23] I follow Aristarchos and Zenodotos in omitting line 416, because it disturbs the elaborated symmetry merely to supply a verb. On the other hand I notice that Phoinix's 'moral' of the *Litai* (Prayers) in 9. 508–12 consists of two lines balanced by three.

[24] See above all Schadewaldt, *HWW* 234ff. This aspect of the scene seems to me far more important than the subdued funerary motifs, for which cf. e.g. Willcock, *Comp.* 201; Schein, 129–32.

Patroklos, and hence that of Hektor. At the height of his dizzy hour of glory Patroklos attempts to assault Troy, and Apollo pushes him back:

> "χάζεο, διογενὲς Πατρόκλεες· οὔ νύ τοι αἶcα
> cῶι ὑπὸ δουρὶ πόλιν πέρθαι Τρώων ἀγερώχων,
> οὐδ' ὑπ' Ἀχιλλῆος, ὅς πέρ cέο πολλὸν ἀμείνων."

'Back, lord Patroklos! It is not fate for the proud Trojans' city to be sacked by your spear, nor even by Achilleus, a far greater man than you.' (16. 707–9)

So when, at 18. 88 ff., Achilleus insists that he must kill Hektor, Thetis' terse two-line prediction falls into place. In book 9 his death was foretold as consequent on rejoining the fighting; by the Homeric technique of increasing precision, it is now more immediately attached by a chain of events to his killing of Hektor.

Achilleus' great speech at 18. 98–126 displays his characteristic percipience at its most cogent, made vivid by unpredictable diction and syntax. The keynote is, however, the passionate urgency sounded by his seizure of his mother's αὐτίκα ('directly'). This is sustained by the reiteration of νῦν ('now') in 101, 114, 121, the optatives in 98, 121, 124, 125, and above all by the direct first-person future verbs δέξομαι ('I shall take') in 115 and κείcομαι ('I will lie') in 121.

A pedant might complain that Thetis, with her knowledge of the future, should have warned Achilleus at the start that his plea to Zeus would lead to the death of Patroklos. But this would destroy the whole portrayal of Achilleus as human, a man of extraordinary insight yet still mortal, and still at least partially ignorant. Hektor does not see the hidden cost of usurping Achilleus' armour; so, less rashly, Achilleus does not see the concealed cost of the *tīmē* he has from Zeus. So, for narrative purposes, Thetis is made ignorant of the fate of Patroklos when she first says:

> "τέκνον, τί κλαίεις; τί δέ ce φρέναc ἵκετο πένθος;
> ἐξαύδα, μὴ κεῦθε· τὰ μὲν δή τοι τετέλεσται
> ἐκ Διός, ὡς ἄρα δὴ πρίν γ' εὔχεο χεῖραc ἀναςχών,
> πάντας ἐπὶ πρύμνηισιν ἀλήμεναι υἷας Ἀχαιῶν
> cεῦ ἐπιδευομένους, παθέειν τ' ἀεκήλια ἔργα."

'Child, why are you crying? What pain has touched your heart? Tell me, do not hide it. Look, all that you asked has been brought about by Zeus, when you held out your hands and prayed that all the sons of the Achaians should be penned back by the sterns of their ships through want of you, and be put to terrible suffering.' (18. 73–7)

On the other hand, Achilleus does clearly see the ambivalence of Zeus' favour (brought out by . . . μέν . . . ἀλλά . . . ('yes . . . but . . .')):

"μῆτερ ἐμή, τὰ μὲν ἄρ μοι 'Ολύμπιος ἐξετέλεccεν·
ἀλλὰ τί μοι τῶν ἦδοc, ἐπεὶ φίλοc ὤλεθ' ἑταῖροc,
Πάτροκλοc, τὸν ἐγὼ περὶ πάντων τῖον ἑταίρων"

'Mother, yes, the Olympian has done all this for me. But what pleasure can I take in it, when my dear friend is killed, Patroklos, a man I honoured above all my companions . . .' (18. 79–81)

He also recognizes his analogy with his father (82 ff.): Peleus was favoured with marriage to a goddess and with wonderful armour, *yet* this armour has been lost to Hektor, and his mortal son will never return home.

Now that his great favour from Zeus has brought him no ἦδοc ('pleasure'), Achilleus wants in effect to undo everything that has happened in the poem so far. He suddenly repents of his anger against Agamemnon, the Trojan successes, and his own inactivity (ἦμαι (I sit) 104). And by regretting his failure to save Patroklos *and* the others (102–3) he regrets his inclusion of *all* the Achaians in the damnation of Agamemnon—see above, pp. 62–3.[25] In sum, Achilleus renounces all the ἔριc (*eris*) and χόλοc (*cholos*) which have pervaded the *Iliad* since its very beginning.

Achilleus' extraordinary 'mixed similes' of lines 107–10—arising perhaps from the practice of smoking bees—powerfully convey the fast-spreading satisfaction of indulging anger, while at the same time extending his regret of his own indulgence to all mankind and even to the gods. Thus, half-way through a speech, the passions of book 1 are renounced: the *mēnis* poem is over. When Achilleus turns his attention to Hektor in 114 ff., he shows no awareness that what has happened is not that he has given up *eris* and *cholos* altogether, but that Hektor has replaced Agamemnon as his target.[26] The timing of this realization by the audience may vary; but there will be no shortage of *eris* and *cholos*, verbal and

---

[25] Note how, at 19. 61, he refers not to Patroklos but the τόccοι Ἀχαιοί (all those many Achaians) who have died during his withdrawal.

[26] *Od.* 3. 135–6 seems to show awareness of *eris* as a key motif of the *Iliad*.

physical, in books 20 to 22. There are verbal signals even sooner, for example Achilleus' promise to Patroklos that he will have vengeance ϲέθεν κταμένοιο χολωθείϲ (in anger for your killing) (18. 337), and the growing *cholos* inspired by his new armour at 19. 16. So the poet infiltrates the awareness that Achilleus is caught up in the 'Homeric paradox' (see pp. 121–2 above). Hektor has won glory, and thus necessarily bereaved his victim's *philoi*. So Achilleus will now go out to win glory and to bereave the *philoi* of the previous victor in his turn. We see his determination of 121 ff. duly fulfilled through Andromache and the other Trojans. Eventually Achilleus himself will come to appreciate the human meaning of this paradox. By the time that Andromache and the Trojan women lament Hektor properly, it will be thanks to Achilleus' collaboration, and he will have overcome even this second fury.

For all the eagerness of his αὐτίκα τεθναίην ('then let me die directly') speech, it is not until the next day comes and his new armour is delivered, that Achilleus can even begin to put it into action. In between comes a sequence of striking scenes—and somewhere among them comes the major structural articulation between part II and part III.

The Achilleus–Thetis scene is 'clamped' into the great central day by the resumption of the battle at 18. 148 where it left off at 17. 761. It does not last long, however, once Hera has roused Achilleus to appear at the ditch. Once the body of Patroklos is back with Achilleus, the sun sets (239–42). The scenes which follow clearly belong with the day of battle. I have already discussed in § 6.2 above how the scene in 18 is similar to, and different from, the Trojan *agorē* in the field after the sunset in book 8, and how Hektor here takes a turning towards death. Schadewaldt has brought out well how Hektor's 'choice' is closely juxtaposed with that of Achilleus—he too is μινυνθάδιοϲ (short-lived) (15. 612, cf. 1. 359). While Achilleus makes his decision consciously in the desperation of grief, Hektor makes his unwittingly in the flood of untimely over-confidence. Achilleus has his mother as infallible ratifier: Hektor has the blind witness and support of his *lāos*. And yet Hektor will still take full responsibility for his misjudgement when the time comes—p. 234 below.

On the Achaian side the *agorē* will have to wait for the morning. For now, there is Achilleus' first lament for Patroklos, where he recognizes his failure towards Menoitios (324–7), and publicly connects this with the certainty of his own death:

"ἀλλ' οὐ Ζεὺς ἄνδρεςςι νοήματα πάντα τελευτᾷ·
ἄμφω γὰρ πέπρωται ὁμοίην γαῖαν ἐρεῦςαι
αὐτοῦ ἐνὶ Τροίηι, ἐπεὶ οὐδ' ἐμὲ νοστήςαντα
δέξεται ἐν μεγάροιςι γέρων ἱππηλάτα Πηλεὺς
οὐδὲ Θέτις μήτηρ, ἀλλ' αὐτοῦ γαῖα καθέξει.
νῦν δ' ἐπεὶ οὖν, Πάτροκλε, ςεῦ ὕςτερος εἶμ' ὑπὸ γαῖαν,
οὔ ςε πρὶν κτεριῶ, πρίν γ' Ἕκτορος ἐνθάδ' ἐνεῖκαι
τεύχεα καὶ κεφαλήν, μεγαθύμου ςοῖο φονῆος·"

'But Zeus does not bring about all that men intend: and both of us are fated to redden the same earth here in Troy, as I shall not return home either to be welcomed in his house by the old horseman Peleus or my mother Thetis, but the earth will cover me here. But now, Patroklos, since I shall be going under the ground after you, I shall not give you burial until I have brought here the armour and the head of Hektor, the great man who murdered you.' (18. 328–35)

The body is then washed and laid out. At this point the narrative leaves earth for Olympos, first for a brief conversation (356–68) between Zeus and Hera, registering the decisive shift of fortune against the Trojans, and then for the meeting of Thetis with Hephaistos (369–467, picking up from her departure from Achilleus at 148).

In structural terms it is clear, I think, that the description of the making of Achilleus' new armour belongs with part III of the *Iliad* and is not a pendant to part II. This is the armour that Achilleus will wear back into battle: the shield will defend him against Aineias (20. 259–72, with allusion to Hephaistos), and against Hektor, at 22. 289–91. The way that the armour leads into the next day is reflected by the narrative continuity between 18. 614–17 and 19. 1 ff., with ἡ δέ in 19. 3 showing that the dawn of 19. 1 is not the opening (any more than was the dawn of 2. 48). The dialogue between Zeus and Hera is, however, a beginning rather than an ending, and leads into Thetis' arrival, at 368 ff. This all points to the conclusion that the division between parts II and III comes at 18. 353/4, where there is not even a paragraph division in the Oxford Classical Text!

In that case, part II ends with the pictures of the death-bound Hektor and then of the dead Patroklos, the two who have dominated the central day. Achilleus is left in grief, but full of menace for the Trojans. Part III begins with a brief résumé of Zeus' perspective on events. His dialogue with Hera, albeit a prickly one, contrasts with his single-handed action at 11. 3 ff., the start of part II. So whether or not my theory about performance has any truth, I suggest that a major closure and opening should be recognized at this juncture. Thus:

(a)   γάστρην μὲν τρίποδος πῦρ ἄμφεπε, θέρμετο δ' ὕδωρ·
        αὐτὰρ ἐπεὶ δὴ ζέσσεν ὕδωρ ἐνὶ ἤνοπι χαλκῶι,
        καὶ τότε δὴ λοῦσάν τε καὶ ἤλειψαν λίπ' ἐλαίωι,
        ἐν δ' ὠτειλὰς πλῆσαν ἀλείφατος ἐννεώροιο·
        ἐν λεχέεσσι δὲ θέντες ἑανῶι λιτὶ κάλυψαν
        ἐς πόδας ἐκ κεφαλῆς, καθύπερθε δὲ φάρεϊ λευκῶι.

The fire worked on the belly of the cauldron, and the water warmed. Then when the water had boiled in the gleaming bronze, they washed him and rubbed him thickly with oil, and filled his wounds with long-stored ointment. Then they placed him on a bier, and covered him from feet to head with a soft sheet of fine linen, and over that a white cloak.
(18. 348–53)

—end of part II. Opening of part III:

(b)   παννύχιοι μὲν ἔπειτα πόδας ταχὺν ἀμφ' Ἀχιλῆα
        Μυρμιδόνες Πάτροκλον ἀνεστενάχοντο γοῶντες·
        Ζεὺς δ' Ἥρην προσέειπε κασιγνήτην ἄλοχόν τε·
        "ἔπρηξας καὶ ἔπειτα, βοῶπις πότνια Ἥρη,
        ἀνστήσας Ἀχιλῆα πόδας ταχύν· ἦ ῥά νυ σεῖο
        ἐξ αὐτῆς ἐγένοντο κάρη κομόωντες Ἀχαιοί."

Then all night long the Myrmidons gathered round swift-footed Achilleus and mourned in lamentation for Patroklos. And Zeus spoke to Hera, his sister and wife: 'So you have achieved it in the end, ox-eyed queen Hera—you stirred swift-footed Achilleus into action. It must be then that you are mother to all the long-haired Achaians, and they your children.'
(18. 354–9)

8

Vulnerable Places

8.1 Achilleus' dismissal of social ties

"ἐγὼ δ' οὐκ αἴτιός εἰμι,
ἀλλὰ Ζεὺc καὶ Μοῖρα καὶ ἠεροφοῖτιc Ἐρινύc,
οἵ τέ μοι εἰν ἀγορῆι φρεcὶν ἔμβαλον ἄγριον ἄτην,
ἤματι τῶι ὅτ' Ἀχιλλῆοc γέραc αὐτὸc ἀπηύρων.
ἀλλὰ τί κεν ῥέξαιμι; θεὸc διὰ πάντα τελευτᾶι.   90
πρέcβα Διὸc θυγάτηρ Ἄτη, ἣ πάνταc ἀᾶται,
οὐλομένη·

.   .   .   .

ὣc καὶ ἐγών, ὅτε δὴ αὖτε μέγαc κορυθαίολοc Ἕκτωρ
Ἀργείουc ὀλέκεcκεν ἐπὶ πρύμνηιcι νέεccιν,   135
οὐ δυνάμην λελαθέcθ' Ἄτηc, ἧι πρῶτον ἀάcθην.
ἀλλ' ἐπεὶ ἀαcάμην καί μευ φρέναc ἐξέλετο Ζεύc,
ἂψ ἐθέλω ἀρέcαι, δόμεναί τ' ἀπερείcι' ἄποινα·
ἀλλ' ὄρcευ πόλεμόνδε, καὶ ἄλλουc ὄρνυθι λαούc.
δῶρα δ' ἐγὼν ὅδε πάντα παραcχέμεν, ὅccα τοι ἐλθὼν   140
χθιζὸc ἐνὶ κλιcίηιcιν ὑπέcχετο δῖοc Ὀδυccεύc.
εἰ δ' ἐθέλειc, ἐπίμεινον ἐπειγόμενόc περ Ἄρηοc,
δῶρα δέ τοι θεράποντεc ἐμῆc παρὰ νηὸc ἑλόντεc
οἴcουc', ὄφρα ἴδηαι ὅ τοι μενοεικέα δώcω."
    Τὸν δ' ἀπαμειβόμενοc προcέφη πόδαc ὠκὺc Ἀχιλλεύc·
"Ἀτρείδη κύδιcτε, ἄναξ ἀνδρῶν Ἀγάμεμνον,   146
δῶρα μὲν αἴ κ' ἐθέληιcθα παραcχέμεν, ὡc ἐπιεικέc,
ἤ τ' ἐχέμεν παρὰ coί· νῦν δὲ μνηcώμεθα χάρμηc
αἶψα μάλ'· οὐ γὰρ χρὴ κλοτοπεύειν ἐνθάδ' ἐόνταc
οὐδὲ διατρίβειν· ἔτι γὰρ μέγα ἔργον ἄρεκτον."   150

'But I am not to blame, but rather Zeus and Fate and Erinys that walks in darkness: they put a cruel blindness in my mind at the assembly on that day when by my own act I took away his prize from Achilleus. But what could I do? It is god who brings all things to their end. This blindness is Ate, eldest daughter of Zeus, the accursed goddess who blinds all men ... So it has been for me in my case now. When great

Hektor of the glinting helmet kept destroying the Argives by the sterns of the ships, I could not forget Ate and the blindness she brought on me on that first day. But since I was blinded and Zeus took away my wits, I am ready to take it back and offer the appeasement of limitless reparation. So rise now for battle, and rouse the rest of our people. As for the gifts, I am here ready to offer all that godlike Odysseus promised yesterday when he came to your hut. Or if you like, hold your eagerness for war while my servants fetch the gifts from my ship and bring them here, so that you can see how my offer will please your heart.'

Then swift-footed Achilleus answered him: 'Most glorious son of Atreus, Agamemnon, lord of men, do as you will with the gifts—either give them, as is right, or keep them with you. But now our spirits should fill for battle, and straightaway. We should not stay here making delays and wasting time in talk—there is still a great task to be done.' (19. 86–92, 134–50)

On my analysis, part III begins with Thetis' acquisition of new armour. Then there is an *agorē* to correspond with book 1. The scene between Thetis and Hephaistos in book 18 is certainly very different from her previous visit to Olympos, in book 1. It is also very different from the scenes with Achilleus on earth. Hephaistos' house reveals a world of comfort, courtesy, and imperishable marvels.[1] He can create an immortal masterpiece, which is as sure to be a wonder as it is sure that Achilleus must die:

"αἲ γάρ μιν θανάτοιο δυσηχέος ὧδε δυναίμην
νόσφιν ἀποκρύψαι, ὅτε μιν μόρος αἰνὸς ἱκάνοι,
ὥς οἱ τεύχεα καλὰ παρέccεται, οἷά τιc αὖτε
ἀνθρώπων πολέων θαυμάccεται, ὃc κεν ἴδηται."

'If only I could be as certain of hiding him away from grim death, when his cruel fate comes on him, as I am that there will be beautiful armour for him now, such that all the many men who see it will marvel at the sight.' (18. 464–7)

The god's exuberant artistry is also a showpiece of the poet's artistry—and it takes him no longer to make than it takes the poet to sing it. Homer's words are, after all, as near as any member of the audience is ever going to get to seeing Achilleus' shield. Appropriately, then, the shield is, like the *Iliad* as a whole, a

---

[1] Contrast the tripod to wash mortality (18. 343 ff.) with the twenty robot tripods that Hephaistos is manufacturing (372 ff.)—though in different sessions of performance on my theory. Note, by the way, the nice touch of humour in the immortal application of ζωιάγρια ('debt for life') in 407 (see Leaf).

celebration of life in the midst of death and destruction.² The microcosm on the shield is dominated by pleasure, plenty, and civilization, but violence and slaughter are there also. For those fighting at Troy the shield presents the world which they have left behind and to which they hope to return. For many it is a vain hope—vain for almost all the Trojans—but they do not know that. Only Achilleus, the recipient, knows for certain that he will have no *nostos*, and will never live in that world again.

Achilleus' urgent desire to get out and exact revenge is renewed as soon as he receives his new armour—νῦν δ' ἤτοι μὲν ἐγὼ θωρήξομαι ('so, now I shall arm myself for battle') (19. 23). But the poem is not ready yet: it is some 350 lines after the dawn before he actually arms and departs, 750 before he sheds blood, and 1,500 before he and Hektor draw near for the final clash. Within each stage there is much that needs to be established before the narrative can sustain the death of Hektor.

The opening human scenes of part III complete the sequence of 'confrontations' between Achilleus and Agamemnon, complementing in various ways those of books 1 and 9. Thetis advises her son of the need for an *agorē* μῆνιν ἀποειπὼν Ἀγαμέμνονι (to declare the end of your anger against Agamemnon) (35), cf. μῆνιν ἀποειπόντος . . . Πηλεΐωνος in 75 (the son of Peleus had declared an end to his anger): in other words this is to undo the *agorē* of book 1.³ As there (see 1. 54, 386), Achilleus summons the meeting; and it is emphasized that this time even more people attend (19. 42–5). Achilleus' initial speech (56–73) is brief, direct, and unqualified: he does not even raise the subject of apologies or gifts. He opens with the simple Ἀτρεΐδη ('Son of Atreus');⁴ and he uses conciliatory duals (cf. ἐμῆς καὶ σῆς ('yours and mine') in 64):

> "Ἀτρεΐδη, ἦ ἄρ τι τόδ' ἀμφοτέροισιν ἄρειον
> ἔπλετο, σοὶ καὶ ἐμοί, ὅ τε νῶι περ ἀχνυμένω κῆρ
> θυμοβόρωι ἔριδι μενεήναμεν εἵνεκα κούρης;"

'Son of Atreus, could we possibly say that this has proved good for both of us, for you and for me, that the two of us in our passions quarrelled in heart-consuming anger over a girl?' (19. 56–8)

---

² I would still stand by the general thesis of my essay in *G & R* 1980 (with biblio.), though much I would now put differently—some in the light of the trenchant deconstruction by J. Henderson in *Farrago*, Lent 1 (1981) (the strategies and ideas of that might in their turn be revealingly dismantled).

³ Cf. Reinhardt, *ID* 413; Lohmann, 173.

⁴ As at 1. 59—contrast the elaborate abusive vocatives of 1. 122, 149, 225.

Agememnon's lengthy reply (78–144) is in great contrast.[5] He starts with uncomfortable parrying (see Leaf on 78–85), and then hastily diverts into prolix mythological paradeigma, getting back to the matter in hand only in his last eleven lines. He addresses Achilleus only at the very end, and he never uses a vocative or any dual or first-person plural. In fact he names Achilleus only once:

"Πηλείδηι μὲν ἐγὼν ἐνδείξομαι· αὐτὰρ οἱ ἄλλοι
cύνθεcθ' Ἀργεῖοι, μῦθόν τ' εὖ γνῶτε ἕκαcτοc."

'Now I shall address the son of Peleus: but the rest of the Argives should listen, and mark well what I say, every one of you.' (19. 83–4)

This is like his speech at 9. 115–61, where he could not bring himself to name Achilleus at all.

Agamemnon's 'apology' needs to be taken in its dramatic context. He is more interested in the picture he presents to the *lāos* as a whole than to Achilleus—particularly as Achilleus is clearly no longer concerned with him. The night before last he attempted to undo the damage before the *gerontes* (9. 115 ff.), and now he is coming before everyone in the *agorē*. If quotations are taken from Agamemnon's speech and treated as though they were autonomous 'philosophy', then there is a danger of extracting some seriously misleading ideas about early Greek ethics.[6] This is, I believe, what Dodds and others have done to arrive, on the strength of this passage, at the conclusion that in Homer's Greece ethical (or moral) responsibility is as yet separate from issues of reward and punishment, credit and blame.

The larger context makes it clear that Agamemnon is definitely in the wrong, and has been since the start, both in ethical terms and because of the disastrous consequences of his behaviour. Even without the implicit evaluation of book 1—see § 2.2 above—he is well on the way to admitting his fault by the time of book 2:

---

[5] It is not forgotten (51–3) that he was wounded the previous morning by the otherwise unknown son of Antenor, Koön. The wounds of Odysseus and Diomedes are also remembered (47–9) (though they will have been forgotten by the time of the funeral games). The three leaders have been entirely out of action since book 11 except for their meeting at 14. 29–152, 377–81.

[6] I have already made a start on this topic in 'Agamemnon', 75–7, where Dodds, Adkins, Lloyd-Jones, and Willcock are cited for the orthodox view. I am delighted that my argument was accepted by C. Gill in the same volume, 16–17. On Agamemnon's apology see also Lesky, 'Motivation'; Lohmann, 75–80.

"ἀλλά μοι αἰγίοχος Κρονίδης Ζεὺς ἄλγε' ἔδωκεν,
ὅς με μετ' ἀπρήκτους ἔριδας καὶ νείκεα βάλλει.
καὶ γὰρ ἐγὼν Ἀχιλεύς τε μαχεσσάμεθ' εἵνεκα κούρης
ἀντιβίοις ἐπέεσσιν, ἐγὼ δ' ἦρχον χαλεπαίνων·"

'Zeus who holds the aegis has dealt me troubles, throwing me into useless quarrels and contention—so I and Achilleus fought with wrangling words over a girl, and I was the first to grow angry.' (2. 375–8, (cf. Odysseus at 19. 183))

In book 9 (106 ff.) Nestor spells out Agamemnon's culpable mistakes, and he himself accepts his fault and responsibility:

"ὦ γέρον, οὔ τι ψεῦδος ἐμὰς ἄτας κατέλεξας·
ἀασάμην, οὐδ' αὐτὸς ἀναίνομαι. ἀντί νυ πολλῶν
λαῶν ἐστιν ἀνὴρ ὅν τε Ζεὺς κῆρι φιλήσῃ,
ὡς νῦν τοῦτον ἔτεισε, δάμασσε δὲ λαὸν Ἀχαιῶν.
ἀλλ' ἐπεὶ ἀασάμην φρεσὶ λευγαλέῃσι πιθήσας,
ἂψ ἐθέλω ἀρέσαι δόμεναί τ' ἀπερείσι' ἄποινα."

'Old man, your talk of my blindness is no lie: I was blinded, I do not deny it myself. A man loved from the heart by Zeus is worth many armies—just as now Zeus has honoured this man, and broken the army of the Achaians. But since I was blinded and listened to my heart's wretched persuasion, I am ready to take it back and offer the appeasement of limitless reparation.' (9. 115–20)[7]

The element of *ātē* implied by the verb ἀασάμην ('I was blinded') does not contradict his responsibility, and is not claimed to diminish his double motivation (cf. 1. 411–12, 9. 377, etc.). In the *agorē* in 19, however, he wishes as far as possible to save face and to preserve his standing in the eyes of the Achaians. So, early in his speech, he attempts to diminish his blameworthiness. Since he cannot possibly, in the context, say anything against Achilleus, he has to put the blame on a third party, the gods—as he does in 86–90.

I have discussed earlier (pp. 98–100) how the attribution of *aitia* is an attribution of blame which expects the payment of the price for the fault. Conversely the claim that one is οὐκ αἴτιος (not to blame) (or ἀναίτιος (blameless)), and the claim that someone else is, amounts to a proposal that one should not have to pay the price

---

[7] Note how Poseidon's sentiments at 13. 95 ff. (esp. 111–12) only make sense on the assumption that Agamemnon is widely held to be *aitios* among the Achaians, and that the *lāos* attributes κακότης (fault) to him. For a full discussion of ἄτη and related words in Homer, see W. F. Wyatt in *AJP* 103 (1982), 247–76.

and that the other party should.[8] So Achilleus exonerates Agamemnon's heralds (1. 335), Telemachos pleads for Phemios (*Od.* 22. 356) and so forth. Generally speaking, however, the *Iliad* does not allow a claim that the gods are to blame to override the standard notion of double motivation. In other words, men may excuse themselves by blaming the gods for their own behaviour; but that behaviour is seen none the less as the outcome of human motivation as well, and as liable to due blame or punishment. Agamemnon's speech in book 9 is completely consistent with this. In 119–20 (quoted above), even taking ἀασάμην completely passively ('I was blinded'), rather than as a middle, Agamemnon still concedes the element of active error in φρεσὶ λευγαλέῃσι πιθήσας ('and listened to my heart's wretched persuasion'): hence his willingness to offer reparation. I suggest therefore that Agamemnon's claim ἐγὼ δ' οὐκ αἴτιός εἰμι ('but I am not to blame') at 19. 86 is a retraction, or at least a contradiction, of what he said in book 9. Since his audience within the poem, and (if I am persuasive) the audiences hearing or reading the poem, all know that he is indeed αἴτιος (to blame), his blaming of the gods is clearly special pleading. When heard in context, Agamemnon is asking the Achaians to be sympathetic towards him and not to contest his face-saving excuses.

The digression from 19. 81 to 19. 133 about Zeus and *Ātē* serves, then, to conceal the *contradiction* between Agamemnon's claim that he is not *aitios* and his willingness to pay reparation. When he eventually emerges from it, he picks up the situation from book 9 and his own language: compare 19. 137–41 with 9. 119–20, quoted above. Yet even now, while conceding the *apoina*, and hence conceding that he *is aitios*, Agamemnon cannot resist special pleading. In 9. 119 φρεσὶ λευγαλέῃσι πιθήσας ('and listened to my heart's wretched persuasion') conceded his fault, and so ἐπεί ('since') made good sense. Here the half-line is altered to καί μευ φρένας ἐξέλετο Ζεύς ('and Zeus took away my wits'), thus making his own role entirely passive, and thus depriving ἐπεί of its argumentative sense. 'Although' might have made sense, but 'because I am innocent, I am ready to pay the price' is, I suggest,

---

[8] For some passages showing that those who are *aitioi* are liable for punishment, and that those who are not are not, see p. 99 n. 28 above and *Il.* 13. 775, 15. 137, 19. 410, 20. 297, 21. 370; *Od.* 11. 553 ff., 22. 48.

a blatant *non sequitur*, and one that is so blatant precisely because it is meant to be perceived as such. In his reply at 146 ff. Achilleus no longer has any interest in making life difficult for Agamemnon. He doesn't care about the material compensation, let alone the repayment of all the θυμαλγέα λώβην (wrong that pains my heart) (see pp. 72–3 above). He is not allowed to move so fast, however, and finds that he has to respond once more, after Agamemnon has taken his oath that he has not touched Briseïs (258–65—in fact the last words of direct speech that Agamemnon utters in the *Iliad*). For all his impatience, Achilleus' words are perfectly diplomatic:[9]

"Ζεῦ πάτερ, ἦ μεγάλας ἄτας ἄνδρεσσι διδοῖσθα·
οὐκ ἂν δή ποτε θυμὸν ἐνὶ στήθεσσιν ἐμοῖσιν
Ἀτρεΐδης ὤρινε διαμπερές, οὐδέ κε κούρην
ἦγεν ἐμεῦ ἀέκοντος ἀμήχανος· ἀλλά ποθι Ζεὺς
ἤθελ᾽ Ἀχαιοῖσιν θάνατον πολέεσσι γενέσθαι.
νῦν δ᾽ ἔρχεσθ᾽ ἐπὶ δεῖπνον, ἵνα ξυνάγωμεν Ἄρηα."

'Father Zeus, you do bring great blindness on men. Otherwise the son of Atreus would never have roused my heart to such lasting anger in my breast, or taken the girl from me in stubborn crossing of my will. But Zeus must have wished that death should come to great numbers of the Achaians. But go now to take your meal, so that we can then join battle.' (19. 270–5)

Thus he manages to acknowledge Agamemnon's appeal to Zeus and *Ātē*, while at the same time restoring his double motivation by attributing the active verbs ὤρινε ('roused') and ἦγεν ('taken') to Agamemnon's own will and activity.

Odysseus (taking his cue, perhaps, from Agamemnon's allusion to him in 141) intervenes after Achilleus' response, and comes close to taking over the chief role. His first line μὴ δὴ οὕτως ἀγαθός περ ἐών, θεοείκελ᾽ Ἀχιλλεῦ ('No. You are a brave man, godlike Achilleus, but . . .') (19. 155) ominously repeats Agamemnon's at 1. 131, but he goes on to be far more conciliatory. It is Odysseus, not Achilleus, who takes it upon himself to read Agamemnon a little lecture on the ethics of leadership:

"Ἀτρεΐδη, σὺ δ᾽ ἔπειτα δικαιότερος καὶ ἐπ᾽ ἄλλωι
ἔσσεαι. οὐ μὲν γάρ τι νεμεσσητὸν βασιλῆα
ἄνδρ᾽ ἀπαρέσσασθαι, ὅτε τις πρότερος χαλεπήνηι."

[9] Cf. Reinhardt, *ID* 417 f.; also on Odysseus and the following debate.

'And you, son of Atreus, will be readier after this to give others their due: there can be no blame in a king giving a man recompense, when he was the first to grow angry.' (19. 181–3)[10]

Agamemnon bridles slightly in 185 ff., and he makes sure to delegate to Odysseus the task of fetching the gifts (192 ff.); nevertheless he appreciates that for the sake of collective morale he must publicly hand over the recompense and take the oath as Odysseus proposes.

Achilleus does not care about the *apoina* or food or drink or morale or social coherence:

$$\text{``}τό \; μοι \; οὔ \; τι \; μετὰ \; φρεςὶ \; ταῦτα \; μέμηλεν,$$
$$ἀλλὰ \; φόνος \; τε \; καὶ \; αἷμα \; καὶ \; ἀργαλέος \; ςτόνος \; ἀνδρῶν.\text{''}$$

'So what you speak of is of no interest to my heart, but my thought is on blood and slaughter and the groans of men in pain.' (19. 213–14)[11]

He is driven by a unique and preternatural passion. At the same time, Zeus and Athene make sure to fuel him with nectar and ambrosia (340–54), and so to some extent undercut his lack of human realism.[12] Odysseus, on the contrary, represents common humanity, and bases his arguments on common sense and on unsentimental facts of physiology: γαςτέρι δ' οὔ πως ἔςτι νέκυν πενθῆςαι Ἀχαιούς (starving the belly is no way for the Achaians to mourn a dead man) (225).

It seems incredible now that the analytic attacks on this part of the poem used to concentrate on complaints about the emphasis on food and drink, which was alleged to be beneath epic dignity.[13] Feasting carries deep significances in this scene, both personal and social, significances which are fully in keeping with the anthropology of the *Iliad*. On the personal level, a leader's food is prepared and served by his closest companions, as, for example, Patroklos and Automedon do for Achilleus and his guests at 9. 201 ff. (cf. 24. 472 ff., 622 ff., and p. 79 above). This is the setting behind the opening of Achilleus' lament at the end of this debate-scene:

[10] There is some ambiguity, not without effect (see Leaf), in 182–3; but τιc ('someone', viz. 'he') must refer to Agamemnon.
[11] Note that line 214, plain, powerful, and full of Iliadic matter, is none the less unique in diction—as are so many of the most striking lines in Homer.
[12] The only other human infused with nectar and ambrosia is the dead Patroklos, shortly before, at 19. 58–9. While marking Achilleus' uniqueness this favour also, perhaps, confirms his nearness to death.
[13] For good defences, see Schadewaldt, *IS* 131–4; Griffin, *HLD* 14–17.

"ἦ ῥά νύ μοί ποτε καὶ cύ, δυcάμμορε, φίλταθ' ἑταίρων,
αὐτὸc ἐνὶ κλιcίηι λαρὸν παρὰ δεῖπνον ἔθηκαc
αἶψα καὶ ὀτραλέωc, ὁπότε cπερχοίατ' Ἀχαιοὶ
Τρωcὶν ἐφ' ἱπποδάμοιcι φέρειν πολύδακρυν Ἄρηα.
νῦν δὲ cὺ μὲν κεῖcαι δεδαϊγμένοc, αὐτὰρ ἐμὸν κῆρ
ἄκμηνον πόcιοc καὶ ἐδητύοc, ἔνδον ἐόντων,
cῆι ποθῆι·"

'Oh, there was a time when you, poor ill-fated man, dearest of my
companions, you yourself would set out a pleasing meal in my hut, so
quick and ready, whenever the Achaians were eager to carry the misery
of war against the horse-taming Trojans. But now you lie there torn, and
my heart goes without food and drink, though it is here in plenty, out of
longing for you.' (19. 315-21)

On the broader political level the *basileus* should lay on feasts for
his followers, and the 'summoner' of an army for the *basilées* he
has summoned (see pp. 57-8 above). This is part of the followers'
expected *tīmē*, and it cements communal bonds. This is illustrated
by Agamemnon's invitations at 2. 402 ff. and 7. 313 ff. (where he
does special honour to Aias). When he feasts the *gerontes* at 9. 89 ff.
it is on the suggestion of Nestor, who is desperately trying to hold
morale together:

"Ἀτρείδη, cὺ μὲν ἄρχε· cὺ γὰρ βαcιλεύτατόc ἐccι.
δαίνυ δαῖτα γέρουcιν· ἔοικέ τοι, οὔ τοι ἀεικέc.
πλεῖαί τοι οἴνου κλιcίαι, τὸν νῆεc Ἀχαιῶν
ἠμάτιαι Θρήικηθεν ἐπ' εὐρέα πόντον ἄγουcι·
πᾶcά τοί ἐcθ' ὑποδεξίη, πολέεccι δ' ἀνάccειc."

'But then you, son of Atreus, should take the lead, as you are the greatest
king among us. Give a feast for the elders: it is right for you to do this,
and quite what is proper. Your huts are full of the wine that the Achaians'
ships bring daily over the broad sea from Thrace: all hospitality rests
with you, as you are the king over many people.' (9. 69-73)[14]

This institution, with its ceremonial, reflected in epic formulae,
is the background in poetic anthropology to Odysseus' proposal
that Agamemnon should feast Achilleus:

"αὐτὰρ ἔπειτά cε δαιτὶ ἐνὶ κλιcίηιc ἀρεcάcθω
πιείρηι, ἵνα μή τι δίκηc ἐπιδευὲc ἔχηιcθα."

'And then he should appease you with a rich feast in his hut, so that you
can have all that is due to you.' (19. 179-80)

[14] Compare 4. 343f. Also cf. the institution of γερούcιον οἶνον (elders' wine) at
4. 259, *Od.* 13. 8.

So when Achilleus refuses, this is not a crudity of narrative, beneath epic dignity, it is the denial of a significant act of social solidarity.[15]

8.2 The broken hopes of Briseïs

"Πάτροκλέ μοι δειλῆι πλεῖcτον κεχαρισμένε θυμῶι,
ζωὸν μέν cε ἔλειπον ἐγὼ κλιcίηθεν ἰοῦcα,
νῦν δέ cε τεθνηῶτα κιχάνομαι, ὄρχαμε λαῶν,
ἂψ ἀνιοῦc᾽· ὥc μοι δέχεται κακὸν ἐκ κακοῦ αἰεί.   290
ἄνδρα μὲν ὧι ἔδοcάν με πατὴρ καὶ πότνια μήτηρ
εἶδον πρὸ πτόλιοc δεδαϊγμένον ὀξέϊ χαλκῶι,
τρεῖc τε καcιγνήτουc, τούc μοι μία γείνατο μήτηρ,
κηδείουc, οἳ πάντεc ὀλέθριον ἦμαρ ἐπέcπον.
οὐδὲ μὲν οὐδέ μ᾽ ἔαcκεc, ὅτ᾽ ἄνδρ᾽ ἐμὸν ὠκὺc Ἀχιλλεὺc   295
ἔκτεινεν, πέρcεν δὲ πόλιν θείοιο Μύνητοc,
κλαίειν, ἀλλά μ᾽ ἔφαcκεc Ἀχιλλῆοc θείοιο
κουριδίην ἄλοχον θήcειν, ἄξειν τ᾽ ἐνὶ νηυcὶν
ἐc Φθίην, δαίcειν δὲ γάμον μετὰ Μυρμιδόνεccι.
τώ c᾽ ἄμοτον κλαίω τεθνηότα, μείλιχον αἰεί."   300
Ὣc ἔφατο κλαίουc᾽, ἐπὶ δὲ cτενάχοντο γυναῖκεc,
Πάτροκλον πρόφαcιν, cφῶν δ᾽ αὐτῶν κήδε᾽ ἑκάcτη.

'Patroklos, more than any of the pleasure of my poor heart, you were alive when I went away from the hut and left you, and now I come back, leader of your people, and find you dead. So it is always in my life, pain following pain. My father and honoured mother gave me to a husband, and I saw him torn by the sharp bronze in front of our city, and my three brothers, borne by the same mother, my beloved brothers all met the day of destruction. But when swift Achilleus killed my husband and sacked the city of godlike Mynes, you would not let me even weep, but you said you would make me godlike Achilleus' wedded wife, and take me back in your ships to Phthia, and celebrate my marriage-feast among the Myrmidons. And so I weep endlessly for your death. You were always gentle.'

[15] This may help to explain the strange episode at 19. 303 ff., where six named leaders, including Agamemnon, stay with Achilleus, trying to comfort him (τέρπον-τεc) and to persuade him to eat. But it is strange that all they do is to grieve along with Achilleus (338–40), and that apparently they never get their meal. This makes me wonder about the authenticity of 310–14—without the lines they would leave Achilleus. It is true that Zeus pities them in line 340, yet his speech in line 342 ff. concerns only Achilleus. This prompts me to observe that 338–9 might be omitted and τούc ('them') in 340 emended to τόν ('him').

Such was her lament, and the women joined with their keening—the cause was Patroklos, but each of them wept over her own sorrows. (19. 287–302)

The conveyance of Agamemnon's gifts to Achilleus, including the seven fine women plus Briseïs (who has been preparatorily named in 246 and 261), sets up the transition from the male *agorē* to the female lament. The affinity between Patroklos and Briseïs, and the subtle linking of this scene of her return in 19 with her departure in book 1, have already been sketched—see pp. 80–2. She—like Nestor, see pp. 175–6 above—knew that Patroklos was the way to Achilleus' heart. Thus Homer finds the opportunity for a vivid portrait of Patroklos' human out-of-battle qualities before Achilleus takes to the field for vengeance. Her lament sets the seal on the poem so far; and marks the end of Achilleus' *mēnis* in a different and more poignant way than his terse contributions to the *agorē*, and even than his great speech at 18. 98 ff.

Briseïs' threnody has significant features in common with Helen's for Hektor, at 24. 762 ff. (on which see further pp. 119–20, 282). The two leading casualties of the poem are each lamented by a woman—not his wife—because he has been considerate to her, even though she is awkwardly marginal or alienated within her society. μείλιχος, ἤπιος, ἀγανός ('gentle', 'kind', 'tender'), and words related to them, are used for Patroklos and Hektor more than of any others in the *Iliad*.

Briseïs is presented as far more than merely a possession or a sex-object.[16] While the captive women in the Achaian camp are usually given no role beyond housework and bed, there is some recognition of other qualities, qualities which in some later stories are reflected by their mothering of Greek heroes. Agamemnon, for instance, puts φρένες (good sense) among the qualities for which he rates Chryseïs more highly than Klytaimnestra:

"καὶ γάρ ῥα Κλυταιμνήϲτρηϲ προβέβουλα
κουριδίηϲ ἀλόχου, ἐπεὶ οὔ ἑθέν ἐϲτι χερείων,
οὐ δέμαϲ οὐδὲ φυήν, οὔτ' ἄρ φρέναϲ οὔτέ τι ἔργα."

'. . . and indeed I prefer her to Klytaimnestra the wife of my marriage, as she is in no way her inferior in body or stature, or good sense or the craft of her hands.' (1. 113–15)

---

[16] In general on Briseïs, see Reinhardt, *ID* 50–9, 421–2.

Hekamede, captured by Achilleus from Tenedos, was selected for
Nestor for her beauty and intelligence (11. 624 ff.).[17] So Briseïs'
hopes that with the support of Patroklos she might in due course
become Achilleus' κουριδίη ἄλοχοc (*kouridiē alochos*) were not
'anthropologically' absurd. I do not agree, then, with Willcock (ad
loc.) that 'Briseis, a captive slave, could not become the κουριδίη
ἄλοχοc of Achilleus. Patroclus has been trying to console her.'
Furthermore there are other suggestions of a special 'romantic'
relationship between Achilleus and Briseïs. There may be a hint
in the narrative at 1. 429–30, and in Thetis' words to Hephaistos
at 18. 446, and there is the fleeting ἀέκουσα ('reluctantly') at 1. 348
(see p. 81 above). But above all there is Achilleus' own language
in his reply to Odysseus in the Embassy. His lines about men
caring for their women are a digression arising out of his central
complaint against Agamemnon's ingratitude:

> "ἄλλα δ' ἀριcτήεccι δίδου γέρα καὶ βαcιλεῦcι,
> τοῖcι μὲν ἔμπεδα κεῖται, ἐμεῦ δ' ἀπὸ μούνου Ἀχαιῶν   335
> εἵλετ', ἔχει δ' ἄλοχον θυμαρέα· τῆι παριαύων
> τερπέcθω. τί δὲ δεῖ πολεμιζέμεναι Τρώεccιν
> Ἀργείουc; τί δὲ λαὸν ἀνήγαγεν ἐνθάδ' ἀγείραc
> Ἀτρεΐδηc; ἦ οὐχ Ἑλένηc ἕνεκ' ἠϋκόμοιο;
> ἦ μοῦνοι φιλέουc' ἀλόχουc μερόπων ἀνθρώπων   340
> Ἀτρεΐδαι; ἐπεὶ ὅc τιc ἀνὴρ ἀγαθὸc καὶ ἐχέφρων
> τὴν αὐτοῦ φιλέει καὶ κήδεται, ὡc καὶ ἐγὼ τὴν
> ἐκ θυμοῦ φίλεον, δουρικτητήν περ ἐοῦcαν."

'All the other prizes he gave to the kings and leading men stay safe with
their owners. I am the only Achaian he has robbed. He has taken my
wife, my heart's love—let him lie with her and take his pleasure. Why
is it that the Argives must fight the Trojans? Why did the son of Atreus
raise an army and sail it here? Was it not because of lovely-haired Helen?
Are the sons of Atreus the only ones of humankind to love their wives?
No, any good man of sense loves his own wife and cares for her—as I
too loved this girl from my heart, even though I won her by my spear.'
(9. 334–43)

Briseïs is not yet *kouridiē*, but she is his ἄλοχον θυμαρέα ('my wife,
my heart's love')—a phrase that comes in only one other place in
the whole of Homer, namely *Od.* 23. 232, when Odysseus at last

---

[17] She takes good care of Nestor and his guest, skilfully mixing a brew and
providing *mezes* (11. 628–31, 638–41). Later Nestor can entrust Machaon to her
with confidence (14. 5–7).

holds Penelope in his arms. He adds ἐκ θυμοῦ φίλεον ('I loved her from my heart'),[18] precisely to make the point that his feelings go deeper than the 'official' φιλία (*philia*) which any right-minded man should feel for τὴν αὐτοῦ (his own woman). Clearly his feelings are more 'romantic' than those that Agamemnon feels for *his kouridiē alochos*!

Of course Achilleus speaks in the rhetorical heat of the moment. It might even be disputed whether his use of ἄλοχος (wife) in 9. 336 is strictly legitimate; but I see no good reason for rejecting his whole argument as empty, especially when he has recently abhorred those who say what they do not feel (312–13). Three passages might be cited to question the genuineness of the feelings that Achilleus expresses. Ironically all three, if relevant, would attribute rather more sentimentally 'romantic' feelings to Homer than the passages that they are claimed to disprove. First, not much later in book 9 (393 ff.), Achilleus speaks of finding, with the approval of Peleus, a *kouridiē alochos* from among the rich choice of eligible women back at home. But by that stage Achilleus is assuming that he is going home without being reconciled with Agamemnon—who will keep Briseïs. The point he is making is that there are plenty of eligible women besides Agamemnon's daughter. Secondly, after the departure of the embassy, Achilleus sleeps with Diomede. Since Agamemnon has Briseïs, he is not actually preferring Diomede. The main point is that, while Achilleus has a good time, Agamemnon has no joy of his abduction— it is emphasized that he never has sex with Briseïs (9. 132–4, 274–6; 19. 175–7, 187–8, and finally 19. 258–65).[19] Third, and most substantial, is the opening of Achilleus' speech to the book 19 *agorē*:

"Ἀτρεΐδη, ἦ ἄρ τι τόδ' ἀμφοτέροισιν ἄρειον
ἔπλετο, coὶ καὶ ἐμοί, ὅ τε νῶϊ περ ἀχνυμένω κῆρ
θυμοβόρωι ἔριδι μενεήναμεν εἵνεκα κούρης;
τὴν ὄφελ' ἐν νήεςςι κατακτάμεν Ἄρτεμις ἰῶι,
ἤματι τῶι ὅτ' ἐγὼν ἑλόμην Λυρνηςςὸν ὀλέςςας·"

---

[18] The only other use of this phrase is by Phoinix at 9. 486 of his feelings for Achilleus.

[19] Diomede's birthplace of Lesbos (664) may be a glancing reminder of the non-availability of Briseïs. Reinhardt infers that the daughter of Briseus is to be thought of as coming from Brēsa on Lesbos (like Chryseïs from Chryse); and certainly ὀγδοάτην ('the eighth') at 19. 246, after the seven women from Lesbos, implies that she came from there as well.

'Son of Atreus, could we possibly say that this has proved good for both of us, for you and for me, that the two of us in our passions quarrelled in heart-consuming anger over a girl? I wish that Artemis had killed her with an arrow on board my ships, on that day when I destroyed Lyrnessos and won her.' (19. 56–60)[20]

I do not see this as incompatible with Patroklos' past assurances to Briseïs. However strongly Achilleus may feel about her, Patroklos was still more important. He would rather she were dead than have regained her at this price.

Briseïs does not know that Achilleus has chosen never to go home, and hence never to have a *kouridiē alochos*, neither her nor any other. But the nearest that he ever comes to marriage in the *Iliad* is at his very last participation in the poem, when he goes to bed with her for the first time since Agamemnon took her. He may have wished her dead at Lyrnessos, but he does not spurn her:

αὐτὰρ Ἀχιλλεὺς εὗδε μυχῶι κλισίης ἐϋπήκτου·
τῶι δὲ Βρισηὶς παρελέξατο καλλιπάρηιος.

And Achilleus slept in the interior of his well-built hut, and the beautiful Briseïs lay beside him. (24. 675–6)

It has been seen already (pp. 84–5 above) that the sacked cities of the Troad (above all Thebe—see p. 126) are given attention in the *Iliad*, and are more than merely past conquests for the Achaians. Andromache was not at Thebe to see her father and brother killed: instead she will witness the sack of her husband's city. This was also the ordeal of Briseïs at Lyrnessos, where Achilleus killed her brothers and husband (whether or not he is to be equated with Mynes).[21] The two cities are associated when Lyrnessos is first named:

---

[20] Dr E. Hall adds this observation: 'When Achilleus says that it has done neither him nor Agamemnon any good to quarrel over a girl (εἵνεκα κούρης), it perhaps recalls his statement that he will not do battle with Agamemnon or anyone else for the sake of a girl (εἵνεκα κούρης) back in 1. 298 (cf. also 2. 377). The destruction caused to the Achaean camp by the quarrel over Briseïs also, on a smaller scale, is a kind of mirror of the destruction caused to Achaians "for the sake of" Helen, ἧς εἵνεκα πολλοὶ Ἀχαιῶν ἐν Τροίηι ἀπόλοντο (2. 161–2) ("for whose sake many of the Achaians have lost their lives in Troy").'

[21] If Briseïs came from Lesbos (see n. 19 above), why were her brothers fighting at Lyrnessos? Presumably the audience was aware that there were close links between Lesbos and the towns on the mainland coast opposite (as in classical times).

κεῖτο γὰρ ἐν νήεσσι ποδάρκης δῖος Ἀχιλλεύς,
κούρης χωόμενος Βρισηΐδος ἠϋκόμοιο,
τὴν ἐκ Λυρνησσοῦ ἐξείλετο πολλὰ μογήσας,
Λυρνησσὸν διαπορθήσας καὶ τείχεα Θήβης,
κὰδ δὲ Μύνητ' ἔβαλεν καὶ Ἐπίστροφον ἐγχεσιμώρους

Swift-footed godlike Achilleus was keeping by his ships, in anger over
the girl, the beautiful Briseïs, whom he had chosen as his spoil from
Lyrnessos after he had laboured hard for its taking, and sacked Lyrnessos
and the walls of Thebe, and felled the spearmen Mynes and
Epistrophos . . . (2. 688–92)

Not long after Briseïs' lament there will be further references to
the expedition against Lyrnessos. Aineias explains to Apollo (in
the guise of Lykaon) why he is reluctant to face Achilleus:

"οὐ μὲν γὰρ νῦν πρῶτα ποδώκεος ἄντ' Ἀχιλῆος
στήσομαι, ἀλλ' ἤδη με καὶ ἄλλοτε δουρὶ φόβησεν
ἐξ Ἴδης, ὅτε βουσὶν ἐπήλυθεν ἡμετέρῃσι,
πέρσε δὲ Λυρνησσὸν καὶ Πήδασον· αὐτὰρ ἐμὲ Ζεὺς
εἰρύσαθ', ὅς μοι ἐπῶρσε μένος λαιψηρά τε γοῦνα."

'This will not be the first time I have faced swift-footed Achilleus, but
before now there was a time when he drove me away from Ida with his
spear, when he came to attack our cattle and sacked Lyrnessos and
Pedasos. But Zeus protected me then, spurring strength in me and speed
to my legs.' (20. 89–93)[22]

Achilleus will also refer to this incident when he confronts Aineias:

"ἦ οὐ μέμνῃι ὅτε πέρ σε βοῶν ἄπο μοῦνον ἐόντα
σεῦα κατ' Ἰδαίων ὀρέων ταχέεσσι πόδεσσι
καρπαλίμως; τότε δ' οὔ τι μετατροπαλίζεο φεύγων.
ἔνθεν δ' ἐς Λυρνησσὸν ὑπέκφυγες· αὐτὰρ ἐγὼ τὴν
πέρσα μεθορμηθεὶς σὺν Ἀθήνῃ καὶ Διὶ πατρί,
ληϊάδας δὲ γυναῖκας ἐλεύθερον ἦμαρ ἀπούρας
ἦγον· ἀτὰρ σὲ Ζεὺς ἐρρύσατο καὶ θεοὶ ἄλλοι."

'Or do you not remember when I cut you off alone from your cattle and
sent you running down the mountains of Ida with all speed of your legs?
You ran away quickly then, without looking back at all. Then you took
refuge in Lyrnessos. But I came after you and sacked the town with the
help of Athene and father Zeus, and took the day of freedom from the

---

[22] An inconsistency here: elsewhere Pedasos seems to be still unsacked, since it
supplies the warrior Elatos at 6. 33–5, and it is still ruled over by old Altes,
grandfather of the real Lykaon (21. 86–7). The sack of Pedasos figured in the
Cypria, frg. XVIII Allen (= 27 Bernabé = 21 Davies).

women I carried away captive: but you were saved by Zeus and the other
gods.' (20. 188–94)

In this context Briseïs is only one of a crowd of captured women,
but it is part of the great-heartedness of the *Iliad* that elsewhere—
δουρικτητήν περ ἐοῦcαν (even though won by the spear)—she is far
more than a mere foreign chattel.

8.3 The surrenders of Lykaon and Skamandros

αὐτὰρ ὁ τῆι ἑτέρηι μὲν ἑλὼν ἐλλίccετο γούνων,
τῆι δ' ἑτέρηι ἔχεν ἔγχος ἀκαχμένον οὐδὲ μεθίει·
καί μιν φωνήcαc ἔπεα πτερόεντα προcηύδα·
"γουνοῦμαί c', Ἀχιλεῦ· cὺ δέ μ' αἴδεο καί μ' ἐλέηcον·
ἀντί τοί εἰμ' ἱκέταο, διοτρεφέc, αἰδοίοιο·   75
πὰρ γὰρ coὶ πρώτωι παcάμην Δημήτεροc ἀκτήν,
ἤματι τῶι ὅτε μ' εἷλεc ἐϋκτιμένηι ἐν ἀλωῆι,
καί με πέραccαc ἄνευθεν ἄγων πατρόc τε φίλων τε
Λῆμνον ἐc ἠγαθέην, ἑκατόμβοιον δέ τοι ἦλφον.
νῦν δὲ λύμην τρὶc τόccα πορών· ἠὼc δέ μοί ἐcτιν   80
ἥδε δυωδεκάτη, ὅτ' ἐc Ἴλιον εἰλήλουθα
πολλὰ παθών· νῦν αὖ με τεῆιc ἐν χερcὶν ἔθηκε
μοῖρ' ὀλοή· μέλλω που ἀπεχθέcθαι Διὶ πατρί,
ὅc με coὶ αὖτιc δῶκε· μινυνθάδιον δέ με μήτηρ
γείνατο Λαοθόη, θυγάτηρ Ἄλταο γέροντοc,   85
Ἄλτεω, ὃc Λελέγεccι φιλοπτολέμοιcιν ἀνάccει,
Πήδαcον αἰπήεccαν ἔχων ἐπὶ Cατνιόεντι.
τοῦ δ' ἔχε θυγατέρα Πρίαμοc, πολλὰc δὲ καὶ ἄλλαc·
τῆc δὲ δύω γενόμεcθα, cὺ δ' ἄμφω δειροτομήcειc.
ἤτοι τὸν πρώτοιcι μετὰ πρυλέεccι δάμαccαc,   90
ἀντίθεον Πολύδωρον, ἐπεὶ βάλεc ὀξέϊ δουρί·
νῦν δὲ δὴ ἐνθάδ' ἐμοὶ κακὸν ἔccεται· οὐ γὰρ ὀΐω
càc χεῖραc φεύξεcθαι, ἐπεί ῥ' ἐπέλαccέ γε δαίμων.
ἄλλο δέ τοι ἐρέω, cὺ δ' ἐνὶ φρεcὶ βάλλεο cῆιcι·
μή με κτεῖν', ἐπεὶ οὐχ ὁμογάcτριοc Ἕκτορόc εἰμι,   95
ὅc τοι ἑταῖρον ἔπεφνεν ἐνηέα τε κρατερόν τε."
    Ὣc ἄρα μιν Πριάμοιο προcηύδα φαίδιμοc υἱὸc
λιccόμενοc ἐπέεccιν, ἀμείλικτον δ' ὄπ' ἄκουcε·
"νήπιε, μή μοι ἄποινα πιφαύcκεο μηδ' ἀγόρευε·
πρὶν μὲν γὰρ Πάτροκλον ἐπιcπεῖν αἴcιμον ἦμαρ,   100
τόφρα τί μοι πεφιδέcθαι ἐνὶ φρεcὶ φίλτερον ἦεν
Τρώων, καὶ πολλοὺc ζωοὺc ἕλον ἠδὲ πέραccα·

νῦν δ' οὐκ ἔcθ' ὅc τιc θάνατον φύγηι, ὅν κε θεόc γε
'Ιλίου προπάροιθεν ἐμῆιc ἐν χερcὶ βάληιcι,
καὶ πάντων Τρώων, πέρι δ' αὖ Πριάμοιό γε παίδων.   105
ἀλλά, φίλοc, θάνε καὶ cύ· τίη ὀλοφύρεαι οὕτωc;
κάτθανε καὶ Πάτροκλοc, ὅ περ cέο πολλὸν ἀμείνων.
οὐχ ὁράαιc οἷοc καὶ ἐγὼ καλόc τε μέγαc τε;
πατρὸc δ' εἴμ' ἀγαθοῖο, θεὰ δέ με γείνατο μήτηρ·
ἀλλ' ἔπι τοι καὶ ἐμοὶ θάνατοc καὶ μοῖρα κραταιή·   110
ἔccεται ἢ ἠὼc ἢ δείλη ἢ μέcον ἦμαρ,
ὁππότε τιc καὶ ἐμεῖο Ἄρηι ἐκ θυμὸν ἕληται,
ἢ ὅ γε δουρὶ βαλὼν ἢ ἀπὸ νευρῆφιν ὀϊcτῶι.''
    "Ὡc φάτο, τοῦ δ' αὐτοῦ λύτο γούνατα καὶ φίλον ἦτορ·
ἔγχοc μέν ῥ' ἀφέηκεν, ὁ δ' ἕζετο χεῖρε πετάccαc   115
ἀμφοτέραc·

Lykaon began to beg for mercy, grasping Achilleus' knees with one hand,
and with the other he took hold of the sharp spear and would not let it
go: and he spoke to him with winged words: 'Achilleus, I am entreating
you by your knees—respect my claim and have mercy on me. I count as
your suppliant, my lord, with a claim that should be honoured—because
you were the first man with whom I ate the grain of Demeter on that
day when you captured me in our well-laid orchard, and took me away
from my father and friends and sold me in sacred Lemnos. I fetched you
the worth of a hundred oxen, and I was freed for a ransom three times
as much. This is the twelfth day since I came back to Troy after great
hardship—and now cruel fate has put me once more in your hands. I
think father Zeus must hate me, to have given me up to you a second
time, and it was a short life that my mother Laothoë bore me to, the
daughter of the old man Altes, Altes who is king of the war-loving Leleges
and lives in steep Pedasos by the river Satnioeis. His daughter was taken
to wife by Priam, but he has many other wives. There were two of us
born to her, and you will have butchered both. You brought down godlike
Polydoros among the leading foot-fighters with a cast of your sharp spear:
and now the end will come for me here—I do not think I shall escape
from your hands, now that god has brought me to them. But I say one
thing more to you, and you mark it well in your mind. Do not kill me,
because I am not from the same womb as Hektor, who killed your kind
and strong friend.'
    So the glorious son of Priam spoke to him with words of entreaty, but
the answer he heard was hard: 'Fool, do not offer me ransom or talk of
it. Before Patroklos met the day of his fate, then perhaps it was more my
mind's liking to spare Trojans, and there were many I took alive and sold
elsewhere. But now there is no-one who will escape death when god puts
him into my hands in front of Ilios, none among all the Trojans, and

above all none of the sons of Priam. No, friend, you die too—why all
this moaning? Patroklos died also, a far better man than you. Do you not
see how fine a man I am, and how huge? And I am the son of a great
father, and a goddess was the mother who bore me. And yet I tell you
death and strong fate are there for me also: there will be a dawn, or an
evening, or a noonday, when some man will take my life too in the
fighting with a cast of his spear or an arrow from the string.'
So he spoke, and Lykaon's strength and spirit collapsed there and then.
He let go of the spear and sat down with both his arms outstretched.
(21. 71–116)

When Achilleus arms, his passion rises (19. 364 ff.); once on the
field he is bloody and ruthless, especially in the mass slaughter
between 20. 381 and 21. 33. At the same time it would be a mistake
to regard him as a berserker, or a mindless butcher, or even, to
select a typical description 'a force of sheer destructive energy'.[23]
Far from being mindless, there is a kind of terrifying reasoning
behind Achilleus' killing, a merciless 'logic' which finds its fullest
expression in the reply to Lykaon.

This note is already sounded as he first sets off to the field.
Automedon's place as charioteer (19. 392 ff.) is a reminder of
Patroklos' departure at 16. 152 ff. and of his fate—see pp. 188–90
above.[24] With grim humour Achilleus tells his horses to bring him
safe back, unlike Patroklos (400–3); and Xanthos is allowed to
reply that they were not to blame, since Apollo was against
Patroklos:

> "νῶϊ δὲ καί κεν ἅμα πνοιῆι Ζεφύροιο θέοιμεν,
> ἥν περ ἐλαφροτάτην φάσ' ἔμμεναι· ἀλλὰ σοὶ αὐτῶι
> μόρσιμόν ἐστι θεῶι τε καὶ ἀνέρι ἶφι δαμῆναι."

'We two could run even with the speed of the west wind's blowing, which
men say is the fastest of all things: but it is your own fate to be brought
down in battle by a god and a man.' (19. 415–7)[25]

Achilleus' reply begins like Hektor's to the dying words of
Patroklos: "Ξάνθε, τί μοι θάνατον μαντεύεαι;" ('Xanthos, why proph-

---

[23] Schein, 145.
[24] Achilleus' taking-up of the Πηλιάδα μελίην (the spear of Pelian ash) corresponds to Patroklos' failure (19. 388–91 = 16. 141–4). This bodes ill for Hektor,
of course.
[25] The portentousness of a talking animal (commonplace in so many other story-
telling traditions) is emphasized by Hera's enabling (407) and its limitation by the
Erinyes (418).

esy my death?') (19. 420); cf. "Πατρόκλεις, τί νύ μοι μαντεύεαι αἰπὺν ὄλεθρον;" ('Patroklos, why make me this prophecy of grim death?') (16. 859). But while Hektor in his overheated confidence goes on to cast doubt on the prediction, Achilleus accepts it. He rejects it, however, as a reason to hold back. He has worked through to the conclusion that it matters more to him to kill Trojans than to live:

"εὖ νυ τὸ οἶδα καὶ αὐτὸς ὅ μοι μόρος ἐνθάδ' ὀλέςθαι,
νόςφι φίλου πατρὸς καὶ μητέρος· ἀλλὰ καὶ ἔμπης
οὐ λήξω πρὶν Τρῶας ἅδην ἐλάςαι πολέμοιο."

'I know well myself that it is my fate to die here, away from my dear father and mother. But even so I shall not stop until I have driven the Trojans to their fill of war.' (19. 421–3)

Achilleus' first main opponent is Aineias.[26] Their actual battle is long delayed by divine jockeying for position and by prolix challenges—only to be stopped in the end by Aineias' supernatural rescue. Aineias in the *Iliad* is a non-tragic figure, and a foil to Hektor. Of the two it is in fact Achilleus who indulges more in verbal sparring. The message of Aineias' colourful 'Hesiodic' folk-wisdom (especially 20. 242–55) is that this kind of indulgence is for children or women not for warriors. The similarities which recall the Aineias–Diomedes encounter in book 5 (166 ff., especially 297 ff.)[27] accentuate the complexity of Achilleus' mentality by contrast. Like Diomedes, however, Achilleus comes to see that no amount of prowess can prevail over someone who is still under the protection of the gods.

Lykaon is the culmination of a series of Trojans in the *Iliad* who supplicate to be spared in battle.[28] First there is Adrestos, killed by Agamemnon despite Menelaos' first reaction (6. 37 ff., see pp. 51–2); then Peisandros and Hippolochos also fall foul of

---

[26] On the problems of the Aineias scene, its relation to *H. Aphr.* etc., see H. Erbse, *RhM* n.s. 110 (1977), 1 ff.; P. M. Smith, *HSCP* 85 (1981), 17–58; Willcock, *Comm.* on 20. 302–8.

[27] There are also some ironic distant echoes of the Glaukos–Diomedes scene—e.g. 20. 213–14 = 6. 150–1; 20. 241 = 6. 211.

[28] I do not count Dolon at 10. 377 ff., as he is not in battle, and there can be little *aidōs* or pity for him. Contrast the successful supplication of Phemios and Medon at *Od.* 22. 330 ff., after the unsuccessful plea of Leodes. On supplication in the *Iliad*, see, among others, J. Gould, *JHS* 103 (1973), 74 ff., esp. 76–7; Fenik, *TBS* 83–4; Griffin, *HLD* 53–6; V. Pedrick, *TAPA* 112 (1982), 125–40; also Thornton, 113 ff., though she takes in a wide variety of scenes under this label.

Agamemnon (11. 122ff., see pp. 162–3).[29] Finally, not long before Lykaon, Tros, who ominously shares the name of the eponymous early king of Troy (cf. 20. 230–1) hopes that Achilleus might pity his ὁμηλικίη (being the same age):

> νήπιος, οὐδὲ τὸ ἤιδη, ὃ οὐ πείσεσθαι ἔμελλεν·
> οὐ γάρ τι γλυκύθυμος ἀνὴρ ἦν οὐδ᾽ ἀγανόφρων,

... the fool, he did not realise that Achilleus would never listen—this was no sweet-minded man, no gentle heart ... (20.466–7)

Yet Achilleus has not always been like this. In the past, as he says at 21. 100–3, he has spared Trojans and ransomed or sold them. At 11. 101 ff. Agamemnon kills two sons of Priam who had been spared at his hands; at 22. 45 Priam, when he cannot see Lykaon's return, recalls that Achilleus has sold many of his sons; and Hekabe in her lament contrasts Hektor with the many of her sons whom Achilleus has sold (24. 751–3). Above all, Lykaon himself was spared and sold when Achilleus captured him on a previous occasion—23. 741–9 adds yet more, and consistent, detail to the narrative of 21. 35ff.[30] He has previously been captured οὐκ ἐθέλοντα (when he did not want it) (36), and now Achilleus is to send him on another trip οὐκ ἐθέλοντα—down to Hades (47–8). This is the narrator's touch of grim humour. Achilleus himself muses in a similar vein: the sea did not restrain Lykaon, so now let's see if earth is more effective:

> "οὐδέ μιν ἔσχε
> πόντος ἁλὸς πολιῆς, ὁ πολέας ἀέκοντας ἐρύκει.
> ἀλλ᾽ ἄγε δὴ καὶ δουρὸς ἀκωκῆς ἡμετέροιο
> γεύσεται, ὄφρα ἴδωμαι ἐνὶ φρεσὶν ἠδὲ δαείω
> ἢ ἄρ᾽ ὁμῶς καὶ κεῖθεν ἐλεύσεται, ἤ μιν ἐρύξει
> γῆ φυσίζοος, ἥ τε κατὰ κρατερόν περ ἐρύκει."

'... but the deep of the grey sea could not hold him away, though it confines many other men whatever their will. Well now, he will taste the point of my spear this time, so that I can see and make certain in my

[29] 11. 137 almost = 21. 98. Schadewaldt (*IS* 49–50) argues that the scene in 11 has been modelled to correspond with Lykaon.
[30] The consistency of detail between 21. 34–135, 22. 46–53, and 23. 741–7 should not necessarily lead to neo-analytic theories of pre-existent sagas (thus most fully Kullmann, 284ff.). The details might just as well have been worked up over many years to give substance to this important scene. Indeed the closely related deaths of both the sons of Laothoë support this hypothesis.

mind whether he will equally come back even from that place as well, or whether the life-giving earth will hold him down, as she holds even the strongest of men.' (21. 58–63)[31]

Lykaon bases his appeal not on the offer of ransom, though his previous history implies that he is worth a lot, but on *aidōs* and ἔλεοc (*eleos*).[32] Not only is he a defenceless suppliant, which gives him a claim to *aidōs*, but the two have eaten together (note the γάρ (for) in 76)—the same claim to *aidōs* as Aias made at 9. 640 αἴδεσσαι δὲ μέλαθρον· ὑπωρόφιοι δέ τοί εἰμεν ('remember the welcome owed by your house: we are under your roof'). In his appeal for *eleos* Lykaon does not emphasize Priam, father of Hektor, but his mother Laothoë, daughter of old Altes (the genealogy is reiterated at 22. 49–51). His words in 84–5 seem to verge on an 'overhearing' (see p. 150 for this device) of Achilleus' first words to Thetis μῆτερ, ἐπεί μ' ἔτεκές γε μινυνθάδιόν περ ἐόντα ('Mother, since you bore me to a life doomed to shortness') (1. 353). Thetis bore only one son, Laothoë two. But Achilleus comes hot from brutally slaughtering the other at 20. 407 ff.: Polydoros, Priam's youngest and favourite son.

Finally Lykaon appeals to Patroklos' special qualities, the qualities which softened Achilleus' heart to him. He even 'knows' the epithet ἐνηής which is especially associated with him—see p. 192. But now (νῦν δέ 103) all is changed: Achilleus is interested in no bargain except death (cf. p. 244 below for Hektor). He turns all the affinities claimed by Lykaon into arguments in favour of his death instead of life.[33] Patroklos, for all his virtues, is dead; Thetis is immortal, but she too will be bereaved of her son. The greatest affinity between them is their imminent death. Lykaon, by far the lesser, will die somewhat sooner. φίλος, 'friend' (106) is not sarcastic or merely colloquial, it arises from the 'familial' bond of mortality.[34]

[31] Cf. Reinhardt, *ID* 348. There may be macabre humour in γεύcεται ('he will taste') in 61, seeing that Lykaon has in the past tasted Achilleus' food.

[32] On the larger significance of the Lykaon scene, see e.g. W. Marg, *Die Antike*, 18 (1942), 175–6; Strasburger, 85–6; Thornton, 138–9. This combination of *aidōs* and *eleos* occurs first in the *Iliad* in 21. 74, and will recur five times more. See 22. 32 (Hekabe to Hektor); 22. 124–5 (Achilleus will not show them for Hektor); 24. 44 (Apollo, negative); 24. 207–8 (Hekabe, negative of Achilleus); 24. 503 (Priam's plea to Achilleus). Cf. also 24. 309 (and *Od*. 6. 327).

[33] Cf. Owen, 209; Griffin, 55; Schein, 148.

[34] Wilfred Owen shows little sign of Homeric influence, but an exception is, I suggest, 'Then, when much blood had clogged their chariot wheels . . .' in 'Strange Meeting'. This is close enough to *Iliad* 20. 498–503 to make me believe that the

Lykaon understands this grim logic. His gesture of acceptance[35] releases Achilleus from the technical inhibition of suppliancy and establishes a kind of complicity between them. The *coup de grâce* is none the less gruesome (116–19), and Achilleus still relishes the thought of the mutilation of Lykaon's corpse by the fishes in the river (122 ff.).

> "ἀλλὰ καὶ ὣς ὀλέεσθε κακὸν μόρον, εἰς ὅ κε πάντες
> τείςετε Πατρόκλοιο φόνον καὶ λοιγὸν Ἀχαιῶν,
> οὓς ἐπὶ νηυσὶ θοῇσιν ἐπέφνετε νόσφιν ἐμεῖο."

'No, for all that you will die a vile death, until all of you have paid for the killing of Patroklos and the ravage of the Achaians you slaughtered by the fast ships when I was not with them.' (21. 133–5)

These are words of terrifying ambition, yet they are not the spewing of an incomprehensible or pathological blood-lust. Audiences are encouraged to come, like Lykaon, to understand Achilleus. He was not like this before the death of Patroklos; but now, now that he is certain to die himself at Troy, there is no reason in his eyes why the Trojans should die later rather than sooner.

Next (139 ff.), Asteropaios, like Lykaon, emerges from the river; it is his eleventh day since arrival at Troy, rather as it was the twelfth since Lykaon's return. But while the Trojan is the most acquiescent victim in the *Iliad*, the Paionian fights with exceptional skill and bravery.[36] He is the only opponent to inflict a wound on Achilleus, and he dies courageously trying to break the great Pelian ash-spear.

Asteropaios' grandfather was the river Axios, as is emphasized in the narrative at 141–3 and in his own speech at 157–60. The river Skamandros favours him:

> τῶι ῥ' Ἀχιλεὺς ἐπόρουσεν, ὁ δ' ἀντίος ἐκ ποταμοῖο
> ἔστη ἔχων δύο δοῦρε· μένος δέ οἱ ἐν φρεσὶ θῆκε
> Ξάνθος, ἐπεὶ κεχόλωτο δαϊκταμένων αἰζηῶν,
> τοὺς Ἀχιλεὺς ἐδάϊζε κατὰ ῥόον οὐδ' ἐλέαιρεν.

key sentence of the poem 'I am the enemy you killed, my friend' is an echo of Lykaon. This is not the 'friend' of the gospels: they are both in 'Hell', and share the 'hopelessness'.

[35] This physical movement is made elsewhere only by those who have already been mortally struck—4. 523, 13. 549, 14. 495 (*contra* Gould, op cit. (n. 28 above), 81 and n. 41).

[36] Even Fenik (*TBS* 146) finds him unusual. He was already singled out by Sarpedon for his bravery at 12. 101–4.

Achilleus sprang forward to attack Asteropaios, and he stood facing him
from the river with two spears in his hands: and Xanthos put courage in
his heart, as he was angered at the carnage of the young men whom
Achilleus was slaughtering along his stream without pity. (21. 144–7)

All the same he cannot help him to wrench Achilleus' spear from
his bank, nor save his corpse from the eels and fish that take over
the carrion role of the dogs and birds (283–4, cf. 125–7).[37]
Rivers, though occasionally envisaged in dangerous flood, as in
the similes at 5. 87 ff. and 16. 384 ff., are generally in the *Iliad*
associated with lands and their fertility, as in the fleeting references
in the catalogue of ships, or more fully in Sarpedon's thoughts of
Xanthos in Lycia (12. 313–14), or Achilleus' of Spercheios in
Phthia (23. 140 ff.). In the dozen or so references to Skamandros
before book 20 (including Astyanax's nickname at 6. 402), he is
simply the great river of Troy (Simoeis is treated as a lesser
brother). He is, however, lined up among the opposed gods at
20. 67 ff., and from 21.1 (see p. 292 on the book-division), the
scene is localized on his banks and in his waters.

When Achilleus throws Lykaon into Skamandros he specifically
includes the river in his taunting:

"οὐδ' ὑμῖν ποταμός περ ἐΰρροος ἀργυροδίνης
ἀρκέσει, ὧι δὴ δηθὰ πολέας ἱερεύετε ταύρους,
ζωοὺς δ' ἐν δίνηισι καθίετε μώνυχας ἵππους."

'And your lovely silver-swirling river will not save you, for all the many
bulls you have long sacrificed to it and the strong-footed horses you have
thrown alive into its eddies.' (21. 130–2)

In triumph over Asteropaios, Achilleus deprecates all watery deit-
ies, including Skamandros and even Ocean (190 ff.)—they cannot
rival his great-grandfather Zeus with his thunder and lightning.
The river's anger aginst Achilleus grows and finally finds vocal
expression at 212 ff.,[38] when Achilleus renews the mass slaughter.
Once he jumps in, Skamandros directly assaults him,[39] and is so
strong that friendly gods have to reassure Achilleus that he will

---

[37] Cf. Segal, 30–2.
[38] I take ἀνέρι εἰσάμενος ('taking the form of a man') (213) to refer only to his
voice not whole bodily shape.
[39] Unnecessarily heavy weather has been made of lines 223 ff.: the river has
tricked Achilleus into his waters (as a scholiast rightly pointed out). I do, however,
have a real problem with 228–32: Zeus has given no such instruction in the
narrative, and such lines belong, if anywhere, on the previous day.

not be drowned (272 ff.), and eventually Athene intervenes (298 ff.). The river tries to protect his locals. This is first indicated as a response to the Lykaon insult:

> Ὣc ἄρ' ἔφη, ποταμὸc δὲ χολώcατο κηρόθι μᾶλλον,
> ὅρμηνεν δ' ἀνὰ θυμὸν ὅπωc παύcειε πόνοιο
> δῖον Ἀχιλλῆα, Τρώεccι δὲ λοιγὸν ἀλάλκοι.

So he spoke, but the river had anger deepening in his heart, and pondered in his mind how he might stop godlike Achilleus in his murderous work, and protect the Trojans from destruction. (21. 136–8)

It then becomes active in conjunction with his assault on Achilleus:

> ζωοὺc δὲ cάω κατὰ καλὰ ῥέεθρα,
> κρύπτων ἐν δίνηιcι βαθείηιcιν μεγάληιcι.
> δεινὸν δ' ἀμφ' Ἀχιλῆα κυκώμενον ἵcτατο κῦμα

... and the living he kept safe along his lovely stream, hiding them in his huge deep pools. The water seethed and rose round Achilleus in a fearful wave ... (21. 238–40)

When Achilleus is encouraged by Athene, Skamandros becomes even more angry, and calls on Simoeis:

> "φίλε κacίγνητε, cθένοc ἀνέροc ἀμφότεροί περ
> cχῶμεν, ἐπεὶ τάχα ἄcτυ μέγα Πριάμοιο ἄνακτοc
> ἐκπέρcει, Τρῶεc δὲ κατὰ μόθον οὐ μενέουcιν.
> ἀλλ' ἐπάμυνε τάχιcτα ..."

'Dear brother, let the two of us join together to contain the strength of this man, because he will soon attack king Priam's great city, and the Trojans will not face him in battle. So come quickly and help me against him.' (21. 308–11)

At this stage Hera intervenes through the agency of Hephaistos and fire.

Fire is ubiquitous in the *Iliad*.[40] From books 8 to 16 it is associated above all with Hektor's attempt to burn the Achaian ships (cf. pp. 147, 173). Once Achilleus is aroused, however, fire is especially associated with him, not least through similes. The link is established at 18. 203 ff., when Athene lights a golden cloud of fire round his head as he stands at the ditch; and this is reinforced by the simile of the beacon lit by islanders under attack.

---

[40] See esp. Whitman, 129 ff.

Achilleus' eyes are then likened to fire when he sees his armour
(19. 17) and when he arms (19. 366); and his shield shines out like
a fire on land seen from the sea (373 ff.). Hektor describes him
with a striking epanalepsis:

> "τοῦ δ' ἐγὼ ἀντίος εἶμι, καὶ εἰ πυρὶ χεῖρας ἔοικεν,
> εἰ πυρὶ χεῖρας ἔοικε, μένος δ' αἴθωνι cιδήρωι."

'Now I am going to face him, even if his hands are like fire, his hands
like fire and his strength like gleaming iron.' (20. 371–2)

This is, perhaps, a reminder that on the previous day it was the
Trojans who had fire in their hands.[41] In a cluster of four similes between 20. 490 and 21. 33 (unfortunately split up by the book-division), two reinforce the alliance
between Achilleus and fire.

> Ὡc δ' ἀναμαιμάει βαθέ' ἄγκεα θεcπιδαὲc πῦρ
> οὔρεοc ἀζαλέοιο, βαθεῖα δὲ καίεται ὕλη,
> πάντηι τε κλονέων ἄνεμοc φλόγα εἰλυφάζει,
> ὣc ὅ γε πάντηι θῦνε cὺν ἔγχεϊ δαίμονι ἶcοc,
> κτεινομένουc ἐφέπων·

As monstrous fire rages through the deep valleys on a parched mountain-
side, and the thick forest burns as the wind drives the flames billowing
all over, so Achilleus stormed with his spear all over the field like some
inhuman being, driving men on and killing them. . . . (20. 490–4)

> ὡc δ' ὅθ' ὑπὸ ῥιπῆc πυρὸc ἀκρίδεc ἠερέθονται
> φευγέμεναι ποταμόνδε· τὸ δὲ φλέγει ἀκάματον πῦρ
> ὄρμενον ἐξαίφνηc, ταὶ δὲ πτώccουcι καθ' ὕδωρ·
> ὣc ὑπ' Ἀχιλλῆοc Ξάνθου βαθυδινήεντοc
> πλῆτο ῥόοc κελάδων ἐπιμὶξ ἵππων τε καὶ ἀνδρῶν.

As when locusts rise in a swarm before the onrush of fire to take refuge
in a river: the fire breaks out suddenly and burns on tireless, while they
huddle away from it in the water—so then before the pursuit of Achilleus
the roaring stream of deep-swirling Xanthos was filled with a mingled
mass of men and horses. (21. 12–16)

The former brings in the destruction of vegetation (cf. 21. 18, 242,
338, 350–2 for vegetation on the banks of Skamandros), the latter
the living creatures which, like the Trojans, seek the river in the

---

[41] I note a small exception to this series: at 20. 423 Hektor with his spear is
φλογὶ εἴκελοc (like a flame).

hope of safety. Skamandros is vital for the fertility of the Trojan plain, and hence for the life of Troy as a whole.[42] The sack of Troy is prophesied or previsioned in various ways throughout the poem (see further pp. 249–50), but it is not until the closing stages that it is specifically foreseen as burning, with the exception of 2. 412 ff., where Agamemnon prays to burn Troy that very day. Otherwise the link is not made until Hera's words to Poseidon:

"ἦτοι μὲν γὰρ νῶϊ πολέας ὠμόccαμεν ὅρκους
πᾶcι μετ' ἀθανάτοιcιν, ἐγὼ καὶ Παλλὰc Ἀθήνη,
μή ποτ' ἐπὶ Τρώεccιν ἀλεξήceιν κακὸν ἦμαρ,
μηδ' ὁπότ' ἂν Τροίη μαλερῶι πυρὶ πᾶcα δάηται
καιομένη, καίωcι δ' ἀρήϊοι υἷεc Ἀχαιῶν."

'Because we two, I and Pallas Athene, have sworn many oaths before all the immortals that we will never keep the evil day away from the Trojans, not even when all Troy is ablaze with devouring fire, and the warrior sons of the Achaians are burning it.' (20. 313–17)

And it is Hera who tells Hephaistos to intervene on the side of Achilleus. Contrary to all common experience, the fire burns the water into submission.[43]

Yet, while there is a tinge of elemental opposition about the battle, the supernatural weirdness is tempered by a detailed realism. The clear symbolism is that, when Hera's agent overcomes the protective river, this is a kind of pre-enactment of the eventual sack of the city.[44] Although Achilleus will be dead by then, he achieves in the *Iliad* the essential prerequisite for the fall of Troy. So it is not enough for Skamandros simply to capitulate to Hephaistos, as in

"λῆγ' ἔριδος, Τρῶαc δὲ καὶ αὐτίκα δῖοc Ἀχιλλεὺc
ἄcτεοc ἐξελάcειε· τί μοι ἔριδος καὶ ἀρωγῆc;"

---

[42] The association is furthered by the simile at 21. 257 ff. comparing Skamandros' attack on Achilleus to a gardener using irrigation. On the other hand the likening of Hephaistos' fire to a drying wind on a garden (346–9) is an ironic reversal.

[43] I wonder whether the phrase in 356 καίετο δ' ἷc ποταμοῖο ('the strong river was being burned') is not more than a mere periphrasis, more like 'the vital strength of the river was being burned'.

[44] Cf. Whitman (139–40, 207), who writes 'the whole passage becomes a dumb-show of the taking of Troy'. On the elemental opposition, cf. Schadewaldt, *HWW* 289–93; Nagler, 149–51.

'...stop your fighting now, and godlike Achilleus can go right on and drive the Trojans out of their city—what need for me to take part in this battle?' (21. 359–60)

He has to go on to take the oath of Hera:

> "ἐγὼ δ' ἐπὶ καὶ τόδ' ὀμοῦμαι,
> μή ποτ' ἐπὶ Τρώεccιν ἀλεξήcειν κακὸν ἦμαρ,
> μηδ' ὁπότ' ἂν Τροίη μαλερῶι πυρὶ πᾶcα δάηται
> καιομένη, καίωcι δ' ἀρήϊοι υἷες Ἀχαιῶν."

'And I shall swear this oath as well, that I shall never keep the evil day away from the Trojans, not even when all Troy is ablaze with devouring fire, and the warrior sons of the Achaians are burning it.' (21. 373–6)

It is worth noting how Skamandros has a range of formulaic epithets—ἐΰρρειος ('fine-flowing'), ἀργυροδίνης ('with silver eddies'), etc.—and how these continue to be used, with the kind of effect special to oral poetry, even when his usual qualities are distorted. When, for instance, he complains to Achilleus πλήθει γὰρ δή μοι νεκύων ἐρατεινὰ ῥέεθρα ('my lovely stream is packed with corpses') (218), the point is that his ῥέεθρα (stream) should be ἐρατεινά (lovely), and that it is an outrage that it is not. So too the formula καλὰ ῥέεθρα ('beautiful stream') is used even when the water is seething in agony (352, 361). Line 382—ἄψορρον δ' ἄρα κῦμα κατέccυτο καλὰ ῥέεθρα (and the stream ran back again along its beautiful channel)—marks the return to familiar (formulaic), natural order.

After the grim conflicts with Lykaon and Asteropaios, and then between Hephaistos and Skamandros, the looser episodic *theomachia* of 21. 385–520 lowers the tone extremely. The comparison which is invited with the pair of *theomachiai* in book 5[45] only serves to accentuate the frivolity and inconsequentiality of this later one. The surrounding context in book 21 is far more harrowing, yet the mutual humiliation of the gods is even more absurd, especially the feminine indignities inflicted by Athene on Aphrodite (424) and by Hera on Artemis (489 ff.). Zeus sets the tone at the start—

---

[45] Especially Ares' explicit allusion at 21. 396–9 to the incident at 5. 841 ff. There are also, for example, similarities between the discomfitures and comfortings of Aphrodite and Artemis (5. 327 ff. and 21. 489 ff., including 5. 373–4 = 21. 509–10). On the poetic function of this *theomachia*, see J. M. Bremer in *BOP* 31 ff.

> ἐγέλαccε δέ οἱ φίλον ἦτορ
> γηθοcύνηι, ὅθ' ὁρᾶτο θεοὺc ἔριδι ξυνιόνταc.

and his heart within him laughed for joy, when he saw the gods joining in conflict. (21. 389–90)

—and there is divine amusement throughout (see especially 408, 434, 491, 508).

The point of all this for the *Iliad* and for its human audiences is brought out when Apollo declines to fight Poseidon:

> "ἐννοcίγαι', οὐκ ἄν με caóφρονα μυθήcaιο
> ἔμμεναι, εἰ δὴ coί γε βροτῶν ἔνεκα πτολεμίξω
> δειλῶν, οἳ φύλλοιcιν ἐοικότεc ἄλλοτε μέν τε
> ζαφλεγέεc τελέθουcιν, ἀρούρηc καρπὸν ἔδοντεc,
> ἄλλοτε δὲ φθινύθουcιν ἀκήριοι."

'Earthshaker, you would not say I was in my right mind if I do battle with you for the sake of wretched mortals, who are like leaves—for a time they flourish in a blaze of glory, and feed on the yield of the earth, and then again they fade lifeless.' (21. 462–6)[46]

Mortals are liable to traumatic suffering, incurable pain, and decay: immortals are by definition exempt from such things. Yet the juxtaposition of all this untragic argy-bargy with what precedes it, and even more with what follows, makes the decay of humanity all the more moving and absorbing.

8.4 *Decision, flight, last stand*

> "ὤ μοι ἐγών· εἰ μέν κε πύλαc καὶ τείχεα δύω,
> Πουλυδάμαc μοι πρῶτοc ἐλεγχείην ἀναθήcει,   100
> ὅc μ' ἐκέλευε Τρωcὶ ποτὶ πτόλιν ἡγήcαcθαι
> νύχθ' ὕπο τήνδ' ὀλοήν, ὅτε τ' ὤρετο δῖοc Ἀχιλλεύc.
> ἀλλ' ἐγὼ οὐ πιθόμην· ἦ τ' ἂν πολὺ κέρδιον ἦεν.
> νῦν δ' ἐπεὶ ὤλεcα λαὸν ἀταcθαλίηιcιν ἐμῆιcιν,
> αἰδέομαι Τρῶαc καὶ Τρωιάδαc ἑλκεcιπέπλουc,   105
> μή ποτέ τιc εἴπηιcι κακώτεροc ἄλλοc ἐμεῖο·
> "Ἕκτωρ ἧφι βίηφι πιθήcαc ὤλεcε λαόν."
> ὣc ἐρέουcιν· ἐμοὶ δὲ τότ' ἂν πολὺ κέρδιον εἴη
> ἄντην ἢ Ἀχιλῆα κατακτείναντα νέεcθαι,

---

[46] This is not as close to Glaukos and Diomedes at 6. 146–9 as it might seem at first glance.

ἠέ κεν αὐτῶι ὀλέςθαι ἐϋκλειῶς πρὸ πόληος.   110
εἰ δέ κεν ἀςπίδα μὲν καταθείομαι ὀμφαλόεςςαν
καὶ κόρυθα βριαρήν, δόρυ δὲ πρὸς τεῖχος ἐρείςας
αὐτὸς ἰὼν Ἀχιλῆος ἀμύμονος ἀντίος ἔλθω
καί οἱ ὑπόςχωμαι Ἑλένην καὶ κτήμαθ' ἅμ' αὐτῆι,
πάντα μάλ' ὅςςα τ' Ἀλέξανδρος κοίληις ἐνὶ νηυςὶν   115
ἠγάγετο Τροίηνδ', ἥ τ' ἔπλετο νείκεος ἀρχή,
δωςέμεν Ἀτρεΐδηιςιν ἄγειν, ἅμα δ' ἀμφὶς Ἀχαιοῖς
ἄλλ' ἀποδάςςεςθαι, ὅςα τε πτόλις ἥδε κέκευθε·
Τρωςὶν δ' αὖ μετόπιςθε γερούςιον ὅρκον ἕλωμαι
μή τι κατακρύψειν, ἀλλ' ἄνδιχα πάντα δάςαςθαι   120
κτῆςιν ὅςην πτολίεθρον ἐπήρατον ἐντὸς ἐέργει·
ἀλλὰ τίη μοι ταῦτα φίλος διελέξατο θυμός;
μή μιν ἐγὼ μὲν ἵκωμαι ἰών, ὁ δέ μ' οὐκ ἐλεήςει
οὐδέ τί μ' αἰδέςεται, κτενέει δέ με γυμνὸν ἐόντα
αὔτως ὥς τε γυναῖκα, ἐπεί κ' ἀπὸ τεύχεα δύω.   125
οὐ μέν πως νῦν ἔςτιν ἀπὸ δρυὸς οὐδ' ἀπὸ πέτρης
τῶι ὀαριζέμεναι, ἅ τε παρθένος ἠΐθεός τε,
παρθένος ἠΐθεός τ' ὀαρίζετον ἀλλήλοιιν.
βέλτερον αὖτ' ἔριδι ξυνελαυνέμεν ὅττι τάχιστα·
εἴδομεν ὁπποτέρωι κεν Ὀλύμπιος εὖχος ὀρέξηι."   130

'What am I to do? If I go back inside the gates and the wall, Poulydamas will be the first to lay blame on me, because he urged me to lead the Trojans back to the city during this last fatal night, when godlike Achilleus had roused himself. But I did not take his advice—it would have been far better if I had. Now that I have destroyed my people through my own arrant folly, I feel shame before the men of Troy and the women of Troy with their trailing dresses, that some man, a worse man than I, will say: "Hektor trusted in his own strength and destroyed his people." That is what they will say: and then it would be far better for me to face Achilleus and either kill him and return home, or die a glorious death myself in front of my city. But suppose I put down my bossed shield and heavy helmet, and lean my spear against the wall, and go out as I am to meet the excellent Achilleus, and promise to return Helen and all her property with her to the sons of Atreus for their keeping, all that Alexandros brought away in his hollow ships to Troy and was the first cause of our quarrel: and also to share equally with the Achaians all the rest of the property stored in this city—then afterwards I could make the Trojans take an oath in their council that they will hide nothing, but divide everything in two parts, all the possessions that the lovely city contains within it. But what need for this debate in my heart? I fear that if I go up to him he will not show me any pity or regard for my appeal, but will simply kill me unarmed like a woman, when I have taken off my armour.

There can be no sweet murmuring with him now, like boy and girl at the trysting-tree or rock, the way a boy and girl murmur sweetly together. Better to close and fight as soon as can be. We can see then to which of us the Olympian is giving the victory.' (22. 99–130)[47]

One moment Zeus is chuckling indulgently over Artemis' discomfiture, and the next (21. 515 ff.) Apollo is grimly occupied with saving those Trojans he can from the rout inflicted by the raging Achilleus. The scene moves, for the first time since book 7, to the city of Troy, as Priam, from the battlements where he watched in book 3, watches the reception of survivors into safety. Those who manage to crowd in through the gates escape ἀσπάσιοι (glad) (607), just as Poulydamas predicted at 18. 270–1 (see p. 158). It is only thanks to Apollo's diversion of Achilleus that casualties are not far worse.

This narrative (unhelpfully separated by the book-division, see p. 292) sets the scene for Hektor's stand outside the gates (presumably closed as commanded by Priam at 21. 535).

> Ἕκτορα δ' αὐτοῦ μεῖναι ὀλοιὴ μοῖρα πέδησεν
> Ἰλίου προπάροιθε πυλάων τε Σκαιάων.

Then his cruel fate shackled Hektor to stay there outside, in front of Ilios and the Skaian gates. (22. 5–6)[48]

Hektor stands alone, as is emphasized by 22. 33, 88; and this means that he fights under far more dangerous conditions than when accompanied by charioteer, companions, and *lāos*. Once released by Apollo, Achilleus advances like a racehorse, and Priam catches sight of the approaching gleam (25 ff., rather as he spotted the distant rout at 21. 526 ff.). By the time the parental pleas are over, Achilleus is nearer, while Hektor waits:

> ἀλλ' ὅ γε μίμν' Ἀχιλῆα πελώριον ἆσσον ἰόντα.
> ὡς δὲ δράκων ἐπὶ χειῆι ὀρέστερος ἄνδρα μένῃσι,
> βεβρωκὼς κακὰ φάρμακ', ἔδυ δέ τέ μιν χόλος αἰνός,
> σμερδαλέον δὲ δέδορκεν ἑλισσόμενος περὶ χειῆι·
> ὡς Ἕκτωρ ἄσβεστον ἔχων μένος οὐχ ὑπεχώρει

---

[47] I take it that line 121, which is not in some mainstream manuscripts (including Π^{27}) and which duplicates line 118, is an unwanted importation from 18. 512. Some such 'concordance' interpolations, on the other hand, infiltrate papyri but not the paradosis, e.g. 22. 10a (from 4. 32) is only in Π^9, and 22. 316abc (from 22. 133–5) are only in Π^{12}.

[48] Note how the formula, commonplace at 4. 517, becomes full of menace in this context.

...but he waited there for huge Achilleus as he came closer. As a mountain snake in his hole waits the approach of a man, when he has eaten poisonous herbs and savage anger has sunk deep into him, and he glares out malevolently, coiling round in his hole: so Hektor kept his fury unabated and would not give back ... (22. 92–6)

And by the next time the narrative turns to him, at 131 ff., he is looming close and terrifying.

Priam pleads with Hektor in 22. 38–76, speaking both as the old *basileus* to the great protector of Troy and as father to son. The constant tendency is, however, towards the personal: πρὸс δ' ἐμὲ τὸν δύστηνον ἔτι φρονέοντ' ἐλέησον ('and have pity on me too— I still live and feel') (59). The sack of Troy is presented through his eyes as menacing, above all, the destruction of his dynasty; and the *thalamoi* of lines 63 are those which stand for his great family network (see 6. 242 ff. and p. 117 above).[49] The culmination of his plea is the vivid envisioning of his own degrading death.[50] Priam tears out his grey hairs with the gesture of mourning, the same grey hairs as his house-dogs will gnaw (74 with 77–8). After him Hektor's mother (she is rarely named in Homer) appeals through the two main roles of women in war: the rearing of babies and the tending of the dead. Her speech moves from the baby at the breast[51] to the corpse on the bier—or rather the danger that she and Andromache will be deprived even of that.

The formulaic repetition of οὐδ' Ἕκτορι θυμὸν ἔπειθε/ον ('but he/ they could not move Hektor's heart') in 78 and 91 economically conveys his unshakeable stance. The explanation is effectively conveyed by the implicit sequence of thought in his 'monologue' (97–130). This is the longest and most significant of four 'shall-I-stand-and-fight?' monologues in the *Iliad*, which all hang on the line ἀλλὰ τίη μοι ταῦτα φίλος διαλέξατο θυμός; ('but what need for

---

[49] The passage is better without line 65, which weakly turns the ἑλκηθείσας ('dragged off') of 62 into ἑλκομένας and spoils the tetracolon of 62–4.

[50] Were it not for the survival of Tyrtaeus fr. 10. 21–30 (West), no one would ever have questioned the Iliadicity of these lines. Without them the power of Priam's plea would be greatly diminished. It is true that αἰδῶ ('private parts') in 75 is unusually explicit (compare and contrast *Il.* 2. 262, *Od.* 18. 85–7, 22. 476); but a special intimacy, like the reference to Hekabe's μαζόν (breast) at 80, is appropriate here, if anywhere.

[51] The wonderful word λαθικηδέα ('trouble-soothing') in 83 could hardly contrast more with the present moment of the narrative.

this debate in my heart?').[52] The third—Agenor's—occurs only 140 lines previously and prepares the way for Hektor—as often, a key scene is anticipated by a less powerful precedent shortly before. Apollo inspires Agenor to his own act of bravery, in 21. 544–98, rather than merely assuming his form throughout. Like Hektor, Agenor stands alone to face Achilleus; in his monologue he similarly rejects flight, rejects a more complicated evasion, and finally determines to fight bravely:

"εἰ δέ κέ οἱ προπάροιθε πόλεος κατεναντίον ἔλθω·
καὶ γάρ θην τούτωι τρωτὸς χρὼς ὀξέϊ χαλκῶι,
ἐν δὲ ἴα ψυχή, θνητὸν δέ ἕ φασ' ἄνθρωποι
ἔμμεναι· αὐτάρ οἱ Κρονίδης Ζεὺς κῦδος ὀπάζει."

'But suppose I go to face him in front of the city. Even his flesh can be wounded by the sharp bronze: there is only one life in him, and men say that he is mortal—only Zeus the son of Kronos is granting him glory.' (21. 567–70)[53]

Fine though this is (and he does hit Achilleus on the greave), it is clear that Agenor would have stood no chance at all without the direct protection of Apollo.

Hektor's monologue has three sections. In the first (99–110) he takes full responsibility for the destruction of his *lāos* (cf. p. 50 above), and acknowledges that this has followed his rejection of Poulydamas' advice. It is the reproach of ἀτασθαλίη (arrant folly), generally an Odyssean word, that his *aidōs* (see p. 53) cannot face. With Andromache (105 = 6. 442), however, *aidōs* kept him in the front ranks, whereas here it keeps him outside for single combat. 'He must now cover the shame that he feels for that act of folly with a hero's death; but this seals the fate of Troy whose only saviour he is.'[54] At least death would restore his *kleos* and cancel the ἐλεγχείη (blame, reproach). Heroic death—ἐϋκλειῶς (gloriously)—would not be a failure.

In the second part (111–25), in an extended conditional clause without an apodosis, Hektor works out the terms of a negotiated surrender. Indeed the occurrence of ἄνδιχα πάντα δάσασθαι ('divide everything in two parts') (120) in a similar context on the shield

[52] See Leaf on 21. 552; Schadewaldt, *HWW* 300–1; G. Petersmann, *Grazer Beitr.* 2 (1974), 147–69; B. Fenik in id. (ed.), *Tradition and Invention* (Leiden, 1978), 68–90 (fuller and better than *TBS* 91–8, 214).

[53] Line 570 seems to be a weak addition to supply an unnecessary infinitive.

[54] Macleod, 9.

of Achilleus at 18. 511 suggests a standard clause in the procedure. The deal that he envisages goes further than that offered in single combat at 3. 67ff., or that discussed in the debate at 7. 345ff. (where Hektor does not participate); yet the possibility is explored only to be rejected. The point is that Achilleus would not be interested, and would not feel any *aidōs* or *eleos*. For anyone else the offer of such favourable terms would be a great triumph. The Achaians are there, after all, for Helen and the *tīmē* of the Atreidai—hence Ἀτρείδηιϲιν ('to the sons of Atreus') in 117. But for Achilleus all that is irrelevant. He is out there now because of Patroklos; and the only possible satisfaction for him is Hektor's life. Hektor realizes that even if he offers himself γυμνόν (unarmed) this will not protect him—any more than it did Lykaon (compare 124 with 21. 50).

Homer could hardly have offered a scene in deeper contrast with Hektor's present than that conjured up in his conclusion (126–30). The combination of παρθένοϲ and ἠΐθεοϲ ('girl' and 'boy'), with its poignant epanalepsis, comes elsewhere only in the idyllic scenes of Achilleus' shield (18. 567, 593): ὀαρίζειν ('murmur') is most memorably used elsewhere at 6. 516, of the conversation between Hektor and Andromache.[55] The fleeting vignette is imaged only to be replaced by the prospect of battle. And, as usual, Hektor has his hopes—see further § **8.5**.

Hektor runs. Yet the narrative of his flight in 136ff. does not present it as an act of gross cowardice: it is only to be expected before the overwhelming terror of Achilleus' approach.[56] Now at last Achilleus' formulaic epithets come into their own—all that pent-up speed is, so to speak, released. It is thanks to his speed that he can keep Hektor on the outside of the cart-track, unable to cut in nearer to the walls within the range of 'covering fire' (145ff., 194ff.).

They are watched as they run by the gods from above, by the Trojans from the walls, and by the Achaians in the plain (Achilleus has to ensure that nobody interferes (205–7)). The simile from games seems obvious:

---

[55] Cf. Stawell, 77; Owen, 221–2. For discussion of the proverbial expression in 126, see M. L. West on Hes. *Theog.* 35.

[56] Cf. Schadewaldt, *HHW* 303–6; Owen, 222–4.

ὡς δ' ὅτ' ἀεθλοφόροι περὶ τέρματα μώνυχες ἵπποι
ῥίμφα μάλα τρωχῶςι· τὸ δὲ μέγα κεῖται ἄεθλον,
ἢ τρίπος ἠὲ γυνή, ἀνδρὸς κατατεθνηῶτος·
ὡς τὼ τρὶς Πριάμοιο πόλιν πέρι δινηθήτην
καρπαλίμοιςι πόδεςςι·

As when champion strong-footed horses wheel round the turning-posts
running at full stretch, when a great prize is there to be won, a tripod or
a woman, in the funeral games for a man who has died: so those two
raced round the city of Priam, circling it three times with all the speed
of their legs ... (22. 162–6)[57]

Yet the obvious is given a poetic twist. The race is *not* being held
because a great man has died, and the prize is *not* a material one.
It is crucial that, in this case, it is the death of the great man
which is itself the prize of the race. So the poet adds lines just
before the simile which are a sort of denial or undercutting of its
similarity:

πρόςθε μὲν ἐςθλὸς ἔφευγε, δίωκε δέ μιν μέγ' ἀμείνων
καρπαλίμως, ἐπεὶ οὐχ ἱερήϊον οὐδὲ βοείην
ἀρνύςθην, ἅ τε ποςςὶν ἀέθλια γίγνεται ἀνδρῶν,
ἀλλὰ περὶ ψυχῆς θέον Ἕκτορος ἱπποδάμοιο.

A brave man was running in front, but a far greater one was in pursuit,
and they ran at speed, since it was no sacrificial beast or oxhide shield
they were competing for—such as are the usual prizes that men win in
the foot-race—but they were running for the life of Hektor the tamer of
horses. (22. 158–61)

Hektor is the native fighting in his own land for his own land.
The specificity of the Trojan landscape emphasizes this:

οἱ δὲ παρὰ ςκοπιὴν καὶ ἐρινεὸν ἠνεμόεντα
τείχεος αἰὲν ὑπὲκ κατ' ἀμαξιτὸν ἐςςεύοντο,
κρουνὼ δ' ἵκανον καλλιρρόω· ἔνθα δὲ πηγαὶ
δοιαὶ ἀναΐςςουςι Σκαμάνδρου δινήεντος.

They sped past the look-out place and the wind-tossed fig-tree, keeping
all the time to the wagon-track a little way out from the wall, and came
to the two well-heads of lovely water: here the twin springs of swirling
Skamandros shoot up from the ground. (22. 145–8)

The pursuit eventually stops for the final battle by these very
springs (208 ff.). In the Mediterranean climate a good, cold spring

[57] A tripod was, indeed, Hesiod's prize in the 'hymn' contest at the funeral
games of Amphidamas, king of Chalkis—see *WD* 654 ff.

is a kind of symbol of the habitability of a place—like the fountain made by Ithakos himself at *Od.* 17. 204 ff. Within the poem it is still less than 400 lines since Skamandros was seethed into submission and made to promise not to protect Troy—see pp. 227–9 above. This is why it is poetically important for the springs of the great river to be right by the city walls, however unrealistic in terms of physical geography.[58]

ἔνθα δ' ἐπ' αὐτάων πλυνοὶ εὐρέες ἐγγὺς ἔασι
καλοὶ λαΐνεοι, ὅθι εἵματα ςιγαλόεντα
πλύνεςκον Τρώων ἄλοχοι καλαί τε θύγατρες
τὸ πρὶν ἐπ' εἰρήνης, πρὶν ἐλθεῖν υἷας Ἀχαιῶν.

There close beside these springs are the fine broad washing-troughs made of stone, where the Trojans' wives and their lovely daughters used to wash their bright clothes, in earlier times, in peace, before the sons of the Achaians came. (22. 153–6)

While the cold spring supplies drinking-water, the hot one provides well-laundered clothes, a token of a prosperous society at peace, like that of Alkinoös in *Od.* 6, for example. During the war the washing-troughs have lain idle; Troy's fine cloth is being used as fruitless offerings (cf. 6. 286 ff.), or for paying ransoms, or for wrapping corpses—see further p. 274. If the great protector of Troy loses the battle by the springs of Skamandros, then the women of Troy will not use them again. Instead their woven work will be looted (or burnt), and they will themselves labour at far-distant springs, as Hektor foresees for Andromache at 6. 456–8.

Two Olympian scenes are interleaved with the pursuit. In the first, at 166–87, Zeus raises the possibility of rescuing Hektor. Behind this lies an even more elaborate scene, at 16. 431–61, when the final confrontation of Sarpedon was approaching. When Zeus considered saving his son, Hera responded with words which (except for an initial vocative) are the same as Athene's in 22. 178–81;

"αἰνότατε Κρονίδη, ποῖον τὸν μῦθον ἔειπες.
ἄνδρα θνητὸν ἐόντα, πάλαι πεπρωμένον αἴςῃ,
ἂψ ἐθέλεις θανάτοιο δυςηχέος ἐξαναλῦςαι;
ἔρδ'· ἀτὰρ οὔ τοι πάντες ἐπαινέομεν θεοὶ ἄλλοι."

---

[58] Cf. Schadewaldt, *HWW* 308; Elliger, 58–61. For a possible poetic fusion of geographical realities see B. Rubens and O. Taplin, *An Odyssey round Odysseus* (London, 1989), 93–5.

'Dread son of Kronos, what is this you are saying? Do you intend to take a man who is mortal and long ago destined by fate, and release him from grim death? Do it then—but we other gods will not all approve you.' (16. 440–3)[59]

Hera went on to suggest supernatural intervention to ensure Sarpedon's burial back in his homeland, and Zeus acquiesced in this compromise, though he wept tears of blood. Hektor is φίλον (dear) (22. 168); Sarpedon was φίλτατον (dearest) (16. 433), yet that still did not save him. The issue of Hektor's burial is not even raised among the gods, though it will come to loom large among the humans, and will in the end be achieved by the humans. In 16 Zeus accepted Hera's protest in silence: in 22 he takes an indulgent tone with Athene, even sanctioning her intervention—ἔρξον ὅπηι δή τοι νόος ἔπλετο, μηδ' ἔτ' ἐρώει ('do as your purpose directs you, and do not hold back any longer') (185).

With this, Athene leaves Olympos for the battlefield. She does not, however, intervene as long as Apollo is with Hektor, and thus observes the polite conventions of athanatology.

πῶς δέ κεν Ἕκτωρ κῆρας ὑπεξέφυγεν θανάτοιο,
εἰ μή οἱ πύματόν τε καὶ ὕστατον ἤντετ' Ἀπόλλων
ἐγγύθεν, ὅς οἱ ἐπῶρσε μένος λαιψηρά τε γοῦνα;

And how could Hektor have kept clear of the fates of death, if Apollo had not come close to him for the last and final time, and spurred strength in him and speed to his legs? (22. 202–4)[60]

The turning-point is marked by the brief second Olympian scene featuring the golden scales.

ἀλλ' ὅτε δὴ τὸ τέταρτον ἐπὶ κρουνοὺς ἀφίκοντο,
καὶ τότε δὴ χρύσεια πατὴρ ἐτίταινε τάλαντα,
ἐν δὲ τίθει δύο κῆρε τανηλεγέος θανάτοιο,
τὴν μὲν Ἀχιλλῆος, τὴν δ' Ἕκτορος ἱπποδάμοιο,
ἕλκε δὲ μέσσα λαβών . . .

. . . but when they came round to the well-heads for the fourth time, then the Father opened out his golden scales. In the pans he put two fates of death's long sorrow, one for Achilleus and one for Hektor the tamer of horses, and he took the scales in the middle and lifted them up . . . (22. 208–12)

---

[59] Although πάλαι πεπρωμένον αἴσηι ('long ago doomed by fate') is as close to 'Fate' as anything in Homer, it is clearly not some power independent of Zeus—see further below.

[60] Cf. πύματόν τε καὶ ὕστατον used of the doomed suitors at *Od.* 20. 13, 116.

This is not some kind of decision by a higher power. The outcome is already settled beyond doubt by Achilleus' prowess and passion, by divine determination, and—for the audience though not the characters—by the whole shape of the narrative. The scales do not decide *who* will win, but show *when* Achilleus will win. It is the same at 8. 68 ff. and in the other passages discussed on p. 141 above. So, to continue the quotation:

ῥέπε δ' Ἕκτορος αἴσιμον ἦμαρ,
ᾤχετο δ' εἰς Ἀΐδαο, λίπεν δέ ἑ Φοῖβος Ἀπόλλων.

... and Hektor's day of doom sank down, away into Hades, and Phoibos Apollo left him. (22. 212–13)[61]

This leaves the field clear for Athene and Achilleus. Hektor is on his own.

Athene's intervention, in strict tactical terms, makes the whole pursuit unnecessary; and Achilleus never does actually catch Hektor up. The goddess displays the passion and pleasure of her involvement, which emerge from the duals she uses to Achilleus (216 ff.), and her verbal relish over Apollo's helplessness (especially the unique προπροκυλινδόμενος ('going through agonies of grovelling') 221). It is also implicit in her assumption of the guise of one of the Trojan royal dynasty,[62] and her clever exploitation (236 ff., cf. 233 f.) of the pleas of Priam and Hekabe, which have recently been heard, though in quite a different way. To Hektor her duals in 243 and 245 are used in deceit. Achilleus duly acknowledges the exalted help he is being given when he warns Hektor (271 ff.) ἄφαρ δέ σε Παλλὰς Ἀθήνη ἔγχει ἐμῶι δαμάαι ('soon Pallas Athene will beat you down under my spear'). This throw misses, but

ἀνὰ δ' ἥρπασε Παλλὰς Ἀθήνη,
ἂψ δ' Ἀχιλῆϊ δίδου, λάθε δ' Ἕκτορα, ποιμένα λαῶν.

unseen by Hektor, shepherd of the people, Pallas Athene pulled up the spear and gave it back to Achilleus. (22. 276–7)

[61] Compare the way that Poseidon's departure at 15. 298 ff. marks the beginning of serious reverses for the Achaians. The relation between Poseidon and Athene in the *Odyssey* is comparable, though on a larger scale.
[62] Deïphobos is a relatively minor son of Priam (cf. 24. 251), though quite active in book 13. Is he chosen because he will take over Helen, and become prominent in stories of the sack (cf. *Od.* 4. 276, 8. 517, etc.)?

8.5   Hektor's dying threat

ἤριπε δ' ἐν κονίηις· ὁ δ' ἐπεύξατο δῖος Ἀχιλλεύς·   330
"Ἕκτορ, ἀτάρ που ἔφης Πατροκλῆ' ἐξεναρίζων
cῶc ἔccecθ', ἐμὲ δ' οὐδὲν ὀπίζεο νόcφιν ἐόντα,
νήπιε· τοῖο δ' ἄνευθεν ἀοccητὴρ μέγ' ἀμείνων
νηυcὶν ἔπι γλαφυρῆιcιν ἐγὼ μετόπιcθε λελείμμην,
ὅc τοι γούνατ' ἔλυcα· cὲ μὲν κύνεc ἠδ' οἰωνοὶ   335
ἑλκήcουc' ἀϊκῶc, τὸν δὲ κτεριοῦcιν Ἀχαιοί."
   Τὸν δ' ὀλιγοδρανέων προcέφη κορυθαίολοc Ἕκτωρ·
"λίccομ' ὑπὲρ ψυχῆc καὶ γούνων cῶν τε τοκήων,
μή με ἔα παρὰ νηυcὶ κύναc καταδάψαι Ἀχαιῶν,
ἀλλὰ cὺ μὲν χαλκόν τε ἅλιc χρυcόν τε δέδεξο,   340
δῶρα τά τοι δώcουcι πατὴρ καὶ πότνια μήτηρ,
cῶμα δὲ οἴκαδ' ἐμὸν δόμεναι πάλιν, ὄφρα πυρόc με
Τρῶεc καὶ Τρώων ἄλοχοι λελάχωcι θανόντα."
   Τὸν δ' ἄρ' ὑπόδρα ἰδὼν προcέφη πόδαc ὠκὺc Ἀχιλλεύc·
"μή με, κύον, γούνων γουνάζεο μηδὲ τοκήων·   345
αἲ γάρ πωc αὐτόν με μένοc καὶ θυμὸc ἀνείη
ὤμ' ἀποταμνόμενον κρέα ἔδμεναι, οἷα ἔοργαc,
ὡc οὐκ ἔcθ' ὃc cῆc γε κύναc κεφαλῆc ἀπαλάλκοι,
οὐδ' εἴ κεν δεκάκιc τε καὶ εἰκοcινήριτ' ἄποινα
cτήcωc' ἐνθάδ' ἄγοντεc, ὑπόcχωνται δὲ καὶ ἄλλα,   350
οὐδ' εἴ κέν c' αὐτὸν χρυcῶι ἐρύcαcθαι ἀνώγοι
Δαρδανίδηc Πρίαμοc· οὐδ' ὣc cέ γε πότνια μήτηρ
ἐνθεμένη λεχέεccι γοήcεται, ὃν τέκεν αὐτή,
ἀλλὰ κύνεc τε καὶ οἰωνοὶ κατὰ πάντα δάcονται."
   Τὸν δὲ καταθνήιcκων προcέφη κορυθαίολοc Ἕκτωρ·   355
"ἦ c' εὖ γιγνώcκων προτιόccομαι, οὐδ' ἄρ' ἔμελλον
πείcειν· ἦ γὰρ cοί γε cιδήρεοc ἐν φρεcὶ θυμόc.
φράζεο νῦν, μή τοί τι θεῶν μήνιμα γένωμαι
ἤματι τῶι ὅτε κέν cε Πάριc καὶ Φοῖβοc Ἀπόλλων
ἐcθλὸν ἐόντ' ὀλέcωcιν ἐνὶ Cκαιῆιcι πύληιcιν."   360
   Ὣc ἄρα μιν εἰπόντα τέλοc θανάτοιο κάλυψε,
ψυχὴ δ' ἐκ ῥεθέων πταμένη Ἀϊδόcδε βεβήκει,
ὃν πότμον γοόωcα, λιποῦc' ἀνδροτῆτα καὶ ἥβην.
τὸν καὶ τεθνηῶτα προcηύδα δῖοc Ἀχιλλεύc·
"τέθναθι· κῆρα δ' ἐγὼ τότε δέξομαι, ὁππότε κεν δὴ   365
Ζεὺc ἐθέληι τελέcαι ἠδ' ἀθάνατοι θεοὶ ἄλλοι."

He crashed in the dust, and godlike Achilleus triumphed over him:
'Hektor, doubtless as you killed Patroklos you thought you would be safe,
and you had no fear of me, as I was far away. You fool—behind him
there was I left to avenge him, a far greater man than he, waiting there

by the hollow ships, and I have collapsed your strength. Now the dogs and birds will maul you hideously, while the Achaians will give Patroklos full burial.'

Then with the strength low in him Hektor of the glinting helmet answered: 'I beseech you by your life and knees and by your parents, do not let the dogs of the Achaian camp eat me by the ships, but take the ransom of bronze and gold in plenty that my father and honoured mother will offer you, and give my body back to my home, so that the Trojans and the wives of the Trojans can give me in death my due rite of burning.'

Then swift-footed Achilleus scowled at him and said: 'Make me no appeals, you dog, by knees or parents. I wish I could eat you myself, that the fury in my heart would drive me to cut you in pieces and eat your flesh raw, for all that you have done to me. So no man is going to keep the dogs away from your head, not even if they bring here and weigh out ten times or twenty times your ransom, not even if Dardanian Priam offers to pay your own weight in gold. Not even so will your honoured mother lay you on the bier and mourn for you, her own child, but the dogs and birds will share you for their feast and leave nothing.'

Then, dying, Hektor of the glinting helmet said to him: 'Yes, I can tell it—I know you well, and I had no chance of swaying you: your heart is like iron in your breast. But take care now, or I may bring the gods' anger on you, on that day when for all your bravery Paris and Phoibos Apollo will destroy you at the Skaian gates.'

As he spoke the end of death enfolded him: and his spirit flitted from his body and went on the way to Hades, weeping for its fate, and the youth and manhood it must leave. Then godlike Achilleus spoke to him, dead though he was: 'Die! I shall take my death at whatever time Zeus and the other immortal gods wish to bring it on me.' (22. 330–66)

Well over half the final battle-scene, from 248 to 366, is taken up with direct speech. This is one indicator that the emphasis is on states of mind, especially the changing perceptions of Hektor. First (250 ff.) he proposes an oath before the gods, as he had before the single combat at 7. 76 ff. (in fact 22. 342–3 = 7. 79–80): they should swear to treat the corpse of the loser honourably. Achilleus harshly rejects this civilized proposal—see further p. 244. This single combat will be fought without umpires or rules.

In his ignorance of Athene's return of Achilleus' spear, Hektor seems to have some reason for his one last over-confident speech in 279–88. Throughout the battle—at 20. 435–7, 22. 129–30, and by implication 22. 256–9—he has expressed hopes of victory, and this seems to be his great chance. His spear hits Achilleus' shield

full on, but simply bounces off without making a mark—τῆλε δ'
ἀπεπλάγχθη cάκεοc δόρυ (but the spear rebounded far from the
shield) (291). At 20. 259–72 lines were lavished on how Hephaistos' new handiwork kept out a good blow; there is also a
reminder when Agenor hits Achilleus' greave (21. 590–4); and
there will be another allusion at 22. 313–16. At this point, however, there is none, and this makes Hektor's failure seem horribly
perfunctory.

> Δηΐφοβον δὲ κάλει λευκάcπιδα μακρὸν ἀΰcαc·
> ᾔτεέ μιν δόρυ μακρόν· ὁ δ' οὔ τί οἱ ἐγγύθεν ἦεν·   295
> Ἕκτωρ δ' ἔγνω ᾗιcιν ἐνὶ φρεcὶ φώνηcέν τε·
> "ὢ πόποι, ἦ μάλα δή με θεοὶ θάνατόνδε κάλεccαν·
> Δηΐφοβον γὰρ ἔγωγ' ἐφάμην ἥρωα παρεῖναι·
> ἀλλ' ὁ μὲν ἐν τείχει, ἐμὲ δ' ἐξαπάτηcεν Ἀθήνη.
> νῦν δὲ δὴ ἐγγύθι μοι θάνατος κακός, οὐδ' ἔτ' ἄνευθεν,   300
> οὐδ' ἀλέη· ἦ γάρ ῥα πάλαι τό γε φίλτερον ἦεν
> Ζηνί τε καὶ Διὸς υἷι ἑκηβόλωι, οἵ με πάρος γε
> πρόφρονεc εἰρύατο· νῦν αὖτέ με μοῖρα κιχάνει."

He called in a great shout to Deïphobos of the white shield, and asked
him for a long spear. But Deïphobos was not there near him. Then
Hektor realised in his heart, and cried out: 'Oh, for sure now the gods
have called me to my death! I thought the hero Deïphobos was with me:
but he is inside the wall, and Athene has tricked me. So now vile death
is close on me, not far now any longer, and there is no escape. This must
long have been the true pleasure of Zeus and Zeus' son the far-shooter,
and yet before now they readily defended me: but now this time my fate
has caught me.' (22. 294–303)

The audience has known since line 213 that Hektor stands alone,
without Apollo, human and vulnerable. The division in the middle
of 295 marks the moment when he sees this truth himself, the
moment when he joins Achilleus in the *certainty* that death is
imminent. Just as Achilleus was told by Thetis (18. 133) and by
his horse (19. 409) that his death is ἐγγύθεν (near), so Hektor
realizes that it is death, not Deïphobos, who is ἐγγύθεν (see 295,
300). Now he is able to use language which is normally only at
the disposal of the narrator: with θεοὶ θάνατόνδε κάλεccαν ('the gods
have called to death') compare 16. 698 of Patroklos, and for μοῖρα
κιχάνει ('fate has caught') compare, for example, 17. 478, 17. 627,
22. 436. Hektor's last two lines before he is mortally wounded are
in their way as heroic as anything in the *Iliad*:

"μὴ μὰν ἀσπουδί γε καὶ ἀκλειῶς ἀπολοίμην,
ἀλλὰ μέγα ῥέξας τι καὶ ἐσσομένοισι πυθέσθαι."

'Even so, let me not die ingloriously, without a fight, without some great
deed done that future men will hear of.' (22. 304–5)

He expresses the idea that his best hopes of overcoming mortality
lie not in victory but in the manner of his losing. In a sense the
success, the *kleos*, that he wins at this moment of failure is confirmed every time that the *Iliad* is heard or read—and, indeed, by
the writing and reading of these very words.[63]
Hektor charges with no weapon but his sword. All that Achilleus, safe in his divine armour (reminder at 315–16), has to do is
impale him on his spear as they close in:

εἰσορόων χρόα καλόν, ὅπηι εἴξειε μάλιστα.
τοῦ δὲ καὶ ἄλλο τόσον μὲν ἔχε χρόα χάλκεα τεύχεα,
καλά, τὰ Πατρόκλοιο βίην ἐνάριξε κατακτάς·
φαίνετο δ' ἧι κληῖδες ἀπ' ὤμων αὐχέν' ἔχουσι,
λαυκανίην, ἵνα τε ψυχῆς ὤκιστος ὄλεθρος·
τῆι ῥ' ἐπὶ οἷ μεμαῶτ' ἔλασ' ἔγχεϊ δῖος Ἀχιλλεύς,
ἀντικρὺ δ' ἁπαλοῖο δι' αὐχένος ἤλυθ' ἀκωκή·
οὐδ' ἄρ' ἀπ' ἀσφάραγον μελίη τάμε χαλκοβάρεια

... looking over his fine body to find the most vulnerable place. All the
rest of his body was covered by his bronze armour, the fine armour he
had stripped from mighty Patroklos when he killed him. But flesh showed
where the collar-bones hold the join of neck and shoulders, at the gullet,
where a man's life is most quickly destroyed. Godlike Achilleus drove in
there with his spear as Hektor charged him, and the point went right
through his soft neck: but the ash spear with its weight of bronze did not
cut the windpipe ... (22. 321–8)[64]

The reminder that Hektor is wearing the armour taken from
Patroklos revives the theme of the chain of vulnerability, most
clearly expressed by Zeus at 17. 192 ff., see pp. 186–8. This leads into
one of the most elaborate and telling architectural correspondences
in the whole poem: the death scene of Patroklos at 16. 829–63 and

---

[63] Apart from Helen—see pp. 97–8 above—this kind of self-referentiality is
more characteristic of the *Odyssey* than the *Iliad*. For some examples of phrases
like this, see *Od.* 3. 204, 8. 580, 11. 76, 24. 433. There is also a future of negative
'fame' foreseen at *Od.* 21. 255, 24. 433 (cf. Agamemnon at *Il.* 2. 119).
[64] Line 329 is probably, as Aristarchos maintained, the addition of a pedant:
ὄφρα ('so that') is too purposeful.

of Hektor at 22. 330–69.[65] Unlike most others they do not come near the beginning or end of a session; but they do come at about the same point in the overall trajectory of part II and of part III. First, the correspondences are particularly close in the victor's speech of triumph (330, ἐπεύξατο ('triumphed over') ∼ 16. 829, ἐπευχόμενος ('in trumph over')). Both speculate on the past state of mind of his victim, the over-confidence which has led to his fate, and taunts him that he will on the contrary be carrion flesh.[66] But while Hektor was quite wrong about Patroklos' departure and Achilleus' instructions to him (see p. 184 above), Achilleus in 331–2 has got Hektor right: in the corresponding scene in book 16 he was indeed scornful of Achilleus (especially 16. 837).

Patroklos in book 16 has one speech in reply, making a sequence of three speeches in all, whereas in 22 Hektor has two replies, making a sequence of five. This opens up room for the question of burial, which is to be so important for the rest of the poem.[67] After the failure of his chivalrous proposal at 254 ff., Hektor now adds, as he is dying, the offer of δῶρα (gifts)—a ransom not for a live prisoner of war, but for a corpse (cf. Glaukos at 17. 160 ff.). Achilleus' reply at 261 ff. was harsh enough, likening his attitude to Hektor to the ways of beasts rather than men: now, in 345 ff., he wishes he could usurp the place of the dogs and birds to eat Hektor's flesh raw. The only other person to speak in such terms is Hekabe, at 24. 212–13 (see p. 282—Zeus' teasing of Hera at 4. 34–6 is only very remotely comparable). Since scholars have tended to talk of 'cannibalism', it should be emphasized that Achilleus (and Hekabe) do not in any way put their wish into practice. That is unthinkable—yet even to wish for the unthinkable is bad enough. The final parts of the poem arise from the question whether Achilleus will be able to relinquish the extreme state of mind which he expresses here. 'If it [sc. Achilleus' anger against Hektor] is to come to an end it must first be represented

---

[65] On the correspondences, see, among others, Reinhardt, *ID* 308–10; G. S. Kirk, *Homer and the Oral Tradition* (Cambridge, 1976), 209–17; Thalmann, 46–51.

[66] Some details of wording: 331 "῞Εκτορ, ἀτάρ που ἔφης . . ." ('Hektor, doubtless you thought . . .') ∼ 16. 830 "Πάτροκλ', ἦ που ἔφησθα . . ." ('Patroklos, you must have thought . . .'); 333 "νήπιε . . . δέ . . ." ('you fool') = 16. 833; 335–6 "cè μὲν κύνες ἠδ' οἰωνοὶ ἑλκήσουσι . . ." ('now the dogs and birds will maul you . . .') ∼ 16. 836 "cè δέ τ' ἐνθάδε γῦπες ἔδονται" ('but you, the vultures will eat you here').

[67] Segal and Redfield (*NCI*) have done much to give this theme proper attention.

as unyielding and horrifying; otherwise the story would lack shape or point or grandeur.'[68]

Achilleus' rejection of any amount of material compensation, however great,[69] sounds a chord which brings it down from the level of rant: in book 9 he made an appealing case for the rejection of any equivalence between material goods and human integrity (9. 378 ff., 401 ff.; 22. 349 almost = 9. 379). There, however, he said that he would not give way until Agamemnon had repaid the heart-rending humiliation, while here there is no 'until', no suggestion of a possible solution.

Hektor's last five lines carry a power that verges on the superhuman. The narrative shaping redoubles the 'usual' prophetic potency of dying words because of the prophecy of Patroklos behind them:

> "ἄλλο δέ τοι ἐρέω, cù δ' ἐνὶ φρεcὶ βάλλεο cῆιcιν·
> οὔ θην οὐδ' αὐτὸc δηρὸν βέηι, ἀλλά τοι ἤδη
> ἄγχι παρέcτηκεν θάνατοc καὶ μοῖρα κραταιή,
> χερcὶ δαμέντ' Ἀχιλῆοc ἀμύμονοc Αἰακίδαο."

'I tell you another thing, and you mark it well in your mind. You yourself, you too will not live long, but already now death and strong fate are standing close beside you, to bring you down at the hands of Achilleus, great son of Aiakos' stock.' (16. 851-4)

Now, just one day later, Hektor is fulfilling these very words. His are no less sure to be fulfilled.

This moment is the climax of a series of predictions of Achilleus' impending death. There have been some ten allusions since his own choice of αὐτίκα τεθναίην ('then let me die directly') in the scene with Thetis in book 18—see §7.3.[70] For the audience, details have gathered by a process of accretion. At 19. 417 the horse Xanthos spoke of a combination of man and god. Achilleus' own words to Lykaon imply that the fatal weapon will be the bow—ἢ ὅ γε δουρὶ βαλὼν ἢ ἀπὸ νευρῆφιν ὀϊcτῶι (with a cast of the spear or an arrow from the string) (21. 113)—since in such altern-

---

[68] Macleod, 21.

[69] It looks as though in Aischylos' play *Phryges* (or *Hektoros Lytra*) Priam actually paid the weight of Hektor's body in gold—see S. Radt, *Tr. G. F.* iii, 365. At *Iliad* 24. 232 he will weigh out ten talents.

[70] Besides the passages about to be cited I have noted 18. 329, 440-2, 458, 464-7; 19. 328-30; 20. 127-8, 337.

atives it is usually the second which proves right.[71] As he fears death in the river, Achilleus complains that this would contradict the prophecy of Thetis (not mentioned before):

> "ἦ μ' ἔφατο Τρώων ὑπὸ τείχεϊ θωρηκτάων
> λαιψηροῖς ὀλέεσθαι Ἀπόλλωνος βελέεσσιν."

'She told me that I would meet my death under the armed Trojans' wall, killed by the quick arrows of Apollo.' (21. 277–8)

The dying words of Hektor add the Skaian gate, which is appropriate enough.[72] What is arrestingly new is the name of the human agent, Paris.

The other telling feature which might give Achilleus pause is the threat of θεῶν μήνιμα ('the gods' fury'). This is quite a strong 'moral' notion, generally more at home in the *Odyssey*, where Elpenor's ghost appeals for burial with the same words.[73] Hektor is well-regarded on Olympos (see especially 22. 167 ff.), and his proposal of a divinely sanctioned agreement was brutally rejected by Achilleus (254 ff.), so his threat here will strike most audiences as far from implausible. 'Hektor's unburied body is thus thrust upon us as a narrative and moral problem.'[74]

The narrative shaping finds its closest correspondence with book 16 as the final reply to the dead victim approaches. The four lines 361–4 are the same as 16.856–8 (with Achilleus instead of Hektor, of course). The beautiful death-couplet, whether or not traditional, comes in Homer only in these two crucial places. In 16 Hektor goes on to challenge Patroklos boldly:

> "Πατρόκλεις, τί νύ μοι μαντεύεαι αἰπὺν ὄλεθρον;
> τίς δ' οἶδ' εἴ κ' Ἀχιλεύς, Θέτιδος πάϊς ἠϋκόμοιο,
> φθήηι ἐμῶι ὑπὸ δουρὶ τυπεὶς ἀπὸ θυμὸν ὀλέσσαι;"

'Patroklos, why make me this prophecy of grim death? Who knows if Achilleus, son of lovely-haired Thetis, might be struck by my spear first, and lose his life before me?' (16. 859–61)

---

[71] See further Macleod on 24. 734–8.

[72] Compare the prayer at 6. 307 that Diomedes might be killed 'in front of the Skaian gates'.

[73] *Od.* 11. 73, cf. 2. 66, 5. 146, 14. 283. It has become a commonplace of Homeric scholarship that the word μῆνις ('fury') is used only of Achilleus among mortals, and is otherwise restricted to gods. The use of the verb ἐμήνιε ('he kept up his fury') of Agamemnon at 1. 249 does, however, seriously undermine this point. There is a good discussion of *mēnis* in Redfield, 'Proem', 97–8.

[74] Macleod, 20, cf. n. on 24. 54. On dying words, see Rutherford, 152–3 and n. 38.

The event has now definitively answered his question—everyone knows now. Achilleus, by contrast, expresses no surprise or questioning in his corresponding couplet, 365–6. His words are not even unprecedented—they are the same as his reply to Thetis at 18. 115–16 (quoted on p. 193). His response to the horse's prophecy also takes the same tone: εὖ νυ τὸ οἶδα καὶ αὐτὸς ... ('I know well myself ...') (19. 421). Achilleus knows full well that in return for the death of Hektor he must accept his own. What he does not take on board at this stage is the threat that his refusal to bury Hector might attract θεῶν μήνιμα (the gods' fury).

8.6 The burning of Trojan cloth

"νῦν δὲ cὲ μὲν παρὰ νηυσὶ κορωνίcι νόcφι τοκήων
αἰόλαι εὐλαὶ ἔδονται, ἐπεί κε κύνεc κορέcωνται,
γυμνόν· ἀτάρ τοι εἵματ' ἐνὶ μεγάροιcι κέονται   510
λεπτά τε καὶ χαρίεντα, τετυγμένα χερcὶ γυναικῶν.
ἀλλ' ἤτοι τάδε πάντα καταφλέξω πυρὶ κηλέωι,
οὐδὲν coί γ' ὄφελοc, ἐπεὶ οὐκ ἐγκείceαι αὐτοῖc,
ἀλλὰ πρὸc Τρώων καὶ Τρωϊάδων κλέοc εἶναι."
Ὣc ἔφατο κλαίουc', ἐπὶ δὲ cτενάχοντο γυναῖκεc.   515

'And now out there by the beaked ships, far away from your parents, the wriggling worms will feed on you, when the dogs have had their fill, where you lie naked—and yet there are fine and lovely clothes stored for you at home, the work of women's hands. But now I shall burn them all in the blazing fire—not for your comfort, as you will never be laid out in them, but to do you honour in the sight of the men and women of Troy.'
Such was her lament, and the women joined with their keening. (22. 508–15)

The response of Andromache is held back. Immediately after the death of Hektor the narrative would be much stronger if lines 395 ff. followed directly on Achilleus' words in 365–6.[75] The inter-

[75] I have even wondered whether lines 367–94 might be interpolated. (1) The stripping of Hektor's armour is emphasized (368–9, 374), yet there is no awareness of this as the recovery of Achilleus' own armour. (2) The ἄλλοι υἷεc Ἀχαιῶν (other sons of the Achaians) (389)—in all their thousands?—admire the beauty of Hektor, even though he has been repeatedly jabbed by them (370–1, 375). (3) Achilleus addresses the Achaian leaders formally as though at a proper meeting (378); yet he does not wait for any response. (4) 385 is quite unsuitable in a public speech—it belongs within monologues. (5) The proposed communal return to the ships carrying the corpse and singing the paean is totally inconsistent with what does

vening anticlimactic lines do, however, recall Hektor's greatest triumph, when he brought fire among the ships (374); and Achilleus' rejection of military advantage because of personal grief (377 ff.) echoes the form and thought of his great monologue at 22. 99 ff. (see pp. 234–5). The humiliation which Achilleus devises for Hektor's corpse is told from the agent's side (on ἀεικέα ἔργα ('shameful treatment') in 395, see p. 51). Yet the narrative is infused with pathos, and subtly coloured by the narrator's use of δυςμενέεςςι ('to his enemies'), which is a view from Hektor's side:[76]

> τοῦ δ' ἦν ἑλκομένοιο κονίςαλος, ἀμφὶ δὲ χαῖται
> κυάνεαι πίτναντο, κάρη δ' ἅπαν ἐν κονίηιςι
> κεῖτο πάρος χαρίεν· τότε δὲ Ζεὺς δυςμενέεςςι
> δῶκεν ἀεικίςςαςθαι ἑῆι ἐν πατρίδι γαίηι.

As Hektor was dragged behind, a cloud of dust arose from him, his dark hair streamed out round him, and all that once handsome head was sunk in the dust: but now Zeus had given him to his enemies to defile him in his own native land. (22. 401–4)[77]

So the shift is made to the responses from within the walls of Troy, which last from 405 to 515. First, as Hektor's hair drags in the dust, Hekabe tears her own (405 f.). But her dirge is delayed until after the longer lamentation of Priam, thus repeating the pattern of their earlier pleas while Hektor was still alive. I can do no better than refer to the fine account of Macleod (p. 22) on the

then follow, i.e. 395 ff. is a *non sequitur* after 391–4.
The lines cannot be removed leaving no trace whatsoever, since Hermes tells Priam:

> "ςὺν δ' ἕλκεα πάντα μέμυκεν,
> ὅςς' ἐτύπη · πολέες γὰρ ἐν αὐτῶι χαλκὸν ἔλαςςαν."

'All the wounds have closed where he was struck—there were many who drove their bronze into him.' (24. 420–1)

On the other hand 24. 18–21 seem to be inconsistent with this passage:

> τοῖο δ' Ἀπόλλων
> πᾶςαν ἀεικείην ἄπεχε χροῒ φῶτ' ἐλεαίρων
> καὶ τεθνηότα περ · περὶ δ' αἰγίδι πάντα κάλυπτε
> χρυςείηι, ἵνα μή μιν ἀποδρύφοι ἑλκυςτάζων.

But Apollo pitied the man even in his death, and kept all disfigurement away from his flesh. He covered him over in the golden aegis, so that Achilleus' dragging of him should not tear his skin. (24. 18–21)

[76] Cf. de Jong 138, 144.
[77] Dr E. Hall points out that Hektor is the only mortal in the *Iliad* to have dark hair, something he shares with Hades, Poseidon, and Boreas in the form of a stallion (20. 224). She suggests that Hektor's hair is, in effect, dark in death.

ways in which Priam's speech in 416–28, here apparently suicidal, foreshadows his eventual journey, when he will indeed move *aidōs* and *eleos* by appealing to his similarity to Peleus. Andromache was not on the walls before or during Hektor's last battle, though she was alluded to at 22. 88. By keeping her in the enclosure of her house—as though in obedience to Hektor's instruction in 6 (see p. 126)—Homer is able to delay and then spotlight the moment when she learns the truth. The pathetic irony of her instruction about the tripod (442f.) is that not only will Hektor not enjoy his homecoming bath, but she will not even be able to wash his corpse. Her first response and the opening of her lament are strongly related to the scene in book 6, as discussed on pp. 126–7 above.

The way that Andromache turns finally to clothing and to fire is unpredictable and effective. The fine woven works of the women of Troy have already been associated with Hektor's death by the washing-troughs—see p. 237. He will not wear them again, nor, Andromache assumes, will he even be shrouded in them in death. Her burning of Hektor's clothes will be a symbolic pre-enactment, not so much of his funeral pyre, as of the burning of Troy as a whole. This significance grows out of a series of premonitions.[78] First there was the burning of Skamandros—see pp. 228–9 above. Then Priam's vivid vision at 22. 54–76—the direct future of 22. 61 is more like a prophecy than an apprehension—closely associates the event (though flames are not evoked) with the death of Hektor: if he falls, Troy falls with him. The death of Hektor and the burning of Troy are eventually brought together in an extraordinary way:

> ὤιμωξεν δ' ἐλεεινὰ πατὴρ φίλος, ἀμφὶ δὲ λαοὶ
> κωκυτῶι τ' εἴχοντο καὶ οἰμωγῆι κατὰ ἄστυ.
> τῶι δὲ μάλιστ' ἄρ' ἔην ἐναλίγκιον, ὡς εἰ ἅπαca
> Ἴλιος ὀφρυόεccα πυρὶ cμύχοιτο κατ' ἄκρηc.

And his dear father groaned pitiably, and around them and all through the city the people were overcome with wailing and groans of lamentation. It was just like it would be if all of beetling Ilios were fired and smouldering from top to bottom. (22. 408–11)

---

[78] On the death of Hektor and the sack of Troy, see, among others, Schadewaldt, *IS* 156–7; Schein, 24. There have, of course, been premonitions of the sack before the sequence elaborated here. See 2. 323 ff.; 4. 163–5 = 6. 447–9; 7. 30; 15. 70, 212 ff.; 16. 707, 18. 363. On Andromache's lament, see Petersmann, 10–16.

This emphasized similarity[79] comes very close to saying that by killing Hektor, Achilleus has in effect burned Troy. The poet could hardly be more explicit without ceasing to be a poet and becoming his own commentator. After this the future of Hektor's clothes, not in the washing-troughs but in the flames, takes its place.

As the day which began at 19. 1 draws to a close, the scene moves finally to the military world of the Achaian camp for scenes of masculine mourning (23. 12 ff.) and the chieftains' feast (28 ff., 55 ff.). In the closing scenes of book 22 the Trojans are deprived of the body of their champion. The opening scenes of book 23 locate him as a hated presence in the camp of Achilleus: he is cast face down in the dirt by the bier of Patroklos.

---

[79] μάλιστ' ἄρα . . .ἐναλίγκιον . . . is not really conveyed by 'just like'.

9

Closing Cadences

9.1 Contest without death

στῆ δ' ὀρθὸς καὶ μῦθον ἐν Ἀργείοισιν ἔειπεν·
"Ἀτρεΐδη τε καὶ ἄλλοι ἐϋκνήμιδες Ἀχαιοί,
ἱππῆας τάδ' ἄεθλα δεδεγμένα κεῖτ' ἐν ἀγῶνι.
εἰ μὲν νῦν ἐπὶ ἄλλωι ἀεθλεύοιμεν Ἀχαιοί,
ἦ τ' ἂν ἐγὼ τὰ πρῶτα λαβὼν κλισίηνδε φεροίμην.   275
ἴστε γὰρ ὅσσον ἐμοὶ ἀρετῆι περιβάλλετον ἵπποι·
ἀθάνατοί τε γάρ εἰσι, Ποσειδάων δὲ πόρ' αὐτοὺς
πατρὶ ἐμῶι Πηλῆϊ, ὁ δ' αὖτ' ἐμοὶ ἐγγυάλιξεν.
ἀλλ' ἤτοι μὲν ἐγὼ μενέω καὶ μώνυχες ἵπποι·
τοίου γὰρ κλέος ἐσθλὸν ἀπώλεσαν ἡνιόχοιο,   280
ἠπίου, ὅς σφωϊν μάλα πολλάκις ὑγρὸν ἔλαιον
χαιτάων κατέχευε, λοέσσας ὕδατι λευκῶι.
τὸν τώ γ' ἑσταότες πενθείετον, οὔδεϊ δέ σφι
χαῖται ἐρηρέδαται, τὼ δ' ἕστατον ἀχνυμένω κῆρ.
ἄλλοι δὲ στέλλεσθε κατὰ στρατόν, ὅς τις Ἀχαιῶν   285
ἵπποισίν τε πέποιθε καὶ ἅρμασι κολλητοῖσιν."

Then he stood up and spoke to the Argives: 'Son of Atreus, and you other well-greaved Achaians, these prizes set out in your gathering here are the prizes that await the charioteers. Now if we Achaians were holding these games at any other man's death, I would certainly take first place and carry the prize away to my hut. You know how far my horses excel all others, as they are immortal horses, given by Poseidon to my father Peleus, and he then handed them to me. But I and my strong-footed horses will stay here, out of the race. They have lost their great and glorious charioteer, that gentle man who so often would pour soft olive oil down over their manes after washing them in bright water. So they stand there grieving for him, and their manes trail on the ground—there is sorrow in their hearts, and they will not move. But the rest of you get ready now, any Achaian in the camp who is confident in his horses and strongly-made chariot.' (23. 271–86)

When the day of Hektor's death comes to an end there is still a lot of unfinished business. This is brought out by the lack of any clear indication of sunset, and the rather ragged dispersal of the Achaians to bed for the night at 23. 58 ff. The dream-spirit of Patroklos heralds a sequence of closures: his irrevocable funeral must be delayed no longer. There are interesting correspondences between him and the dream sent by Zeus to Agamemnon five nights earlier.[1] Agamemnon's dream was a prelude to the battles of the *Iliad*: Achilleus' brings it to a close. The earlier dream was false, it introduced a new motivation, and it led towards conflict: the latter is genuine, it urges Achilleus to what he in any case intends (see 49 ff.), and it leads towards settlement rather than strife. It also brings home, however, the irreversibility of death, both through its words (75-9) and through its fugitive insubstantiality (99-101).

The only meeting that Achilleus and Patroklos can look forward to is the joining of their ashes in a single urn. Patroklos' request for this (82 ff.), with its unlaboured assumption of Achilleus' imminent death, is set in train by Achilleus with the same calm certainty. By line 126 he has chosen a place for their barrow; at 140 ff. he cuts the lock that he had been saving for Spercheios and offers it to Patroklos instead;[2] and next day he gives instructions:

> "καὶ τὰ μὲν ἐν χρυσέηι φιάληι καὶ δίπλακι δημῶι
> θείομεν, εἰς ὅ κεν αὐτὸς ἐγὼν Ἀϊδι κεύθωμαι.
> τύμβον δ' οὐ μάλα πολλὸν ἐγὼ πονέεσθαι ἄνωγα,
> ἀλλ' ἐπιεικέα τοῖον· ἔπειτα δὲ καὶ τὸν Ἀχαιοὶ
> εὐρύν θ' ὑψηλόν τε τιθήμεναι, οἵ κεν ἐμεῖο
> δεύτεροι ἐν νήεσσι πολυκλήϊσι λίπησθε."

'And let us put his bones in a golden jar with a double fold of fat, until I myself am hidden in Hades. For his tomb I do not want you to build a huge mound, but just one that is fitting. Then afterwards the Achaians can make it broad and high, those of you who are left in the many-benched ships after my time.' (23. 243-8)

The slaughter of the twelve Trojan youths on the pyre (the last deaths of the *Iliad*) verges on the perfunctory after the preparation of 18. 336-7, 21. 26-7, 23. 22-3—two lines of narrative (175-6)

---

[1] 23. 68-9 partly = 2. 20, 23. On the dreams see esp. Segal, 51 f.; Macleod, 28-9.

[2] In the language of Aischylos, *Cho.* 6-7, this lock is both θρεπτήριος (in return for nurture) and πενθητήριος (in token of mourning).

without any detail or colouring. Attention is given, rather, to the summoning of the winds, and to the violence of their gusts and of the flames they fan.[3] This accompanies a change in Achilleus' state of mind, towards a kind of burnt-out exhaustion which renders him more sociable.

It is one of the main poetic functions of the funeral games to show Achilleus soothing and resolving public strife, instead of provoking and furthering it. The anger and competitive quarrelling during the games is reminiscent of the early scenes of the *Iliad*; but it never reaches a really ugly or damaging pitch, largely thanks to the courtesy of Achilleus.[4] The first instance (450 ff.) is the dispute over the progress of the chariot race which arises between Idomeneus and the lesser Aias (who is in the wrong and who gets his come-uppance later, at 773 ff.). Achilleus calms them—see further below. It is crucial that, while there is danger and excitement, there is no death and no damage worse than broken bones, or being laughed at.

This huge, bright, public, male set-piece also functions as an opportunity for each of the major Achaians to make some sort of 'curtain call', several of them with nice individualizing touches.[5] All of the Achaians of the 'first division' participate, and all of the second, except for Thoas and Eurypylos.[6] Even those who are too old to compete are given their 'bow'. They are Idomeneus (perhaps also 'represented' by his *hetairos* Meriones?), Phoinix, who is a special umpire (359–61), and, above all, Nestor, who gives prolix advice to his son before the chariot-race (306 ff.) and reminisces afterwards (626 ff.), when Achilleus pays him special respect.

In terms of the internal poetic anthropology, games are held to bring honour to the dead man and by association to the 'sponsor' of the games. The prizes also, of course, carry *tīmē* for the winners. So Nestor recalls the games held for Amarynkeus by his sons (23. 630 ff.), and the ghost of Agamemnon recalls at *Od.* 24. 85 ff.

---

[3] Whether or not this is indebted to an *Aithiopis* model—see Kakridis, *H. Res.* 75 ff.; cf. L. Coventry, *JHS* 107 (1987), 178.

[4] See esp. Macleod, 30 and 32, n. 1.

[5] On the funeral games in general, see Stawell, 89 ff.; Willcock, 'Games'; Redfield, *NCI* 204–10; Macleod, 29–32; J. R. Dunkle, *Prometheus*, 7 (1981), 11–18; A. Schnapp-Gourbeillon in G. Gnoli and J.-P. Vernant (edd.), *La Mort, les morts dans les sociétés anciennes* (Cambridge and Paris, 1982), 77–88; Bannert, 129–51.

[6] Eurypylos was wounded in book 11; but so were Diomedes and Odysseus and yet they are back on top form.

the wonderful prizes that Thetis supplied for the funeral of Achilleus himself:

"ὣς cὺ μὲν οὐδὲ θανὼν ὄνομ' ὤλεcαc. ἀλλά τοι αἰεὶ
πάντας ἐπ' ἀνθρώπους κλέος ἔςςεται ἐςθλόν, Ἀχιλλεῦ."

'And thus not even in death have you lost your name, but for all time among all mankind the fame of you will be great, Achilleus.' (*Od.* 24. 93–4, tr. Shewring)

In this case we know that the anthropology of real life tallied to some extent, since Hesiod (*WD* 651–9) immortalized the name of Amphidamas of Chalkis through the funeral games held by his sons—he himself won a tripod for poetry. Hesiod does not say if there were prizes for the other competitors, but in the Homeric anthropology it is of the essence that there is a prize for every competitor. When Achilleus gives Nestor the jar left over from the chariot-race, he explicitly says:

"τῆ νῦν, καὶ coὶ τοῦτο, γέρον, κειμήλιον ἔςτω,
Πατρόκλοιο τάφου μνῆμ' ἔμμεναι· οὐ γὰρ ἔτ' αὐτὸν
ὄψηι ἐν Ἀργείοιcι· δίδωμι δέ τοι τόδ' ἄεθλον
αὔτωc."

'Here now, old man, here is a treasure for you too to keep, as a memory of the burial of Patroklos, as you will never see him again among the Argives. I give you this prize simply as a gift.' (23. 618–21)

Nestor eventually concludes his reply:

"ἀλλ' ἴθι καὶ cὸν ἑταῖρον ἀέθλοιcι κτερέϊζε.
τοῦτο δ' ἐγὼ πρόφρων δέχομαι, χαίρει δέ μοι ἦτορ,
ὥc μευ ἀεὶ μέμνηcαι ἐνηέος, οὐδέ cε λήθω
τιμῆc ἧc τέ μ' ἔοικε τετιμῆcθαι μετ' Ἀχαιοῖc.
coὶ δὲ θεοὶ τῶνδ' ἀντὶ χάριν μενοεικέα δοῖεν."

'Well, you must go now and see to the games in honour of your own friend's burial. I gladly accept this gift, and my heart is happy that you always remember me as your kind friend, and you do not forget the honour that I should rightly be paid among the Achaians. May the gods give you your heart's desire in recompense for this.' (23. 646–50)[7]

[7] I am not altogether happy with this transmitted text. (1) It is Nestor who should be remembering Patroklos in future. (2) Patroklos is elsewhere the sole recipient of the epithet ἐνηής ('kind'); see p. 192. This leads me to propose the emendation of 648 to ὥc εὖ ἀεὶ μεμνήcομ' ἐνηέος ('but I shall always remember him, the kind one'). The reference of εὖ ('him') would be clear after 646; and for μεμνήcομ(αι) ('I shall remember') see 22. 390. The trouble is that with the present tenses χαίρει ('is happy') before and λήθω ('forget') after, the future makes an

Since he is the supplier of the prizes it would not be right for Achilleus to compete himself. He does not lose the opportunity, however, to remind everyone politely that his horses are the best (274 ff.)[8] He goes on to recall Patroklos' skill as a charioteer. The audience were witnesses of the grief of the immortal horses for his loss (17. 426 ff., see pp. 189–90). Achilleus was not, but his words recall the scene (23. 283–4, 417, 436–40). Like humans, these horses defile their hair as a token of grief.

The great chariot-race takes up 390 of 630 lines devoted to the games. It is excitingly narrated in its own right, but it also raises ethical issues, especially its tensest incident, when Antilochos and Menelaos narrowly avoid collision.[9] As a result Antilochos comes in second. When Achilleus proposes that Eumelos should have second prize nonetheless (see p. 257 below), all the Achaians approve except Antilochos (539 ff.). This echo of Agamemnon and Chryses becomes even clearer when he asserts "*τὴν δ' ἐγὼ οὐ δώσω*" ('but I will not give up the mare') (552) just as Agamemnon had insisted "*τὴν δ' ἐγὼ οὐ λύσω*" ('but I will not release the woman') (1. 29). More *eris* threatens. The solution of this impasse is only achieved by means of magnanimity from Achilleus. It is Antilochos himself who rather 'cheekily' proposes an extra prize (548 ff.):

> Ὣς φάτο, μείδηϲεν δὲ ποδάρκηϲ δῖοϲ Ἀχιλλεὺϲ
> χαίρων Ἀντιλόχωι, ὅτι οἱ φίλοϲ ἦεν ἑταῖροϲ·

So he spoke, and swift-footed godlike Achilleus smiled in delight at Antilochos, as he was a dear friend . . . (23. 555–6)

---

awkward sequence. This would be somewhat relieved by putting a heavier stop after *ἐνηέοϲ* ('the kind one'), and a lighter one between 649 and 650 ('and as you do not forget . . .may the gods . . .'). This construction is perhaps no more awkward than the transmitted text. Another alternative would be to put a full stop after *οὐδέ ϲε λήθω* ('and you do not forget me'), cf. 1. 561, then taking line 649 to be interpolated (or supposing a line missing between 648 and 649).

⁸ This truth was slipped in at 2. 770, where Eumelos' horses were already marked out as second-best (2. 763–7)—but that was before Diomedes captured the horses of Aineias (see p. 109).

⁹ There is a technical discussion of just what did happen during the race by M. Gagarin, *CPh* 78 (1983), 35–9. Those who put trust in Finley (*'The World of Odysseus'*) might care to compare his account of Diomedes' victory in the race on p. 119 with the Greek of 23. 507–13; and to ask what this implies about the relationship between the worlds of Finley and of Homer.

This is, in fact, the first time in the poem that Achilleus has smiled (Odysseus smiles at a comparably late stage at *Od.* 22. 371). This reconciliation through generosity is a far cry from book 1. Next, however, there is Menelaos' complaint against Antilochos. The narrative of the race at 417–47 skilfully sets up a genuine matter of dispute over whether Antilochos' tactics were fair. The incident exploits the way that both have been clearly and affectionately characterized in the poem.[10] Antilochos is quick and bright and goes for a tactic which would have been suicidal were he not certain of the caution of Menelaos (note ἑκών ('deliberately') at 434). The two have collaborated before, and Menelaos is angry precisely because Antilochos has taken advantage of his familiarity to reject his example of good sense (426, 440, 570). Macleod (30–1) has shown how the ugly quarrel which rears its head again resembles the quarrel of book 1. Yet the two settle it between themselves through sensitivity, generosity, and wit. Antilochos admits that his young μῆτιc is λεπτή (his judgement is flimsy)— yet it was just such *mētis* which was counselled by Nestor (306 ff.) and which gave him the lead! He gives Menelaos the prize horse, while still deftly claiming that he actually won it: "ἵππον δέ τοι αὐτὸc δώcω, τὴν ἀρόμην" ('I shall give up of my own accord the mare that I won') (591–2). Menelaos then makes the generous gesture of giving it back:

> "τῶ τοι λιccομένωι ἐπιπείcομαι, ἠδὲ καὶ ἵππον
> δώcω ἐμήν περ ἐοῦcαν, ἵνα γνώωcι καὶ οἵδε
> ὡc ἐμὸc οὔ ποτε θυμὸc ὑπερφίαλοc καὶ ἀπηνήc."

'So I shall be swayed by your appeal, and I shall even give you the mare, mine though she is, so that all our friends here can see that my heart is never stubborn or unyielding.' (23. 609–11)

His delight at the reconciliation is 'smiled on' by the narrator with a vocative and a particularly beautiful simile:

> τοῖο δὲ θυμὸc
> ἰάνθη ὡc εἴ τε περὶ cταχύεccιν ἐέρcη
> ληΐου ἀλδήcκοντοc, ὅτε φρίccουcιν ἄρουραι·
> ὡc ἄρα cοί, Μενέλαε, μετὰ φρεcὶ θυμὸc ἰάνθη.

---

[10] Cf. Reinhardt, *ID* 355–8; Willcock, 'Games', 'Antilochus', 6–8. Antilochos will display further charm when he comes last in the footrace; and will again win special favour from Achilleus (785–97).

And his heart was melted like the dew on the ears of growing corn, when the fields are bristling with the crop—so your heart, Menelaos, was melted within you. (23. 597–600)[11]

The fortunes of Eumelos in the race, which receive what might seem a surprising amount of attention, may supply a kind of miniature 'allegory' within the narrative—see p. 87 above for this notion. His fate has, I suggest, analogies with that of Troy. He is favoured by Apollo in contest with Diomedes, who is favoured by Athene; she ensures his downfall and he loses disastrously. Rather as the audience of the *Iliad* pities Troy, Achilleus pities Eumelos, to the approval of *his* audience, the assembled Achaians. He is given a special prize for his gallant and pitiable defeat: the special prize for Troy is the immortality of poetry.

The remaining contests of the funeral games, as though taking their cue from Achilleus' smile in 555, are infused with humour, a laughter released by the fact that, although the games mimic battle in many ways[12]—and this is reflected in the formulaic diction—life and death are not at stake. This is, then, quite different from the grim or exultant wit of the battlefield. One particularly good joke seems to have been missed, one that would be clear to any audience with an interest in economic calculation.[13] Although there was as yet no coinage, an interest in the calculation of price is scattered through Homer, whether the weighing of gold in talents or half-talents (e.g. 23. 751, 796) or the valuation of objects by equivalent oxen, conveyed by a numeral compounded with -βοιον—as, for example, in 6. 232 ff., in the exchange of armour.

The values of the prizes for wrestling are carefully enumerated:

> τῶι μὲν νικήcαντι μέγαν τρίποδ' ἐμπυριβήτην,
> τὸν δὲ δυωδεκάβοιον ἐνὶ cφίcι τῖον Ἀχαιοί·
> ἀνδρὶ δὲ νικηθέντι γυναῖκ' ἐc μέccον ἔθηκε,
> πολλὰ δ' ἐπίcτατο ἔργα, τίον δέ ἑ τεccαράβοιον.

---

[11] Menelaos is granted no fewer than six fine similes during the *Iliad* (cf. Fenik, *TBS* 161). In 598 ἐέρcη ('the dew') and ἐέρcηι ('with the dew') seem to have been ancient variants to judge from Ap. Rh. 3. 1019 and Aesch. *Agam.* 1390–2. Either way, it seems too simple to regard θυμὸc ἰάνθη as 'figurative' and the implied ἰάνθη in the simile as 'literal', since elsewhere in Homer the verb is more often applied psychologically than physically (only at 10. 359 and 12. 175).

[12] The over-dangerous line 806 should perhaps be athetized.

[13] Cf. Donlan on 'balanced reciprocity' (though he is primarily concerned with other less 'calculated' kinds of economics).

For the winner a great tripod to stand over the fire, which the Achaians
among themselves valued at twelve oxen's worth: and as the prize for the
beaten man he brought a woman into the centre, one skilled in the range
of handcraft, and they valued her at four oxen. (23. 702–5)

But before the struggle between Odysseus and Aias gets too serious, Achilleus intervenes adjudging that both have won—a result
fundamentally alien to the battlefield (the umpired duel of Hektor
and Aias in 7 is the exception that proves the rule):

> "μηκέτ' ἐρείδεςθον, μηδὲ τρίβεςθε κακοῖςι·
> νίκη δ' ἀμφοτέροιςιν· ἀέθλια δ' ἴς' ἀνελόντες
> ἔρχεςθ', ὄφρα καὶ ἄλλοι ἀεθλεύωςιν Ἀχαιοί."
> Ὣς ἔφαθ', οἱ δ' ἄρα τοῦ μάλα μὲν κλύον ἠδὲ πίθοντο,
> καί ῥ' ἀπομορξαμένω κονίην δύςαντο χιτῶνας.

'No more struggling now—do not wear yourselves out with the pain of
it. You have both won. Share the prizes, then, and go on your way, so
that some other Achaians can enter the games.'
  So he spoke, and they listened well and agreed. They brushed off the
dust then and put on their tunics. (23. 735–9)

An audience interested in such things will remember that, while
the value of the prizes in oxen was easily divisible by two, neither
would be much good if split, however equally. In the general
atmosphere of goodwill and generosity the distribution can be left
unresolved.
  The same spirit just about carries through the potentially
difficult participation of Agamemnon. He lets Menelaos have use
of his mare Aithe (295), but otherwise takes no part at all until
889 ff., when he rises to the challenge of the spear-throwing against
Meriones (who with a touch of comedy has entered several competitions). Achilleus seizes the opportunity for diplomacy:

> "Ἀτρεΐδη· ἴδμεν γὰρ ὅςον προβέβηκας ἁπάντων
> ἠδ' ὅςςον δυνάμει τε καὶ ἥμαςιν ἔπλευ ἄριςτος·
> ἀλλὰ ςὺ μὲν τόδ' ἄεθλον ἔχων κοίλας ἐπὶ νῆας
> ἔρχευ, ἀτὰρ δόρυ Μηριόνηι ἥρωϊ πόρωμεν,
> εἰ ςύ γε ςῶι θυμῶι ἐθέλοις· κέλομαι γὰρ ἔγωγε."
> Ὣς ἔφατ', οὐδ' ἀπίθηςεν ἄναξ ἀνδρῶν Ἀγαμέμνων·

'Son of Atreus, we know how superior you are to all others, and how
much you are the best in strength for the spear-throw. So you take this
prize with you on your way to the hollow ships, and let us give the spear

to the hero Meriones, if that might be the wish of your own heart—that is what I suggest.'
So he spoke, and Agamemnon, lord of men, did not fail to agree. (23. 890–5)[14]

Everyone is content. But it is a rather late and lowly 'curtain call' for Agamemnon. His prize is worth only one ox (886), and he makes no kind of direct response. His oath on the return of Briseïs in 19 remains his last speech in the *Iliad* (cf. p. 209). Several of the prizes have a history, and some carry a special significance for the audience because of their particular connections within the poem. The armour which Patroklos took from Sarpedon (800), for instance, is a reminder of his finest hour. Achilleus offers two items of armour from one of his bravest victims on his great day of slaughter (the armour taken from Hektor was, of course, his own): the corslet of Asteropaios (560–2) and his sword (808–9). The silver mixing-bowl offered at 740 ff. draws on the unhappy life-story of Lykaon, with details of his capture and sale all consistent with those in book 21—see p. 222. These reminders of Achilleus at his most relentless bring out this newly regained sociability.

One prize towards the end has a special relevance to the issues of the poem, even though it was acquired before the *Iliad* began (so to speak):

Αὐτὰρ Πηλεΐδης θῆκεν cόλον αὐτοχόωνον,
ὃν πρὶν μὲν ῥίπταcκε μέγα cθένος Ἠετίωνος·
ἀλλ' ἤτοι τὸν πέφνε ποδάρκης δῖος Ἀχιλλεύς,
τὸν δ' ἄγετ' ἐν νήεccι cὺν ἄλλοιcι κτεάτεccι.

Now the son of Peleus set down a lump of pig-iron, which before then had been used as his discus by the mighty Eëtion: but swift-footed godlike Achilleus had killed him, and carried off the iron in his ships together with Eëtion's other possessions. (23. 826–9)

As seen on p. 126 the fate of Thebe and Eëtion becomes a kind of precedent and double for that of Troy and Priam. After Andromache's lament at 22. 477 ff. this prize has the effect, I suggest, of bringing to mind at some deep level of consciousness the body of Hektor, which still lies naked in the dust at Achilleus' *klisiē*.[15]

---

[14] To be ἄριcτοc (best) at spear-throwing, like Epeios for example at boxing (669), is not by any means to be absolutely ἄριcτοc.
[15] Cf. Taplin, *Chios* 18–19.

The point made is that, while Achilleus has achieved a public reintegration, he has yet to find any equivalent private peace of mind. He has yet to grow out of the savagery he expressed to the dying Hektor.

This double level to Achilleus' reintegration, which I have loosely called 'public' and 'private', is made very clear as soon as the Achaians disperse for the last time in the poem (24. 1 ff.). Although he has made his peace within the world of his fellow warriors, Achilleus is still far from finding peace of mind. The series of frequentative imperfects at 24. 12 ff. brings out the repetitiveness of his actions, and by implication the lack of satisfaction he derives from them.

9.2 Priam's resolution

εὖρον δ' εὐρύοπα Κρονίδην, περὶ δ' ἄλλοι ἅπαντες
ἥαθ' ὁμηγερέες μάκαρες θεοὶ αἰὲν ἐόντες.
ἡ δ' ἄρα πὰρ Διὶ πατρὶ καθέζετο, εἶξε δ' Ἀθήνη.   100
Ἥρη δὲ χρύσεον καλὸν δέπας ἐν χερὶ θῆκε
καί ῥ' εὔφρην' ἐπέεσσι· Θέτις δ' ὥρεξε πιοῦσα.
τοῖσι δὲ μύθων ἦρχε πατὴρ ἀνδρῶν τε θεῶν τε·
"ἤλυθες Οὔλυμπόνδε, θεὰ Θέτι, κηδομένη περ,
πένθος ἄλαστον ἔχουσα μετὰ φρεσίν· οἶδα καὶ αὐτός·   105
ἀλλὰ καὶ ὣς ἐρέω τοῦ σ' εἵνεκα δεῦρο κάλεσσα.
ἐννῆμαρ δὴ νεῖκος ἐν ἀθανάτοισιν ὄρωρεν
Ἕκτορος ἀμφὶ νέκυι καὶ Ἀχιλλῆϊ πτολιπόρθωι·
κλέψαι δ' ὀτρύνουσιν ἐύσκοπον Ἀργειφόντην·
αὐτὰρ ἐγὼ τόδε κῦδος Ἀχιλλῆϊ προτιάπτω,   110
αἰδῶ καὶ φιλότητα τεὴν μετόπισθε φυλάσσων.
αἶψα μάλ' ἐς στρατὸν ἐλθὲ καὶ υἱέϊ σῶι ἐπίτειλον·
σκύζεσθαί οἱ εἰπὲ θεούς, ἐμὲ δ' ἔξοχα πάντων
ἀθανάτων κεχολῶσθαι, ὅτι φρεσὶ μαινομένηισιν
Ἕκτορ' ἔχει παρὰ νηυσὶ κορωνίσιν οὐδ' ἀπέλυσεν,   115
αἴ κέν πως ἐμέ τε δείσηι ἀπό θ' Ἕκτορα λύσηι.
αὐτὰρ ἐγὼ Πριάμωι μεγαλήτορι Ἶριν ἐφήσω
λύσασθαι φίλον υἱόν, ἰόντ' ἐπὶ νῆας Ἀχαιῶν,
δῶρα δ' Ἀχιλλῆϊ φερέμεν, τά κε θυμὸν ἰήνηι."

There they found the wide-seeing son of Kronos, and all the other blessed gods sitting gathered round him. Thetis sat down beside father Zeus, and Athene made way for her. Hera put a lovely golden cup in her hand and spoke kind words of welcome: and Thetis drank and handed back the cup. Then the father of men and gods began to speak: 'You have come to Olympos, divine Thetis, for all your grief, and you have lasting sorrow in your heart—I know this. But even so I shall tell you why I have called you here. For nine days now there has been argument among the immortals over Achilleus, sacker of cities, and the body of Hektor—and they are urging Hermes the sharp-sighted, the slayer of Argos, to steal the body. But here is a means of glory I can grant to Achilleus, and preserve your respect and love for the future. You can go quickly to the camp and give this message to your son. Tell him the gods are enraged at him, and my own anger is the greatest among all the immortals, because in the madness of his heart he is keeping Hektor by the beaked ships and has not released him. He may then give Hektor back in fear of me. And I shall send Iris to great-hearted Priam, telling him to go to the ships of the Achaians and ransom his dear son, bringing gifts to Achilleus which will soften his heart.' (24. 98–119)

The narrative does not hurry into the great meeting of Priam and Achilleus. The idea was first proposed at 24. 75–6 (quoted below), yet it is not until 471–2 that the great moment is reached: γέρων δ' ἰθὺς κίεν οἴκου τῆι ῥ' Ἀχιλεὺς ἵζεσκε (and the old man went straight for the house, where Achilleus was sitting). In the meantime Achilleus must be made ready; and, more fully, Priam's state of mind has to be fully established. Without all this preparation the actual scene could not have its swiftness and power.

Their meeting is also given a divine level of motivation in the last Olympian scenes of the poem (24. 23–120 with 143–59). First there is a reminder of the doom of Troy through the poem's one and only direct allusion to the story of Paris before he set off for Sparta with Aphrodite's favour. Hera and Athene

ἔχον ὥς σφιν πρῶτον ἀπήχθετο Ἴλιος ἱρὴ
καὶ Πρίαμος καὶ λαὸς Ἀλεξάνδρου ἔνεκ' ἄτης,
ὃς νείκεσσε θεάς, ὅτε οἱ μέσσαυλον ἵκοντο,
τὴν δ' ἤινησ' ἥ οἱ πόρε μαχλοσύνην ἀλεγεινήν.

persisted in the hatred they had from the beginning for sacred Ilios and Priam and his people, because of the blind folly of Alexandros, who had scorned the goddesses when they came to his sheepfold, and gave his choice for the one who offered him dangerous lust. (24. 27–30)

As Reinhardt showed, the judgement of Paris is taken for granted at an unspoken level throughout the poem, but all allusion to it is avoided, as that would be intrusive and dissatisfying—origins make very incomplete explanations.[16] There may be a suggestion in these lines that the heightened sexuality which Paris won from Aphrodite—μαχλοσύνη (dangerous lust)—is the charm that keeps him safely tolerated at Troy. Is μαχλοσύνη the sweet infection that the Trojans cannot bring themselves to purge? Whether or not this is an over-moralistic interpretation, the allusion sets a dark background to all that follows: not only Hektor but also Priam, and his city will all, before long, come to destruction.

Hera does little more in 56 ff. than calculate men's *tīmē* by their affinity-quotient to the gods. The poetry of Apollo's speech at 33 ff., on the other hand, makes powerful connections with the ethics of the whole poem, and speaks to the human audience. Apollo appeals to the pathos of Hektor's family, and complains of Achilleus in terms that recall Phoinix and Aias in the Embassy. He also taps the cumulative potency of the combination of *aidōs* and *eleos* (44—see p. 223), and insists on the essential humanity of endurance, the 'message' which Priam and Achilleus are going to live out in archetype:[17] τλητὸν γὰρ Μοῖραι θυμὸν θέσαν ἀνθρώποισιν (since the Fates have put an enduring heart in humankind) (49). Without this insight Greek Tragedy would never have happened. The question that Apollo is setting before the gods is far larger than the particular case of Hektor: 'are they to uphold human civilisation, or let it be flouted?'[18] At the end it seems that Apollo appeals to a basic order that goes even beyond ethics:

"μὴ ἀγαθῶι περ ἐόντι νεμεσσηθέωμέν οἱ ἡμεῖς·
κωφὴν γὰρ δὴ γαῖαν ἀεικίζει μενεαίνων."

'Great man though he is, he should be wary of our anger—he is dishonouring the dumb earth now in his fury'. (24. 53–4)

If κωφὴν γαῖαν ('the dumb earth') refers not only to the physical corpse of Hektor but to the natural order, then this implies that 'dumb' nature needs the gods to stand up for her.

In the case of Sarpedon it was Hera who proposed the compromise that his body should be supernaturally buried (16. 450ff.). In book 24 Zeus' compromise is masterly: he manages to satisfy

---

[16] See Reinhardt, 'PU'. There are good further observations by T. C. W. Stinton in *Collected Papers on Greek Tragedy* (Oxford, 1990), 17 ff. (first publ. in 1965).

[17] This 'message' is also conveyed in the *Odyssey* by the man of enduring heart *par excellence*; see e.g. *Od.* 18. 125 ff., esp. 134–5; cf. Nisbet–Hubbard on Horace, *Odes* 1. 24. 19.

[18] Macleod, 90; cf. L. Coventry, *JHS* 107 (1987), 177–80.

Apollo's pressing claims, while still conceding to Hera that Achilleus' *tīmē* should be superior:

> "ἀλλ' εἴ τις καλέσειε θεῶν Θέτιν ἆσσον ἐμεῖο,
> ὄφρα τί οἱ εἴπω πυκινὸν ἔπος, ὥς κεν Ἀχιλλεὺς
> δώρων ἐκ Πριάμοιο λάχῃ ἀπό θ' Ἕκτορα λύσῃ."

'But would one of the gods call Thetis to come here before me, so that I can put a sound plan to her, to see that Achilleus wins gifts from Priam and releases the body of Hektor.' (24. 74–6)

So he will be offered gifts *and* he will have the opportunity to release the body of his own volition, rather than having it merely removed. Zeus finds a way to involve the mortals without divine deceit. It is also Zeus' initiative to involve Thetis as his intermediary. In this way the goddess whose uninvited visit began the suffering of the *Iliad* will now act as an emissary for resolution.

In book 1 Thetis came alone to Olympos, on her son's initiative, to find Zeus by himself; he feared that their agreement would arouse dissent on Olympos, especially from Hera; and this proved all too true. The dawn of 24. 31 (= 1. 493) introduces this balancing and contrasting scene. Though she wears her black veil even on Olympos, to emphasize her close relationship with mortality, Thetis arrives this time by divine summons, to find all the gods together with Zeus, and to be met with courtesy even from Hera. In contrast to his reluctance in book 1, Zeus is now able—while warning of his anger—to favour Thetis by offering additional κῦδος, *kūdos* (glory) to her son (110). The application of the word κῦδος to divine attention and to material gifts does not conform to the standard sense of the word as used of the popularity of the battle-hero:[19] instead the opportunity offered for behaving magnanimously and memorably is apparently a kind of redefinition. It is important that it is not a foregone conclusion that Achilleus will take his opportunity—they will see (αἴ κέν πως . . . (he may then . . .)).

The conveyance of Zeus' message to Achilleus is kept brief (122–42). In her last meeting with her son in the poem Thetis expresses motherly care before she gives the message:

> "τέκνον ἐμόν, τέο μέχρις ὀδυρόμενος καὶ ἀχεύων
> σὴν ἔδεαι κραδίην, μεμνημένος οὔτε τι σίτου

---

[19] Cf. Redfield, *NCI* 33–4.

οὔτ' εὐνῆς; ἀγαθὸν δὲ γυναικί περ ἐν φιλότητι
μίςγεςθ'· οὐ γάρ μοι δηρὸν βέηι, ἀλλά τοι ἤδη
ἄγχι παρέςτηκεν θάνατος καὶ μοῖρα κραταιή.''

'My child, how long will you eat out your heart in sorrow and mourning, with no thought for either food or bed? It is a good thing to join with a woman in love—as I shall not see you live long now, but already death and strong fate are standing close beside you.' (24. 128–32)[20]

This is important foreshadowing for the Achilleus–Priam scene— see §§ **9.3**, **9.4** below. At this stage, however, Achilleus makes no response. Even his agreement to Zeus' proposal is as terse as it could be:

"τῆιδ' εἴη· ὃς ἄποινα φέροι καὶ νεκρὸν ἄγοιτο,
εἰ δὴ πρόφρονι θυμῶι 'Ολύμπιος αὐτὸς ἀνώγει.''

'So be it. The man who brings the ransom can take the body, if the Olympian himself in all earnest wishes it.' (24. 139–40)

Note that Thetis does not pass on Zeus' nomination of Priam as bringer of the ransom, so that this is kept as a surprise for Achilleus, and the real emotional and personal significance of his laconic agreement is saved up. Zeus has laid down *what* will happen: all the interest and uncertainty lies in *how* the humans will achieve it.

Zeus' message to Priam includes clear assurances of his safety (152, 157–8 = 181, 186–7). But all the apprehension which surrounds his departure from Troy should not be seen as impiety or stupidity. It is none the less convincing that the quest should be experienced as desperate and dangerous by the human agents. For one thing Zeus can be deceptive—and there are indeed echoes of the deceptive dream he sent to Agamemnon.[21] Priam is determined to go *even if* the gods are misleading him about his personal safety:

"εἰ δέ μοι αἶca
τεθνάμεναι παρὰ νηυcὶν Ἀχαιῶν χαλκοχιτώνων,
βούλομαι·''

'If it is my fate to die beside the ships of the bronze-clad Achaians, then I welcome it.' (24. 224–6)

---

[20] 131–2 are close to 16. 852–3 (quoted on p. 179), when Patroklos warned Hektor of his imminent death.
[21] 24. 173–4 partly = 2. 26–7—see further Macleod, 33.

Zeus may say of Achilleus

"οὔτε γάρ ἐcτ' ἄφρων οὔτ' ἄcκοποc οὔτ' ἀλιτήμων,
ἀλλὰ μάλ' ἐνδυκέωc ἱκέτεω πεφιδήcεται ἀνδρόc."

'he is not foolish or blind or godless, but will show a suppliant all kindness
and spare him.' (24. 157–8)

but the fact remains that the last time that Priam and Hekabe saw
him he was dragging Hektor's body. On the human evidence,
Hekabe's fears (which were fully justified for Hektor at 22. 79 ff.)
are all too likely to be right:

"εἰ γάρ c' αἱρήcει καὶ ἐcόψεται ὀφθαλμοῖcιν,
ὠμηcτὴc καὶ ἄπιcτοc ἀνὴρ ὅ γε, οὔ c' ἐλεήcει,
οὐδέ τί c' αἰδέcεται."

'If he gets you in his hands and sets his eyes on you—he is a savage beast
and not to be trusted, he will not show you mercy, he will have no regard
for your claim.' (24. 206–8)

Her epithet ὠμηcτήc (savage) is a reminder of Achilleus' wish that
he could eat Hektor raw (22. 345 ff.);[22] and she goes on to show
the same spirit: "τοῦ ἐγὼ μέcον ἧπαρ ἔχοιμι ἐcθέμεναι προcφῦcα" ('I
wish I could sink my teeth in that man's very liver and eat it!')
(212–13). This is the same inhuman vindictiveness that Achilleus
has yet to renounce. Priam's bravery is the one thing that could
bring that about.

The extraordinary courage of Priam's enterprise is brought out
by the protraction of his departure from 188 to 329. This includes
the libation and prayer to Zeus (283 ff.), a procedure found elsewhere only at Patroklos' departure, where Zeus refused the prayer
for his safe return.[23] Despite Priam's favourable omen,

φίλοι δ' ἅμα πάντεc ἕποντο
πόλλ' ὀλοφυρόμενοι ὡc εἰ θάνατόνδε κιόντα.

all his family went with him in constant lamentation, as if he was going
to his death. (24. 327–8)

---

[22] Cf. Segal, 61.
[23] 24. 306–7 partly = 16. 231–2; see further Macleod on 283–320. For θάνατόνδε
('to death') in 328 cf. 16. 693, 22. 297, and p. 242 above. I am grateful to R. B.
Rutherford for pointing out to me how this contrasts with a certain feebleness
earlier in the poem, especially his queasiness in book 3 (303 ff.), his compliance in
the debate at 7. 365 ff., and even his pleading at the start of 22. Priam's first grief
at 22. 412 ff. marks a transition—see Macleod, 21–2.

To them Priam's case seems as dire as Hektor's did to his dear ones who lamented for him at 6. 500 (cf. pp. 124–5): but he will in fact reaffirm life and return safely to Troy the next day. Even so, those with a sharp ear for a tragic cadence might detect a reference to Priam's eventual slaughter at the hands of the son of Achilleus. He makes his prayer as he stands at the altar of Zeus μέcωι ἕρκει (in the middle of the yard) (306): there was a strong tradition that Neoptolemos killed him as he took refuge at the altar of Zeus *Herkeios* (of the yard).[24]

By the time that the two old men stop and water their animals it is dark—δὴ γὰρ καὶ ἐπὶ κνέφας ἤλυθε (by now darkness had come over the earth) (351). This makes the approaching figure of Hermes at 352 ff. all the more alarming. The god builds up a kind of substitute father–son relationship which is easy by comparison with the really difficult one that Priam is about to enter on.[25] Hermes departs just before the encounter, leaving the serious business, so to speak, to the humans. He can get past fortifications and sentries and can open the massive locks of Achilleus' encampment; but it is not so easy for a god to gauge human sensibilities. There is a telling discrepancy between Hermes' closing advice to Priam, and what he actually does:

> "τύνη δ' εἰcελθὼν λαβὲ γούνατα Πηλείωνος,
> καί μιν ὑπὲρ πατρὸc καὶ μητέροc ἠϋκόμοιο
> λίccεο καὶ τέκεοc, ἵνα οἱ cὺν θυμὸν ὀρίνηιc."

'But you should go in and take the son of Peleus by his knees, and appeal to him in the name of his father and lovely-haired mother and his child, so as to move his heart.' (24. 465–7)

Priam, however, senses that it is the old man who must carry the appeal: πατρὸc ('father') is his second word in line 486.

9.3   *Bereavement and endurance*

> Ὣc φάτο, τῶι δ' ἄρα πατρὸc ὑφ' ἵμερον ὦρcε γόοιο·
> ἁψάμενοc δ' ἄρα χειρὸc ἀπώcατο ἦκα γέροντα.

---

[24] This was already in the cyclic *Iliou Persis* (p. 107, l. 31 Allen = p. 88, l. 15 Bernabé = p. 62, l. 20 Davies). For some later allusions see Taplin, *BICS* 34 (1987), 76; add Eur. *Tro.* 17, 483.

[25] Well brought out in Macleod's note on 362. Note the touches of humour in e.g. 371, 377, 430. I am not clear, however, who would feel the indignation of νεμεccητόν ('it would cause anger') in 463, and why, if a god were to be directly

τὼ δὲ μνηcαμένω, ὁ μὲν Ἕκτορο ἀνδροφόνοιο
κλαῖ' ἀδινὰ προπάροιθε ποδῶν Ἀχιλῆο ἐλυcθείc,   510
αὐτὰρ Ἀχιλλεὺ κλαῖεν ἑὸν πατέρ', ἄλλοτε δ' αὖτε
Πάτροκλον· τῶν δὲ cτοναχὴ κατὰ δώματ' ὀρώρει.

αὐτὰρ ἐπεί ῥα γόοιο τετάρπετο δῖο Ἀχιλλεύc,
καί οἱ ἀπὸ πραπίδων ἦλθ' ἵμερο ἠδ' ἀπὸ γυίων,
αὐτίκ' ἀπὸ θρόνου ὦρτο, γέροντα δὲ χειρὸ ἀνίcτη,   515
οἰκτίρων πολιόν τε κάρη πολιόν τε γένειον,
καί μιν φωνήcαc ἔπεα πτερόεντα προcηύδα·
"ἆ δείλ', ἦ δὴ πολλὰ κάκ' ἄνcχεο cὸν κατὰ θυμόν.
πῶc ἔτληc ἐπὶ νῆαc Ἀχαιῶν ἐλθέμεν οἶοc,
ἀνδρὸc ἐc ὀφθαλμοὺc ὅc τοι πολέαc τε καὶ ἐcθλοὺc   520
υἱέαc ἐξενάριξα; cιδήρειόν νύ τοι ἦτορ.
ἀλλ' ἄγε δὴ κατ' ἄρ' ἕζευ ἐπὶ θρόνου, ἄλγεα δ' ἔμπηc
ἐν θυμῶι κατακεῖcθαι ἐάcομεν ἀχνύμενοί περ·
οὐ γάρ τιc πρῆξιc πέλεται κρυεροῖο γόοιο·
ὡc γὰρ ἐπεκλώcαντο θεοὶ δειλοῖcι βροτοῖcι,   525
ζώειν ἀχνυμένοιc· αὐτοὶ δέ τ' ἀκηδέεc εἰcί."

So he spoke, and he roused in Achilleus the desire to weep for his
father. He took the old man by the hand and gently pushed him away.
And the two of them began to weep in remembrance. Priam cried loud
for murderous Hektor, huddled at the feet of Achilleus, and Achilleus
cried for his own father, and then again for Patroklos: and the house was
filled with the sound of their weeping. Then when godlike Achilleus had
had his pleasure in mourning, and the desire for it had passed from his
mind and his body, he stood up from his chair and raised the old man
by his hand, in pity for his grey head and grey beard, and spoke winged
words to him: 'Poor man, you have surely endured many sorrows in your
heart. How could you bear to come alone to the ships of the Achaians,
into the eyes of a man who has killed many of your brave sons? Your
heart must be of iron. But come now, sit down here on a chair, and for
all our sorrow let us leave the pain to lie still in our hearts—no good can
come from chilling tears. This is the fate the gods have spun for poor
mortal men, that we should live in misery, but they themselves have no
sorrows.' (24. 507–26)

After Priam's long preparations and his courteous scene with
Hermes, the narrative suddenly moves with extraordinary swiftness and unpredictability. At the same time powerful associations
with earlier scenes are brought into play, especially the absence
of Patroklos from Achilleus' feasting—see pp. 79–80—and the

entertained by a mortal. Perhaps the other gods would regard it as demeaning;
and it serves at least as a polite excuse for departure.

comparison with Chryses, the old suppliant who comes with
ransom for his child—see pp. 77–8.

τοὺς δ' ἔλαθ' εἰcελθὼν Πρίαμος μέγας, ἄγχι δ' ἄρα cτάς
χερcὶν Ἀχιλλῆος λάβε γούνατα καὶ κύcε χεῖρας
δεινὰς ἀνδροφόνους, αἵ οἱ πολέας κτάνον υἷας.
ὡς δ' ὅτ' ἂν ἄνδρ' ἄτη πυκινὴ λάβηι, ὅς τ' ἐνὶ πάτρηι
φῶτα κατακτείνας ἄλλων ἐξίκετο δῆμον,
ἀνδρὸς ἐς ἀφνειοῦ, θάμβος δ' ἔχει εἰcορόωντας,
ὣς Ἀχιλεὺς θάμβηςεν ἰδὼν Πρίαμον θεοειδέα·
θάμβηςαν δὲ καὶ ἄλλοι, ἐς ἀλλήλους δὲ ἴδοντο.

Huge Priam came in unseen, and moving close to him took Achilleus'
knees in his arms and kissed his hands, those terrible, murderous hands,
which had killed many of his sons. As when a man is held fast by blind
folly—he kills a man in his own country, and then comes to another land,
to a rich man's house, and amazement takes those who see his entry. So
Achilleus was amazed when he saw godlike Priam, and the others too
were amazed, and looked at each other. (24. 477–84)

Astonishment seizes the poem's audience no less than it seizes
Achilleus and his companions, just as it seizes the witnesses within
the simile.[26] The simile arouses strong conflicting responses since,
while it shares the suppliancy with the narrative, there are discrep-
ancies of geography, wealth, and, above all, the relative location
of the killer. According to the usual courtesies, the host should
rise to his feet and speak first, and the guest should eat before
there is any talk of business—the references to Achilleus' recent
meal may be a delicate reminder of this. But here, before there is
time for any reactions except astonishment, Priam speaks.

Priam's concentration on Peleus re-emphasizes what has been
built up as something of an obsession with Achilleus.[27] At 9. 393 ff.
he thinks of Peleus arranging his wedding at home. But that is
the exception; usually it is his failure to return which weighs on
Achilleus' mind, as at 18. 330 ff. and 23. 144 ff., for example. At
19. 321 ff. he laments that even Peleus' death would not have
distressed him as much as Patroklos', yet he still ends with
thoughts of his father:

---

[26] On this simile and the theme of the murderer in exile, see R. M. Schlunk,
AJP 97 (1976), 199 ff., esp. 207–9.

[27] This Iliadic concern may well be directly reflected in the *Nekyia* at *Od.*
11. 473 ff., where the ghost of Achilleus is still worrying about him.

"ἤδη γὰρ Πηληά γ' ὀίομαι ἢ κατὰ πάμπαν
τεθνάμεν, ἤ που τυτθὸν ἔτι ζώοντ' ἀκάχησθαι
γήραΐ τε στυγερῶι καὶ ἐμὴν ποτιδέγμενον αἰεὶ
λυγρὴν ἀγγελίην, ὅτ' ἀποφθιμένοιο πύθηται."

'Because I think Peleus by now will either be dead and utterly gone, or perhaps living on a shadow of life in the pain of hateful old age, and always expecting the terrible news when he will learn that I am dead.'
(19. 334–7)[28]

Priam does not, of course, know of Achilleus' fatal choice of death as the price of revenge on Hektor. So his dwelling on Peleus' expectations of his son's *nostos* is in a sense a terrible *faux pas*:

"ἀλλ' ἤτοι κεῖνός γε σέθεν ζώοντος ἀκούων
χαίρει τ' ἐν θυμῶι, ἐπί τ' ἔλπεται ἤματα πάντα
ὄψεσθαι φίλον υἱὸν ἀπὸ Τροίηθεν ἰόντα."

'But at least he can hear that you are alive, and feel joy in his heart, and look forward every day to seeing his dear son return from Troy.'
(24. 490–2)

It would not be surprising if Achilleus' response were bitterness and anger.

Priam is, however, more aware that he is treading dangerous ground when he shifts his appeal at 493–502 to the extinction of his dynasty of sons. Up till the death of Patroklos, Achilleus had no particular animus against them; but after that he wanted to kill all Trojans περὶ δ' αὖ Πριάμοιό γε παίδων (and above all the sons of Priam), as he put it to Lykaon (21. 105). Priam carefully delays naming Hektor until 501, and in general he puts the emphasis on himself and his fatherhood. It is also significant that he rests no weight on the *apoina* and gives no reckoning of them (though the narrative has enumerated them at 24. 228 ff.). This could hardly be further from Agamemnon, who spent 35 lines on cataloguing his gifts, yet did not think of going himself. Priam ends:

"ἀλλ' αἰδεῖο θεούς, Ἀχιλεῦ, αὐτόν τ' ἐλέησον,
μνησάμενος σοῦ πατρός· ἐγὼ δ' ἐλεεινότερός περ,
ἔτλην δ' οἷ' οὔ πώ τις ἐπιχθόνιος βροτὸς ἄλλος,
ἀνδρὸς παιδοφόνοιο ποτὶ στόμα χεῖρ' ὀρέγεσθαι."

---

[28] This fits with the picture of Peleus conjured up by another old ἱππότα (horseman), Nestor, at 7. 124 ff., when he recalls him as proud but anxious about the expedition to Troy.

'Respect the gods, then, Achilleus, and have pity on me, remembering your own father. But I am yet more pitiable than he. I have endured to do what no other mortal man on earth has done—I have brought to my lips the hands of the man who killed my child.' (24. 503–6)

This, if anything, satisfies the condition that Achilleus missed at 9. 387 (see pp. 72–3): πρίν γ' ἀπὸ πᾶcαν ἐμοὶ δόμεναι θυμαλγέα λώβην (until he pays me the full price for all this wrong that pains my heart). Priam offers himself as a kind of archetype of the human universals of parenthood and of—the great fear of all parents— bereavement. The poignant irony is that, while he believes he is contrasting himself with the happy future of Peleus, he has in fact accentuated their shared lot: both old men will have to live through the death of their greatest hope, their sons.

How will Achilleus respond? Before words there are actions, gestures which are wonderfully expressive of his conflicting sequence of emotions. The initial tableau has Priam kneeling close to Achilleus, who is sitting. With ἀπώcατο ('pushed him away') (508) Achilleus rejects the suppliant who crouches huddled at his feet (510).[29] Yet this is belied by the adverb ἧκα ('gently'). Priam may well expect death, but for the audience there is also reassurance from the grammar in the duals of line 509: the pair of them are united in an unforgettable grouping of grief. Only after the exhaustion of grieving does Achilleus raise Priam to his feet with the gesture which accepts the suppliant (515, cf. Od. 7. 167–9). At this stage his emotions begin to turn outward from his own sorrows to pity for the old man, and pity for those very attributes against which Hektor had to harden his heart: the white hair and beard (516), which Priam foresaw (22. 74) defiled by his dogs.

Instead of refuting Priam's speech, or directly endorsing it, Achilleus sets it in a broader context of the human endurance of suffering. Everyone's troubles seem uniquely terrible to them: yet they are not—and some people are even more abjectly wretched (531–3). The tone of Achilleus' words is not immediately gentle: ἆ δειλέ ('poor man') may be said to victims (as, for example, at

---

[29] With this gesture Menelaos rejected Adrestos at 6. 62—ὁ δ' ἀπὸ ἕθεν ὤcατο (he pushed him away from him)—the moment before Agamemnon slaughtered him. There has been extraordinarily little work on non-verbal communication in Homeric narration. A useful preliminary catalogue has been compiled by D. Lateiner in *Arethusa*, 20 (1987), 108–12, in an appendix to an article on non-verbal communication in Herodotus.

11.452, 11.837), and the three lines 519–21 repeat Hekabe's at
203–5 where she was complaining of Achilleus' savagery (see
above). Only with the courteous imperative of line 522 does the
tone become less harsh, leading into a train of thought (note γάρ
('for') in 524–5) which explains how all men have at least some
wretchedness in their lives—all men, even Peleus, despite what
Priam thought:[30]

> "ἀλλ' ἕνα παῖδα τέκεν παναώριον· οὐδέ νυ τόν γε
> γηράσκοντα κομίζω, ἐπεὶ μάλα τηλόθι πάτρης
> ἧμαι ἐνὶ Τροίηι, cέ τε κήδων ἠδὲ cὰ τέκνα."

'... but he fathered a single son doomed to die all-untimely: and I cannot
care for him as he grows old, since I am sitting here in Troy, far from
my own country, bringing pain to you and your children.' (24. 540–2)

παναώριον ('doomed to die all-untimely'), which links Peleus and
Achilleus, is the word to match πανάποτμος ('my fate is all misery')
in 493, the link between Priam and Hektor. Achilleus has gone to
war when his father needs him, and he will die without giving the
delight of a *nostos*. At 18. 104 Achilleus reproached himself for
not protecting the Achaians—"ἀλλ' ἧμαι παρὰ νηυcὶν ἐτώcιον ἄχθος
ἀρούρης" ('but I sit here by the ships, a useless burden on the
earth'): now in another sense he still 'sits around', but κήδων—
'bringing pain to' rather than 'taking care of', which would be the
middle form of the same verb—Priam and his sons, instead of
taking care of Peleus. Achilleus does not by any means reject the
glory of battle, nor (as is sometimes claimed) does he see human
life as 'meaningless'; but he sets war in the larger framework of
the human condition with its ineradicable admixture of misery.
This is another way of putting 'the Homeric paradox'—see
pp. 122, 200 above.

'It is a fine touch that Achilleus sees both Priam's and Peleus'
sufferings as embodied in one and the same person: himself.'[31]
Instead of setting up the two old men as rivals for the title of
ἐλεεινότερος ('more pitiable'), he simply sets out their lots, one
after the other. Peleus (534–42) *seemed* to be the first of men for
his wealth, power, and marriage (ἐκέκαστο ('he surpassed') 535);
so Priam (543–8) *seemed* first for territory, wealth, and sons (φαcὶ

---

[30] On the jars, see Macleod 13–14 and note on 518–51. Perhaps they are to be
thought of as the jars which store the wool which has been spun by the Moirai.
[31] Macleod on 542.

κεκάcθαι ('they say that you surpassed') 546).³² The good fortune of both has been whittled away—yet

> "ἄνcχεο, μηδ' ἀλίαcτον ὀδύρεο còν κατὰ θυμόν·
> οὐ γάρ τι πρήξεις ἀκαχήμενος υἷος ἑῆος,
> οὐδέ μιν ἀνcτήcεις, πρὶν καὶ κακὸν ἄλλο πάθηιcθα."

'... you must endure, and not grieve endlessly in your heart. You will not gain anything by mourning for your son: you will not bring him back to life, before yet more suffering has come on you.' (24. 549–51)

Achilleus' last three lines, far from counselling despair or even resignation, urge a limit to grieving. The indicative ἄνcχεο ('you have endured') of line 518 turns into the imperative ἄνcχεο ('you must endure') of 549.³³

The 'lesson' that the young Achilleus imparts to the old Priam carries all the more weight because he has freshly learned it himself; and he has learned it from the very situation that they are now in. After the dream-spirit of Patroklos and the cutting of his lock (p. 252 above), he was able to say in public "γόοιο μὲν ἔcτι καὶ ἆcαι" ('men can have enough of lamentation') (23. 157). And in public he has put this into practice. But the opening of book 24 showed him behaving as though there still was some point to his endless maltreatment of Hektor—it is this very lack of sense of proportion that Apollo complains of at 24. 44 ff. Thetis tried to dissuade him from this attitude at 128–32, but at that stage Achilleus did not respond. It is Priam who truly brings the lesson home to him. Even as they weep, Hektor is lying nearby in the dust. Achilleus can raise Priam to his feet (ἀνίcτη ('raised') 515)—and there even now he stands. No one can do that for the dead: πρὶν καὶ κακὸν ἄλλο πάθηιcθα (before yet another suffering has come on you), meaning Priam's own death. Achilleus extends their present into the broad sweep of time: the transition from life to death is always one-way and always irreversible.

But resolution is not achieved yet by any means. Priam cannot rest easy:

---

³² The wealth of Troy as an exemplum of the vulnerability of human prosperity has been building up through e.g. 9. 401–3, 18. 288–92, 20. 219–21 (cf. 17. 225 f.). A recent reminder was the collection of the ransom of Hektor, at 24. 228 ff., fetched from the same treasure-store as Hekabe drew on in book 6 (24. 191 = 6. 288).

³³ Further on the ring-composition here, see Macleod on 549–51; cf. also Nagler, 190–2.

"μή πώ μ' ἐc θρόνον ἵζε, διοτρεφέc, ὄφρα κεν Ἕκτωρ
κεῖται ἐνὶ κλιcίηιcιν ἀκηδήc, ἀλλὰ τάχιcτα
λῦcον, ἵν' ὀφθαλμοῖcιν ἴδω·"

'Do not make me sit on a chair, my lord, while Hektor still lies untended
in your hut, but release him now, so I can see him with my eyes.'
(24. 553–5)

This impatience is not diplomatic. Furthermore his good wishes
in the next lines for Achilleus' safe return home show that he has
not yet fully appreciated the implications of παναώριον ('doomed
to die all-untimely'). This comes close to overturning Achilleus'
hard-won equilibrium:

"τῶ νῦν μή μοι μᾶλλον ἐν ἄλγεcι θυμὸν ὀρίνηιc,
μή cε, γέρον, οὐδ' αὐτὸν ἐνὶ κλιcίηιcιν ἐάcω
καὶ ἱκέτην περ ἐόντα, Διὸc δ' ἀλίτωμαι ἐφετμάc."
Ὣc ἔφατ', ἔδειcεν δ' ὁ γέρων καὶ ἐπείθετο μύθωι.

'So do not stir my heart any further in its grief, or I may not spare you
either in my hut, old man, suppliant though you are—and so offend
against Zeus' command.'
So he spoke, and the old man was afraid and did as he was ordered.
(24. 568–71)[34]

Achilleus realizes that if either of them bursts out from his self-
control then disaster will follow. And he realizes better than the
old father himself that it would be dangerous for him actually to
see Hektor before he departs. The supplying of this kind of
psychological commentary is encouraged by the narrator's own
explanations such as

δμωιὰc δ' ἐκκαλέcαc λοῦcαι κέλετ' ἀμφί τ' ἀλεῖψαι,
νόcφιν ἀειράcαc, ὡc μὴ Πρίαμοc ἴδοι υἱόν,
μὴ ὁ μὲν ἀχνυμένηι κραδίηι χόλον οὐκ ἐρύcαιτο
παῖδα ἰδών, Ἀχιλῆϊ δ' ὀρινθείη φίλον ἦτορ,
καί ἑ κατακτείνειε, Διὸc δ' ἀλίτηται ἐφετμάc.

Achilleus called out his serving-women and told them to wash the body
and anoint it all over, carrying it first to another room so that Priam
should not see his son—in case in his anguish of heart he might not
control his anger on seeing his son, and then Achilleus might have his

---

[34] 571 = 1. 33. But in 24 Achilleus, unlike Agamemnon, does show *aidōs* for the
gods and *eleos* for the old man. For some further details of comparison between
Priam and Chryses, see Reinhardt, *ID* 63–8; Lohmann, 169–72; Macleod, 32–5;
Letoublon in *BOP* 136–42.

own heart stirred to violence, and kill him, and so offend against Zeus' command. (24. 582-6)

Even though he received encouragement from Zeus, Priam's mission takes courage and restraint. Achilleus' speech at 560 ff. shows how he too has to exercise self-control and will-power. He also has received his message from Zeus, and he is well aware that Priam has been helped by the gods (563-7). But he none the less has to motivate his actions for himself. His capacity for disobedience (see 570, quoted above) make his obedience his own action rather than mere passive acquiescence. It is only because it takes a great effort of will from Achilleus that he is able to cancel out Apollo's account of him in 24. 39 ff. and to live up to Zeus' commendation (155-8 = 184-7).

Achilleus' ethical achievement, his new *kūdos*, is perhaps brightest in lines 587-90:

τὸν δ' ἐπεὶ οὖν δμωιαὶ λοῦcαν καὶ χρῖcαν ἐλαίωι,
ἀμφὶ δέ μιν φᾶρος καλὸν βάλον ἠδὲ χιτῶνα,
αὐτὸc τόν γ' Ἀχιλεὺc λεχέων ἐπέθηκεν ἀείρας,
cὺν δ' ἕταροι ἤειραν ἐϋξέcτην ἐπ' ἀπήνην.

... when the serving-women had washed the body and anointed it with olive oil, and put the tunic and a beautiful cloak over it, Achilleus himself lifted it and placed it on a bier, and his companions helped him to lift it onto the well-polished cart. (24. 587-90)

As usual the evaluation is left implicit, to be worked out by audiences. With this action Achilleus in effect begins the funeral rites.[35] It is of the highest importance that he does this himself, just as Priam has himself come with the ransom. No man, however great, should be above making the fundamental ethical gestures, however small. When Priam fetched the ransom from the treasury at 228 ff., there was a special emphasis on the cloth, in fact twelve each of πέπλοι, χλαῖναι, τάπητες, φάρεα, and χιτῶνεc (robes, cloaks, blankets, mantles, and tunics). Two φάρεα and a χιτών are carefully left in the cart (580). And it is these that Achilleus uses. So Andromache's lament of 22. 508 ff. (see p. 249) is delicately contradicted, and by Achilleus of all people. Hektor's corpse is shrouded in fine cloth of the house of Priam: and his ashes will be finally wrapped πορφυρέοιc πέπλοιcι μαλακοῖcιν (in soft purple cloths) in the closing moments of the poem (24. 796).

[35] See Macleod on 587-9.

9.4 Asserting life in despite of death

οἱ δ' ἐπ' ὀνείαθ' ἑτοῖμα προκείμενα χεῖρας ἴαλλον.
αὐτὰρ ἐπεὶ πόςιος καὶ ἐδητύος ἐξ ἔρον ἔντο,
ἤτοι Δαρδανίδης Πρίαμος θαύμαζ' Ἀχιλῆα,
ὅσσος ἔην οἷός τε· θεοῖςι γὰρ ἄντα ἐώικει·   630
αὐτὰρ ὁ Δαρδανίδην Πρίαμον θαύμαζεν Ἀχιλλεύς,
εἰσορόων ὄψίν τ' ἀγαθὴν καὶ μῦθον ἀκούων.
αὐτὰρ ἐπεὶ τάρπησαν ἐς ἀλλήλους ὁρόωντες,
τὸν πρότερος προσέειπε γέρων Πρίαμος θεοειδής·
"λέξον νῦν με τάχιστα, διοτρεφές, ὄφρα καὶ ἤδη   635
ὕπνωι ὕπο γλυκερῶι ταρπώμεθα κοιμηθέντες·
οὐ γάρ πω μύσαν ὄσσε ὑπὸ βλεφάροιςιν ἐμοῖςιν
ἐξ οὗ σῆς ὑπὸ χερςὶν ἐμὸς πάις ὤλεσε θυμόν,
ἀλλ' αἰεὶ στενάχω καὶ κήδεα μυρία πέςςω,
αὐλῆς ἐν χόρτοιςι κυλινδόμενος κατὰ κόπρον.   640
νῦν δὴ καὶ σίτου παςάμην καὶ αἴθοπα οἶνον
λαυκανίης καθέηκα· πάρος γε μὲν οὔ τι πεπάςμην."

Then they put their hands to the food set prepared beside them. When they had put away their desire for eating and drinking, then Dardanian Priam gazed at Achilleus with admiration for the size of the man and his beauty—he looked like the gods face to face. And Achilleus gazed at Dardanian Priam, admiring his noble looks and the talk that he had heard. When they had taken their pleasure in looking at each other, the old man, godlike Priam, was the first to speak: 'Give me a bed now, my lord, as soon as may be, so that we can lie down at last now and enjoy the sweetness of sleep. My eyes have never yet closed under my lids since my son lost his life under your hands, but all the time I have been grieving and brooding on my countless anguish, rolling in the dung in the enclosure of my farmyard. Now I have both tasted food and let gleaming wine down my throat—before this I had tasted nothing.'
(24. 627–42)

The Priam–Achilleus scene achieves an extraordinary combination of the particular with the universal, the unique detail with significance across time and place. Most of the time the universal level is left implicit, and when it does surface, it is, as usual in Homer, only after the implicit has already been active some time. So the audience is not directed to the deeper level, but does have its own inferences and intuitions confirmed.

Thus, the shared meal is, on the particular level, the setting-right of the procedures of hospitality so disrupted by Priam's unconventional arrival. But a universal level is implicit in the dialogue from 596 ff., and in Achilleus' adaptation of the Niobe story. Everyone who is to live must eat, whatever their other differences. Eating means living, and life must go on: 'it is the sign that both men have learned to live with their grief'.[36] This universality all but surfaces at lines 641–2.

Achilleus has been well prepared for this 'lesson'. In the long dispute with Odysseus in 19 he behaved like a man who did not need to eat—see pp. 210–11,[37] and in the Lykaon scene he repudiated the bond of having eaten together, see p. 223. In the evening after the death of Hektor, however, although he refuses to wash (23. 39 ff.), it seems that Achilleus does eat; at least he says to the others "νῦν μὲν cτυγερῆι πειθώμεθα δαιτί" ('for now let us yield to the cursed need for food') (23. 48). It is then not clear whether or not he joins the feasting at 24. 1–2. More importantly, Thetis urges eating as an assertion of life for men who are born to die:

"τέκνον ἐμόν, τέο μέχρις ὀδυρόμενος καὶ ἀχεύων
cὴν ἔδεαι κραδίην, μεμνημένος οὔτε τι cίτου
οὔτ' εὐνῆς; ἀγαθὸν δὲ γυναικί περ ἐν φιλότητι
μίcγεcθ'· οὐ γάρ μοι δηρὸν βέηι, ἀλλά τοι ἤδη
ἄγχι παρέcτηκεν θάνατος καὶ μοῖρα κραταιή."

'My child, how long will you eat out your heart in sorrow and mourning, with no thought for either food or bed? It is a good thing to join with a woman in love—as I shall not see you live long now, but already death and strong fate are standing close beside you.' (24. 128–32)

When Priam arrives, Achilleus is described as having recently finished a meal (415–16), so he has taken her advice. So he reaches the stage when he can use the first-person-plural, in 601, and the dual as well, in 618–19: "ἀλλ' ἄγε δὴ καὶ νῶϊ μεδώμεθα, δῖε γεραιέ, cίτου" ('so come now, we two as well, godlike old man, should have our thought for food') (24. 618–19). He is urging a mutual activity, a token of common humanity, of shared life in the face of shared mortality.

The description of the preparation of the food in 621–8 is in the formulaic diction appropriate to the quasi-ceremonial occa-

---

[36] Macleod, 139; cf. Nagler, 176 ff.; Edwards, 'CHF', 89.
[37] Odysseus' words at 19. 223 ff. are a rough-and-ready forerunner of the Priam–Achilleus meal.

sion.[38] This recalls above all the hospitality in Achilleus' *klisiē* at 9. 199 ff., and hence the absence of Patroklos—see pp. 79–80. The unforced familiarity of the repetition achieves an effect which is simply not open to most literature. It is able to accentuate the *uniqueness* of the occasion without drawing any explicit attention to it: the actions are common, almost automatic, yet the agents are Achilleus and Priam. The mutuality and the strangeness are also conveyed through the wording of 628–32, where the switch of nominative and accusative in 629 and 631 brings out their parity. Both are in different ways amazing; both have been doing remarkable things. Not the least of these is eating together.

Achilleus guided Priam towards eating. Now Priam in his turn takes the initiative and helps Achilleus back to the full resumption of life. He too appreciates that the lessons of mortality must be turned into diurnal reality. After satisfying sorrow and hunger, there should be sleep. The narrative appropriateness of this is so strong that it outrides the extreme lack of realism of Priam's proposal[39]—Hermes will, indeed, have to intervene to get him away before daylight (677 ff.). Unlike Priam, Achilleus has slept since the day of Hektor's death, but not well. When everyone else goes to bed, at 23. 57 ff., he sleeps apart along the beach,[40] and is disturbed by the dream of Patroklos. The next night, when the pyre has burned down, Achilleus has scarcely fallen asleep beside it when he is awoken for the next day (23. 229–32). After the games it is explicit that he does not sleep:

> τοὶ μὲν δόρποιο μέδοντο
> ὕπνου τε γλυκεροῦ ταρπήμεναι· αὐτὰρ Ἀχιλλεὺς
> κλαῖε φίλου ἑτάρου μεμνημένος, οὐδέ μιν ὕπνος
> ᾕρει πανδαμάτωρ,

All others turned their minds to supper, and the enjoyment of sweet sleep. But Achilleus began to weep as he thought of his dear companion, and sleep that conquers all could not take him. (24. 2–5)

---

[38] Line 624, for example, comes three times elsewhere in the *Iliad*, 627 twice (eleven in *Od.*) and 628 six times (fourteen in *Od.*). The very first feast-scene of the poem was at Chryse, in 1. 458 ff.

[39] There is some acknowledgement of this in the arrangement for Priam to sleep outside (650 ff.).

[40] On this 'symbolic geography', see Segal, 51; Elliger, 68. On this scene, see also Kakridis, *H. Res.* 103–5.

Thetis' advice at 128–32, quoted above, is for food *and* bed.
Sleep becomes the token of the assertion of life, as opposed to death, a token made the more powerful by the closeness, yet vital difference, between the twin brothers sleep and death.[41] Achilleus and Priam achieve a reconciliation infused with courtesy, consideration, and even gentleness.[42] It is a model for all humanity; but Homer is too great a poet to extend its peace to all humanity. It does not even extend to the others at Troy. The two of them recognize with grim resignation that any truce for the burial of Hektor will be temporary. Then the war will go on: that is ἀνάγκη (what must be)—see further below.

The closing cadence of the whole scene is sounded by three pairs of lines.

Ὣς ἄρα φωνήςας ἐπὶ καρπῶι χεῖρα γέροντος
ἔλλαβε δεξιτερήν, μή πως δείςει' ἐνὶ θυμῶι.

So speaking he took the old man's right hand at the wrist, so he should feel no fear in his heart. (24. 671–2)

The gentle gesture, like that of Odysseus' farewell from Penelope before the war (*Od*. 18. 258), is the last contact between the two.

οἱ μὲν ἄρ' ἐν προδόμωι δόμου αὐτόθι κοιμήςαντο,
κῆρυξ καὶ Πρίαμος, πυκινὰ φρεςὶ μήδε' ἔχοντες.

So they then lay down there in the porch of the house, the herald and Priam, men with wise thoughts in their minds. (24. 673–4)

The guests bed down in the fashion proper to the end of a hospitality scene, something more in keeping with the *Odyssey*.[43] The nearest thing in the *Iliad* is the end of the Embassy in book 9, where an old man, Phoinix, is similarly taken good care of for the night.

αὐτὰρ Ἀχιλλεὺς εὗδε μυχῶι κλιςίης ἐϋπήκτου·
τῶι δὲ Βριςηῒς παρελέξατο καλλιπάρηιος.

And Achilleus slept in the corner of his well-built hut, and the beautiful Briseïs lay beside him. (24. 675–6)

---

[41] See 14. 231, 16. 454, 16. 672 = 682, Hesiod, *Theog*. 212, 756–9. At *Od*. 13. 80 Odysseus sleeps a sleep θανάτωι ἄγχιστα ἐοικώς (most like death).

[42] Cf. Nagler, 188 ff. See Macleod's notes on e.g. 661, 681 for polite language, often verging on the colloquial; note also γέρον φίλε ('dear old man') in 650.

[43] For example *Od*. 3. 395 ff., 4. 296 ff. (4. 302 = *Il*. 24. 673), 7. 334 ff.

Here Achilleus' active participation in the *Iliad* comes to a close. The restoration of Briseïs is linked one last time with the loss of Patroklos (see p. 80) and with the marriage that she and Achilleus will never formalize (see § 8.2). None the less, love-making is an assertion of life despite death. Thetis connected them with a γάρ ('as'):

> "ἀγαθὸν δὲ γυναικί περ ἐν φιλότητι
> μίςγεςθ'· οὐ γάρ μοι δηρὸν βέηι, ἀλλά τοι ἤδη
> ἄγχι παρέστηκεν θάνατος καὶ μοῖρα κραταιή."

'It is a good thing to join with a woman in love—as I shall not see you live long now, but already death and strong fate are standing close beside you.' (24. 130–2)

9.5 *Homer's memorial*

> λαοῖσιν δ' ὁ γέρων Πρίαμος μετὰ μῦθον ἔειπεν·
> "ἄξετε νῦν, Τρῶες, ξύλα ἄστυδε, μηδέ τι θυμῶι
> δείςητ' Ἀργείων πυκινὸν λόχον· ἦ γὰρ Ἀχιλλεὺς
> πέμπων μ' ὧδ' ἐπέτελλε μελαινάων ἀπὸ νηῶν,   780
> μὴ πρὶν πημανέειν, πρὶν δωδεκάτη μόληι ἠώς."
> Ὣς ἔφαθ', οἱ δ' ὑπ' ἀμάξηισιν βόας ἡμιόνους τε
> ζεύγνυσαν, αἶψα δ' ἔπειτα πρὸ ἄστεος ἠγερέθοντο.
> ἐννῆμαρ μὲν τοί γε ἀγίνεον ἄσπετον ὕλην·
> ἀλλ' ὅτε δὴ δεκάτη ἐφάνη φαεσίμβροτος ἠώς,   785
> καὶ τότ' ἄρ' ἐξέφερον θρασὺν Ἕκτορα δάκρυ χέοντες,
> ἐν δὲ πυρῆι ὑπάτηι νεκρὸν θέσαν, ἐν δ' ἔβαλον πῦρ.
> Ἦμος δ' ἠριγένεια φάνη ῥοδοδάκτυλος Ἠώς,
> τῆμος ἄρ' ἀμφὶ πυρὴν κλυτοῦ Ἕκτορος ἔγρετο λαός.
>
> . . . .
>
> αἶψα δ' ἄρ' ἐς κοίλην κάπετον θέσαν, αὐτὰρ ὕπερθε
> πυκνοῖσιν λάεσσι κατεστόρεσαν μεγάλοισι·
> ῥίμφα δὲ σῆμ' ἔχεαν, περὶ δὲ σκοποὶ ἥατο πάντηι,
> μὴ πρὶν ἐφορμηθεῖεν ἐϋκνήμιδες Ἀχαιοί.   800
> χεύαντες δὲ τὸ σῆμα πάλιν κίον· αὐτὰρ ἔπειτα
> εὖ συναγειρόμενοι δαίνυντ' ἐρικυδέα δαῖτα
> δώμασιν ἐν Πριάμοιο, διοτρεφέος βασιλῆος.
> Ὣς οἵ γ' ἀμφίεπον τάφον Ἕκτορος ἱπποδάμοιο.

Then the old man Priam spoke to his people: 'Bring wood now into the city, Trojans, and have no fear in your hearts of a massed ambush from the Argives. Achilleus promised me, when he sent me on my way back

from the black ships, that they will do us no harm until the twelfth dawn comes.'
So he spoke, and they yoked oxen and mules to their carts, and quickly gathered then in front of the city. For nine days they brought in vast quantities of wood. But when the tenth dawn appeared bringing light for mortals, then they carried out brave Hektor with their tears falling, and placed his body at the top of the pyre, and put fire to it.
When early-born Dawn appeared with her rosy fingers, then the people collected around the pyre of famous Hektor . . . and they quickly placed it in the hollow of a grave, and covered it over with great stones laid close together. Then they piled a grave-mound over it in haste, with look-outs set on all sides, in case the well-greaved Achaians made an early attack. When they had piled the mound they went back. And then they gathered again in due order and held a glorious feast in the house of Priam, the god-ordained king.
Such was the burial they gave to Hektor, tamer of horses. (24. 777–89, 797–804)

The closing cadences of the *Iliad* also look beyond the end to the future. Hektor is laid to rest, but life and death, war and suffering go on. After the closure of the great Priam–Achilleus scene, Kassandra contributes to the opening-up of future perspectives. The return of Priam and the old herald to Troy, accompanied again by Hermes, is a reversal of their outward journey, even to the spreading of dawn (695) at the same stage as night had fallen in the other direction. But, while they arrived at the camp unseen by any human, Kassandra has spotted their return. What she is known for in Homer is not her prophetic power but her beauty. She is ἰκέλη χρυcέηι Ἀφροδίτηι (beautiful as golden Aphrodite) (24. 699; otherwise applied only to Brisëis at 19. 282), and at 13. 365 she is Πριάμοιο θυγατρῶν εἶδοc ἀρίcτην (the most beautiful of Priam's daughters). Indeed Othryoneus came to Troy, and died there, in the hope of winning her hand. At 9. 139 f. Agamemnon had offered Achilleus the twenty most beautiful women captured at Troy—barring only Helen; with Achilleus dead, Agamemnon will, of course, pick the most beautiful princess for himself. The *Odyssey* (11. 405 ff., especially 421–3) tells how the concubine who replaced Chrysëis died at the hands of Klytaimestra, while Aigisthos dealt with Agamemnon. While Kassandra's role is adequately explained by the link it makes to the Trojans crowding round the gates at 707 ff., I suggest that it is enriched for those who hear a forward reference, since she then foreshadows the fate of the women of Troy, and even glances at the fortunes of Agamemnon on his return home.[44] The last quarter of an hour or so—100 lines—of the *Iliad* is set in Troy. It says much about the poem as a whole that half of that time is spent on the laments of the three women—wife, mother, and 'sister-in-law'. It is, in fact, Andromache's which is the closest to an 'official' obituary, and which looks most to the future of the city.[45] She starts from herself and her son, but soon moves on to a further application:

"πρὶν γὰρ πόλις ἥδε κατ' ἄκρης
πέρσεται· ἦ γὰρ ὄλωλας ἐπίσκοπος, ὅς τέ μιν αὐτὴν
ῥύσκευ, ἔχες δ' ἀλόχους κεδνὰς καὶ νήπια τέκνα,
αἳ δή τοι τάχα νηυσὶν ὀχήσονται γλαφυρῆισι,
καὶ μὲν ἐγὼ μετὰ τῆισι·"

'Before that this city of ours will be sacked from top to bottom: because you, her guardian, are dead—you used to protect the city, and keep safe her loved wives and little children. They will soon now be carried away in the hollow ships, and I among them.' (24. 728–32)[46]

At the sack of Troy she will become one woman among many, and the men . . . their fate is left unspoken. Only Astyanax is singled out for a kind of prophecy, the victim of his own father's prowess in battle (732–9). Finally, in 742–5, she comes, through the grief of the *lāoi*, to her own lot: she has no intimate last memory. Yet, paradoxically, she will have the memory of this lament.

Hekabe's lament is the one most closely related to the Achilleus–Priam scene of the previous night. It begins and ends with the favour of the gods which has brought back Hektor's body and kept it sound. Her central lines sound a note of defiance:

"σεῦ δ' ἐπεὶ ἐξέλετο ψυχὴν ταναηκέϊ χαλκῶι,
πολλὰ ῥυστάζεσκεν ἑοῦ περὶ σῆμ' ἑτάροιο,
Πατρόκλου, τὸν ἔπεφνες· ἀνέστησεν δέ μιν οὐδ' ὣς."

---

[44] This leads me to open up the single allusion to Klytaimestra, at 1. 113–15, about the same distance, as it happens, from the beginning as Kassandra is from the end. Just when Agamemnon's possessiveness and lust is fuelling the initial strife, there is a fleeting reminder, for those who hear it, that he will not die of old age with his loving family round him.

[45] Cf. Macleod on 723–76.

[46] Line 730 alludes both to the 'popular etymology' of Hektor, see p. 116 above, and to the explanation of the name Astyanax given at 6. 403.

'But when he had taken the life from you with the long-pointed bronze, he dragged you time after time around the tomb of his companion you had killed, Patroklos—yet for all this he did not bring him to life.' (24. 754–6)

Taken in the context of divine favour, this is apparently a renunciation of the brutal vindictiveness of 24. 212–16 (see above), rather than a continuation of it.[47] Above all there is the echo of the key phrase in Achilleus' speech to Priam: *"οὐδέ μιν ἀνcτήceιc"* ('you will not bring him back to life') (551). Achilleus found his own way to the truth, the 'lesson' that no amount of grief or vengeance or resurrectionary magic can make a dead person stand up: by applying this 'lesson' to Achilleus, Hekabe also reaches it for herself. Hektor will no more stand up than Patroklos: *"νῦν δέ μοι ἑρcήειc καὶ πρόcφατοc ἐν μεγάροιcι κεῖcαι"* ('But now I have you lying here in the house sweet and fresh as dew') (757–8).

Helen's lament, finally, is the most immediate and private, yet it too also has an implicit 'political' level, as has been discussed already on pp. 119–20 above. Helen's past has led to this present, and will lead to the fall of Troy. It is also, in a sense, Hektor's kind heart that has brought them here. Yet for most audiences it is for that very kindness, no less than his bravery in war, that Hektor is admirable. Briseïs' lament for Patroklos gives the same depth to his portrait—see pp. 213–4. The two kindest characters in the *Iliad* are the two most important to die in its battles.

Hektor's actual funeral begins one line before the last page of the Oxford Classical Text, probably less than five minutes from the end in performance. It takes a much shorter performance-time than that of Patroklos, while being spread over a longer narrative-time. For instance, the wood-gathering of 23. 110–26 took only one day while that of 24. 777–84 takes nine days.

The narrative-time framework was set up by agreement between Priam and Achilleus. When asked how long is needed, Priam replied:

> *"ἐννῆμαρ μέν κ' αὐτὸν ἐνὶ μεγάροιc γοάοιμεν,*
> *τῆι δεκάτηι δέ κε θάπτοιμεν δαινῦτό τε λαόc,*
> *ἐνδεκάτηι δέ κε τύμβον ἐπ' αὐτῶι ποιήcαιμεν,*
> *τῆι δὲ δυωδεκάτηι πολεμίξομεν, εἴ περ ἀνάγκη."*

---

[47] 'Something not far from pity' (as put in Macleod's note on 746–50), rather than 'only perpetuates the venomous passion of war' (Segal, 69).

'We would lament him for nine days in our houses, then bury him on the tenth day and hold the funeral feast for the people. On the eleventh day we would build the grave-mound over him, and on the twelfth day let us fight again, if that must be.' (664–7) These rituals are followed through with slight variation in 784–804. The twelfth day grows inexorably closer as the *Iliad* sounds its closing coda. Only six lines before the end Homer expends two (799–800) on an apparently mundane detail about setting look-outs. Leaf was offended: 'the reason for this precaution is not very obvious; as they have trusted Achilleus' word so long, they might be expected to trust to the end'. But this is to think in terms of military strategy rather than poetic strategy. The Trojans look out from the eleventh day in anticipation of the twelfth. And they lead the inner eye of the audience beyond line 804: τῆι δὲ δυωδεκάτηι πολεμίξομεν, εἴ περ ἀνάγκη (and on the twelfth let us fight again, if that must be). The resignation of that plain (and unformulaic) line presupposes a whole world of suffering. It is indeed ἀνάγκη.

The look-outs set up a subliminal glimpse of the unfolding future, of the unsung lines: 'And on the twelfth day battle was resumed. And before long Achilleus was killed, and buried along with Patroklos. And not long after that Troy was sacked. Priam was killed, Astyanax thrown from the walls, Andromache taken into slavery . . .'[48] All these events, insistently foreseen within the *Iliad*, hang over its closure. War and suffering are not buried with Hektor; dark perspectives are fitfully lit by the future flames of Troy. As Colin Macleod (16) says of the end of the *Iliad*, 'its humanity does not float in shallow optimism; it is firmly and deeply rooted in an awareness of human reality and suffering.'

Yet, silhouetted against the prospects of death and waste, Hektor's *sēma*, memorial of his bravery and his kindness, stands constant. When he issued the challenge to single combat in book 7 he promised his opponent honourable burial:

"εἰ δέ κ' ἐγὼ τὸν ἕλω, δώηι δέ μοι εὖχος Ἀπόλλων,
τεύχεα cυλήcαc οἴcω προτὶ Ἴλιον ἱρήν,
καὶ κρεμόω προτὶ νηὸν Ἀπόλλωνος ἑκάτοιο,

---

[48] On Hektor's funeral, see Edwards, 'CHF', 85–6. Edith Hall has raised with me the question whether the removal of Ἕκτορος ἱπποδάμοιο (Hektor, tamer of horses) opens up a glance at the future vulnerability of Troy to the horse of wood?

τὸν δὲ νέκυν ἐπὶ νῆας ἐϋccέλμουc ἀποδώcω,
ὄφρα ἑ ταρχύcωcι κάρη κομόωντεc Ἀχαιοί,   85
cῆμά τε οἱ χεύωcιν ἐπὶ πλατεῖ Ἑλληcπόντωι.
καί ποτέ τιc εἴπηιcι καὶ ὀψιγόνων ἀνθρώπων,
νηῒ πολυκλήϊδι πλέων ἐπὶ οἴνοπα πόντον·
'ἀνδρὸc μὲν τόδε cῆμα πάλαι κατατεθνηῶτοc,
ὅν ποτ' ἀριcτεύοντα κατέκτανε φαίδιμοc Ἕκτωρ.'   90
ὥc ποτέ τιc ἐρέει· τὸ δ' ἐμὸν κλέοc οὔ ποτ' ὀλεῖται."

'And if I kill him, and Apollo grants my prayer. I shall strip his armour
and carry it back to sacred Ilios, and hang it in dedication at the temple
of Apollo the far-shooter, but his body I shall return to the well-benched
ships, so that the long-haired Achaians can give him the rites of burial
and heap a mound for him by the broad Hellespont. And people will say,
even men of generations not yet born, as they sail by over the sparkling
sea in their many-benched ships: "This is the mound of a man who died
long ago. He was the greatest of men, and glorious Hektor killed him."
That is what they will say: and my glory will never die.' (7. 81–91)

The poem ends with his own burial. His tumulus is not by the
sea, which is where Patroklos was buried, but in front of his city.
Any audience, any individual, who embarks on the voyage of the
Iliad, wherever they live, whether they hear or read, will end with
the image of Hektor's *sēma* before their eyes: "τὸ δ' ἐμὸν κλέοc οὔ
ποτ' ὀλεῖται" ('and my glory will never die').

It is not only Hektor's *kleos* that remains indestructible; so does
the *kleos* of the poet. Homer has already foreseen the hearing of
his poem as a voyage, his audiences as the sailors of future ages,
and the *Iliad* as his own memorial, his immortality.

APPENDIX

THE DIVISION OF THE *ILIAD* INTO TWENTY-FOUR BOOKS

It is as near certain as such things can be that the familiar division of the *Iliad*—and of the *Odyssey*—does not go back to the formation of the poems.[1] There are twenty-four sections because each, instead of being merely numbered, was labelled with a letter of the Ionic alphabet, the standard alphabet of later Greece. (The alphabet of Homer's day had between twenty and twenty-six letters depending on local variations.[2]) So the divisions are the work of a librarian or scholar or book-merchant. This does not alter the fact that they are deeply ingrained in everyone's perception of the poems, that all texts and translations make conspicuous use of them, and that they are an indispensable convention for exact citation. At the same time, I maintain that it helps the appreciation of Homer to undo them to some extent, to see that they have become ingrained from outside.

The 'Plutarch' *Life of Homer*, 2. 4, actually attributes the book-divisions to the school of Aristarchos (mid-second-century BC). I am inclined to accept this testimony, even though the best modern discussion, by S. West, attributes it to the fourth-century book trade.[3] There is no evidence of any labelled book-divisions at all

[1] Scholars who have defended the book-divisions as organic and authentic include P. Mazon, *Introduction à l'Iliade* (Paris, 1948), 137–40; G. Brocchia, *La forma poetica dell'Iliade e la genesi dell'epos omerico* (Messina, 1967); G. P. Goold in *ICS* 2 (1977), 1–34 esp. 26 ff.; cf. also Notopoulos, 'Studies', 9–12; Whitman, 283. Many others, who would not claim special authority for the book-divisions, still analyse the poem(s) in terms of blocks of books (see p. 13), or analyse the internal structures of each book, or the balancing relationships of separate books, etc. The new Cambridge *Iliad* and La Valla/Oxford *Odyssey* commentaries proceed very much book by book. This is all, to a greater or lesser extent, misguided and misleading.

[2] See Heubeck, 'Schrift', 164–5 and 102. Jeffery, 23–35 in fact catalogues twenty-four letters for 'the first alphabet'—they include *wau, heta, san*, and *qoppa*.

[3] S. West, *PPH* 18–25; cf. Pfeiffer, 115–6. But the books are too variable in length, and generally too short, to have been determined by the capacity of papyrus rolls. It is not a fatal objection against Aristarchos that there is no book division at *Od* 23. 296/7 (or 299/300), since that would make an unacceptably short book; and, given the text including 23.297 to the end, a division at 23. 296/7 would leave incomplete the day and long evening which began right back in book 20.

(e.g. of the historians) before the fourth century. None of the early
quotations of Homer, down to Aristotle at least, use the book-
divisions, or numbers, or letters: they cite by episode, and do so
by what seem to have been pretty rough and vague labels. For
example, Herodotos (2. 116) cites 6. 289 ff., the robe taken by
Hekabe for Athena, as from Διομήδους ἀριστείη (the *aristeia* of
Diomedes)—a label that later becomes attached to book 5—and
Thucydides (1. 9. 4) cites the cκήπτρου παράδοcιc (handing-down
of the sceptre), a scene that, strictly speaking, is only a few lines
long. About forty of these loose labels continued to be used in
later Antiquity.

As West (20–1) has shown, the early papyri do not have any
space or any other indicator at the locations of our book-divisions
(nor a priori do they end rolls at these places). *P. Genavensis*, 90
(West, 107–17) is the only one, as it happens, with the left-hand
edge of the column intact, and book 12, line 1 follows immediately
on 11. 848. After the late second century BC at the earliest, this
changes (cf. West, 22–3). All the usual indicators of textual division begin to appear in the papyri of Homer, with increasing
prominence as time goes by—coronis, 'chapter titles', and the
beginning of a new column or roll.

On the whole the book-divisions are well placed. They seem to
be the work of someone who has given thoughtful attention to the
poem—one reason for preferring Aristarchos to the book-trade.
Given the division into twenty-four parts, there are not many
places, though there are some, where the dividing-line might, in
my opinion, have been better placed. But had nine books, say,
been called for, or twenty-one, or thirty-six, just as good a division
could have been made. As I have argued in chapter 1, I believe
that at a fundamental level of narrative construction the *Iliad* can
only be divided into three parts.

The traditional twenty-four books are so deeply stamped in the
mind of scholars (not so much of students and less specialist
readers, I find) that I propose now to look at each dividing-point
one by one, and to ask why it is placed where it is, and where else
it might have been put. The extraordinary continuity of Homer's
narrative technique emerges clearly from this analysis; and it is
also sometimes quite revealing of the interpretative priorities of
'Aristarchos' (as I shall call the agent). As the book-divisions have
achieved a special, largely unconscious, authority, it sometimes

emerges that they can be positively damaging to the understanding of the poem.

1. 611/2. 1

The strongest division in the first 2,000 lines or more of the *Iliad* undoubtedly comes somewhere in between the great *agorē* of book 1 and the long day which is begun by Agamemnon's dream. Going to bed obviously marks a closure—indeed I have myself argued (pp. 24, 152–4) that the going-to-bed at the end of book 9 is the end of part I. The division is, however, obviously less sharp when there is an exception to the sleepers (one of the many problems with 10. 1!). So here Zeus warned Hera that he would act as he saw fit (1. 561–7), and in 2. 3 ff. he is eager to put that into effect. Similarly at 24. 679 Hermes is the exception to the divine and human slumbers.[4]

There is in fact a significant rival to the traditional juncture for this first significant division in the poem (and conceivably the first interval in performance). At 1. 492 the human world is left by the narrative with a picture of Achilleus' withdrawal; and at 1. 493 ff. a twelfth-day resumption returns to the mission of Thetis to Zeus, which will on the very next day, set in motion the battles of the *Iliad*. ('Aristarchos' does in fact favour a move to Olympos as a division-point, see 4. 1, 13. 1, 15. 1, 20. 1.) The first section would then end with chronic human strife rather than with the temporary good cheer of the gods.

2. 877/3. 1

The switch from the marshalling/catalogues to the advance of the armies towards each other is a perfectly good place to put the break, though there is obviously a continuity across it. Two earlier places where divisions might as well have been are 2. 431/2—the end of the flowing sequence of debates and the turn from words to deeds (see Nestor at 2. 435–61)—or the move from the Achaians to Troy at 2. 785/6. Note that a patriotic Greek would be happy to make 3. 1 ff. prominent—see p. 113.

---

[4] 2. 1–2a = 24.677–8. These are the only two places where the phrase θεοί τε καὶ ἀνέρες ('the gods and the warrior men') occurs; yet they stand in great contrast.

3. 461/4. 1

The sequence from the making of the truce in 3 to its breaking
in 4 is strong, and no one would have complained if there had
been no division in this area in the *Iliad*. Slightly better, perhaps,
than the shift to Olympos from the battlefield (where the situation
at the end of 3 is resumed at 4. 86 ff.) might have been 3. 447/8:
Paris and Helen go to bed, while the others are still in the field.

4. 544/5. 1

It is ironic that, on the analysis of Kirk and Thornton, this is
their first major division, since it is one of 'Aristarchos" less good
choices. The most important narrative juncture in the entire
sequence from 2 to 7 comes not here but at the first actual clash
of the armies. It is, however, a good illustration of the narrative
continuity that that point is not easily pinned down: it is shared
between 4. 421/2 (from *epipōlēsis* to main narrative), 445/6
(advance turns into clash of ranks—the most important of the
three), and 4. 456/7 (from mass battle to individual hits). Between
4. 457 and 5. 83 there are two series of hits, first alternating, then
all in favour of the Achaians. 'Aristarchos' patriotically chose the
switch for his book-division.

The more immediate motive is the singling-out of Diomedes.
Yet this has encouraged the misleading supposition that book 5
forms a unified *aristeia* of Diomedes. Lines 37 to 84 concern other
warriors, and it is only at 5. 85 ff., that his exploits really get under
way. (The culminating defeat of Pandaros is a crucial link with
book 4—see § **3.5**.) Then Diomedes plays a relatively small part
in 5. 445–792, before returning to prominence for the wounding
of Ares, and for the meeting with Glaukos (6. 119–236).

5. 909/6. 1

This is a fairly arbitrary point to select, with no better claims
than, say, 5. 792/3 or 6. 72/3.

6. 529/7. 1

The return from Troy to battle by Hektor and Paris makes a fair
dividing-point—though in many ways the new sequence begins

at 7. 16 ff., when the gods begin to think of ways of drawing the battle to a close. In so far as the scenes in Troy form a structural unit, the section ending at 6. 529 should have begun at 6. 237, or perhaps 6. 73, where Helenos first advised Hektor to visit the city. Presumably 'Aristarchos' regarded the scenes in Troy as too short—and too concentrated on the 'enemy'?—to constitute a whole book.

7. 482/8. 1

This is, indeed, the most significant dividing-point in between the joining of battle in 4 and the end of book 9—it would make an obvious place for an interval. Book 7 ends with the closure of sleep, and book 8 presents the aperture of a new dawn and a divine assembly. At the same time the sequence of meetings and diplomacy towards the end of 7 anticipates the rejoining of battle. And the divine assembly of 7. 443 ff. leads into Zeus' all-night planning in 7. 478–82,[5] which leads into the Olympian gathering at 8. 2 ff. In some ways the combination of closure and anticipation foreshadows the major juncture between 9 and 11—see pp. 23–4.

8. 565/9. 1

The Trojan night-camp—with the fine spondaic cadence of line 565—gives a memorable moment of closure. Yet it is only a momentary pause in the standard pattern of 'post-mortem scenes'—see p. 22. The contrasting similes of 8. 555 ff. and 9. 4 ff. are a signal of the continuity (across another division in the Cambridge commentaries).

9. 713/11. 1

I have explained elsewhere why I take this to be one of two fundamental divisions of the *Iliad*—see § 1.3—and why I regard book 10 as intrusive—see pp. 152–3.

---

[5] ϲφιν ('for them') in 7. 478 surely refers only to the Achaians.

11. 848/12. 1

The sequence of Patroklos' first active participation, from 11. 596
to 848, is a distinct narrative section, well marked off from the
battles before it and after it. It is, however, presumably too short
to have comprised one of twenty-four books. The decision whether
to tack it on to what precedes or to what follows is arbitrary—or
was arbitrary for 'Aristarchos'.

12. 471/13. 1

Hektor breaks into the Achaian camp, Zeus turns his attention
away, and thus begins the 'great retardation', which lasts until the
middle of book 15. This is the most significant dividing-point in
between book 11 and 15, though it is an overstatement to say that
it has 'strong organic authority' (Kirk, i. 45). It is probably not
(in my view) one of the eight most important division-points in
the *Iliad* as a whole—for those see p. 27. So it is rather unfortunate that it marks the single great break in two-volume editions,
including the Oxford Classical Text.

13. 837/14. 1

The move from battlefield to a relatively brief scene in the Achaian
camp makes a pretty weak break. It might just as well have come
at 13. 672/3, where the mêlée turns to the focus of Hektor—but
that would not have been philhellene, of course—or at 14. 152/3,
where the narrative turns from earth to Olympos. The sequence
of the *Dios apatē* forms a nice set-piece (14. 153-360), the only
clear sectioning within the battle sequence from books 13 to 15.

14. 522/15. 1

It seems that 'Aristarchos' was determined to make the re-
awakening of Zeus the division-point. The trouble is that that
happens half-way through a line (15. 4); as it is, the last three and
a half lines of the rout of 14. 508-22 have become detached as the
opening of book 15 (15. 1-4a).

15. 746/16. 1

The objection to this division is that it cuts off the protracted struggle between Hektor and Aias from its climax, in 16. 101–23. It thus obscures the most important turning-point in the whole sequence from 11 to 18 (part II): the synchronism of the firing of a ship and the dispatch of Patroklos—see pp. 177–8. The juncture at 16. 123/4 would in fact make a good interval-point. The climax of the battle for the ships is marked by the invocation of the Muses in 112–13, and by the cadence of 122–3, with their monosyllabic line-endings πῦρ and φλόξ ('fire', 'flame'). Then the resumption is marked by the sudden activity of Achilleus and by his urgent imperatives in 126–9, starting ὄρσεο ('up now'). The thinking behind the far less telling division at 16. 1 is not hard to see: 'Aristarchos' wanted to turn a single book into a 'Patrokleia' (as with Diomedes in book 5).

16. 867/17. 1

The same 'Patrokleia' motive leads to this division at the first narrative shift after his death. The fact is, however, that there is a fine flow of narrative all the way from 16. 124 until well into the book 18, and there are no satisfactory break-points. This particular one damagingly divides the death of Patroklos from the death of Euphorbos, and indeed from all the following narrative, which is centred on his corpse. (Actually, if there has to be a division here, it would be more dramatic at 16. 861/2.)

17. 761/18. 1

The scene between Achilleus and Thetis (18. 35–147) is a crucial episode, but it should not be sectioned off from what goes before. The arrival of Antilochos at 18. 1 ff. is tightly linked to his dispatch at 17. 651–701; and the battle which is left at 17. 761 is tightly bound to its resumption at 18. 148 ff.

18. 617/19. 1

I have argued (pp. 201–2) that the second fundamental division in the construction of the *Iliad* comes at 18. 353/4. Thus 18. 354 ff. leads into the making of the arms; and, after the set-piece description in 18. 478–613, the narrative presses on without break. Thetis receives the arms and takes them to Achilleus in 18. 614–7, 19. 1–13; and ἥ (she) in 19. 3 signals the continuity. In other words, the dawn in 19. 1 does not here mark the major structural resumption, unlike 11. 1, where it did. So the manufacture of the armour is a kind of prelude to the day—the technique of Agamemnon's dream at 2. 1–47 before the dawn at 2. 48 is remotely similar.

19. 424/20. 1

This is a perfectly reasonable place for a minor division, coming between the Achaian preliminaries and the Olympian line-up (though three lines later might have been better). There is just as great a division at 20. 75, but it comes in mid-line.

20. 503/21. 1

This is perhaps the least acceptable of all of 'Aristarchos'' divisions (so, needless to say, it coincides with a Thornton–Kirk division!). On a larger scale it breaks up the onrush of Achilleus' slaughter, and the Lykaon scene is cut off from the closely related deaths of his brother Polydoros and of Tros, another suppliant. On a closer scale the division cuts apart both the sequence of mass slaughter which runs from 20. 490 to 21. 26 and the cluster of four long similes in the 44 lines from 20. 473 to 21. 33. There is, in fact, no significant break within the run of Achilleus' day on the battlefield from book 20 to 22, or even early 23.

21. 611/22. 1

I can see no reason for preferring this particular point to 21. 513/14, the end of the *theomachia*, or 22. 24/5, the start of the sequence which leads up to Hektor's death. 'Aristarchos' may have pin-pointed the naming of Hector in 22. 5 and gone back to the nearest possible division before that.

22. 515/23. 1

'Aristarchos' chose the point where the narrative leaves the Trojans—for over 1,000 lines—and so gives the new book an Achaian opening. But this cuts across the 'post-mortem' scene-sequence at the end of the day's battle, see pp. 22–3 and on 8/9 above. This is positively misleading in that it puts a wedge in between the sides instead of allowing their juxtaposition to have its effect: both are overwhelmed with grief, yet one camp contains the bodies of both the dead. Burial preoccupies the Achaians: the denial of it haunts the Trojans.

There is, in my view, an important juncture in the narrative structure in this vicinity, one that might be suitable for an interval. In terms of narrative-time, the day which has lasted since 19. 1 (or even, in a sense, since 18. 354) comes to an end, and everyone goes to bed—the classic closure. The actual division-point is not, however, very distinct: it seems to come at 23. 56/7,[6] so that the ghost-dream of Patroklos follows it, leading towards the funeral and the games.

23. 897/24. 1

There is, indeed, an important division at this point as the scene moves from the public games and Achilleus' chivalry there to his private grief and vindictiveness. At the same time, it is worth observing that, had there (in another scheme) been a further division at 24. 140/1, when the scene moves from Thetis and Achilleus to Iris and Priam, then more justice might have been done by critics ever since to the importance of the old king and of Ilios in the *Iliad*.

---

[6] It is some objection that this would split line 56 from 57, when elsewhere they occur in a formulaic sequence. It is worth noting, however, that they are also somewhat divided between two narrative sequences at 2. 431/2.

SELECT BIBLIOGRAPHY

This Bibliography selects only those works which I have found most helpful or most relevant to the writing of this book. This means that some works cited in footnotes are not listed here; and that a few are listed here but cited nowhere else. The Bibliography also serves as a key to abbreviated titles.

COMMENTARIES

Iliad

Ameis–Hentze	K. F. Ameis and C. Hentze, latest edns. (Leipzig and Berlin, 1894–1900).
Kirk	G. S. Kirk, i. *Books 1–4* (Cambridge, 1985); ii. *Books 5–8* (Cambridge, 1990).
Leaf	W. Leaf, 2nd end. (London, 1900).
Macleod	C. M. Macleod, *Book XXIV* (Cambridge, 1982).
Willcock, *Comm.*	M. M. Willcock, (London, 1978, 1984).
Willcock, *Comp.*	M. M. Willcock, *A Companion to the* Iliad (Chicago, 1976).

The commentaries on the *Odyssey* by S. West (books 1–4), J. B. Hainsworth (5–8), A. Heubeck (9–12, 23–4), A. Hoekstra (13–16), J. Russo (17–20), and M. Fernández-Galiano (21–2), first published by Fondazione Lorenzo Valla (1981–5), are cited in the English versions (3 vols.; Oxford, 1988–91).

Hesiod: M. L. West's editions with commentary of the *Theogony* (Oxford, 1966) and the *Works and Days* (Oxford, 1978).

BOOKS AND ARTICLES

Andersen	Ø. Andersen, 'Myth, Paradigm and "Spatial Form" in the *Iliad*', in *BOP* 1–14.
Arend	W. Arend, *Die typischen Szenen bei Homer* (Problemata, 7) (Berlin, 1933).
Armstrong	J. I. Armstrong, 'The Arming Motif in the *Iliad*', *AJP* 79 (1958), 337–54.

296   *Select Bibliography*

Bannert   H. Bannert, *Formen des Wiederholens bei Homer*
                   (*WSt* Beiheft 13) (Vienna, 1988).
BOP   J. M. Bremer, I. de Jong, and J. Kalff (edd.),
                   Homer: Beyond Oral Poetry (Amsterdam, 1987).
Bowra   C. M. Bowra, *Heroic Poetry*, 2nd edn. (London,
                   1961).
Burkert, 'Theben' W. Burkert, 'Das hunderttorige Theben und
                   die Datierung der *Ilias*', *WSt*, n.s. 10 (1976),
                   5–21.
Burkert, 'Kynaithos' W. Burkert, 'Kynaithos, Polycrates and the
                   Homeric Hymn to Apollo', in G. W.
                   Bowersock, W. Burkert, M. C. J. Putnam
                   (edd.), *Arktouros: Hellenic Studies for B. M. W.
                   Knox* (Berlin, 1979), 53–62.
Burkert, 'Making' W. Burkert, 'The Making of Homer in
                   the Sixth Century BC: Rhapsodes versus
                   Stesichorus', in *Papers on the Amasis Painter
                   and his World* (Malibu, Calif., 1987), 43–62.
Camps   W. A. Camps, *An Introduction to Homer*
                   (Oxford, 1980).
CH   A. J. B. Wace and F. H. Stubbings (edd.), *A
                   Companion to Homer* (London, 1963).
Collins   L. Collins, *Studies in Characterisation in the
                   Iliad* (Beitr. zur klassischen Philologie, 189)
                   (Frankfurt, 1988).
Cook   J. M. Cook, *The Troad: An Archaeological and
                   Topographical Study* (Oxford, 1973).
de Jong   I. J. F. de Jong, *Narrators and Focalizers: The
                   Presentation of the Story in the* Iliad (Amster-
                   dam, 1987).
Di Benedetto   V. Di Benedetto, 'Nel laboratorio di Omero',
                   RFIC 114 (1988), i. 257–85; ii. 385–410.
Dodds   E. R. Dodds, *The Greeks and the Irrational*
                   (Berkeley, Calif., 1951).
Donlan   W. Donlan, 'Reciprocities in Homer', *CW* 75
                   (1981–2), 137–75.
Edwards, 'Type-scenes' M. W. Edwards, 'Type-scenes and Homeric
                   Hospitality', *TAPA* 105 (1975), 51–72.
Edwards, 'CI'   M. W. Edwards, 'Convention and Individuality
                   in *Iliad* I', *HSCP* 84 (1988), 1–28.
Edwards, 'CHF'   M. W. Edwards, 'The Conventions of a
                   Homeric Funeral', in J. H. Betts (ed.), *Studies
                   in Honour of T. B. L. Webster* (Bristol, 1986),
                   i. 84–92.

Edwards, *HPI*　　　　M. W. Edwards, *Homer, Poet of the* Iliad (Baltimore, 1987).

Elliger　　　　W. Elliger, *Die Darstellung der Landschaft in der griechischen Dichtung* (Berlin, 1975).

Erbse, 'Betr.'　　　　H. Erbse, 'Betrachtungen über das 5. Buch der *Ilias*' (first publ. 1961), in *Ausgewählte Schriften zur klassischen Philologie* (Berlin, 1979), 19–46.

Erbse, 'HI'　　　　H. Erbse, 'Hektor in der *Ilias*' (first publ. 1978), in *Ausgewählte Schriften zur klassischen Philologie* (Berlin, 1979), 1 ff.

Fenik, *TBS*　　　　B. Fenik, *Typical Battle Scenes in the* Iliad (*Hermes* Einzelschr. 21) (Wiesbaden, 1968).

Fenik, *SO*　　　　B. Fenik, *Studies in the Odyssey* (*Hermes* Einzelschr. 30) (Wiesbaden, 1974).

Fenik, 'Monologues'　　　　B. Fenik, 'Stylization and Variety: Four Monologues in the *Iliad*', in B. Fenik (ed.), *Tradition and Invention* (Leiden, 1978), 68–90.

Finley　　　　M. I. Finley, *The World of Odysseus* (New York and London, [1st edn. 1954] 2nd edn. 1978).

Finnegan　　　　R. Finnegan, *Oral Poetry* (Cambridge, 1977).

Geddes　　　　A. G. Geddes, 'Who's Who in Homeric Society?' *CQ*, n.s. 34 (1984), 17–36.

Gentili　　　　B. Gentili, *Poet and Public in Ancient Greece* (Baltimore, 1988) (first publ. in Italian in 1985).

Griffin, *Homer*　　　　J. Griffin, *Homer* (Oxford, 1980).

Griffin, *HLD*　　　　J. Griffin, *Homer on Life and Death* (Oxford, 1980).

Griffin, 'Words'　　　　J. Griffin, 'Words and Speakers in Homer', *JHS* 106 (1986), 36–57.

Hall　　　　E. Hall, *Inventing the Barbarian* (Oxford, 1989).

Hägg　　　　R. Hägg (ed.), *The Greek Renaissance of the Eighth Century BC: Tradition and Innovation* (Stockholm, 1983).

Hatto　　　　A. T. Hatto, 'Towards an Anatomy of Heroic Epic Poetry', in *THEP* ii. 147–294.

Hellwig　　　　B. Hellwig, *Raum und Zeit im homerischen Epos* (Spudasmata, 2) (Hildesheim, 1964).

Herington　　　　J. Herington, *Poetry into Drama: Early Tragedy and the Greek Poetic Tradition* (Berkeley, Calif., 1985).

Heubeck, 'Form'　　　　A. Heubeck, 'Zur inneren Form der *Ilias*', *Gymnasium*, 65 (1958), 37–47.

Heubeck, *HF*　　　　A. Heubeck, *Die homerische Frage* (Darmstadt, 1974).

298   *Select Bibliography*

Heubeck, 'Schrift'   A. Heubeck, 'Schrift', in *Archaeologia Homerica*, iii, ch. 10 (Göttingen, 1979).

Janko   R. Janko, *Homer, Hesiod and the Hymns* (Cambridge, 1982).

Jeffery   L. H. Jeffery, *The Local Scripts of Archaic Greece* (1st edn. 1961, rev. A. Johnston, Oxford, 1990).

Jensen   M. S. Jensen, *The Homeric Question and the Oral-Formulaic Theory* (Opuscula Graecolatina, 20) (Copenhagen, 1980).

Kakridis, *H. Res.*   J. T. Kakridis, *Homeric Researches* (Lund, 1949).

Kakridis, *H. Rev.*   J. T. Kakridis, *Homer Revisited* (Lund, 1971).

Kannicht   R. Kannicht, 'Thalia: Über den Zusammenhang zwischen Fest und Poesie bei den Griechen', in W. Haug and R. Werning (edd.), *Das Fest* (Poetik und Hermeneutik, 14) (Munich, 1989), 29–52.

Kirk, *SH*   G. S. Kirk, *The Songs of Homer* (Cambridge, 1962).

Krischer   T. Krischer, *Formale Konventionen der homerischen Epik* (Zetemata, 51) (Munich, 1971).

Kullmann   W. Kullmann, *Die Quellen der Ilias* (*Hermes* Einzelschr. 14) (Wiesbaden, 1960).

Lesky, 'Motivation'   A. Lesky, 'Göttliche und menschliche Motivation im homerischen Epos', in *SB Heidelberg Akad.* 1961.4.

Lesky, *RE*   A. Lesky, 'Homeros', repr. from *RE* Suppl. vol. 11 (Stuttgart, 1967).

Letoublon   F. Letoublon, 'Défi et combat dans l'*Iliade*', *REG* 96 (1983), 27–48.

Lohmann   D. Lohmann, *Die Komposition der Reden in der Ilias* (Berlin, 1970).

Lord   A. Lord, *The Singer of Tales* (Harvard, 1960).

Lynn-George   M. Lynn-George Epos: *word, narrative and the Iliad* (London, 1988).

Macleod, 'HP'   C. Macleod, 'Homer on Poetry and the Poetry of Homer', in *Collected Essays* (Oxford, 1983), 1–15.

Martin   R. P. Martin, *The Language of Heroes: Speech and Performance in the* Iliad (Ithaca, NY, 1989).

Morris   I. Morris, 'The Use and Abuse of Homer', *Class. Ant.* 5 (1986), 81–138.

Motzkus	D. Motzkus, *Untersuchungen zum 9. Buch der Ilias* (diss. Hamburg, 1964).
Mueller	M. Mueller, *The Iliad* (London, 1984).
Nagler	M. N. Nagler, *Spontaneity and Tradition: A Study in the Oral Art of Homer* (Berkeley, Calif., 1974).
Nagy	G. Nagy, *The Best of the Achaeans* (Baltimore, 1979).
Nicolai	W. Nicolai, *Kleine und große Darstellungseinheiten in der* Ilias (Heidelberg, 1973).
Notopoulos, 'PH'	J. Notopoulos, 'Parataxis in Homer', *TAPA* 80 (1949), 1–23.
Notopoulos, 'CI'	J. Notopoulos, 'Continuity and Interconnection in Homeric Oral Composition', *TAPA* 82 (1951), 81–101.
Notopoulos, 'Studies'	J. Notopoulos, 'Studies in Early Greek Oral Poetry', *HSCP* 68 (1964), 1–77.
Owen	E. T. Owen, *The Story of the* Iliad (Toronto, 1946; repr. Bristol, 1989).
Parry, 'LA'	A. Parry, 'The Language of Achilles' (first publ. 1956), in *The Language of Achilles and Other Papers* (Oxford, 1989), 1–7.
Parry, *HHI*	A. Parry, 'Have we Homer's *Iliad?*' (1966), in *The Language of Achilles and Other Papers*, 104–40.
Parry, 'LCH'	'Language and Characterization in Homer' (1972), in *The Language of Achilles and Other Papers*, 301–26.
Patzer	H. Patzer, *Dichterische Kunst und poetisches Handwerk im homerischen Epos* (*SB Frankfurter Akad.* 1971. 1) (Wiesbaden, 1972).
Petersmann	G. Petersmann, 'Die monologische Totenklage der *Ilias*', *RhM* n.s. 116 (1973), 3–16.
Pfeiffer	R. Pfeiffer, *History of Classical Scholarship from the Beginnings to the End of the Hellenistic Age* (Oxford, 1968).
Rabel	R. T. Rabel, 'Chryses and the Opening of the *Iliad*', *AJP* 109 (1988), 473–81.
Redfield, *NCI*	J. M. Redfield, *Nature and Culture in the* Iliad: *The Tragedy of Hector* (Chicago, 1975).
Redfield, 'Proem'	J. M. Redfield, 'The Proem of the *Iliad*: Homer's Art', *CPh* 74 (1979), 95–110.
Reinhardt, 'PU'	K. Reinhardt, 'Das Parisurteil' (first publ.

1938), in C. Becker (ed.), *Tradition und Geist* (Göttingen, 1960), 16–36.

Reinhardt, *ID* K. Reinhardt, *Die Ilias und ihr Dichter*, ed. U. Hölscher (Göttingen, 1961).

Robbins E. Robbins, 'Achilles to Thetis: *Iliad* 1. 365–412', *EMC*, n.s. 9 (1990), 1–15.

Rutherford R. B. Rutherford, 'Tragic Form and Feeling in the *Iliad*', *JHS* 102 (1982), 145–60.

Schadewaldt, *IS* W. Schadewaldt, *Iliasstudien*, [1st edn., 1943] 3rd edn. (Darmstadt, 1966).

Schadewaldt, *HWW* W. Schadewaldt, *Von Homers Welt und Werk*, 4th edn. (Stuttgart, 1965).

Schadewaldt, *Aufbau* W. Schadewaldt, *Die Aufbau der* Ilias (Frankfurt, 1975).

Schein S. Schein, *The Mortal Hero* (Berkeley, Calif., 1984).

Scodel R. Scodel, 'The Word of Achilles', *CPh* 84 (1989), 91–9.

Segal C. Segal, *The Theme of the Mutilation of the Corpse in the* Iliad (*Mnemosyne* Suppl. 17) (Leiden, 1971).

Silk M. Silk, *Homer: The Iliad* (Cambridge, 1987).

Stawell F. M. Stawell, *Homer and the Iliad* (London, 1909).

Strasburger G. Strasburger, *Die kleinen Kämpfer der* Ilias (Frankfurt, 1954).

Taplin, 'Shield' O. Taplin, 'The Shield of Achilleus within the *Iliad*', *G&R* 27 (1980), 1–21.

Taplin, *Chios* O. Taplin, 'Homer's Use of Achilles' Earlier Campaigns in the *Iliad*', in J. Boardman and C. E. Vaphopoulou-Richardson (edd.), *Chios* (Oxford, 1986), 15–19.

Taplin, 'Agamemnon' 'Agamemnon's Role in the *Iliad*', in C. Pelling (ed.), *Characterization and Individuality in Greek Literature* (Oxford, 1990), 60–82.

Thalmann W. G. Thalmann, *Conventions of Form and Thought in Early Greek Epic Poetry* (Baltimore, 1984).

THEP ii J. B. Hainsworth (ed.), *Traditions of Heroic Poetry*, ii (London, 1989).

Thornton A. Thornton, *Homer's* Iliad: *Its Composition and the Motif of Supplication* (Hypomnemata, 81) (Göttingen, 1984).

Tsagarakis	O. Tsagarakis, *Form and Content in Homer* (Hermes Einzelschr. 48) (Wiesbaden, 1982).
Wade-Gery	H. T. Wade-Gery, *The Poet of the* Iliad (Cambridge, 1952).
West, *PPH*	S. West, *The Ptolemaic Papyri of Homer* (Papyrologica Coloniensia, 3) (Cologne, 1967).
Whitman	C. H. Whitman, *Homer and the Heroic Tradition* (Cambridge, Mass., 1958).
Willcock, 'Games'	M. M. Willcock, 'The Funeral Games of Patroclus', *BICS* 20 (1973), 1–11.
Willcock, 'Antilochus'	'Antilochus in the *Iliad*', in *Mélanges Édouard Delebecque* (Aix-en-Provence, 1983), 479–85.
Wilson	J. R. Wilson, 'The Wedding Gifts of Peleus', *Phoenix*, 28 (1974), 385–9.

GLOSSARY

Note: what follows is not a lexicography of each word, but only an account of the meaning which is given to the word when used in transliteration in this book. Often a reference to a fuller discussion is given.

agorē (ἀγορή): a public gathering, usually of all the *lāos*, usually summoned by a *basileus*.

aidōs (αἰδώς): a sense of compunction which inhibits ethically dubious behaviour—see pp. 52–3.

aitios (αἴτιος, neg. *anaitios*): responsible for something, to blame—see p. 99.

apoina (ἄποινα): material compensation, ransom—see p. 53.

ātē (ἄτη): a foolishness leading to disastrous consequences, often spoken of as somehow sent by the gods.

aristeia (not Homeric): a concentration of success in battle for a particular character.

atīmia: see *tīmē*.

basileus (βαςιλεύς, pl. *basilēes*): a chief, lord, baron. There is some vagueness over how many any particular locality has, and over their hierarchy both locally and in allied war—see pp. 47–50.

boulē (βουλή): a meeting of the *gerontes/basilēes* to discuss policy.

charis (χάρις): a favour done to someone, within an ethical system of expecting mutual benefit in the long run—see pp. 59–60.

cholos (χόλος): anger (much more common than *mēnis*).

Dios apatē: the deceit played by Hera on Zeus in book 14 when she seduces him into a post-coital slumber.

Dios boulē (Διὸς βουλή): the plan or determination of Zeus. The (or a) *Dios boulē* is said in 1. 5 to be fulfilled by the slaughter resulting from Achilleus' quarrel with Agamemnon.

eleos (ἔλεος): pity (see p. 223 for combination with *aidōs*).

epikouroi (ἐπίκουροι): allies who come to the help of a place in difficulties, used of the allies of Troy—see pp. 58–9.

epipōlēsis: Agamemnon's 'inspection' of the Achaian leaders and troops in book 4 (based on the verb in 4. 231).

eris (ἔρις): conflict, strife, whether or not in battle.

geras (γέρας): a special privilege, used particularly for a special prize picked out from spoil for the leaders and bestowed by the *lāos*—see pp. 60–4.

gerontes (γέροντες): the inner council of leaders, not necessarily old, at least not in war.

hetairos (ἑταῖρος): companion, used especially of a man of high standing who is chief friend, assistant, charioteer, etc. to an even greater man, such as Patroklos to Achilleus, Sthenelos to Diomedes.

kleos (κλέος): the subject of talk, hence fame, and above all the immortal glory won by great heroes. Poetry, in effect, arbitrates on *kleos*—see p. 5 and *passim*.

klisiē (κλισίη): living quarters, used of the encampment, chiefly of wood, that the Achaians have built along the shore during the siege.

kouridiē alochos (κουριδίη ἄλοχος): lawful wedded wife.

kūdos (κῦδος): glory, especially perhaps the aura of recent success.

lāos (λαός, pl. λαοί): the people, the host, the army as a whole. This may even include the *basilēes* unless they are separated out, as they usually are—see pp. 49–50.

mēnis (μῆνις): resentful fury—Achilleus' *mēnis* supplies the first word of the poem.

mētis (μῆτις): cleverness, cunning.

nekyia: the scene in *Odyssey* 11 when Odysseus makes contact with the dead.

nostos (νόστος): return home, especially from war.

philos (φίλος): in a close relationship, usually but not necessarily affectionate.

sēma (σῆμα): a marker, a token, in particular a grave-mound—see pp. 283–4.

teichoskopia: the conventional title for the scene in *Iliad* 3, when Helen and Priam are on the walls of Troy.

thalamos (θάλαμος): an inner chamber, especially the marital bedroom of a house.

theomachia (not Homeric): a battle between gods, as in books 5 and 21 of the *Iliad*.

tīmē (τιμή, neg. *atīmia*, ἀτιμία): proper recognition, due esteem—see pp. 50–1 and *passim*. The deprivation of this is a state of *atīmia*, of being underrated.

INDEX TO PASSAGES OF HOMER

ILIAD

ODYSSEY

INDEX